THE BITTER PILL

THE BITTER PILL

Worldwide Reaction to the Encyclical *Humanae Vitae*

Edited by F. V. JOANNES of IDO-C
Translated by IDO-C

Pilgrim Press
Philadelphia Boston

SBN 8298–0157–X
Library of Congress Catalog Card Number 70–117186

Copyright © 1970 United Church Press
Philadelphia, Pennsylvania

Published originally in Milan, Italy as *L'Humanae Vitae,
in appendice il testo dell'enciclica.* © Arnoldo Mondadori
Editore, *I edizione maggio 1969. Inchieste* IDO-C.

CONTENTS

FOREWORD

Honesty is the first virtue. This is also true when writing a book, for writing a book is like having a conversation—one must reflect on the topic, go beyond bias and prejudice, and then squarely face the issue itself.

This is all the more true if the conversation dwells on an event like *Humanae Vitae*. It is an *event* and not just a *document* because Paul VI's encyclical, when the classical costume of papal documents has been removed, is something that can be reduced to concrete, real-life situations. Beyond its statement of principles and beyond the motives underlying it, which not everyone has succeeded in grasping, it touches a too real and too controversial sphere of modern life to be anything less than an event —an event that has without a doubt left its mark on our age and that has possibly opened up a new era in the presence of the Church and the Papacy in the world. The world holds a different attitude toward the Church today. For better or for worse? The predictions will necessarily differ according to who formulates them. It depends on whether that person views the Church as a purely historical fact, subject to all the ups and downs of history, or whether he views it as a value that, although conditioned— and at times led astray—by historical influences, is at the same time the bearer of a message which transcends history. Be it one or the other, one thing is certain: *Humanae Vitae* will not be passed over like any other papal document. This is shown by the extent and the intensity of the debate it has provoked.

One thing that has immediately become evident is that while

1

the first reactions centered rather on one precise point, the ban on the use of contraceptives, this, paradoxically, very soon came to be seen as a side issue. A host of other problems have slowly accumulated around the initial nucleus and have sparked off a real debate, a round table conference on a world scale. It would seem that the number of interlocutors on the famous Pontifical Commission has been increased to include even those who have never taken any interest in the matter in question, and who have seen it only from the point of view of eventual permission to use progestative drugs for birth-control purposes.

The most significant repercussion up to date, however, has been the way that the issue has broadened so as to reach not just beyond the circle of specialists, but also beyond the sphere of the Catholic Church and, what is more, beyond the strictly religious sphere itself. Whether the reactions be ones of rejection, of criticism, of delusion, or on the other hand, of optimism, of acceptance, and of convinced adhesion, they are never trivial or superficial. Even though they betray at times a lack of cultural background or the technical knowledge necessary to discuss the problems that have arisen, they all bear witness to an authenticity and a passionate concern which reveals and makes us aware of a phenomenon to which great importance is to be attached. It is the fact that people today are extremely involved in the problems of their situation in life and of their destiny in a civilization of which the outlines are now being shaped and of which they want to become full-fledged participants and not just actors moved by directors, no matter who they be.

Another fact which is emerging, tending to support a realistic, wise optimism, is the fact that it is simply not true, as is often heard, that men have completely lost their capacity for making moral judgments or all their ethical sensitivity in their actions and their decisions. This issue must not be confused with the question of classical moral language. Possibly the negative reactions to *Humanae Vitae* are more the result of an inability to understand its language, which, no one would deny, modern man has great difficulty in making intelligible. Possibly it is this which is the real bone of contention rather than the deeper issues and the real concerns that led Paul VI to draw conclusions which have been enthusiastically shared by only a handful. It is becoming all the more apparent, too, that the basic issue is not even the encyclical and its decisions, but one involving man, his present problems and his hopes for the future. This issue involves the encyclical only in a secondary way, and even then not so much by criticizing or accepting the document as such, but rather by asking it several fundamental questions which may have radical and revolutionary consequences. Is Christianity capable of understanding the man of today? Will it be capable of understanding the man of tomorrow? Does its message of transcendence and salvation have any real raison d'etre today when man has in his grasp such enormous possibilities for building his own world, his own future, and his own salvation? Speaking more generally, is the religious and ethical ideal an advancement of man and an inspiration for his future? Is it capable of accepting the future in all the dimensions that it will assume, or is it rather an unnecessary intrusion and a dangerous extrapolation which impedes this process?

These questions provoke innumerable others that besiege not only the religious man or the man of faith but any man who is concerned with his future and his present situation as directed toward that future. In this sense *Humanae Vitae* may be said to have the positive function of being an interrogation mark placed over the central problem of human life itself, that of the birth of life, its insertion into the family and into society. It is almost certain that the text of the encyclical as such will be superseded before long, but it will probably always remain a fundamental interrogation mark. Paul VI struggled with this basic problem for years and it eventually forced him to make a decision which to many appears as a prophetic gesture for the future, over and above its immediate significance which probably will soon be superseded.

Moreover, the entire present moment in which we are living is one great interrogation mark. Very few things are secure and many are passing through a period of crisis. Could not a papal document also humbly participate, as is true to its Christian vocation, in this great interrogation mark which is our age? The Christian knows that nothing, not even any of his wise and carefully considered choices, is ever the "last word," for the last word always lies beyond human choices. Every choice that the Christian makes, even though provisional and susceptible to evolution, has in it something of the truth which, together with all men, it is approaching.

The scope of this book is precisely this "approaching together." It is not a book written for specialists. It is simply a dialogue "together with all men," whether they be believers or nonbelievers, credulous or critical, disillusioned or enthusiastic, specialists or simply people concerned with themselves, their families, and their countries. We have read their statements with the desire of understanding the vastness of the issues and problems brought to light by the encyclical. *Humanae Vitae* has unexpectedly become a catalyst that has revealed all the distress, the searching, and the uncertainties of today. More than 4,000 texts in 15 different languages have accumulated at IDO-C. It is an enormous and variegated mass of documents, extremely complex and difficult to grasp in their extreme diversity of attitudes, backgrounds, perspectives, and styles.

A selection was necessary, but many different factors had to be taken into consideration: their backgrounds, particular significance, originality, and nonexcessive degree of specialization. From all this it was first necessary to establish the basic outlines of the discussion and then follow this discussion through the dialectic which emerged after an initial reading of the texts.

The book has no intention of proving anything, either "for" or "against." On some occasions a comment has been added or a mention made of some weakness or ambiguous statement. On other occasions the reader, by comparing and contrasting the various texts himself, has been left with the margin necessary for his personal, honest reflection.

The first problem to rear its head was that of space. The final result would have consisted of several thousand pages of text and would hardly have been accessible to the nonspecialized public for which it is intended. Several chapters, therefore, had to be excluded and others given a more modest size. It was with particular regret that we excluded the chapter dedicated to the large number of interesting reactions from the bishops of the world. We say "with particular regret" because these represent the first known case of a reconsideration and, one could well say, a "rescaling" of a papal document. The specialist will certainly look elsewhere for his more detailed research, but even he may be able to discover in these lines something hidden from his scientific research: the concrete, living voice of the man in the street, the doctor, the demographer, the biologist, the politician, and the journalist. What do they think? What do they say? What do they do? It is vitally important to know this. Does the much-feared "public opinion" have any value for the magisterium or for the religious community which is the Church? Is it possibly even necessary? Might it not be the modern translation of the old aphorism "Vox populi, vox Dei"?

This is why we have spoken of honesty as being the first virtue: honesty in attempting to understand a document entailing looking farther than just at its rather antiquated language, honesty in considering and understanding the language and ideas of the men of our time. In any case, is not the Church itself this reality, made up of the men on the street more than of the men in Curias and technical commissions?

Chapter 1   A Controversial History

There is more to morality than the "Pill"
Two different views of man—love and natural law
A new look at sexuality
The Pope wants enlightenment
A sensation in the English-speaking world and a hot
      July 25
What values have majorities and minorities?

There Is More to Morality than the "Pill"

What has just been stated must be made quite clear. Although the discussion arose over one specific problem, its field has now been greatly extended and many more issues have been brought into consideration. Unfortunately the debate ended up in the arena of public opinion. Not least responsible for this was the immense press coverage concentrated almost entirely on the question of contraceptives. This gave rise to a kind of "pill war" not only among the general public but also among the experts, as if nothing more were involved in the question than contraceptives. True, this was an important aspect of the question, but it came after a series of other far more important and fundamental considerations. A discussion which should have been carried much farther forward thus degenerated into little more than a fragmentary, casuistic skirmish. People found themselves caught up in a casuistic morality at the very time when the general desire was to leave it behind.

The encyclical, too, showed signs of this, having been set in motion as it was by an issue too easily reduced to the level of contraceptive devices, even though it was published some time after the discussion had broken out. In a way, the encyclical recognizes this when it encourages "the men of science, who can considerably advance the welfare of marriage and the family, along with peace of conscience, if by pooling their efforts they labor to explain more thoroughly the various conditions favoring a proper regulation of births" (No. 24).

The encyclical recognizes the fact that scientific research can lead to further openings on this moral problem, even if it seems to maintain, immediately afterward, that scientific research will do little more than prove what the encyclical has already taught. In his first general audience at Castel Gandolfo after the promulgation of the encyclical, Paul VI stated that not all the problems of family and married life had been touched in the encyclical, and he added that the magisterium would be able and would be forced to deal with them in a fuller way later. In addition, the same encyclical says that "the problem of birth, like every other problem regarding human life, is to be considered beyond partial perspectives—whether of the biological or psy-

7

chological, demographic or sociological, orders—in the light of an integral vision of man and his vocation" (No. 7).

In spite of the fact, then, that this concern is evident in the encyclical, it ends up giving the general impression of being little more than a ban on the use of contraceptives and an undue intrusion into the intimate problems of marriage.

In the *Ami du Clerge* of September 12, 1968, M. Huftier observes:

The encyclical, it must be remembered, is concerned with a precise point and does not encompass the whole of morality. This very limited sector of human, moral behavior has become more important today not only as a result, as some people are eager to point out, of the "aphrodisiacal" atmosphere in which we live, but above all because today, more so than in the past, people are marrying for love. Couples want to integrate their sexual life with their moral life. There is no such thing as moral behavior on one hand and the reality of married life on the other. The goal conscientiously assigned to marriage by numerous young couples is the growth of their love, both spiritually and bodily. It is true that procreation is also an essential objective of this mutual love, but it may not take its place. It is even less right to ask the couples, for the sake of procreation, to sacrifice this growing understanding of the true meaning of their love.

The majority of the reactions reported in this "dossier" will show that the more serious public opinion agrees with Huftier, and that it devotes more attention to those controversial, basic issues already being discussed before the appearance of the encyclical. Normally it is on these points that the encyclical is either attacked or defended. And, besides, it is certainly not the encyclical's intention to freeze far wider and more accurate research into the basic issues already discussed. What, then, are these fundamental topics which go to make up the "prehistory" of the encyclical? Their basic outlines may be sketched as follows: the understanding of man and the natural law, the relationship between the law of love and the law of nature, the meaning of sexuality and fertility in marriage, the moral norm in relation to individual conscience, the value of married intimacy, and the purpose of marriage. Clearly the encyclical deals more with the concrete results of this deeper anthropological and moral reflection. Even though the encyclical on its side gives one particular solution to such problems, all the same it cannot abolish the problems. Several of them are still being analyzed, and they are all so linked together that this delays a better understanding of them and their interdependence. What, then, is the encyclical's history?

Two Different Views of Man—Love and Natural Law

From the beginning of the nineteenth century, ecclesiastical authority has repeatedly criticized certain practices affecting the integrity of intercourse. The *copula interrupta* is condemned in a "responsum" of the Sacred Penitentiary in 1822, then in 1823, and in 1824. In a responsum of 1851 this practice is defined as "scandalous, wrong, and contrary to the natural law of marriage." In a responsum of 1853 from the Holy Office, the use of the "condom" is said to be "intrinsically evil." In a responsum of 1916 the Sacred Penitentiary speaks in general terms of "an instrument," and states that a man who uses an instrument should be put on the same level as someone who rapes a woman.

The teaching of the encyclical *Casti Connubii* is identical. It has, furthermore, become the classical statement on the matter. The most important passages are the following:

> But no reason whatever, even the gravest, can make what is intrinsically against nature become conformable with nature and morally good. The conjugal act is of its very nature designed for the procreation of offspring. Therefore those who in performing it deliberately deprive it of its natural power and efficacy, act against nature and do something which is shameful and intrinsically immoral. . . .
>
> The Catholic Church . . . raises her voice . . . and through our mouth proclaims anew that any use of matrimony whatsoever in the exercise of which the act is deprived, by human interference, of its natural power to procreate life, is an offense against the law of God and of nature, and that those who commit it are guilty of a grave sin.

Pius XII endorses this declaration of his predecessor issued on December 31, 1931 in an allocution of October 29, 1951. Very soon, however, a certain fact starts becoming clear. A gap is growing between the opinions of an increasing number of Catholics and the ecclesiastical directives. Headway starts being made, too, with the idea that Catholics have the right to follow a line of behavior which departs from the norm if it is their personal conviction. It thus becomes clear that it is not enough to simply repeat what has been said in the past. This only leads to an ever-widening gulf between the voice of the Church and the behavior of Catholics. What is in fact happening is that the problem is becoming progressively clearer on the anthropological level and in the growth of modern thought. The ecclesiastical texts quoted above obviously presuppose a line of thought in anthropology which affects Catholic theology as well as contemporary philosophical thought. When the conclusions that this anthropology leads to are developed it becomes patently clear why Catholics are finding it more and more difficult to accept the ecclesiastical directives. If it is true that ethical norms in marriage are, in the last analysis, anthropological questions, it is obvious that the difficulty will not be solved so long as moral theology persists in concentrating on the natural law as an absolute norm. From here onward the question must be studied on another level, the anthropological.

In the space of a few years the fact starts dawning that one vision of man is slowly being replaced by another and that the two easily finish up clashing.

At the base of the ecclesiastical declarations quoted above is a vision of man which has prevailed in the philosophical and theological thought of the Church for many centuries and is still partly accepted. It betrays its Greek origins by the fact that it attempts to grasp the essence of man, and consequently has a rather static character about it. Man consists of a body and a soul, called matter and form by the philosophers. In this fundamental definition of man, saving grace becomes an attribute of the soul (for St. Thomas, however, the body considered as locus of the moral virtues also has this meaning). In this way the body becomes the object of moral actions. From here onward theology concentrates almost exclusively on the soul and its beatific vision.

Even this view attempts to defend the unity of human life. The body belongs to the essence of man himself and is God's creation. It and the soul are interdependent and together form man. There are other ways, however, to express this fundamental duality. One has slowly become more accepted in modern existentialist philosophy.

This philosophy tries to approach man's existential experience with as few prejudices as possible and goes about it without any a priori reference to any type of existing metaphysics. For this reason it has found notable points of contact with biblical thought. Hence modern philosophical thought is making itself felt more and more in dogmatic as well as in moral theology. This anthropology devotes its attention to man's existence, maintaining that nothing can be learned about man unless by means of this. Rather than give abstract definitions of the essence of man, it studies man's relationship with other men and with God.

In this way man is seen as the subject of different relationships with his subjectivity being manifested in his body. Man is at the same time a subject in his body and an embodied subject. From this point of view it is no longer possible to consider the body as simply the object of moral actions arising from the soul. Corporality is one aspect of this acting subject and every action, even the most elevated, bears the mark of this corporality. Thus man's unity is asserted in a radically new way. At the same time it steers clear of the danger always lurking in the background of the former view of man, that of giving less importance to the body and the sexuality which is part of it. This explains the present reevaluation of the body, of sexuality, and of the whole mission of man on earth.

Marriage morality is coming to be seen more and more in the framework of this new view of man. What is more, theologians and moralists are seeing it as all the more valid not only because this "new" anthropology does not come into conflict with revelation about the dignity and destiny of man, but above all, because it gives a shot in the arm to a number of different doctrinal points, such as the saving meaning of the resurrection of Christ and the cosmic view of redemption. Even though the question is being faced in a positive and not intentionally polemical way, it necessarily involves a criticism of the former view of man. Whenever any new thinking arises, it automatically puts the previously accepted teaching in a precarious position.

11

Criticism begins to be leveled not only at its basic assertions but also at those ecclesiastical laws formulated along the lines of the old thinking.

One essential element directly bound up with the reappraisal of man is the understanding of the rights of nature, or natural law. This is especially important because the greater part of the reasoning of *Humanae Vitae* is based on it. It has become, in fact, the point most vulnerable to philosophical and theological criticism in the encyclical.

With this outlook it is becoming progressively clearer that the classical opinion that intercourse is permitted only with a view to procreation is giving place to the opinion that intercourse has a value if it answers the personal needs of the couple, even if procreation is no longer possible. This change of perspective anchors the definition of the natural law of marriage. Following the logic of the classical ecclesiastical declarations on marriage relations, such relations are in harmony with natural law only if there exists the natural capacity for procreation in the act of intercourse. This means, in fact, that the male seed must be deposited in the woman's vagina. Therefore coitus interruptus, or the use of mechanical and chemical means to prevent ovulation, is forbidden because these means are contrary to nature. Now it is precisely at this view of natural law that criticisms have been leveled. The criticism can be summed up in one precise question: Is this act which is held to fulfill the natural law really the total act—totally fulfilling the conditions of the natural order?

It has been tacitly accepted from the start that pregnancy results from this act. In nature the act of coupling consists in the fact that the male impregnates the female. On the human level it is also impossible to divide the event into act and effect. Impregnation is part of the whole of the sexual act. According to the natural law it then follows that intercourse is permitted only when it has procreation as its objective, because only then does it conform to the natural order of things. This was the reason for not allowing intercourse except when, explicitly or implicitly, it was performed with the intention to procreate. If, however, because of the personal needs of the couple, the sexual act is permitted during periods in which pregnancy is impossible, then an intention is given to the sexual act which it does not have in nature. At the same time, it is presumed that there is no need for the natural intention to be adhered to at that moment. If, then, it is presumed that conjugal relationships may be licit without their being necessarily fecund, this is to admit at the same time that it is now a question of human and not animal sexuality, and that on this level the personal relationships of the couple have more importance than the preservation of the natural order.

This was the decisive step taken in establishing the principle of morality in marriage. But this principle could not be held so long as it was affirmed at the same time that the natural order must be preserved. It could only be accepted by separating intercourse from procreation and relating natural law only to intercourse. The definition of natural law in marriage, that is becoming more and more common, was introduced in this way.

Moral theology began to give an absolute value to this norm, and it is the criterion by which all the various contraceptive methods are at present morally evaluated.

Another problem presented itself when couples themselves found it difficult to see how intercourse could possibly be allowed when the fertile periods were avoided, and yet not be allowed when pregnancy was avoided by using contraceptives. In both cases the natural order is being put in danger in circumstances that make it incomplete. In both cases the sexual impulse is being aroused with full knowledge that it will not be able to attain its natural objective. It is difficult to be theoretically convincing in such cases by saying that in one case the male seed is "lost" and in another case it is not. Therefore, even by looking at impregnation in the total context of the sexual act, one does not get a complete picture of the reality which is the starting point for a formulation of natural law.

Sexuality is more than a psychological structure, for it includes sense and psychic elements which together compose the complete whole along with the psychological structure. Even animal sexuality has these elements. They belong to corporality. Nature determines the psychic elements of sexuality as well as

13

the biological structure of the organism. Moral theology put so much stress on the organism in its definition of the natural law that it gave the impression that the natural law had nothing to do with the psychic elements. Possibly this overemphasis on the organic structure came from the old anthropology where the soul-body and spirit-matter formulas easily led to reducing sexuality to simply something material and tangible.

Absolute endorsement of the natural law is the end result of an anthropology which sees the immutable organic structure as the objective. Obviously a norm that has as its point of departure an objectivized organism will tend to become both absolute and static; the individual must act according to the norm as legislated by nature itself. But if a truly human sexuality is composed of all the biological, sense, and psychic elements of sexuality, then the norm will change. In such a case the individual must take into consideration not only his physical makeup but also and above all the psychic aspects of his sexuality. In this way the highest norm of moral action is found to be the law of love. Just as the fact of being a person represents a higher value in the whole of human life than the isolated sexuality that man shares with animals, so the law of love, which corresponds to the higher dignity of man considered as a person, is a higher law than the natural law which corresponds to the sexual faculties.

In the same way that reason enlightens and humanizes the sexual element in human relationships, so the law of love enlightens and humanizes the natural law. It is impossible to talk of natural law by itself. It can only be talked of in relation to the law of love.

These were the kind of basic considerations which catalyzed further thought on sexuality and its meaning and value in a balanced married life.

A New Look at Sexuality

Not only did the conclusions of a large part of contemporary thinking lead to a fuller appreciation of human sexuality, they also led to establishing a link between natural law and love. These two consequences are connected. If a person's sexuality is bound up with his love, then sexuality is once again placed in the framework of human dignity. This excludes any other criterion for defining the norm of morality.

First, then, human sexuality gains in importance. Consequently, this destroys the taboo surrounding sex, or at least it establishes the premises which will do so. Seen from the vantage point of the new anthropology, the natural law does not disappear but becomes part of the grandeur of love. Intercourse should be rooted in mutual, personal love. Without it, the act loses its human qualities. The couple's intercourse is incomplete until not only love but also the natural order is shown in all its fullness. As a general rule, then, it can be presumed that the use of technical means which undermine the integrity of intercourse is not to be allowed. Such interferences have their repercussions on the emotional level which is, in turn, closely bound up with married love itself.

A better appreciation of sexuality, however, shows that the natural law is relative. The natural sexual order cannot be investigated by itself since it is included in the reciprocal love of the couple. For this reason the moral norm deduced from the law of love is not absolute. In the name of love, it may be found necessary to break the natural order of sexuality. Even if the use of contraceptives is against the natural physical order, it can become allowable in certain cases. In such a perspective the personal responsibility of the couple is stressed far more than before. As long as the moral norm is derived from an immutable fact such as the physical organism, it is possible to make laws that apply in theory to every particular case. Under such circumstances it would make good sense to say that the use of contraceptives and coitus interruptus are never allowed and there is nothing that a couple can do except submit to this ruling.

But the theologians would ask if it is still possible to speak of a Christian moral code. There is no chance, in such a case, of love ever becoming a joyful inspiration for morality. It can only be a moral strength that helps one to put into practice the norms which are imposed from outside. Nature is put above the person and law is put above love. Setting norms of action becomes the domain of an outside authority, and the only thing left for love is to put the norms into practice. What meaning, then, have the words which St. Paul uses to describe the new state of life of Christians? "But if you follow the leading of the Spirit, you stand clear of the law (Gal. 5:18)." Because of all these difficulties, a different way of viewing marriage morality from the classical one was put forward. It was not done without exposing to strong criticism the old morality and the anthropology on which it was based.

The moral theologian A. Valsecchi in his book *Regolazione delle nascite. Un decennio di riflessioni teologiche,* Brescia, 1967, summed up the main issues and indicated the problems which would arise over the use of contraceptives in these words:

The initial criticism directed against the traditional position took it upon itself to show up that position's extremely fragile rational arguments, and carried the offensive against its basic point that every act of intercourse must always be directed toward procreation, thus coming up with the distinction, later to strike such good fortune, between the fertility of the act and the fertility of marriage. Its conclusion was that it was not the particular act but sexuality as a whole which possessed that intrinsic orientation to a fertility—and to a fertility worthy of man—that through all of married life would never be frustrated. Each individual act had to fulfill what was demanded in the expression of conjugal love, and this love found its main area of growth precisely in sexuality. But if, at first, more than one theologian felt he could retain the duty of complete intercourse in this way, a duty which was evidently no longer required just for the sake of procreation (intercourse, it began to be said, had to be complete in order to be totally integrating for the couple), it was not long before the weaknesses in even this line of reasoning became evident. For in what way is the physical completion of coitus absolutely necessary for an adequate expression of conjugal love? Would not this kind of thinking bring in through the back door the "physicism" refuted previously?

A series of studies was added to these speculations with the intention of showing the correct Christian position on the issue. Biblical and patristic thought came to be seen as far less categorical than first thought. The observant eye of the historian noticed that traditional thought on the matter, although opposed to contraception, did not appear to be irreversible, either because it was based at the time on reasons no longer tenable or because it became clearer how much it depended on ideas of sexuality in which the influence of imported anthropologies was far more visible than the influence of the original Christian thought. There were still the declarations of the magisterium, especially those of Pius XI and Pius XII. An attempt was made, however, to put them in their historical context, showing how much even these owed to a reformable view of sexuality or else simply responded to the urgent pastoral need of erecting a comfortable bulwark to defend important values in married life. The conciliar document went no farther than to state what these values were [*Gaudium et Spes,* in those passages which treat of marriage—EDITOR], just as the magisterium's partial insight into these values had already led it to show the benefit of sterile days.

The couple tending toward that community of love on which marriage is built, could make these sexual acts a mature expression of that love and in this way work at bringing about a generous, responsible fertility in which their union would find its fulfillment. Sexuality would thus be put at the service of love. It became clear, therefore, that the conjugal act, even if no longer bound up with the normative principle of biological completion, did not on account of this lose all intrinsic possibility of being subject to a norm.

The Pope Wants Enlightenment

The theological debate had to have repercussions in the Council. The starting point of discussion in the Council, however, was clearly the traditional teaching, notably that of *Casti Connubii* and of Pius XII. A schema, *De castitate, virginitate, matrimonio, familia,* drawn up by the preparatory commission and presented to the Fathers on July 13, 1962, put forward a doctrinal synthesis on marriage in the 4 chapters of the second part. In this, the primary end of marriage was put "solely" in the procreation and education of the offspring, while the "mutual help of the couple" and the "remedy for concupiscence" were proposed as "secondary" ends. Contraceptive practices, including "conjugal onanism," were condemned as intrinsically and gravely sinful. The right was upheld, however, of making the number of offspring proportionate to the economic conditions of the respective families and of society in general. It was to be a prudent judgment that also took into account the providential help of God. This was simply the teaching normally given in moral theology, presented without any changes. The Schema, besides, was characterized by a canonical-juridical mentality together with a polemical attitude against errors and deviations (by the end of the 4 chapters, 21 condemnations had been uttered).

The Schema was never discussed. At the end of the first session of the Council it was decided to reduce to 17 the number of schemas to be examined. It was also decided that the subject matter on marriage and the family would make up part of a new schema which was to deal with the relationship between the Church and the modern world. Neither did this new text get as far as the Council floor. Its history is complex and intricate. It is sufficient to note that both it and the following drafts rose above the dispute over the ends of marriage (the word ends is completely missing from the text), and gave a nonjuridical formulation of the sum of the values which marriage must attain. The first of these values emphasized was married love, described as "a mutual, free gift of oneself in one spirit and in one flesh and through an interior union of sentiments; a tender affection kept alive and proved by deeds, overcoming a simple, superficial affective inclination." It was stated, moreover, that fertility should be the result of this kind of love, but that the absence of love does not deprive marriage of its fundamental value and indissolubility. It is all a matter of a generous fertility which is brought about with "a full and conscious responsibility according to the gifts of God and the norm of true love" (cf. the whole development of Schema XIII and the evolution of the teaching, also the incidents that held the conciliar assembly and public opinion in astonishment for a long time, in Jan Grootaer's essay, *Il Concilio di fronte ai problemi di matrimonio e della famiglia—Le tre letture dello Schema XIII*, in *Diritti del sesso e matrimonio*, Milan, 1968, pp. 133–72).

In the meantime, Pope John XXIII had established in March 1963 an extraordinary commission of 6 members (3 theologians and 3 laymen) to study the extent to which the Catholic Church should reexamine its teachings on marriage morality. This commission met for the first time in October 1963. Pope John wanted to be enlightened and so started off a discussion among the experts. At the same time, however, it was a recognition that even the Pope should be and wanted to be kept informed. But Pope John died on June 3, 1963 after a short, fascinating pontificate. He did not get the chance even to be present at the first sitting of his commission. In January 1964 the new Pope Paul VI increased to 12 the number on the commission, the members of which he kept secret. On June 23, 1964, Paul VI announced to the cardinals that the question of birth control was continuously being studied with the collaboration of highly reputed experts, and that he would give a conclusion as soon as possible in the way he considered most suitable. He said at that time:

Everyone is talking of this problem. . . . It is an extremely complex and delicate one. The Church is aware of its many aspects. And the Church will have to proclaim this law of God in the light of the scientific, social, and theological truths which have been made the object of very wide study and documentation in the last few years. We hope to quickly bring this study to an end with the collaboration of highly reputed experts. . . . But we frankly state that up to now we do not have sufficient reason to consider out-of-date and consequently not binding, the norms given by Pius XII in this regard. These norms must be considered valid, at least until we feel obliged in conscience to change them.

When the conciliar sessions resumed between October 28 and 30, 1964, a lively debate flared up in the Council hall. The different points of view on the problem were by now clear. One of the four "moderators" of the Council, Cardinal Suenens, made a particularly strong intervention and stressed the work that the commission was to engage in:

The commission's first task is in the area of faith and consists in seeing if we have brought all aspects of the teaching of the Church on marriage sufficiently into light up till now. Of course, this does not mean modifying or putting in doubt the really traditional teaching of the Church. It means knowing if we will fully open our hearts to the Holy Spirit to understand the divine truth. The gospel remains always the same. But no age can pride itself on having fully penetrated the unfathomable riches of Christ. The Spirit has been promised us to progressively introduce up into the fullness of truth.

Thus the Church must never repudiate a truth she has taught in the past, but as she progresses into a fuller understanding of the gospel, she may and must integrate this truth into an ever richer synthesis and reveal the ever more fruitful quality of these principles. In this way the Church draws from her treasure house things new and old. With this agreed upon, it is important to examine whether we have maintained in perfect equilibrium all the dimensions of the Church's teaching on marriage. Maybe we have emphasized the words "increase and multiply" to such an extent that we have left in the shade the other divine pronouncement, "And they shall become two in one flesh." These two truths are central and both are from sacred scripture. They must illuminate each other in the light of the full truth revealed to us in our Lord Jesus Christ.

It is the commission's task to tell us whether we have put too much stress on the primary end of procreation, to the detriment of an equally vital end which is the growth in conjugal unity. . . . Let it not be said that this is going to open up the way to moral laxity. This problem does not exist because the faithful are trying to satisfy their passions and their egotism, but because the best of them are anxiously trying to live this double fidelity to the teaching of the Church and to what marital and parental love has taught them. The commission's second task is in the area of scientific progress and a deeper knowledge of natural ethics. The commission will have to examine whether the classical doctrine, especially that of the manuals, takes sufficient account of the new insights of modern science. We have made some progress since Aristotle, and we have discovered the complexity of the reality where what is biological interferes with what is psychological and the conscious with the subconscious. New possibilities are constantly being discovered in man in his power to direct the course of nature. Hence there arises a deeper awareness of the unity of man, both in his being as an embodied spirit and in the dynamisms of all his life—a unity that is as it were the heart of Thomistic anthropology: there follows equally a more exact estimate of his rational power over the world entrusted to him. Who does not see that thus we are perhaps being led to further inquiries on the quest of what is according to or against nature? We shall follow the progress of science.

I beg you, my brothers; let us avoid a new Galileo case; one is enough for the Church.

It will pertain to the commission to integrate new elements into the total vision and to submit its conclusions to the supreme magisterium.

And I hope it will not be said that by this new synthesis we are giving way to what is called situation ethics. It is fitting that the exposition of doctrine, which is unchangeable in its principles, should take account of contingent factors which are in evolution in the course of history. That is what was done by the Popes who successively wrote *Rerum Novarum, Quadragesimo Anno* and *Mater et Magistra* in order to express with greater precision the same principle in terms of a new age.

On the same day, October 29, Patriarch Maximos IV Saigh intervened along the same lines:

This problem is at the base of a grave crisis of the Catholic conscience. Cannot we almost call it a division between the official teaching of the Church and the opposite behavior on the part of the immense majority of Christian couples? The authority of the Church is being questioned on a large scale. The faithful are finding themselves forced to live separated from Church law, far. from the sacraments, in continual anxiety, unable to find a suitable solution between the two contradictory imperatives: conscience and normal married life. . . . Frankly, ought not the official position of the Church on this matter be revised in the light of modern science, both theological and medical, psychological and sociological?

In marriage, the blossoming out of the personality and his or her integration into God's creative plan form a whole. The end of marriage ought therefore not to be dissected into a primary end and a secondary end. This consideration opens the horizon onto new perspectives concerning the morality of conjugal behavior in its totality.

And moreover are we not in the right to ask ourselves if certain official positions are not to be attributed to outdated conceptions and perhaps also to a psychosis of celibates who are strangers to this sector of life? Are we not, without wishing it, burdened by that Manichaean conception of man and of the world for which the work of the flesh, vitiated in itself, is only tolerated in view of the child?

Is the external biological correctness of actions the sole criterion of morality here, independent of the life of the couple, its moral climate as a marriage and as a family, and the weighty imperatives of prudence, the fundamental rule of all human activity?

This aged Eastern patriarch gave a speech which was extremely clear, intelligible, cognizant, and up-to-date, while at the same time deeply loyal (so characteristically Eastern) to *tradition*. This put not a few against him. But he was not the only one to speak in this way. On the same day Cardinal Léger of Montreal, who was later to leave his cardinal's see to go to work in a leprosarium in Africa, intervened. His words, too, were along the lines of those of Patriarch Maximos IV.

On the following day, however, Cardinal Ottaviani replied with his customary sureness and frankness, strongly criticizing, on the basis of the classical view, what had been said by the other Fathers the day before. He stated: "It is clearly against the purpose of marriage, for marriage puts no limit to procreation. The problems brought up by the Schema—except those dealing with health reasons—can be solved, especially if we are penetrated by the Spirit of the cross of Christ." And Ottaviani concluded by saying, "I am surprised by what was said in the Council yesterday, putting in doubt the teaching up to now on the principles of married life. Does not this way of looking at the question put in doubt maybe the inerrancy of the Church? Or in past centuries was the Holy Spirit not in the Church to illuminate minds on this point of doctrine?"

In an interview granted by Ottaviani to the weekly *Vita* of June 3, 1964, he said that the new outlook would have made the use of the Pill lawful and this "could favor hedonism." When in the Council the debate was under way and a clear break started to become apparent, Paul VI removed the problem from conciliar discussion and took it upon himself, delegating the study of it to the Papal Commission, which was increased in size in March 1965. It had its fourth sitting in Rome with the work being done in secret. In fact, it was understood to be a purely consultative organ of the Pontiff. To its ranks were added new experts, doctors, sociologists, theologians, and some Catholic married couples. On March 27, the Pope received in audience the members of the commission and asked that its work be speeded up. Among other things he told them:

We ask you insistently not to lose sight of the urgency of a situation that demands unambiguous indications from the Church and from its supreme authority. Men's consciences cannot be exposed to the uncertainties that too often hinder married life today from developing according to the design of the Lord. . . . Here are the guidelines which your research has to follow: on the one hand a better knowledge of physiological and medical laws, of demographic movements and of social change; on the other hand, and above all, there is the level of superior illumination that the data of faith and the traditional teaching of the Church project on these facts. The Church, like a careful mother, is concerned in every age with giving a proper reply to the great problems that men are faced with. . . . In this present case the problem presented can be summed up in this way: in what way and according to what norms must the couple fulfill, in the exercise of their mutual love, this service to life to which their vocation calls them? The Christian conscience will always be inspired by the consciousness of its duties, of the dignity of the married state in which the love of the Christian couple is ennobled by the grace of the sacrament, and of the greatness of the gift made to a child called to life.

Hesitations and divergent trends were in any case evident in the commission. It was admitted by Cardinal Ottaviani in an interview in the weekly *Amica* of June 2, 1966:

It is not possible to say at the moment when the work of the Pontifical Commission will be finished, especially because the scientific factors on which the examination of the question turns are still uncertain, and the experts themselves are not in agreement in their conclusions. Disagreement is particularly evident as to how certain discoveries function and still more as to their immediate and long-term effects.

This seems to suggest that in the commission there was a particular area of scientific discussion—one of the two aspects stressed by Paul in his allocution—which was especially difficult, and those upholding the classical position found support for their solution in this difficulty. Almost at the same time, however, the well-known moral theologian, Bernard Häring, a Council expert and member of the commission, let it be understood that the discussion had taken on far wider proportions. He wrote an article in the bimonthly *Rocca* of January 1–15, 1966, where, among other things, he states:

In the conciliar text on the Church and in the world of our time, the chapter on marriage clearly states that in the end it is the couple themselves that have to decide in conscience before God if they must bring new life into the world. Neither the confessor nor any other earthly authority may take their place in this decision. But this decision has to be made "before God" taking Providence into consideration as far as the couple are able to interpret it. Faith in Providence does not mean allowing oneself to be led by blind instinct, but on the contrary, examining God's gifts with wide-open eyes and with a grateful heart. In this way the couple will be able to foresee if they are capable of giving their children a suitable upbringing. The responsible attitude on the part of parents is something entirely different from what is commonly called "birth planning" where the parents say that they will have two children and no more. Responsible parents do not make a once-for-all plan, but always reconsider the real possibilities.

Häring then underlined the fact that the Council texts concerning families and married life "offer a splendid vision of the couple's vocation," and that in them the Council Fathers "give proof of a great understanding of the difficulties of husbands and wives." This amounts to an admission on the part of one of the most up-to-date theologians today that a real evolution has occurred since the drafting of the first text of the Schema, which was characterized by a moralism and legalism criticized and found unacceptable by the greater part of the Council members.

In the meantime *L'Osservatore Romano* of March 7–8, 1966, reported that the Pope had increased the size of the Commission, nominating seven cardinals (among them were Suenens and J. Lefebvre) and nine bishops. He also nominated as president of the same commission, Cardinal Ottaviani, and as vice-presidents Cardinals Döpfner and Heenan. The Dominican P. H. de Riedmatten was nominated secretary.

The Papal Commission carried on its work at an intense pace, finishing on June 25, 1966, and handed over its conclusions to the Pope, who took it upon himself to study them with a view to his decision. The experts had come together from April 14 to June 4, and in the course of the six successive sessions had studied the problem in its entirety under all its aspects: theological, moral, pastoral, social, medical, and demographical. From June 6 to 18 the experts had met in plenary session and had studied the conclusions of the different specialized commissions in order to coordinate them. From July 19 to 25 the members of the commission of cardinals and archbishops set up by the Pope had put together a report of the conclusions and proposals that the commission of experts had reached. An overview of the entire work of the commission and of the subcommission of

and the crucial period which the teaching and disciplinary authority of the Church, or more modestly, Rome, was undergoing.

A Sensation in the English-speaking World and a Hot July 25

This was the state of affairs during the first months of 1967. Some people were simply expecting a restatement of the traditional teaching. Others were expecting the same but were convinced that there would be a certain openness toward the theological movement felt to be by now irreversible. This opinion seems to have been strengthened by a new and rather sensational occurrence. The American *National Catholic Reporter* and the English *Tablet* published in their entirety the three reports drawn up and submitted to the Pope by the Papal Commission. Up till this time only the existence of a report was known of, but now not only was there proof that a huge majority favored and brought forward proofs to justify a change and development in the teaching, but also the final texts themselves could be seen side by side. They did nothing other than reaffirm and sharpen even more the positions which had slowly been crystallizing for several years in the debate. The reports in fact represented the two positions held in the commission: on one side that of the "classicists," and on the other that of the "personalists," or "renewalists." No compromise was reached by a synthesis expressed in a single document. This was certainly for the better for it avoided superficiality and expressed exactly what the two positions maintained.

The title of the first document, *Schema of the Document on Responsible Parenthood*, suggested a clear line of reasoning. Its authors were reputed to be Fr. Joseph Fuchs, German Jesuit professor at the Gregorian University; Fr. Raymond Sigmond, Hungarian Dominican, president of the Institute of Social Sciences and Developmental Research at Paris; Paul Anciaux, professor at the major seminary at Malines; Prof. A. Auer of Wurzburg, specialist in sexological problems; Michel Labourdette, Dominican theologian at Toulouse; and Pierre de Locht, of the National Center of Family Pastoral Care at Brussels. The document was signed, however, by thirteen other theologians and by various other experts in different specialized matters that the commission dealt with. It can be considered as the basic document and as most faithfully portraying the positions reached not only in the commission itself but also in the whole contemporary thought on the problem. It was not endorsed by a minority which instead drew up its own document. This very wordy document does nothing other than fully expound the classical difficulties and reasoning as found in the manuals of moral theology, and the interventions both inside and outside the Council (with particular reference to Ottaviani and Ruffini).

But there was also a third document called *Synthetic Document on the Morality of Birth Regulation.* It is a very interesting document for it is the first draft drawn up by the majority. Neither was this document accepted by the commission minority. Its interest lies in the different way that it treats the specific problem of birth control. The fact that it is well removed from the moralistic tradition places it rather in line with the more recent tradition of thought which has emerged in the past few years. In any case, both documents of the majority are completely different from all previous approaches to the problem in the past. The treatment, the terminology, the concerns, and the realism which support them are all far more theological, biblical, human, and Christian. Their simple, straightforward style make them readable and understandable to the vast public. Even in the most delicate and technical matters it does not require a great effort at concentration to see how the work done during those years by the group of experts has really renewed a doctrine previously held to be irreformable and quite "traditional." At the same time, their broad, rich treatment of thought not only prevents them from ever falling off into abstruse technicalities but also keeps them close to the complexity and continually changing nature of a problem so closely tied up with the concrete conditions of marriage and family life.

Even though *Humanae Vitae* chose the direction of the minority document, for reasons explained in the encyclical itself, credit should be given to the majority documents for the value they really have. Moreover, even after the encyclical, it is still possible to hold that it is precisely these documents which are open to a more conscious, profound, and responsible develop-ment in the future, not only on the part of the specialists and experts mentioned by the encyclical but also on the part of those people who every day live out a problem which clearly has not been solved just by an encyclical. The secretary of the Papal Commission, H. de Riedmatten, in *Courrier de Genève* and in *La Liberté* of Freiburg of September 2–3, 1967, made a declaration on his sole responsibility, in which he deplored the "document leak" as a "profoundly sad fact" since the texts were owned by neither the translator-commentator nor the editor, and their publication was a "grave injustice to those people who worked under prudent safeguards."

This small scandal in the English-speaking world soon spread very rapidly, however, for the texts were published first in book form with ample notes and comments by Jean-Marie Paupert (Seuil, Paris, 1967), and then in Italian. Even if the reasons de Riedmatten gives for deploring their publication are true, the texts have helped the public to get quick, clear information on the whole issue.

In the meantime the attitudes expressed by the majority documents became more and more those taken up by broad strata of Catholics as well as by theologians and moralists. The press continued reporting the issue from time to time, but un-fortunately on a rather scandal-mongering, superficial level, and from a limited point of view. The bone of contention was the "Pill" instead of the deeper problems involved.

A most striking fact that occurred on the eve of the publi-cation of the encyclical was the stand taken by the Third World Lay Congress assembled in Rome. Their fourth and eighth reso-lutions had been preceded by long, animated group discussions and were accepted by almost the whole of the Congress on October 17, 1967. They were quite clear and made no small impression in Roman curial circles. In fact, they state that the Congress

remembers the social duty of couples to bring about a conscientious procreation; the duty of Christians to take part in the efforts for world-wide education; the very live awareness that Christian lay people have of the need of the teaching authority of the Church to limit itself to the fundamental moral and spiritual values, leaving the choice of the scientific or technical means for realizing responsible parenthood to the parents themselves who will act in conformity with their Christian faith and on the basis of medical and scientific consultation.

The text is extremely concise and clear. On one hand there is the demand that the problems be treated in the widest possible way by taking into account all the moral and spiritual values in married life. On the other hand there is the demand that the concrete choice of methods be left to the individual couples. To all appearances then, after the discussions of the lay people at the Congress, the problem of methods in relation to the natural law and to the risks involved had been solved. Naturally there was still the Pope's decision.

In the months that followed it was known that Paul VI had created a further commission of twelve experts whom he was probably consulting during the examination he was engaged in. It was also known that the French Jesuit Gustave Martelet had been called to Rome. He was known to be against the principle of "totality"—that is, the principle that the duty of procreation is in the totality of married life and not in the individual act of intercourse—and as the theologian who, although against the new outlook on the whole, had at the same time dealt with it in a very intelligent way.

Toward the middle of July 1968 the rumor became more and more insistent that an encyclical on the question was imminent. The Press Office of the Holy See, however, flatly denied such rumors. On July 25, *Humanae Vitae* was signed by Paul VI.

Someone stated that the Vatican had categorically denied it several days before to avoid possible intervention and pressure. One journalist asked himself if this was a generous gesture on the part of one of the Pope's collaborators in order to free him from further distress, or the gesture of a far less authoritative attaché, spurred on by the same filial concern. Another journalist asked if the Press Office really knew nothing or whether it was decided in such cases, in deference to the principle of the higher good, to use "epieikeia" of professional journalist morality as customarily employed by the Vatican newspaper in its dealings with its confreres "outside the walls."

What Values Have Majorities and Minorities?

Even if one does not want to give too much credibility to these well-meant calumniations, it is a fact that the last phase of the decision-making process and of the preparation of the encyclical was veiled in a jealously guarded secrecy. Apart from the fact that the Pope had already declared on several occasions that the final decision was up to him as the one responsible for the supreme magisterium of the Church, it is also easy to understand how a new way of discussion and public dissent was not welcome just after the Pontifical Commission's work had been brought to a close.

It seems that a rough copy of *Humanae Vitae* was already in the hands of the Episcopal Synod which met for the first time in Rome in the autumn of 1967. After the encyclical had been issued, criticisms came from several sources that the decision had not been made collegially. This would have given a wider basic outlook on the problem and would have brought out the fact that after the Council had just started its running-in period, "Episcopal collegiality" was being taken seriously. It is certain, however, that Paul VI submitted the rough copy of the encyclical as well as a copy of the general discussion of the topic to quite a few bishops. This came from a piece of news given by Ivan Yates in the *Observer* of August 4, 1968:

At least three West European cardinals, Suenens of Mechelen, Brussels, Döpfner of Munich, and Koenig of Vienna, have pleaded with the Pope in the last twelve months not to issue his draft. Cardinal Suenens, in particular, has told friends he sent a warning letter to the Pope in stronger terms than he had ever before thought it right to use. But although all three cardinals had every opportunity to put their case when they were in Rome, they were obviously not in such a favorable position as those who were there all day every day, working within the Curia in a Byzantine atmosphere of intrigue and secrecy.

Maybe it is not true that the greater part of the episcopate was in favor of a change of attitude on contraceptives. But the whole issue must have been far clearer for those bishops and cardinals who made up the Papal Commission. Therefore, the problem now becomes: Granted that on several occasions the Vatican and even Paul VI himself had stressed the adequate representation and competence of the Papal Commission, and seeing that its final conclusions gave a good indication of the more widespread opinions inside the Catholic Church, then what value has the majority in this case? The editorial of *Le Monde* of July 30, 1968 notes that it is

quite significant that after he himself had nominated the members of the commission who were to study this problem, the Pope finally chose the minority position and insisted very forcefully on his condemnation of the use of every artificial means of contraception. He based himself on arguments from the natural law—the very arguments which the majority report had challenged.

As regards the majority itself, not only of the experts but also of the cardinals and the bishops on the commission, *The Times* of September 16, 1968 came out with some unexpected news, certainly revealed by some bishop who had been part of the Papal Commission. *The Times* wrote:

Were the majority of the bishops and cardinals who in 1966 were asked by the Pope to elaborate the preparatory texts for the encyclical on birth control in favor of the use of the Pill? This hypothesis has already been put forward by very authoritative and usually well-informed sources. But it is now almost certain that in pronouncing himself against the use of the so-called contraceptives the Pope has acted against the opinion of the majority of the prelates to whom he had entrusted the study of the problem; this is confirmed by the extracts from their conclusions contained in a secret document that the Vatican would have published only in the event that birth control by means of the use of contraceptives had been approved by Paul VI. . . .

In June 1966 the Pope received two documents. One of these was the report of the "consultative commission" consisting of 23 theologians. . . . As many as 19 of these 23 scholars declared themselves in favor of a reform that would also include approval of the Pill. This report came to the knowledge of the press and was published all over the world. During the same period, however, the Pope received a second document, the report prepared by the 15-member episcopal commission consisting of cardinals and bishops. This text, entitled *Pastorales indicationes,* would have constituted the draft of an encyclical in the event that Paul VI had decided to pronounce himself in favor of birth control.

32

If the document disclosed by *The Times* is genuine, and there is no reason to think that it may have been, just because it was not denied, it means that the majority was made up not only of experts—theologians, doctors, psychologists, biologists—but also of members of the special episcopal commission. What significance did such a majority have? What, also, were the reactions of its members after the promulgation of *Humanae Vitae*? If one were to search through the declarations of the individual bishops who were part of the commission, one would be hard pressed to detect a sense of delusion. It even appears that they tried to avoid altogether the problem of an episcopal majority, or else—and this seems the most likely possibility— they presupposed that there was no question as to whether a majority could induce the Pope to choose in a definite direction. Put in these terms, however, it gives rise to another more delicate problem, to be treated below, of the magisterium which belongs to the whole Church and the magisterium which belongs to the body of bishops and the Sovereign Pontiff.

The position of the majority of the bishops who could well have been those endorsing the document revealed by *The Times* was possibly best expressed by a passage from the pastoral letter which Cardinal Heenan had read on August 4 in all the Churches of the Archdiocese of Westminster:

Some are now saying that the Pope had no right to dissent from the opinion of the majority of the members of the commission. This is a question which deserves an answer.

On this I can speak with some authority because I was pro-president of the final commission which reported to the Pope. No member of the commission thought that we could resolve the problem by a majority vote. We were asked to sift evidence and present the Pope with our findings. It was always understood that the decision must be by him alone as Christ's Vicar. The law of God cannot be decided by a majority vote.

It was the Dominican M. R. Gagnebet, professor at the Angelicum University in Rome who gave the best conceptual expression of the issue as given in classical theology on papal teaching authority. In a series of articles he unambiguously and forcefully answered—and with arguments that have left not a few theologians puzzled—the objections which were raised against the Pope's way of arriving at a decision. In *L'Osservatore Romano* of September 5, 1968 Gagnebet wrote an article entitled "The Pope Decides by Himself," where he attacked those views which wanted to give importance to the opinion of majorities of bishops, theologians (clearly referring to the study commissions), or the "common opinion of the faithful" which, in the Catholic understanding of the search for religious truth, also plays an important role.

Gagnebet argued as follows:

Finally, the criticisms center around a third point (Gagnebet had previously treated of other criticisms of the encyclical.—EDITOR): The Pope has decided alone. He has pronounced himself against the opinion of his advisors. He did not get the College of Bishops to intervene to decide together with them. He did not have confidence in the common opinion of the faithful. "Is not this the first time," one journalist asks, "that one man alone was ever right and everyone else wrong?"

It is certainly extraordinary to hear that the Pope has been reproached for not following the opinion of the commission majority. After all, it was up to the Pope to decide. It is he who is assisted by the Holy Spirit to do so and it is he who has the inalienable responsibility for this decision, since it is to him that Christ conferred the authority to make it as well as the mission to lead the faithful to eternal life. This mission, this authority, this assistance, cannot belong to any commission of experts, no matter how intelligent and prudent. Their joy was to give information and to gather together all the elements which will clarify the decision. If a majority was found to be in favor of an opinion that did not exist in the Church before, this means that it was extremely important to listen to these learned, intelligent and loyal men who felt they could go against the traditional teaching of the Church. Seeing that they had so earnestly put their views forward, they had to be given the chance to fully explain their arguments and objections. What one could now say if the Pope had decided without listening to them! The encyclical explains why the Pope was not of the same opinion. There is no need to labor the point.

The Pope has decided by himself without the College, and also, as some insinuated, against the College. This objection rests on a false notion of College as spread by a certain theologian before the Council — a notion that the Council itself did not agree with. According to this notion, the supreme power in the Church should always be exercised collegially. The Pope should be left with the job of day-to-day government and current affairs in the same way that reigning rulers are encharged with speeding up ordinary matters. The important decisions should be made collegially either in a Council or in a meeting of representatives of the College in a Synod. Such an opinion is false. As the very people who hold this position will recognize, it is not what is taught in the Constitution *Lumen Gentium*. Let us reread the text of the Constitution: "For in virtue of his office —that is, as Vicar of Christ and pastor of the whole Church—the Roman Pontiff has full, supreme, and universal power over the Church. And he can always exercise his power freely" (No. 22).

The explanatory note expounds the authentic meaning of the passage as follows: "The care of the whole flock of Christ has been entrusted to the Supreme Pontiff. It belongs to him, according to the changing needs of the Church during the passage of time, to determine the way in which it is fitting for this care to be exercised, whether personally or collegially. . . . As supreme pastor of the Church the Sovereign Pontiff can always exercise his authority as he chooses, as is demanded by his office itself. While the College always exists, it does not for that reason permanently operate through *strictly* collegial action, as the tradition of the Church shows. . . . Indeed, it operates through collegial actions at intervals and only *with the consent of its head.*" These passages are quite clear. There is no need to give arguments to prove them. It is evident that no one in the Church can reproach the Roman Pontiff for preferring to exercise his supreme power personally in dealing with any particular question. When the Holy Father reserved these problems to himself after the commission had done its work, no one in the Council protested, nor could anyone have protested. The Pope did not neglect to consult the bishops, and in any case any of them could have freely offered their observations on this point, as mentioned in the encyclical itself.

What do certain journalists base themselves on when they write that the majority of the episcopal body favored the new opinion which was rejected by the Holy Father? Certain speeches that had echoes in the Council, of course, have not been forgotten. But there is nothing to prove that these were the expression of the majority of the Fathers' opinions.

Finally, a declaration by American theologians spread by the world press expresses another extraordinary line of thought. The Pope did not take into account the common opinion of the faithful. The faithful, although wanting to remain in the grace of God, do not hesitate to use contraceptives. How can the same Holy Spirit who guides them be pushing them into intrinsically evil actions? No Catholic doubts that the Pope has the assistance of the Holy Spirit. This assistance, however, is not the privilege of him alone out of the whole people of God. All have it. People then are quick in calling this the work of the Holy Spirit. It can be explained, however, in other ways, particularly by the unbridled propaganda on a world scale in favor of these devices and also by the green light that certain theologians imprudently gave them in spite of what the Pope had said before his decision. What must be kept in mind above all, however, is that this so-called opinion of the faithful is far from being unanimous. . . .

It is true that the assistance of the Holy Spirit in the Church is not limited to the Pope and bishops. It reaches out to all its members and even extends beyond the visible limits of the Church. Beyond the common assistance promised to all to fulfill their personal and social duties as Christians, however, there is a special assistance reserved to those who have public functions in the Church. It is not the function of all the faithful to settle controversies which arise in questions of faith and morals. This mission belongs, first and foremost, to the Vicar of Christ. So it is first and foremost to him that such special assistance is given. Why disturb the faithful with sophisms of this kind?

There is no need to add that what Gagnebet calls "sophisms," many other theologians and members of the faithful look at as serious questions. They see the very structure of the "people of God" put in danger if too much weight is given to Gagnebet's arguments, which is not to deny them at the same time a measure of truth. There are those, too, who feel that the sophisms are precisely one-sided arguments such as these.

For alongside Gagnebet's "totalitarian" judgment which represents one way of looking at the magisterium and, consequently, majorities and minorities in the Church, there is the judgment of other theologians, far more subtle and searching, and possibly nearer the direction that theological thinking has been taking in the past few years. It is well expressed by a well-known German theologian, Franz Böckle, in his *Osservazioni Teologiche* in which he added a commentary on *Humanae Vitae*. In this work he develops the ideas he had already expressed in *Neue Zürcher Zeitung* of August 4, 1968. Böckle, besides being lecturer in moral theology at Bonn University, was also a member of the Papal Commission. In his *Osservazioni Teologiche* (in *Humanae Vitae*—note *teologico-pastorali*, Brescia, 1968), he says:

We have to be very grateful to those bishops who, when faced with the Pope's decision, sympathetically referred it back to individuals' decisions of conscience. It has to be clearly understood, however, that this only shifts and covers over the real problem. When there is a very clear reaction on the part of the body of the Church to a decision on a disputed point, only a straightforward decision by those responsible in the Church can help. For them to withdraw from this responsibility by leaving it up to the faithful to make an eventual decision against the clear command, can only result in a catastrophic rejection of authority itself. On the other hand, the Pope has the right to make a binding solution in disputed points of faith and morals. On these occasions one applies Pius XII's encyclical *Humani Generis,* which expressly states that in the case of a papal decision on a clearly delineated, controversial issue, the point is no longer open to discussion.

This statement was inserted *ad literam* in the first Schema on the Constitution on the Church presented at the Council in 1962. In fact, in the final text it was dropped in a very obvious way. This is not because it has lost all value but because it has come to be seen that in making all these decisions a far more differentiated decision is necessary. Normally a Pope's magisterial intervention expresses the more solid opinion of the Church as a whole. So the degree to which the individual is bound rests, as well as on theological reasoning, to a great extent on this magisterial intervention. We are not referring here to the idea that truth can be discovered democratically, but to the consequences of the *collegiality between the Pope and the episcopacy of the whole world,* correctly understood. Certainly it is the Pope's duty to give a kind of arbitrational decision. But in my opinion too little attention has been paid to the function which this duty plays.

The Pope's vote is not like the deciding vote of a president before two equally divided groups. When a president in such a case votes in favor of a particular opinion, he is, in fact, giving one group victory by democratic process. This system is certainly an efficient decision-making process in concrete law problems. It is not a reliable method in the objective search for truth or in interpreting the divine will. The Pope's power of decision, therefore, according to a reasonably wide theological opinion, has a completely different function. *Decidere* here rather means *recidere.* The Pope's decision resembles cutting what the prevailing majority without a doubt holds from what is still seen only vaguely and uncertainly.

It is a well-known fact that no progress is made in a discussion if everything is always being questioned. It has to be clearly seen where everyone agrees. The Pope, as the president and defender of unity in the episcopate, must, practically speaking, gauge what the bishops agree on. On this, there should no longer be any free discussion. Because of the function that the Pope's decision plays, it is expected that it be in general agreement with the decision of the Church. The point of the matter is that the Pope did not stop here in his decision on birth control. His encyclical is not limited to recalling the fundamental principles established by all the bishops in council, such as the real commitment that intercourse leads to in marriage, the valid reasons for limiting the number of children, even the affirmation that the choice of methods should not be left just to the individual person's decision but that the first criterion is the dignity of the human person. Rather, Paul VI intervened in the one question that, from the Council onward, was most widely and intensely debated by the bishops and theologians.

Böckle then describes how the question went from the Council to the Pope personally, then asks himself the far-reaching question of how Paul VI understands "magisterium" when he refers to it in the encyclical.

When the Pope uses the word magisterium he refers either to himself, in other words to the *ordinary magisterium of the Pope,* or else he refers to the *universal magisterium* of the Church, which, however, only applies to the Council's statements of principles. . . . What the Pope considered should not be done by means of the Council or by means of the bishop members of the extraordinary commission, he now decided to do by exercising his personal office through the judgment of his conscience.

In a footnote to this text, Böckle makes a short observation which tends to put in a wholly new light the judgment given by Gagnebet when quoting, as proof of his reasoning, the explanatory note included in *Lumen Gentium* on the exercise of collegiality. Böckle notes: "The *nota explicativa praevia* on the Constitution on the Church, *Lumen Gentium,* states that the Pope could use his powers even *seorsim* and *solus,* but only *sicut ad ipsum suo munere requiritur* ('as is required by his office'). The lone journey of the Pope does not cut him off from the whole Church." This "not cutting him off from the whole Church" is the very difficulty experienced by anyone who has grown in his understanding of the Church as the "people of God." This is not to deny or disobey authority but simply to follow the logical steps that, after all, the Constitution *Lumen Gentium* itself had first paced out when it envisaged the Church as *Populus Dei*.

It is along these lines that Prof. P. C. Sporken, a well-known teacher at the University of Nijmegen, in *De Tijd* of August 3, 1968, in a long article that will be further dealt with later, sums up a few of the objections brought against the way in which the encyclical was drawn up.

The first objection deals with the encyclical's origins. At the Council the Pope had imposed silence on the bishops and reserved the whole question to himself. Now he gives his pronouncement without any clear, open consultation with the world episcopate (the rather vague reactions of the bishops themselves bear witness to it). This is not all. We have a right to expect the commission, created by John XXIII and then filled out by Paul VI, to represent the whole of Catholicism. Was not the whole intention of the Pope to be informed on what the Church thought, so as then to be able to make a wise decision? Yet we know what a sad path this commission took (see *De Tijd* of July 29, 1968). Cardinal Ottaviani refused to pass the final report on to the Pope but instead handed the minority report to him. Instead of having the report confirmed, a new—secret—commission was nominated which was made up only of prelates. These are undoubtedly the spiritual parents of this encyclical, for it really does little more than repeat the minority opinion. It must be said that the course of affairs has been quite bizarre.

When Prof. Sporken refers to the "sad path" of the commission, he is alluding to the fact that possibly an attempt was made to put the minority opinion across as the majority opinion. The fact mentioned by Sporken goes back to what *The Tablet* of September 21, 1968 wrote, giving unpublished details regarding the last short period of the commission's work. When the work of the commission up to that stage had ended it was June 24, 1966. Three questions had to be put to the vote. The first was, "Is contraception illicit in itself or intrinsically harmful?" The other two questions would depend on the reply given to the first, and dealt with contraceptive methods and the feasibility of the "magisterium's" making a pronouncement on them. After the voting on the first question (2 Yes, 1 Yes with reservations, 3 abstaining, 9 No) there followed the drafting of the two texts which made up the official report of the commission. We have already referred to them: the introductory pastoral document (French original: *Indications pastorales*), and the theological document (*Schema documenti de responsabili paternitate*). These were the new details revealed by *The Tablet*:

On June 28 the Bishops' Commission met under the presidency of Cardinal Ottaviani, who apparently did not take a very active part in the discussions. The final report, officially ratified by the commission, was taken to the Pope by Cardinal Döpfner and Rev. H. de Riedmatten, O.P., general secretary of the commission. The fact that the president of the commission did not take it himself was of no significance, though it was later interpreted as indicating that he refused to do so and Cardinal Döpfner took his place. It is known that Cardinal Ottaviani later submitted another document to the Pope himself. This occasion was dated July 1, 1966 by the UPI and KNP press agencies, and the document was said to be the *Report of the Minority of the Papal Commission,* a doctrinal document defending the position taken by Pope Pius XI in *Casti Connubii* and Pius XII in his address to the midwives in 1951.

This is what has given rise to the term "minority report," which is inaccurate, as the document that Cardinal Ottaviani presented had not been considered or approved by the Papal Commission. There is no evidence to connect it with the document published under the heading *Minority Report* (*The Tablet,* April 29, 1966). This was in fact a working paper by a group of four theologians of the minority tendency.

It was replied to four days later in the document published on the *Argument for Reform* (*The Tablet,* May 6, 1966), which is likewise only a working paper. Neither of these two documents can claim the status of "reports." This must be confined to the theological report, previously called the "majority report," and the document, added by the cardinals and bishops, and published here.

So the real voice of the majority of the Papal Commission was the text published as that "of the majority" and presented by C[illegible]öpfner to the Pope. Cardinal Ottaviani sent the Pope j[illegible]rking document of four theologians. All this goes to show [illegible]ad path" of the commission but certainly takes nothing awa[illegible]om the *post factum,* since even though the Pope chose the opin[illegible] the "minority," what he did, in fact, was to express a personal [illegible]on that on occasions coincided with that of the minority. The problem now takes on deeper implications, involving the role that public opinion plays in the Church both on theological questions dealing with interpreting the faith and on practical problems of behavior bound up with its moral teaching. We have seen how Böckle treated the problem of majorities and minorities of opinion in a more detailed way. The same problem will turn up again in a more acute form when we contrast the direction and style of the encyclical with the Church structures involved in doctrinal and disciplinary matters.

For the moment, after considering the statements of Gagnebet that "integrally" reflect the classical teaching, and those of Böckle that repropose the same doctrines in a far more evolved framework and, in fact, mirror a wide area of theological thought today, let us hear what a German Catholic intellectual, Walter Dirks, writer and lay theologian, has to say. He has never put himself forward as being either provocative or progressive. His reaction could well be an indication of the irritation which a sector of Catholics feel when noticing the lack of thorough dialogue—one aspect to which they are extremely sensitive—in the study of what Christians have to hold as doctrine revealed by God. In the September 1968 issue of *Frankfurter Hefte,* Walter Dirks fully discusses the theme "The Pope and the Church," and observes that the encyclical is a "unique fact in the history of the modern papacy." Dirks says:

> This Pope who, in and with the living Church, wants to be the arbiter and guarantor of unity, has put himself in opposition to the Church, autocratically making "decisions" in which there is a total lack of the spirit of dialogue. This is a unique fact in the history of the modern papacy. Certainly Pius XII taught and made his "decisions" in complete independence, but at the same time in full agreement with the Church, and could base himself on the attitudes of the bishops and the Catholics. They, on their part, gave their agreement.

The very dogma which in 1951 defined, amid general horror, the bodily assumption of the Virgin Mary, was preceded by a survey of all the bishops' views. Even Pius IX found it difficult, at Vatican Council I, to get a majority of the Fathers to accept the declarations on papal primacy and infallibility. These facts show how even before Vatican II, that is when the modern papacy was at its apogee, the Pope made his decisions not in solitary confinement without any other guide than that of the inspiration of the Holy Spirit, reserved to him and to him alone, but by uniting himself to the apostolic College and linking himself with the theological consciousness of the Church.

What value, then, do majorities and minorities have? The problem cannot be solved at the present moment. *Humanae Vitae* put the question in the most acute and complex form that it has ever been put. This is probably related to a new awareness of the Church and a new sense of responsibility which perhaps the ecclesial body has never had until today.

The lay people present in the Papal Commissions of the future will know that they are just "consultants" of the Pontiff. They will also have an even greater awareness of being living, responsible members of the "ecclesial body," whose visible head is the Pope. But how will the equilibrium between these two elements come about? *Humanae Vitae* has only opened up the road for further thinking promising to be more and more interesting and enlightening.

Some idea may be had of the growing attitude on the part of the Christian laity by considering the somewhat energetic reaction of a group of American lay people who made up part of the now-famous Papal Commission. The *Religious News Service* agency, dating its service from Washington, October 1, 1968, communicated that

Donald Barret, Thomas Burch, Mr. and Mrs. Crowley, Dr. John Cavanagh, Dr. Andrew Hellegers and Prof. John Noonam, who formed part of the Pontifical Commission on birth control, have declared themselves to be in disagreement with what the Pope has said in his encyclical. These laymen maintain that a married couple must decide this question in accordance with its conscience and that the Pope's teaching in this respect is not infallible. Prof. Noonam says that the Pope has taken no account of the opinion of the commission he had nominated and that the Pope had decided to prepare the encyclical in secrecy, availing himself of only half a dozen theologians. Prof. Noonam then said that the commission had disapproved and rejected the Pope's decision. He went on to compare the papal encyclical to a series of encyclicals whose affirmations were later clamorously belied by the Church itself (such as, for example, the statements made by Gregory XVI against the admissibility of freedom of conscience) and concluded that the encyclical *Humanae Vitae* leaves the question exactly where it was before.

It may not be quite true to say that the specific question dealt with by the encyclical remains in the same state as before, not only because the study and discussion is not yet completed. It is certain, however, that the fundamental question raised by the encyclical not only remains as before, but has become more insistent. When value has the thought of the whole Church when a "decision" has to be taken; that is, when the divine law has to be interpreted? Certainly this will become one of the biggest problems of the next few years. The extraordinary Episcopal Synod which came together in the fall of 1969 dealt with the theme which underlies the question of the value of majorities. It is the topic of Episcopal collegiality. What is it, and if it exists, how will it be expressed?

Chapter 2 Real Reasons and Underlying Motives for the Encyclical

Why an encyclical? A crisis in the Church and the purity
of the faith
The features of an encyclical and of *Humanae Vitae*
A total vision of man and his vocation
Criticism and honest searching by lay people

What prompted the Pope to express himself in so straightforward and strong a manner? Evidently it was because he felt that the truth could not be stated today differently from the way it was stated in the past. In any case, he could have couched this "doctrinal" rigor in "pastoral" considerations which would have made its effects less staggering. But this he did not want, and for a very precise reason. The Pope knew exactly the risk he was taking. On the one hand, he risked coming out against a considerable number of bishops, priests, theologians, and lay people in the Church. On the other, he risked alienating the majority of Protestants and nonbelievers and thus reversing the strong tide of sympathy in his favor that he was fortunate enough to enjoy.

This is how Louis Salleron in *Le Monde* of August 6, 1968 sees the question of the motives underlying the encyclical. Salleron attempts to explain why the encyclical was written. His reasons, however, clearly show how hazardous an undertaking it is to start attributing motives to Paul VI that go beyond those which he himself indicated in the encyclical and shortly afterward in his various appearances.

Why an Encyclical? A Crisis in the Church and the Purity of the Faith

Salleron's opinion, and even he admits that he was surprised by the encyclical, is worth listening to if only because it represents quite a widespread line of thought in those areas where the encyclical's appearance was seen from the point of view of the present crisis in the Church. Paul VI's more recent actions have also all been judged from the same point of view. This kind of reply to the question of the encyclical's underlying motives, probably more than any other, helps to shed light on those reasons that the Pope himself has revealed. It gives a more accurate picture of the encyclical by removing all hint of political maneuvering. Even if this were noble politics—politics without vested interests—it would still be ecclesiastical politics rather than pastoral concern. In fact, just to ask the question, even with the best of intentions, about a contrast or conflict between the doctrinal and the pastoral, as already mentioned by Salleron, is to risk falling into a political outlook on the whole issue.

Salleron himself admits that "one can only guess why the

Pope was led to put his responsibilities as pastor after those of teacher." Yet, as Salleron mentions:

The reasons put forward by us do not seem altogether incorrect. The Church has been hit for several years now, and especially since the Council, by a vast movement of "contestation." It is not only the mass media which are completely confusing people and shaking all religious ideas. It is the clergy themselves who have everywhere given in to innovations. The *Index* has been suppressed. Everyone is preaching his own private truth. The clergy are now agreed that the institution must give way to the prophetic spirit so as to renew and develop the Church. Using the excuse of collegiality, bishops are tending to found national Churches and are drawing up new catechisms which differ among themselves and gradually go farther and farther from the traditional teaching. In a word, if it is not a state of anarchy, it is at least the beginning of anarchy. Week after week Paul VI has increased the number of his interventions, but he gets almost no response. So he then decides to speak through official documents which have come one after another, the Profession of Faith on June 29 and then the encyclical *Humanae Vitae*.

The analysis of the entire process that led up to *Humanae Vitae* is done, then, from the point of view of the crisis which the Church is at the moment going through. It may also be noted, however, that to look at *Humanae Vitae* in this way is to reduce it to something pitiful, to an example of power politics all the more controversial because of the influence it exercises over people's consciences. This way of looking at the encyclical would turn it into a "political game" where some of the most important values of faith are used as pawns: loyalty to and acceptance of the magisterium, and adherence to the religious truths in both the Credo of June 29 and in *Humanae Vitae*. Possibly Salleron feels the incongruity of the situation when he observes:

The bishops had insisted with Paul VI that he stop condemning errors and express himself in a positive way. This he did, and his voice now sounds like thunder. Was it a risk? Certainly, but a clearly calculated one. What bishop, after all, will say, "I am leaving the Church"? And if he does not leave it, how can his Credo be any different from that of the Pope and of tradition?

Much can be said about "leaving" and "staying in" the

Church and about the Pope's Credo and tradition. At least the most elementary ethical norms of theological investigation, however, should be kept in mind. These norms have been accepted and used in the Church since at least the time of Vincent of Lerins, but it has unexpectedly come to light that many people have forgotten them through an unforeseen loss of memory. The fact remains, however, that to put the motives underlying *Humanae Vitae* on the level of "risks" to be taken in a moment of "crisis" in the Church, is at least to bring the Church down to the level of what the subtle game of religious politics involves and affects. It would be like the case of the Bernini pope who turned his back on Galileo because between them stood the whole history of the king of Spain, the grand duke of Tuscany, and a Europe being pulled to pieces, not to mention the sad fact of the Reformation. Maybe the comparison is strained, but not too strained. If the situation were like this, then we could close the whole case and only much later begin thinking of *Humanae Vitae* and the problems it involves.

Either the motives are clean and honest, as we believe those of Paul VI to be, or else they are something entirely different and experience will bear it out. If people then discuss Paul VI's motives, it does not mean that this will have catastrophic effects on the Church; it means exactly the opposite. The debate must take place within the Church. One does not leave the Church to acquire the right to debate. The Church of the tradition, as understood by those obsessed with what *Humanae Vitae* states, has never existed. There was, admittedly, the Church of principles written in blood, of grandson cardinals, of grand inquisitors, of the "four musketeers" of sad memory in the sacred game reserve of a not-too-distant modernism. This was not, however, the Church of the Word of God where the Vicar of Christ is precisely a Vicar of the Word of God made flesh for all, and not just a representative of huge, anonymous interests protected by his blessings and excommunications.

It is vital, from the beginning, to ask only those questions which will shed light on the underlying motives of the encyclical. We must make a clear break, at the same time, with all those answers which suggest a Church in the process of falling to pieces. The simple Christian who knows where ideas of this kind come from will have enough sense to turn a deaf ear to them and wait for the Word of God to come to him in better times. If one were to follow the hypothesis—too simple to be true—developed by Salleron, it would be possible to be led finally to believe that all kinds of "dramatic" and "catastrophic" reports were arriving at the Vatican both before and after the publication of the encyclical. On the basis of these reports, a certain "minority group radical," as he describes himself, writing in *Il Borghese* of October 3, 1968, has constructed a whole *positio* that would do justice to the golden age of the Inquisition. (No wonder people come out of the cinema convinced that the Dominicans of the time of Galileo were dull, disreputable types. Nothing helps to tranquilize present-day consciences more than violent accusations against the past.)

The minority group radical says:

Even the progressive episcopate has lost control of the situation and cannot keep in check the spreading centrifugal left- and right-wing movements in their respective countries. The more perceptive bow their heads. "We should have foreseen it," they utter bitterly. One hears more and more often, thus confirming the wildest possible rumors, that the Pope himself has expressed his concern over this dangerous situation developing in Europe as well as in both Americas, Africa, and Asia.

Here the minority group radical goes to great lengths to describe the horrifying things now happening in the German Catholic world, including the *Katholikentag* of Essen where

things not believed possible have occurred in the past year. To think that this assembly was considered for centuries the bulwark of faith in the Protestant world! . . . These good German Catholics have borrowed from their former enemies the phrase book and idea of anti-papism, mixing it all together in an incredible cauldron of reformist notions and attempts at contestation.

The minority group radical concludes:

This is the stage that the situation has reached. We think it rather logical, then, that in the Section of the Secretariat of State entrusted with non-Italian Catholicism, there must be an atmosphere of foreboding. No one knows any longer what course to follow in order to get out of this situation in an honorable way without either provoking a schism or diminishing the hierarchical authority of the Church.

Leaving aside the Secretariat of State occupied with non-Italian Catholicism (giving the impression of a foreign ministry entrusted with the eternal salvation of nations both far and near), there is nobody today who is thinking of a schism and who would consequently want to destroy the hierarchical authority of the Church. Probably this was said because the Church is still seen as a monolith of secure politico-economic guarantees whose cohesion is held secure because of the fact that nobody says anything. The concepts of obedience, authority, and research in the Church which arose from this outlook give more the impression of being political programs of the Kremlin rather than the Church, the mystical body of Christ. However, and this is the first point, if it is true that Paul VI wrote the encyclical to prevent an avalanche, how is it that this very catastrophe has occurred just several months afterward? If so many Catholics criticize the encyclical, then either the Church is at its lowest ebb or else the reasons attributed to the encyclical are ridiculous.

Admittedly, Alberto Giovannini, once again in *Il Borghese* of August 1, 1968, interpreted the encyclical as "an indication, in spite of everything, that Catholicism in its basic tenets, intends remaining something serious." The Council, then, and whoever took it seriously, evidently wanted to turn Catholicism into a glorious barbecue party! But here is also where the doubt arises. Is not Paul VI's whole concern precisely that the Church should not fall into the hands of the left- and right-wing movements? "The encyclical," continues Giovannini, "was enough to sweep away all the unquestioned popularity that Paul VI had won with the left-wing elements of all confessions. It was even enough to have Pope Montini branded 'Pacellian,' short-sighted, and reactionary." It is the left-wing elements of all confessions, then, who are the ones whispering into the ear of the simple Christian.

Giovannini then applies this to the Council: "It is the 'conciliar' Catholics who want to sin with the Church's blessing. The Council will allow them, among other things, to avoid their

interior and almost always hypocritical efforts at 'repentance.'"
It would be difficult to find in so few words a better monument
to the ignorance of Christianity, seeing that a Christian is one
who is engaged in interior and almost always hypocritical efforts
at repentance. What a pathetic sight this trivial, lay translation
of *simul justus et peccator* is. This section of the Church then
becomes the leftist element and the Church finally blocks its
path. Giovannini then follows with an examination of conscience
of a Church which has unconsciously given way to the "left-wing
elements of all confessions" (no need to state that such confessions are probably not ecclesial confessions) and that now is
pulling itself together and is returning to the right path:

Let us be frank. How could we have pretended that all this would
not happen when for years the Church gave the impression that religion, her teaching and her dogmas, were, let us say, like the skin on
one's neck, that each could pull to the left or to the right as he
preferred? The progressives of all philosophical (sic!) and religious
confessions, Catholics no less than others, had become accustomed in
these years to the Church's unconditional surrender to so-called progress and to the actions of a Pope who was more and more intent on
embracing the "world." It is evident, then, that they could not remain
indifferent, nor could they simply accept the "revelation" of Pope
Montini that the Church still has moral principles which, in the light
of the present situation in the world, are disputable, such as procreation and the indissolubility of marriage, but which the Church itself
cannot touch. They were not expecting it, and after seeing everything
which had happened up till then as in their favor, they cannot be
entirely blamed for considering Paul VI's moral rigorism as almost a
kind of "Pacellian" affront.

Those who hold this Pacellian affront to the left wing have
lead many crusades which have had little to do with "intangible"
moral principles, seeing that their satisfaction in the reaffirmation
of such principles comes from a platform which usually becomes
irate when these principles are restated. It also becomes irate
when Paul VI, no longer healthily "Pacellian," receives some
suspicious character from the *East* or sends a representative of
his to see if some agreement can be reached with the "devil"
who has taken up his dwelling in the East, all for the same
reasons that he wrote the encyclical: to be a pastor always and

for all. There is also a small oversight, easily forgiven for one who indulges in dropping theological judgments "en passant" in the context of what could hardly be called theological reasoning. Moral principles are not "disputable" in the light of the present situation in the world, but are disputable only in the light of the whole Christian teaching and within the sphere of the ecclesial community. No Catholic who "discusses" them intends destroying them, seeing that today he can remain in the Church if he wants to; but if he does not remain and discusses them, it is precisely because he feels it is his task to do so.

Nobody in the Church denies this—even if, let us be honest, we are still far from agreed upon the forms, limits, and organization of this discussion. Moreover, conceiving of this "Church" as giving the impression of treating religion and dogmas as "the skin on one's neck" (with the stress on pulling it to the "left") sounds much like reducing the Church to a Secretariat of State. Seeing, however, that Paul VI entrusted his encyclical to the Church and not to the Secretary of State, it is the Church as it is today (no worse, and possibly a good deal better than it has ever been) which has received his encyclical and passed it into its life stream, and in which, thank God, there flows blood and not water (or does it hurt to think that blood is red, bringing back to mind those "left-wing elements of all confessions"?).

Faced with the real motives underlying the encyclical, a simple Christian remains a Christian and becomes more a Christian on account of it even though he discusses or criticizes the encyclical. He knows full well that he does so because he is a Christian; as, for example, the unknown person who, writing in the weekly *La Chiesa nel Mondo,* gives some very simple but very Christian thoughts. These are far more relevant to the whole question of the motives of the encyclical than those motives from on high where the Church is either put on a pedestal or ironized according to whether the "left-wing elements of all confessions" are felt to be dangerous or harmless. This simple Christian who signs his name as Mario Panico has put his reflections down in writing and states among other things:

Paul VI's encyclical, defined as "a document of the ordinary magisterium of a noninfallible and hence nonirreformable nature, even though authoritative" could not but spark off, on account of the expectations and of the vital importance of the issue, a widespread debate both inside and outside the Church. I maintain that this fact is an important event and a sign of vitality, a reason for encouraging dialogue in every form both for and against the encyclical as a basis for further study, research, and drawing up of guidelines to help resolve so burning a problem for Catholics and for the human race. I have noticed, unfortunately, how the debate has been seen by many as just one more chance to profess their a priori faiths and as a motive to accuse those who disagree with them of everything from "lack of faith" to suspected heresy, or even an open break with the ecclesiastical hierarchy.

These episodes appear to me to be painful things which I had hoped by now had completely disappeared. Instead, there is a noticeable persistence and growth of this second-rate phenomenon which is indirectly robbing Christians of their freedom! It also seems to me that *L'Osservatore Romano* itself has indirectly promoted this type of attitude. While praising every agreement with the encyclical, even the most senseless and acritical, it has, at the same time, placed those who disagree with it on at least an inferior level, even though it cannot ignore what they say. . . . But the most offensive thing of all which I wish to highlight is the fact that the most vigorous champions of the encyclical's cause have felt it necessary to write their "cry of rejoicing" in publications like S— and B—, well-known for their wide experience in scandal-mongering and for their reactionary, factious spirit in their treatment of issues. These periodicals did not spare among others, the then Cardinal Montini and now Pope Paul VI from harmful criticism, from calumnious suspicions, and from offensive statements which involve, as well as the Pope, a large part of the clergy and Catholic laity. Nevertheless, these periodicals find Italian clergy who collaborate and contribute their news items, complaints, and firsthand reports. They also find "Catholics" who can find no other place to let it be known that they "approve of the encyclical."

In the face of events of this type we would have expected—and not for the first time—a correction by *L'Osservatore Romano,* but in vain. In vain also we would have desired that stiff note of warning which punctually comes every time anyone writes in *L'Espresso,* or if he has had the bad luck of being quoted by the Marxist press. Once again *L'Osservatore Romano* says one thing and does another. It is useless and superficial to restate how little use all this is for the maturation of the "Church, the people of God" and the education of Catholics toward becoming "responsible, free, and mature in conscience." This leads us to note the length of the path in Italy toward renewing even one sphere of life in a Church which often embitters, saddens, and offends us, precisely because we feel and believe that the Church is our mother and because we feel committed to making even its human side the Bride of Christ.

This simple, direct reaction of a believer passes beyond the question of the encyclical itself, even if prompted by it. This reaction is interesting, however, for a number of reasons and not solely on account of the Church in Italy to which it refers. First, this Christian experiences the difficulty of trying to put forward the motives underlying the encyclical when he even finds it difficult to explain to a believer the motives underlying the existence and mission of the Church. Second, he affirms what, for a believer, is unshakable and inalienable, but for reasons of faith that go far deeper than any simple reasons of expediency. Third, because of this faith, he affirms the possibility and the loyalty of criticism seen as an act of faith and confidence in the Church and as a responsibility shared with the whole people of God. This is the reason that, while the first duty is to accept the word of him who stands at the apex of pastoral service in the Church, the next duty is that of reflecting on what he says and its meaning, even if this should give rise to a criticism of it. Certainly this will be no more subversive or destructive than all those "unconditional" approvals. After all, it is more offensive to say that "one approves" of the magisterium of the Church than it is to say "one discusses it." The believer does not "approve" of the magisterium because it is not a thing that comes to him from outside but arises from within the Church, and it is by living in the Church that "one lives" the magisterium, where there is no distinction between the "doctrinal" and the "pastoral," both being aspects of the one reality.

Hence the believer must first ask himself what an encyclical is (and *Humanae Vitae* has put this issue forward for reflection once again), then how he must act in conscience in regard to the encyclical. The next step will be to ask himself what its content is, what line of reasoning it is based on; and then he must evaluate and discuss it. He may, in the end, even disagree with the reasoning. He will keep in mind the fact that a teaching of the magisterium of itself does not depend on the arguments it puts forward. Since this magisterium is not infallible, however, he holds that it is not irreformable, and therefore will pursue his reflections in order that his effort may contribute to a homogeneous evolution while accepting this magisterium as the Church's present conviction.

The Features of an Encyclical and of Humanae Vitae

First, then, it must be made clear what an encyclical is and what its value is. In this way we shall have some idea of how to judge *Humanae Vitae,* and a better idea of the attitude that a believer should have toward the encyclical.

The South American theologian Jorge Mejia, writing in *Criterio* of August 22, 1968 first asks himself the "why" of this particular method of teaching; that is, the encyclical. He then passes on to the issue which we have mentioned:

The teaching of the See of Rome is not absolute. On this matter the See of Rome teaches and commands by virtue of what is commonly recognized as its duty and right to interpret the natural law in the light of the gospel. In spite of what one would like to think, it is a most delicate region, the "twilight zone" of the magisterium's functioning. When revelation clearly teaches something or at least sheds sufficient light on a revealed truth, the magisterium has no difficulty in recognizing and stating this. We know what serious consideration goes into the exercise of the solemn magisterium in the form of dogmas, to such an extent that Vatican Council II abstained from proclaiming even one, while the last two dogmas have been directly proclaimed by the See of Rome—the Immaculate Conception and the Assumption of Mary. The matter is entirely different when the ordinary, or solemn, magisterium, whether papal or conciliar, intends proclaiming teachings that refer to reason, to nature, or to natural law. In the Roman Catholic idea of the magisterium, the Church has an unquestionable right to do this precisely on account of the "historical" and not systematic nature of the revelation of scripture. Now, however, we are entering a sphere where the progress of human knowledge, cultural limitations, and historical change all play their part.

If there exists an unchangeable natural law expressing the divine will as such—and not insofar as simply incarnated in biology and chemistry—and the principle of moral behavior, then it does not follow that we all know it at first sight, nor is it immediately evident in the sphere to which it applies. The Church certainly uses the normal methods of research and the various means available for arriving at conclusions which are natural as such, even if we believe that in doing this she is guided by the permanent inspiration of the Spirit, not only in order not to say something she should not say but also—and possibly, especially—in order not to say more than she should say. This shows that, over and beyond the margin of error and imperfection which the various traditions can contain, they are, at the same time, subject to a continual process of growth, maturation, and correction. Perhaps the most striking example of this in modern times is the doctrine of religious liberty. If the present teaching is correct, then we can understand how difficult it is for the See of Rome to break with these traditions and that it is the duty of the See of Rome to subject them, whenever necessary, to observation and testing. This testing and correcting process can be done by means of a Council, as in the case of religious liberty.

This, however, leads us to reflect on the method used by the Sovereign Pontiff in making known his decision on birth regulation—an encyclical. An encyclical, it is often said, is not a document of the solemn magisterium, does not require external assent, is not irreformable, and is always subject to criticism. Or one can go to the other extreme and say that it is a definitive document requiring internal assent; will, in fact, never be reformed, and whoever dares to criticize the Pope's statements is to be classed among the hidden and open adversaries of the Catholic faith that are to be found today even in ecclesiastical circles.

It is neither one nor the other. Encyclicals do not claim to take the place either of Councils or of dogmatic definitions, whether it be the Pope or a Council that defines them. Encyclicals contribute to making up part of a dynamic magisterium which chooses this method of communicating with the faithful because it is direct and efficient, and the issues involved almost always depend on some concrete circumstances of a period of the Church's history or some area of the Church's concern. As such, they are not intended to be read out of context, as if each of them were an absolute principle or a definite statement of which nothing had ever been said previously and after which nothing new could ever reasonably be expected to turn up. Anyone who reads the encyclicals in this absolute way—as, for example, the social encyclicals of Leo XIII when applied to today—will immediately find himself faced with insurmountable difficulties, or else will be due for a big surprise.

In other words, the encyclicals are moments, possibly decisive moments, of a doctrine's unfolding itself in time but not exhausted in any one of these moments. Something similar can be said of the conciliar magisterium and even, finally, of solemn definitions. . . . This does not mean, however, that an issue should be made of an encyclical as if it were more important than an opinion made official by the head of the hierarchy. This would be a dangerous conclusion because it would lead to denying the very meaning of the teaching magisterium which belongs to the structure of the Church as understood by Catholics. The variable way in which this magisterium functions does not give us an excuse to begin questioning basic principles. On the other hand, too, it does not give us the right to accept some encyclicals and to reject or ignore others if we so choose. Not all of a Pope's encyclicals are equally important, nor do all fulfill all the conditions we have just described. On the other hand, we have no right, either, to simply prescind from *Humanae Vitae* by hoisting up the flag of *Populorum Progressio* against it. It is not enough to say that the latter corresponds more to the modern mentality. This could possibly explain some things but it would justify nothing.

At the same time, however, *Humanae Vitae* cannot be transformed into the touchstone of fidelity to the See of Rome, as if no other encyclical had ever been written before it and as if *Populorum Progressio,* for example, did not merit as much adhesion, acceptance, and above all, practical application, as its more recent sister document. The same principle applies here as mentioned above, but in the opposite way. What, too, of the Council? Was adhesion required of the clergy and Catholics to the Declaration on Religious Freedom or to the Declaration on Non-Christian Religions or to ecumenism? Were the theological faculties asked to sign the theological teaching of *Lumen Gentium* or of *Gaudium et Spes*? No, because it was already presupposed, although no one can or may ignore the fact that if theologians, priests, religious, lay people, and finally members of the hierarchy had this alternative put before them, they would not always have responded with absolute peace of mind and with total acceptance of the adhesion required. We may also observe how much is being said, done, and not done about the things commanded, in theory and in practice, by the Council.

Faced with the backlash created by an encyclical that undoubtedly took up a stand against an opinion which had already made considerable headway in the Church, Mejia's treatment is extremely balanced and realistic. The problem remains of the type of adhesion required of a magisterium expressed by means of an encyclical, and will be dealt with later.

Another theologian, who has wanted to preserve his anonymity but who shows himself to be both competent and possessing a remarkable critical ability, has taken even farther the examination of the meaning of an encyclical. At the same time he has approached it from the difficult standpoint of the believer who must live his faith interiorly while belonging to a religious community which possesses an external magisterium. Besides putting Jorge Mejia's reasoning in a more dynamic and personalist framework, the theologian's reflections in *Le Monde* of August 8, 1968 take up again Mejia's reflections on historical verification. As Mejia in fact notes, *Humanae Vitae*, like every other encyclical, is "neither an absolute nor the last word."

The writer says:

The faith of the believer, like all the deepest convictions which we find within ourselves, prevents the apparent paradox of being both extremely and candidly simple, and yet gives us a free hand to investigate into it. The fact is that faith, in its very fervor, employs all the rational and critical faculties against any infantile or fideistic monolithism which may be found mixed together with it. In this way it respects its participation in the Mystery of God by overcoming its weaknesses and sociological conditionings. This is particularly true of the faith of Christians where the freedom of the spirit feeds this permanent search as well as giving it a necessary guarantee in the guidance of the magisterium and in the juridical machinery. The reading and understanding of scripture, even on the grammatical level, is given real assistance by this.

If this rule is always true for the supreme enunciation contained in scripture, how much more true will it be for the "secondary documents" in which divine revelation reechoes in the course of history. Of these documents, which vary according to their historical circumstances and the form of their redaction as well as the higher authorities to which they appeal, the letters called "encyclicals" from higher authorities constitute a specific literary type which has been developed by the Church's teaching magisterium particularly since the nineteenth century. Theologians call it the "ordinary" magisterium in the sense that while supplying an authentic expression of the tradition in a given historical epoch, nonetheless it is not proposed as a definitive interpretation of the Word of God. This distinction, already of considerable significance, becomes even more important when the encyclicals' development, textual superstructure, and modes of expression are considered. This is not subtle casuistry, but once again, respect for the transcendence of the Mystery, which never finds an adequate incarnation in history. The solemn statements themselves, called "dogmas," in spite of their infallibility, are subject to this relativity of formulas, concepts, and situations, and the inevitable partial nature of even the most adequate pronouncements.

Instead of reflecting on these theoretical qualifications, the more helpful course of action to adopt is the actual observation of the facts and textual variations themselves. Historians do not express surprise when faced with all this relativity. They remember one of the most significant examples, the papal bull *Unam Sanctam*, which Boniface VIII solemnly proclaimed against Philip the Fair. It is all the more important a text because it terminates with a dogmatic definition which explicitly proclaims that "the political behavior of sovereigns is subject to the law of the gospel and, therefore, to the authority who represents this law."

Our anonymous theologian observes that Boniface VIII's "definition" is the product of a theological system typical of the era of "Christendom," which was very much akin to a theocracy. This theological system has since declined and has been publicly rejected by the magisterium itself. He then passes on to more recent texts which share these same features; for example, Gregory XVI's encyclical *Mirari Vos* against the liberalism of Lammenais and Lacordaire, and Pius IX's encyclical *Quanta Cura*, which led to the *Syllabus* "against the errors of our time" (1864). Vatican II's Declaration of Religious Freedom is in great part a revision of many ideas that were authoritatively proposed in the past. One event, however, which caused a sensation in its time—and not many years ago—is particularly significant:

Pius XII's encyclical *Humani Generis* (1950), if read in the context of its underlying motives, not mentioned in the document, has been surpassed today by the theological renewal, for the encyclical criticized too summarily the very principle of this renewal and it misunderstood the historicity of the Christian economy and of human nature itself.

Following the principles suggested at the beginning and keeping in mind the facts handed down by history, the theologian makes his conclusion. He does not directly mention *Humanae Vitae* but takes into consideration the problems to which it has given rise in the exposition of his thought:

Thus, encyclicals are written on different levels according to the subject matter they treat. They include several other finer points belonging either to the dogmatic field or to that of directives, especially in scientific, psychological, economic, and social matters. The repercussions of both a culture's progress and its underdevelopment are found in encyclicals since both the discoveries and the real problems in a culture cannot be seen clearly until much later. They need not be read word for word or treated in either a literal or dialectical fashion. A believer's healthy faith knows how to unite a proper respect for the pastoral magisterium that the community is vitally in need of, especially in periods of upheaval, with a serene, personal investigation which follows the patient research carried out by qualified experts and which gives careful attention to both scientific progress and the growth of conscience, and which, at the same time, joyfully trusts in the evangelical "sense" of the "people of God" (*Lumen Gentium*, No. 12).

Those who decry this "historicization" of the magisterium, of faith, and of theology, should pay more attention to a believer's "healthy" faith. It would seem, in fact, that all those reactions which either glorify or criticize the encyclical reveal a faith which is in a rather hysterical condition, whereas it should be eminently serene and conducive to even greater serenity.

On the other hand, our investigation of the underlying motives of the encyclical has really shown to what extent faith can fall under "foreign" influences, from the politico-economic (the "left-wing elements of all confessions") to politico-religious (a "beginning of anarchy"), and even to religious and spiritual syndromes that almost certainly require clinical attention.

That balanced attitude which does not allow *Humanae Vitae* to be transformed into either the touchstone of orthodoxy or the starting point for an infantile questioning of the magisterium (and even less of Christian faith), possibly can only be acquired if we allow the encyclical itself to become a new, positive opportunity for dialogue. If this does not happen, then we shall find ourselves falling into hardened attitudes which do nothing other than dig moats around something which is not the faith in its essential purity. This "something" will have taken the place of faith and given rise to power struggles of various descriptions that are nothing but the projection of all kinds of uncertainties and the search for salvation in pseudo-liberty on the one hand and in all-encompassing authority on the other. When we have reached this stage, we are no longer in the field of *faith*—much less of Christian faith—but in the field of psychoanalysis. It is to be hoped that *Humanae Vitae*, either in the writing or the reading of it, has little in common with this stage.

That this stage has not yet arrived—at least from a non-specialist's point of view—may be observed from a serene analysis and criticism of the underlying motives of the encyclical. Criticism does not destroy the encyclical's motives but, to the extent that the believer lives his faith, makes them real to him, as we have heard from the two theologians whom we have just read.

A Total Vision of Man and His Vocation

The one point of the encyclical which has been most responsible for provoking the general outcry against it, is its exclusion as a lawful means of birth control, the direct interruption of the generative process once it has begun. Above all, it has been that fact that "similarly excluded is every action which, either in anticipation of the conjugal act, or in its accomplishment, or in the development of its natural consequences, proposes, whether as an end or as a means, to render procreation impossible" (*Humanae Vitae*, No. 14). In the eyes of the public this meant but one thing: the Pill was out. It is clear that the magisterium had no intention of interfering in an issue of this kind unless it saw it in a far wider context and unless the issues affected this context in some way. Also, it is only by starting with this context that it is really possible to grasp the motives underlying the encyclical. The encyclical itself (in No. 7) gives the context in which the exclusion of contraceptive methods must be put:

The problem of birth, like every other problem regarding human life, is to be considered beyond partial perspectives—whether of the biological or psychological, demographic or sociological orders—in the light of an integral vision of man and of his vocation, not only his natural and earthly but also his supernatural and eternal vocation.

From this text several things immediately follow: a perspective on married love and its characteristics, a judgment on responsible parenthood, and finally, an affirmation of respect for nature and the finality of the marriage act in which the two aspects of union and procreation are inseparable and which consequently do not allow the use of any means which separates them, since this would be contrary to nature and hence against God's plan. This whole process follows a strict logic upheld by the encyclical for the above motives and on account of the grave consequences that follow on from artificial methods of birth regulation (as explained in No. 17 of the encyclical).

There is almost unanimous agreement on the general context in which the encyclical's decision is placed: married love in all its entirety, nobility, and fullness. Disagreement, however, has arisen over two points: its concept of "human nature" or, more generally, "nature" used as the basis for the exclusion of "unnatural" means, and the motives militating against the use of these means. We shall see later how these two points always reappear in the whole discussion on the encyclical.

It is sufficient at the moment to note two immediate reactions which, if not typical of the hysteria mentioned previously, do not indicate, at least, that healthy faith mentioned above by the anonymous theologian. They help us, besides, to be wary of uncritically accepting any attribution to the encyclical of motives differing from those given by Paul VI in the encyclical itself, which we shall examine after having observed the following reactions.

The Economist of October 7, 1968, after some statements very offensive to the Pope says:

Why, then, has the Pope taken the stand he has? It has to be suspected that one factor is that he desires to preserve the prestige and authority of the Roman See. If so, he has made an error of judgment in the means chosen to achieve this end. . . . What is likely to happen now? Although it will become the focus of bitter controversy, the encyclical within days of its issue is intellectually deader than the dodo. . . . It should also have convinced all but the most triumphal that the structure of a medieval monarchy is entirely unsuitable to that Church in the modern world. This encyclical is not the fruit of papal infallibility, but papal isolation. And if it be argued that all this criticism is an unacceptable and ignorant intrusion into the world of theology, then the answer must be that His Holiness has this week made a most uninstructed foray into the no doubt lesser world of sociology and economics.

The opposite reaction was given by Rome's *Il Tempo* the following day:

This is the living, triumphant outcome of *Humanae Vitae*; and this outcome, if its great importance is to be fully grasped, must be seen separately from the more or less justifiable concern over its social repercussions or over how wise the papal condemnation is, politically speaking. These anxieties and fears must be left to the sociologists to fight over. Here, then, are two historical and memorable events. The "Credo" has dispersed, once and for all, the theological deviations and heretical views which already seemed to be undermining the foundation of the bimillennial edifice of the Church. *Humanae Vitae*, by its insistence on the natural beginnings of life and its sublime morality, has ensured that the mystery of birth remain untouched.

It is true that the second text is right in excluding all those issues which should be left "to the sociologists to fight over" and for insisting that the "mystery of birth" remain "untouched." Unfortunately, however, both texts have some very unsettling things to say when they begin examining the motives of the encyclical. One article gives us the "structure of a medieval monarchy" while the other insists on the live, "triumphant outcome." The two phrases, in the long run, are identical, seeing that the Church of God has no more need of a triumphant outcome than it has of a structure of medieval monarchy. Which of the two statements, one "for" and the other "against" the encyclical—but both, seemingly, equally wide of the mark—will be more appreciated? Probably neither, or at least a good Christian would hope this—for even though he be fuming with rage against the encyclical, he wants his criticisms to remain within the area outlined by the encyclical itself. In any case,

L'Osservatore Romano on August 11 gave an energetic answer to the first but not to the second.

Our primary concern, however, is to penetrate deeper into the real motives underlying the encyclical. Our best guide here is Paul VI himself, who, in an audience at Castel Gandolfo several days after the publication of *Humanae Vitae*, said:

Its essential content, . . . is not merely a declaration of a negative moral law that excludes every action aimed at rendering procreation impossible, but it is above all a positive presentation of conjugal morality in regard to its mission of love and fertility in the light of an integral vision of man and his vocation, not only his natural and earthly but also his supernatural and eternal vocation. It clarifies a fundamental chapter in the personal, married, family, and social life of man.

The motives of the encyclical are clearly laid out here. The different, ambiguous motives proposed so far which went to the extent of suggesting that it was a political move calculated to ensure the "reentry" of the post-conciliar period, can now be rejected. There is, however, one further danger, that of thinking that now the last word has been uttered on what the Church thinks concerning the person, the encounter of human love, and the family. This view would tend toward seeing everything in the light of a prohibition, that of the "pontifical condemnation" (this is possibly how the second writer above, by an oversight, understood the "essential content, . . . is not merely a declaration of a negative moral law"; moreover, this prohibition would be seen in the squalid light of the Pill). To counter this, Paul VI adds a comment indicating his awareness of the fact that even if "today" he *had* to say "an unwelcome word" (Castel Gandolfo, August 5), this "is not a complete treatment of marriage, the family, and their moral significance. This is an immense field to which the magisterium of the Church could and perhaps should return with a fuller, more organic, and more synthetic treatment."

With this taken into account, Paul VI then outlines the direction of the program followed by him in *this* encyclical: "This encyclical is an answer to the questions, doubts, and trends about which, as everyone is aware, there has been such wide and lively discussion in recent times. This has led us to take a wide interest in it from the doctrinal and pastoral point of view."

Even though the direction and the limits of the encyclical have been outlined in this way, it is always to be read in its proper context as we have found indicated in No. 7 of the encyclical. In No. 8 this context takes on such a new dimension that people are known to have said that it is not understandable how the encyclical can then simply claim to be deducing all the details of its exclusion of various contraceptive practices from this text. In No. 8 the encyclical says, in fact:

Conjugal love reveals its true nature and nobility when it is considered in its supreme origin, God, who is love, "the Father, from whom every family in heaven and on earth is named (Eph. 3:15)." Marriage is not, then, the effect of chance or the product of the evolution of unconscious natural forces; it is the wise institution of the Creator to realize in mankind his design of love. By means of the reciprocal personal gift of self, proper and exclusive to them, husband and wife tend toward the communion of their beings in view of mutual personal perfection, to collaborate with God in the generation and education of new lives. For baptized persons, moreover, marriage invests the dignity of a sacramental sign of grace, inasmuch as it represents the union of Christ and of the Church.

Only after the treatment of the issue has been presented in this way and every believer is ready to give it total acceptance, is it then possible to approach the whole discussion on motives which we have mentioned and in the way we have mentioned. This is all the more so because Paul VI himself tells priests in No. 28 of the encyclical:

Be the first to give, in the exercise of your ministry, the example of loyal internal and external obedience to the teaching authority of the Church. That obedience, as you well know, obliges not only because of the reasons adduced, but also because of the light of the Holy Spirit, which is given in a particular way to the pastors of the Church in order that they may illustrate the truth.

Gustave Martelet, the Jesuit who was very near to Paul VI in the final stage of the encyclical's preparation, and hence closely listened to in his statements after the appearance of the encyclical, asks himself in *Nouvelle Revue Théologique* of December 1968 regarding the phrase quoted by the encyclical:

Does this possibly mean that the reasoning used in the encyclical is completely separate both from the exercise of the charisma and from the doctrine itself? If this were true, then Catholics and priests would find themselves faced with the strange duty of having to submit in spite of the reasons adduced for the teaching. This would make impossible that rational obedience of the spirit which presupposes interior assent to the Church's teaching. Moreover, there would be no possibility of anyone ever advancing in this interior understanding of spiritual things without which there can exist no living tradition in the Church, nor a "sense of faith" of the people of God (*Lumen Gentium*, No. 12). Therefore, when the Pope speaks of this assent in which the "reasons advanced" do not have the main role, he is not demanding blind obedience. . . . Rather, he is indicating the necessity of following a type of illumination which, at first, may not give us fully satisfactory reasons but which does put us in contact with an absolute realm of values of which we can have an overall intuition even before the final basis of these values has been demonstrated.

This type of attitude, not unknown even to the scientist, is not so new as it may at first sight seem (cf. B. D'Espagnat, *Conceptions de le physique contemporaine. Les interpretations de la mécanique quantique et de la mesure*, Paris, 1965: "When analyzing first principles in depth, the difficulty in understanding them becomes particularly apparent," p. 140).

Martelet gives some examples from the early history of the Church where a stand by the Roman Church on a controversial issue later proved to be a wise one, even if the reasons were not evident at the beginning. In these cases it was necessary, above all, to act within the limits of basic "fidelity" to the "Spirit who has in his Church the body of his community (St. Augustine)." Martelet then concludes:

There is more need for this kind of fidelity in the Church than is usually thought. It is all the more painful when it deals with matters on which every man and every woman, humanly speaking, are rightful authorities, as in the case of marriage. If a conflict arises between the opinions of a large number of persons and an authentically proclaimed Church teaching, it is often necessary without becoming self-satisfied or closed, to decide to "hold" what is seen as evident together with the costly affirmations of an authoritative magisterium which appears to a considerable number of people to be lacking in authority on the given question. But this fidelity must be as far as possible a creative one. Man's cultural history gives some very remarkable examples of it.

This principle proposed by an authoritative commentator on the encyclical is undoubtedly very positive and full of possibilities which would be missed by a senseless, irrational exaltation of the encyclical (unfortunately, the greater part of the "adhesions" published on several occasions by *L'Osservatore Romano* are to be included here) as well as by a radical and violent attack on it.

Nonetheless, it is essential that the underlying motives of the encyclical be clarified even further within the limits of the context we have mentioned. Once again it is Martelet who first quotes the text of No. 7 of *Humanae Vitae*—the text where it is stated that the encyclical intends to put "the problem of birth . . . in the light of an integral vision of man and of his vocation, not only his natural and earthly, but also his supernatural and eternal vocation." He then puts the concern of the encyclical in this overall context so that its teaching is read in its correct frame of reference as first and foremost a religious teaching. "This declaration," Martelet affirms, "which focuses on the height of the Mystery of which the Church is servant and sign, has guided the drawing-up of the encyclical. It must also guide its interpretation, as well as the necessary deepening of some points. Therefore, its exact sense must be clearly understood."

The encyclical, penetrating deeper than the Council's affirmations, states:

Conjugal love reveals its true nature and nobility when it is considered in its supreme origin, God, who is love (1 John 4:8), "the Father, from whom every family in heaven and on earth is named (Eph. 3:15)" (No. 8). This is an important statement. It immediately shows that love is inseparable from a creative generosity which is the guarantee of love's deep, perfect growth and also its final fulfillment. Besides, "by means of the reciprocal personal gift of self, proper and exclusive to them, husband and wife tend toward the communion of their beings in view of mutual personal perfection, to collaborate with God in the generation and education of new lives" (Nos. 8, 2). "Fully human" married love, insofar as it is at the same time "material and spiritual," is a "total" love, "faithful and exclusive." It is also a "fertile love, for it is not exhausted by the communion between husband and wife, but is destined to continue, raising up new lives" (Nos. 9, 2–5). It is here where concern is shown for the fact that it is often believed that married love is quite justified in closing in on itself and regarding the birth of a child as unimportant.

This is precisely the critical point—when the principle that the finality of every marriage act must always be open to pro-creation, is taken to its logical conclusion. Therefore Martelet himself admits immediately afterward:

Certainly, the fact that married love finds its source in a love "from whom every family in heaven and on earth is named" does not imply that it must reproduce, in *each* of its acts, that eternal fruitfulness from which it is derived and of which it is the image. "In fact, as experience bears witness, not every conjugal act is followed by a new life" (No. 11). Rather, there can be a "positive will of avoiding children for plausible reasons" (Nos. 16, 4). The eternal fruitfulness of God in the generation of the Son, as also in his creative fruitfulness with regard to us, is of a strictly *spiritual* order which we cannot imitate in a purely *biological* way. It is the *whole* of married life, as also the whole of human existence, in which man and woman must represent, to a greater or lesser extent, the inexhaustible vitality of the eternal love of God.

The encyclical, by seeing the couple's love as a sign of God's love, wants to recall an essential truth about love. Right and deep as married love's desire and capacity for total communion are, love does not fully become what it ought to become unless it allows the fruit of its intimacy to appear. Maybe this fruit will be hard to desire and even to accept. As soon as it systematically begins excluding this fruit, how-ever, love immediately injures itself so that it leads to death—that death which is the eventual destination of every introverted *eros* and every couple who enjoy a life they refuse to spread. . . . Made in the image of God who is love himself, married love is not directed solely by the secret impulse to unfathomable intimacy between the sexes but also the "newness" (Nos. 8, 3; 9, 5) of life which it has the mission of giving—and of giving forever. Love is truly surpassed by the sign of its fruitfulness.

Martelet's long exposition is conducted in the serene tone coupled with solid theological thought, not to mention a truly remarkable display of human wisdom. In any case, the central nucleus of the way in which *Humanae Vitae* reasons is already contained in the short text just quoted.

It is not in every instance, however, that a defense of the "reasons adopted" is expounded in this tone. If this were the style of thinking of all the theologians supporting the encyclical, the discussion would probably remain on a dignified and gentlemanly level. But matters change when this central nucleus begins to be used as the point of departure for salvaging a whole list of motives which encompass the entire globe, its present faults, the sins of theologians and moralists, etc. It is striking, for example, that all the undeniably true things which a patristic scholar like the Jesuit Jean Daniélou says, fade into insignificance before his *"j'accuse"* which embraces the universe—certainly not, it seems, in the manner of him "from whom every family in heaven and on earth is named." In *La Croix* of September 13, 1968 Daniélou faces the whole question in "The Significance of *Humanae Vitae*." He says:

I know the problem that so many Christian families are faced with. I know what sublime ideas they have of love and marriage. I know that they want as many children as they can bring up. I know that if they limit their number it is to be better able to fulfill their duties. I know that it is for them that *Humanae Vitae* will bring problems and decisions affecting conscience.

Daniélou then adds that he knows the Church is the Church of the poor and not of an elite, and this includes above all, those families who will have problems.

Daniélou continues:

And yet I feel—and how many others there are who do not dare to say the same!—how right Paul VI was to speak the way he did. What was in question was the end result of an immensely long process. One of the gravest struggles of our age turns on the whole question of love and marriage. All the demons have been let loose into the fray, each with his apparently valid arguments. There was the conspiracy of the libertarians and the technocrats. The former wanted to extend their universal desire for planning into the realm of the family. Others saw in sexual liberty one of the principal means of contestation. The sinister influence of psychoanalysis was finally even persuading people that chastity was a myth and that sexual perversion is found everywhere. Huge financial gains were being made on the exploitation of eroticism in films and in the press. To oppose all these forces and to turn the tide back, extraordinary courage was necessary. And we shall never be grateful enough to Paul VI for having, in spite of everything and first against theologians, taken the part of man against himself.

The basic question is far more important than it might seem at first glance. Initially the issue is one of distinguishing between legitimate means of birth control from reprehensible contraceptive practices. This practical question, however, includes within itself a whole understanding of man. There is, first, the intrinsic relationship between genital sexuality and the transmission of life. Certainly not every sexual act is fertile, but every sexual act is open to fertility. Genitality emancipated from fertility is a great menace. Whether one likes it or not, the recognition of the lawfulness of those contraceptive practices mentioned in the encyclical favored this emancipation. Certainly, it could be used for legitimate reasons. These reasons could even appear to be in harmony with the higher objectives of marriage. This cannot remove the fact, however, that in themselves they deprive the sexual act of an essential element without which its full significance cannot be grasped.

This does not come from a superseded concept of human nature. Modern anthropology is the first to tell us that the body as such has a meaning and does not acquire a meaning from the intention given to it. It is patently clear that here we are touching on a basic point. In fact, the question today is whether man arbitrarily decides what to do with himself according to the plans he makes for himself and without reference to any objective order, or whether there is a meaning already written into the reality of man himself so that he cannot reach his fulfillment unless he conforms to this order written into things. It does not really matter if this objective norm is called "nature" or "law." In any case it acquires its value from the fact that it is the expression of God's design. It is the interior necessity of being in harmony with the will of God which constitutes the fundamental reason for following this norm. For many people today all objective morality gives the appearance of being an alienation and a repression. The opposite is true. It is the condition for true freedom. . . . Paul VI's teaching has recalled the sacred character of human love at a time when, as with so many other things, civilization is tending to desacralize it and to take the mystery from it.

The encyclical is really a solemn witness to the fact that technology does not have absolute rights and that there is a limit beyond which it may not go. Another manifestation of this is the revolt against technocracy, witnessed, for instance, in the student movement. The encyclical expresses this revolt not from the point of view of anarchy, instinct, or imagination, as does Marcuse, but from the point of view of the depths of man. . . . It is a fundamental conflict; either one accepts the fact that sexuality may become one more product in a consumer society and hence it must be rationally organized in its use, or else one accepts the fact that human love is always an encounter between man and God—that it is an essential entry point for the sacred into human existence . . . which man misses if he uses it arbitrarily. It is this sacredness of love that the Church will defend to the end. The Church will defend it because the Church knows that it is defending human values in this way.

The question of birth regulation is not the only one where the Church has faced the pretenses of secularism. The Church is just as intransigent when it condemns divorce and defends the indissolubility of marriage. It knows that here also some tragic situations can develop. It would be easy for the Church to find followers by making broad concessions to all the customs being introduced today. This kind of Church, however, degraded in its morality, would be just as contemptible as a Church emptied of its dogmas, as some would like to see done.

The violent reactions stirred up by the encyclical reveal that it has touched a vital point. It has unleashed the fury of all those who in the pretense of reconciling the Church and the world do nothing other than make the Church conform to the world. The slogans on the Church's contempt for the flesh, on post-conciliar integrism, and even on the anxious character of Paul VI have been brought out from under their dust covers. The partisan-type arguments brought against the encyclical are its best justification.

These affirmations certainly make no small impression seeing that the best justification of the encyclical would be exactly those reactions which nobody, even those who criticized the encyclical, would think of accepting. Just as striking are the "demons let loose" and the condemnations against everything and everyone. A faint smell of the stake can be detected between the lines. One would agree, however, with the fundamental, forcefully expressed comments on the short statements of Paul VI. Daniélou concludes by recognizing the fact that, though the encyclical rejects the modern line of thought which desecrates both love and man, destroys morality, and gives a free rein to technology, yet it is "a teaching of love and not of condemnation, an orientation given for all and not a constitution for a small sect of the faithful."

It is important to realize this: if the encyclical were more a condemnation than a teaching of love, then it would immediately have had to face not a few awkward facts—what would have happened to the countless theologians who had presented their objections to the encyclical's reasoning in great length, the episcopates who gave it a pastoral interpretation, and the vast numbers of Christians who are certainly neither "technocrats" nor "libertarians" and yet who composed all those Catholic sectors which expressed reserves and criticism? Unfortunately it is not possible to develop and report all these numerous statements, but some will appear later in the relevant sections.

Two particular reactions, however, cannot be forgotten: the Schema on marriage and the family presented to and voted on by the plenary session of the Dutch Pastoral Council of January 5–8, 1969 and the speech that Prof. Scherer gave at the 82d *Katholikentag* of German Catholics in Essen on September 5, 1968.

Criticism and Honest Searching by Lay People

From some of the expressions we have reported in the course of our discussion, it would appear that all dissent or questioning of the encyclical is by now quite futile. The impression, in fact, seems to be that any intervention might well represent that "conspiracy of technocrats and libertarians" who are bent on extending the influence of their plans even over love and the family, and who are trying to put sexual freedom forward as one of the principal means of contestation.

In the reactions of both the Dutch Pastoral Council and the *Katholikentag*, it becomes clear that their reflections center mainly on the fundamental motives underlying the encyclical. They are themes which we have already heard in the quiet way that Paul VI and Martelet have expressed them. Why, then, do these Catholics take them up once again? It is not simply because they cannot accept them. Rather, it is precisely their acceptance of the principles justifying the encyclical that is the starting point of their criticism, and they also present from another point of view the motives which have led many Christians to adopt a variety of positions before the same fundamental values. This reveals a different, seemingly more optimistic evaluation of present-day developments in the understanding of human love—developments that are not felt to be destructive or dangerous to the "integral vision of man and his vocation." We may note as well that in these two Catholic positions can be found, practically speaking, reactions which in a clear and precise but also balanced and solid way, are more or less common on all levels of the Catholic world.

The text of the Schema of the Dutch Pastoral Council is developed in three sections: the content of the encyclical's doctrine, the meaning of the authority of the magisterium, and the individual judgment of conscience. In spite of its brevity, the text is very important both because of the particularly alive and dynamic, even if critical, Catholic environment from which it comes, and because it takes into consideration objections that could be brought against those Catholics who criticize the encyclical. The text is written in the plural because its intention is to speak in the name of the Dutch Catholics—or at least the majority of them—fully represented in the plenary session of the Pastoral Council. It says:

In the encyclical taken as a whole we appreciate, first, the appeal for responsibility in sexuality and marriage (cf. Letter of the Dutch Bishops, July 31, 1969), and the care taken to recognize the will of God which is understood as the main guide of human activity and of the Church's faith, and which, in the divine ordering of things, is also the true good of man. When, however, we study the content of the encyclical more clearly, we notice that it is not evident how from biological data on sexual union and the process of generation we can directly know the will of the Creator and the natural moral law which is valid for human activity. It is true that the encyclical recognizes "an integral vision of man and of his vocation" as a fundamental norm (No. 7), but what it then does is restrict this norm to the structure and workings of the human organism. These, therefore, acquire a value which is uninfringeable and must not be interfered with by man even to serve higher, personal values (Nos. 10, 11, 17, 31).

In our opinion, such personal values as the relationship between married love and human fertility, the dignity of woman, the greatest possible seriousness before man's sexual life, respect for the Creator and for the origin of life, are not in themselves threatened by the use of so-called artificial methods. The categorical condemnation here applies to all artificial methods without distinction and does not take into consideration individual persons, their intentions, and the circumstances they find themselves in. In this way every medical, psychological, and social consideration either for or against any particular method has been rejected from the beginning. In certain marriages the use of the Pill or other contraceptive methods could well meet with serious objection. Just as periodic continence for some couples can enrich their mutual union, so it can for others represent a serious threat.

These considerations show the importance of responsibility and moral seriousness on the part of couples, but cannot in any way contribute toward the formation of a moral judgment since, according to the encyclical, this can be based only on the "law of the generative process" (No. 13). The encyclical simply states, "it is allowed" or "it is not allowed." We fear that it is precisely this which will lead to superficial attitudes and a comfortable norm of action. We think that by highlighting in *this* way the concrete rejection of various methods, the encyclical has failed to give an authoritative statement and guide in favor of the dignity of marriage and sexuality which, in fact, in our society is often threatened and given little serious consideration.

As for the magisterial authority of the papal encyclical, the commission has come to the conclusion that the authoritative teaching to which the head of the Church is called by God is correctly exercised only when an attempt has been made, in concepts and words, to communicate with the life of faith and the awareness of values of the faithful today and with the authentic thought of the whole ecclesial community as it is also expressed by the episcopate of the whole world. Vatican Council II attaches great importance to the agreement of all the faithful in questions of faith and morals. This agreement is not purely and simply the result of an efficient magisterium (cf. *Lumen Gentium*, No. 12). It is not shown by a unanimous mass decision or even by a numerical majority, but emerges in the serious, public discussion carried on by believers. We doubt that all this has been sufficiently expressed in the encyclical. Moreover, when ecclesiastical authority speaks in the field of morals (as distinguished from the mysteries of faith in the true and proper sense), it is speaking of truths which are already open to people's moral sentiment and thought, and present to them through individual consciences. For this reason, even if the Church must say things which are unpleasant and unpopular, it can lead to light being shed on moral issues, and in these cases the warning is heard and understood.

When, however, a moral teaching does not lead to a clearer and more correct understanding for many of the devout faithful, then whether this teaching is correct must be seriously queried. This is precisely what seems to be the case with the statements of *Humanae Vitae* on the unlawfulness and sinfulness of so-called artificial methods of birth regulation. According to the encyclical, every honest man must be able to understand the truth of the teaching put forward (No. 17; cf. No. 12). We must admit, however, that in our country and elsewhere, many believing, very honest, and competent Catholics do not see how the condemnation is justifiable, and what is more, they criticize it with arguments which go to the root of the matter. This is also true for many Reformed Christians and for numerous non-Christians. If we did not keep these in mind, we would find ourselves lacking in respect for a conscience which is honestly searching for the truth (cf. *Gaudium et Spes,* No. 16).

As regards the individual judgment of conscience, we are convinced that not accepting the rules of behavior proposed by the encyclical is not equivalent to acting "arbitrarily" (Nos. 10, 17, 18). The appeal to conscience as the ultimate norm is not an appeal to disobedience, obstinacy, and disorderliness, but to commitment to the moral truth which, in the opinion of many people, the concrete statements of the encyclical do not seem to have grasped faithfully. There are many factors which influence the judgment of conscience on the question of methods of birth regulation, such as the mutual love of man and woman, family relationships, and social conditions. These factors are mentioned in the encyclical (Nos. 8, 9, 10) but do not appear in any way to be of influence in the judgment of conscience. Moral truth, "man's true good" (No. 18), is found, in our opinion, only through a spiritual union with the whole ecclesial community and through readiness to search together for an understanding of the commitments demanded from a Christian in the world.

The text, which was fully discussed and drawn up after numerous consultations, typical of the Pastoral Council's way of working, almost caused a scandal in the public eye. In reality, it is not a rejection of the encyclical. Unfortunately, the direct way of speaking which the Dutch have, often leads to what they say being interpreted in an entirely different light. It is all a matter of culture and a completely different way of thinking. The text of the Pastoral Council reflects, basically, that manner of dealing with the texts of the magisterium which the "anonymous" theologian and even, to some extent, Gustave Martelet have spoken of. It is, nonetheless, an honest stand adopted by a local Church. It would be dishonest to begin to make judgments insinuating a loss of moral sense or a loss of the meaning of faith, etc. The text itself, drawn up by authentic believers, expresses how anxious it is to take into consideration not only Catholics but also Reformed Christians and non-Christians who, although not fully accepting the intrinsic value of the teaching of the encyclical, are still serious and very responsible people who want to promote the good of the family and of mankind.

The topics raised by the Dutch Pastoral Council had already been fully treated by the *Katholikentag* at Essen. Besides the sensation that the assembly's demands made, the theme treated by Dr. Scherer gives us some measure of the earnestness with which the Catholics devoted their energies to considering the encyclical:

If we care to investigate, we shall see that our traditional Catholic idea of marriage is being questioned by the man of today. It can be rightly said that the findings of modern science, as well as the more or less clear understanding of man today, have a certain right to our consideration when we start defending something as unchangeable Catholic truth. We must also reflect, however, using the yardstick of faith, on what the man of today is questioning in the field of marriage, man-woman relationships, and human sexuality.

The criterion of all these is the radical nature of the love of God as it has appeared in Christ in the world. We must continually be open to allowing ourselves to be converted by love. But this also demands of us that we critically examine many things happening in the world, and to the extent that they affect us, reject them and even, in certain cases, eliminate them from us. This sets up a dynamic tension which includes and goes beyond our limited topic: we must become all things to all men so that they can perceive the demands and the promise of the message of Jesus Christ and so that we do not become conformed to the world. It is impossible to examine here every single issue which our subject matter includes. Only a few topics that I hope are important can be dealt with. The following points must be discussed: (1) the concept of marriage and married love as it is beginning to be more and more delineated in contemporary Catholic thought, (2) the relation between married love and sexuality, (3) the question of birth regulation where a position will be adopted with regard to the encyclical *Humanae Vitae.*

In the course of the last few decades there has prevailed in the Catholic sphere, in spite of opposition, a concept of marriage which sees it as the personal community of love between man and woman. This view had come to be more and more prevalent up to the time of the declarations of Vatican Council II on marriage. It began to be understood that the task of marriage, that of generation, does not militate against a personalist view of marriage but that this view, precisely because it involves a married community of persons, can also contribute to the birth of a new personal life.

Let us now try to clarify where the concepts of "personal community of love" or "the total love of the couple" will lead us.

I would first like to distinguish three essential aspects of married love: the loving gaze, the reciprocal giving of oneself, and the fullness of union. I shall make some observations on each of these three aspects. We shall begin with the loving gaze. To understand what is meant by this phrase we must put ourselves in the context of the unique experience of the beginning of a loving encounter between a man and a woman. Persons discover the other in themselves in the moment when they are drawn by the other from the very depths of their own person. Their partner seems like a unique miracle whose nearness transforms their whole world. It is often said that this fascinating, erotic passion makes a person blind. Exactly the opposite is true: a love like this, like every love, opens our eyes to what we would otherwise so easily overlook in our interpersonal relationships; that is, the fact that each person individually is unrepeatable, worthy to exist in himself, a person who is valuable for who he is.

For the first time, this uncovers for us the meaning of the words "personal love" in their most exact sense. Love is personal if it grasps the other for himself. The word person also means the material and spiritual totality of man. Even in this sense the loving gaze remains something personal. That is, it wants the person in all his qualities of knowledge and freedom but also those involving sentiment, vital attraction, and the mutual appeal of the sexes. This loving gaze springs from where all the forces of a person's being intertwine with each other and in each other. This depth of the person can be best indicated by the image of the heart. In this sense we can say that the loving gaze means looking with the eyes of the heart.

We must be careful not to confuse this movement of the whole person, which we have just mentioned, with so-called projections which also have an important part to play in the encounter between man and woman. By projections we mean the fixations of the mother or of the father, of ideals, of images, of desire for the other sex, which are possibly of a very ambiguous nature. The individual is not even aware of them, especially seeing that stereotyped images abound everywhere. These stereotypes have been inculcated into him from his childhood, and he now transfers them on to his partner. In the projection, which is often very similar to the stereotype, the individual mirrors himself in the other. Even in this way there can develop a strong sentimental link. These cases, however, cannot be called personal love since the other is not discovered and loved for himself alone but solely as an extension of one's own self. The shadow of the self is projected on to him so that he cannot reveal his own being.

Usually when a story of love begins, the first signs of the loving gaze are mixed together with various projections. Therefore, among the most important duties of love, which in an advanced stage of marriage must already have been fulfilled, is that of continually eliminating projections, leaving the gaze toward the other freer in order to give the other more room in which to reveal his true being. According to the degree in which projections have been eliminated, to that same degree a partner can be appreciated because he is himself, he has his own being and must realize himself by himself. The person who can look in this way acquires a new, deeper, and higher joy. We may call it "objective joy" because in it the person no longer thinks just of himself but rejoices in the other person as he is in himself. This objective joy will no longer be carried forward by the fierce rush of sentiments typical of a newly born love, but rather, will shine like a bright light in which its beginning, the loving gaze, is not simply put into the background but returns in all its depth.

Balancing what has just been said, however, certain other considerations can be advanced. In every marriage the loving gaze is put to the test by another experience with one's partner. The longer a person lives with another, the clearer it becomes to him that all these things mean so little. Admittedly, the other is an exclusively unique being but at the same time delusive with his failings, his emptiness, and his transitory existence finally destined for death. Precisely for this reason it is rightly stressed that in marriage the most important thing is to mutually accept each other in spite of one's weaknesses, to be patient, to support each other, and to forgive.

Here already we are touching a point that for Christians consists in not being conformed to the world, since what is called "love" and is disseminated as such, often enough knows very little of these powers of forgiveness and mutual support.

We must, however, face the problem of where marriage gets the strength for this perseverance and why it is prudent that love have such a radical character. The answer to this question must be given, in my opinion, in the following way: love, as long as it remains faithful to itself, hopes that the first experience of love, the loving gaze, already possesses the definitive truth in itself. Love cannot stop believing that it is worth the effort to have a partner in spite of all the experiences to the contrary, that that unique, precious object of which the loving gaze is a foretaste, is too much a part of him and that it is worthy and proper that it exist. For this reason, the two remain beside each other, no matter what happens. While they are like this, one is telling the other with all his existence: it is good for you to be here, I believe in you, you can hope, you have a future. Married fidelity is not bourgeois respectability, or even necessity disguised as the virtue of the sexually underdeveloped man. It is a fecund secret (G. Marcel) by which the person who receives the gift of fidelity feels himself called and sustained by the primordial force of being, and hence of God.

Up to this point even someone who, for any reason, does not call himself a Christian can follow what has been said since the loving gaze we have mentioned belongs to the human structure of love and is an experience that can arise in the life of every person. He may even view the fidelity which is the fruit of an undying hope as a prudent, human possibility in life, seeing that every person can experience in various ways—for example, in philosophical meditation—that beyond our existence there rules a nonobjective hope which even conquers death. This hope both makes our life a continuous risk and gives a meaning to fidelity to another person.

The Christian faith now enters to remind man of the real reason which justifies his holding a hope as boundless as this. It first turns to the resurrection of Jesus from the dead, its central content. In Jesus' resurrection and through it, each man personally and the history of mankind as a whole are made participants in the promises of a never-to-be-equaled perfection in boundless measure and in the inexhaustible power of the being of God himself. In fact, this has already become a reality in the risen Christ. His resurrection is his elevation to the fullness of being with God. In his elevation there are included all men of goodwill. He represents them before God and makes them participants in the fullness of his life.

As long as Christ lives, we shall also live. Our future is fixed and founded in him. For this reason, we can experience in our faith in him that it is not death, absurdity, emptiness, guilt, and dissolution which determine man's last destiny, but an infinite meaning that takes all of man's hopes into the inexpressible because it is God himself who became in Christ the goal and the content of man's future.

Christian marriage also lives on this serenity. It gives the couple hope that the loving gaze, when faced with all the experiences with their partner which put it in question, will finally be vindicated before God. In their faith in the risen Christ, which embraces and saves us all, both husband and wife can hope in each other: all the emptiness and death-bound transience that are found in you at this moment no longer have a future. They are already overcome and finished, overcome with the death and resurrection of the Lord. You will find yourself in an inexpressible state that surpasses every expectation, that the loving gaze prefigures, as long as our "life is hidden with Christ in God. But when Christ is revealed—and he is our life—you too will be revealed in all your glory with him (Col. 3:3–4)." This hope forms the ultimate, basic reason for married fidelity. Where fidelity lives on this hope, it makes the persons who live in marriage witnesses to Christ and to the love of God which has appeared in him. It utters a word to the partner that has been gradually forming as long as this love has existed: you are loved by an infinite love; in it your future and the meaning of your existence have been saved beyond death.

Where marriage is lived with this fundamental attitude, there is not only the love of God which is communicated. Marriage, rather, becomes filled with this love; the couple live it. Precisely because this love itself becomes present, it also can be said to show itself and appear. This is exactly what Catholic doctrine means when it says that marriage is a sacrament. It lets God's love appear as such. It points to God's love and makes visible what that is which lives in its depths, and from which it attains life: the very love of God irrevocably offered in Christ to the world. We can hope that this love shows itself efficacious not just in Christian marriage but wherever there are persons who are welded together by love. Christian marriage, however, knows this profound meaning explicitly, and consciously wants to be one of the great signs of the Church which shows that unique secret which surpasses, sustains, and unites all things.

As regards the second essential moment in married love, the mutual self-giving, we can doubtless be briefer because the most important element of this subject has already been clarified in the statements on hope and fidelity that we mentioned in relation to the loving gaze. In marriage, as it is rightly said, persons must commit themselves to each other, put themselves at each other's disposition, and the I must flow into the Thou. Marriage is a higher form of existence for the other. For many people, in fact, it is the one form that it will take. This altruistic sentiment must be proved by many small daily services. In all this the important thing, first and last, is that one accept the other, adhere to his being, utter the "Yes of letting be" to him (M. Buber). This is total love between person and person which the pastoral constitution of Vatican II speaks of in relation to marriage. It is above all found in a fidelity without reservations in the words, "I am near you; I am for you, whatever happens." In this way the first and second aspects of married love are intimately connected with each other. The lovers discover by the give-and-take of their loving gaze the form that their existence takes on (first aspect). They want to exist for each other (second aspect).

These two persons would like also—and with this we find ourselves at the third aspect—to be united forever. This union finds its expression in many ways; for example, in the many things done in common in everyday life, in the destiny which the couple must experience together, in the common task of raising their children. Spiritual communion also makes up part of married love. This only goes to illustrate the fact that persons can find no fulfillment in their love if they gaze exclusively at each other. They also need something to look at together, and in which their love can resonate. The greater, deeper, and more essential this "something" is in which the persons are related to each other, the more radically will they be united to each other, the richer will one become for the other.

This is particularly true of love between man and woman. It seeks in its most intimate moments of yearning for something in which is hidden the correlationship of the I and the Thou and which, at the same time, surpasses both of them in infinitude. This can possibly be best expressed by two basic statements of love. One says, "I would like to give you everything, wish you your total, whole, and unsurpassable self-completion for which I cannot find a word because it surpasses all understanding." The other says, "I wish to be with you for eternity—forever." Both statements express the intimate secret of every human being: our being called to God who is the infinite horizon; the fullness of the deepest, unfathomable love. Wherever eros between the sexes reveals itself, there also appears this source of intimate desire in man which is so far from being fulfilled. Here it is again true that that which can be experienced by all and which is part of the inalienable structure of man, in Christian marriage is so well understood that the Christian can proclaim what every place and generation thinks and intimately desires: me with you, hidden forever in the secret of the living God who is love itself.

The central affirmation on the meaning of the sexual encounter, taking the word in its strictest sense, between man and woman can possibly be formulated in this way: sexual commitment is required to be the bodily expression of married love. Just as we can communicate with our tongues to other people, in a way that is experiential and perceptible to the senses, both what we are thinking and the vital element in us, so the playful tenderness and the pleasure that one experiences by means of the other must communicate and express love. In the language of the body, one must become touchable for the other: I love you; I think of you and exist for you; I rejoice in you because you are this remarkable woman, this remarkable man. Both should be able to experience again and again in this action that they are a single thing, two persons, a man and a woman, who are united in a We which embraces them.

Perhaps we bring out the deepest meaning of sexual union when we give back to the much-abused word appeasement its true meaning. To obtain appeasement and satisfaction (*befriedigung*) means, literally, to enter into peace. The one who obtains peace is he who finds some place in the midst of this perverse, battle-scarred world where he can have a foretaste of a possible world totality and of universal harmony. As a person, however, man only finds peace when he has arrived at an interior harmony because another Yes tells him that it accepts him and helps him by means of this Yes to more deeply possess himself. This place is found in the loving, married encounter when it is really filled with love, and if the love begins to resound in this encounter. Certainly no human couple can give itself that ultimate peace for which every person longs. For this reason, the peace that man and woman can experience in union points to a higher peace which they must pursue together in the eternal Thou of God. "When a man is intimately united with his wife they are driven by the desire for the eternal hills (M. Buber)."

Love and sexuality, then, must be perceived in their reciprocal relationship. They are neither simply the same thing as a mistaken modern view sees them nor are they in opposition to each other, as an ancient prejudice against human sexuality could lead one to believe. This prejudice can be historically explained by the spiritualistic and Manichaean thought of the better-known intellectual movements of the late classical age. These movements have had a decisive influence on Christian spirituality and ethics—as opposed to the anthropology of biblical origin. Christians of all creeds have the task today of re-examining and renewing this patrimony. Much has already been done toward this objective, but a considerable amount still remains to be done.

Thus one still often comes across Catholics who hold that the humanization of man's sexual impulses is achieved above all by dominating one's instincts. Yet nobody can deny that respect for one's partner, as well as not reducing sexual union in marriage to a trivial affair, also demands from the couple renunciations in the sexual sphere.

On the other hand, it must be made clear that man's basic task with regard to his sexual impulses does not consist in dominating them but in integrating them. "Integration" requires that these impulses be inserted into the totality of the human person. Man must be able to rediscover himself in the fact of sexuality in such a way that it no longer just stands there as a strange, painful, and basically inhuman weight in his life. This is achieved precisely when love is expressed in sexuality and man's sexual instincts become more and more the powers which realize this love the more they concretize the love which bursts forth from the center of the person. What then is most spiritual, love, acquires, not by any abstraction, the concrete closeness of the experience of bodies. The self, then, when it is only understood as dominion of oneself can easily shut itself up in itself. By an openness, however, toward the Thou and toward life, it can reach the *We* which is a vitally important constituent of a person's basic attitudes during the whole period of his married life.

The sexual union, and in this way we can sum it up together with the pastoral constitution *Gaudium et Spes,* must be the realization of sexual love. This requirement is not a law imposed on sexuality from outside, but has its origins in the nature of man, understood as a person who possesses a body. All which is really human must be the concretization of the spirit. For this reason, the more that human sexuality withdraws from the demands of love, the more it will lose its proper meaning. Even the man of today who, with a certain amount of justification, supports the liberation of sexuality from taboos and from the prejudices mentioned above, does not evidently live his sexual life as a means of pleasure. Often enough it appears absurd and humiliating to him that sexuality unveils only emptiness, fear, and nausea. This is an important revelation because it indicates the widespread misunderstanding today about sexuality which sees it solely as an instinctive, biological need (before which human reason has at the most the task of hygiene), and on the best of occasions can be considered simply an innocent society game.

Sexuality wants to be drawn by love. Love and sexuality belong to one and the same realm and consequently cannot be separated in such a deplorable way either by traditional prejudices or by a naturalism which, in the last analysis, is the same thing. With the insertion of this positive *ethos* into sexuality it is now possible to make some carefully considered statements on many other questions, especially on various problems of premarital relationships. Certainly we must not be too ready to criticize the sexual behavior of many people of our time. At times the lack of growth in the sexual field is the result of an impulsiveness not yet brought under control, a cynical naturalism, a straightforward consumer mentality which puts aside all ethical considerations in the field of sexuality. Often, however, the unfulfilled desire to possess security with another Thou and to have bodily communication with him is an important factor.

The fact must not be ignored that the sexual experiences of modern man often help him overcome the limitations of a world still dominated by reason and technology. All this demands a differentiated idea of pastoral care, which at times we Catholics tend to lack.

When debating birth regulation, questions concerning two areas must be carefully distinguished: (1) the parents' responsibility for the number of children and the spacing of births, (2) morally permissible methods of birth regulation. In the Catholic Church there is at least agreement on questions about the first area. In the last few decades it has gradually become more common to hear that there are, with the conditions of present-day society, serious reasons for making birth regulation a duty for couples. This has also been highlighted by *Humanae Vitae*.

It is well to remember what the Council in the pastoral constitution *Gaudium et Spes* said on this question: "Parents should regard as their proper mission the task of transmitting human life and educating those to whom it has been transmitted. They should realize that they are thereby cooperators with the love of God the Creator, and are, so to speak, the interpreters of that love. Thus they will fulfill their task with human and Christian responsibility. With docile reverence toward God, they will come to the right decision by common counsel and effort. They will thoughtfully take into account both their own welfare and that of their children, those already born and those which may be foreseen. For this accounting they will reckon with both the material and the spiritual conditions of the times as well as of their state in life. Finally, they will consult the interests of the family group, of temporal society, and of the Church herself" (No. 50).

The second group of problems—that is, the controversy over the choice of methods—has really very little ethical importance in relation to the basic problem, just mentioned, of the motives which allow a parent to prevent the birth of a child. In relation to the decision of whether a human being, a unique person, should or should not come into existence, the problem of contraceptive methods seems quite secondary. In the Church, however, while a greater agreement has been reached on the basic question, there has been a debate raging for years on the choice of methods. This kind of debate is doubtless necessary. We Catholics, however, are slowly falling into the danger of wasting our energy and our minds on disputes over details involving the authority of the ecclesiastical magisterium on one side and secular commitments on the other.

Today's world is really dominated by greater concerns. It is a world through which the fearful word of the death of God is passing. It is a world where not just hunger and atomic weapons menace our existence but also where the meaning of this existence itself is becoming desperately problematical for man. It is also a world dominated by slavery, violence, and power worship masquerading as ideology. Should we Christians not fear that we shall lose this world's confidence if it sees us continually wasting our energies in unending disputes over a secondary issue?

The fact that the encyclical *Humanae Vitae* stresses more than any previous papal document the fundamental importance of love in marriage is surely a fact which deserves our praise. Here it is unquestionably developing the lines laid down by the Council. The Pope also clearly indicates the significance of sexual union for married love. But let us now consider this from the point of view of methods. The encyclical teaches that the marriage act has a twofold meaning, the union of love and procreation. Their inseparable connection is willed by God so that man cannot arbitrarily reject this connection. If he does not keep it in mind, then he is going against the intimate structure of marriage and the will of the author of life (No. 13).

Even if the Pope demands this basic openness to fertility not just for marriage in its totality but for every single marriage act, he states that the use of infertile periods in the woman's monthly cycle is permissible. In the former case he says: "The married couple make legitimate use of a natural disposition"; in the latter, they "impede the development of natural processes" (No. 16). Therefore, medical science is invited to work so that "a sufficiently secure basis is provided" for birth regulation, "founded on the observance of natural rhythms" (No. 24). The couple is often urged to "respect the laws of the generative process" (No. 13) and thus live "in respect for the order established by God" (No. 16). This demand is made at a point where it is noted that man cannot be considered as the arbiter of the source of human life. Whoever respects the laws of the generative process is obedient to this law (No. 13).

The Pope then finally makes a reference to the possible consequences of artificial methods of birth regulation. The couple could, it is said, open up a wide and easy road to infidelity in marriage and to a general lowering of morality. There is the danger that if the man grows used to contraceptive practices he may finally lose his respect for the woman. There is also reference to the special vulnerability of the young in the realm of sexual morality (No. 17). The Pope's declarations were severely criticized. In some ambients, however, they have evoked enthusiasm and have been favorably received. If, on such an issue, emotional reactions are understandable, then we must attempt to see exactly what is involved in the debate. For the sake of an objective discussion let us mention several points:

1. It is the encyclical's desire that every intervention which interferes with the biological structure of the sexual act be excluded. On the same point, the encyclical goes on to show that the human understanding of man's sexual powers must keep in mind the biological laws which are part of the human person (No. 10). It highlights, as well, that man does not generally possess unlimited dominion over his body. This is especially true, the encyclical continues, of the generative faculties because of their intrinsic ordering to the birth of life, which is sacred (No. 13).

It goes without saying that basic recognition must be given to the principle that man may not order his organism in an arbitrary way. It becomes even more important in this period when man is continually acquiring greater control over his biological makeup. This principle must be considered a defense of the dignity of the human person. On the other hand, it must be kept in mind that there are also some interferences with man's organism which are for the good of the person and hence permissible. This is also true of birth regulation. It is understood, of course, that it can only be used when serious reasons require that the married sexual union be infertile. This would include the case where positive values in married life which are more important than the physiological process and act of ovulation and its undisturbed development, are endangered.

The question, then, is one of making the consummation of married love possible under given conditions. This is vitally important for marriage because it will lead the couple to reciprocal joy, will make their reciprocal gift visible, and will allow them to experience the fact that they form a single body.

The good of man in his bodily and spiritual totality—and in our case the good of marriage—depends for its existence and value on the preservation of biological structures. These really exist for man and not vice versa. Everything material, even the material structure of one's own organism, is at the service of the person. If this is not kept in mind, the truth underscored in the encyclical—that man may not arbitrarily interfere with his body—is being used against man even though it should serve for his well-being. Neither can this truth, in turn, be considered in isolation. It must also be seen in reference to the totality of the human person; otherwise it loses its meaning. This incongruity is very strongly felt by the couple when they are asked to abstain from the marriage act so as not to infringe on biological laws. When a person recognizes that something is absurd, then no moral obligation can arise from it, for this would really be going against the very essence of his nature, which is what is meant by a person's awareness of his desire and its fulfillment. This has absolutely nothing in common with the situation where respect for the good of the partner necessitates abstinence from married union. Domination of self can have a meaning if it is done for love of the living Thou, the person loved.

2. The encyclical seems to me to be illogical on a fundamental question. It asserts that whoever interferes with the laws of the process of procreation makes himself arbiter of the source of human life. Naturally it must be asked whether man can become lord of the origins of life so easily, seeing that he is always cooperating in the events of creation. Does not the same reasoning apply, in any case, to someone who makes use of the infertile periods? He has just as much intention of preventing conception, as the encyclical is forced to admit farther on. It is not even understandable how an act consummated on an infertile day can give the act that basic openness to procreation.

There is an inner contradiction in the encyclical here. It must consider that the meaning of the marriage act is to be found also in the expression of love and not just in procreation. It admits that the marriage act is also an act of love, but it is still tied to the old view by not drawing the logical conclusion that a sexual act is morally justified solely on account of love. However, it does in some way reach this conclusion when it allows the use of infertile days. If one is to be logical, it must be admitted that the sexual act is for the service of married love and is always morally good when it promotes this love. Or else it must be said that sexual union is a question of procreation and nothing else. Then, even the method recommended by the Pope for birth regulation is illicit.

3. Present-day biological research has confirmed, moreover, that in sexual union, love and fertility need not necessarily be found together on every occasion. Human sexuality is not tied up with the mating or breeding period when intercourse is performed exclusively for the sake of procreation. There is no correlation even between a person's inclination to intercourse and the procreative powers, as found in many animals. It must be noted, too, that the ovum remains fertile for about three hours after the bursting of the follicle. It has been calculated that a woman can become pregnant in only thirty-nine hours of a year. As H. Domas stressed, this represents a considerable disproportion to a woman's copulative capacities. It must be remembered, finally, that from the great number of spermatozoa that a man produces during his lifetime, only very few will probably fertilize an ovum. All this clearly shows that the gift of oneself in marriage more often than not is a sign and expression of love rather than a procreative act.

4. As for the Pope's fear that the use of artificial methods of birth regulation would favor a general trend to give instincts free rein, it must be recalled that the abuse of a thing does not mean that it cannot be rightly used. It must be definitely presupposed that the couple know very well the difference between its right use; that is, birth regulation necessary for serious motives, and sexual license. It would also be bad to want to overcome infidelity and irresponsible consumer sex not by an ethos of personal commitment and of love but by using fear of undesirable consequences as a motive.

5. Anyone who puts forward these or any other possible objections against the encyclical's position can do no less than again ask that the decision of the choice of birth-regulation methods be left to each individual couple. Those methods, however, which do not regulate births but are abortive are rejected from the start, according to the common Catholic conviction. The following points must be

kept in mind: (1) Every instance of sexual contact must be motivated by love and must allow love to be expressed in one's body. (2) The couple cannot deprive the sexual act of its natural fruit unless for a serious motive, which puts the burden of responsibility on them. (3) All the presently known methods of birth regulation disturb the expression of love in some way. Therefore, the following principle applies for each individual couple: according to the state of your sexual experience, your sentiments, and your sexual powers, try to find the method of birth regulation where your sexual life can speak even better the language of love. What has been said here on the question of birth regulation must not be taken as the Church's teaching. This has been established in another direction by the encyclical *Humanae Vitae*.

What is an encyclical's authority and what attitude should Catholics adopt with regard to it when they are convinced that they are not able to follow it? On these issues the German bishops have spoken quite clearly. This is not the place for interpreting the bishops' words more exactly. The theologians with their individual contributions will certainly take care of that. Let one thing be noted however. What has been said here is more than a humble, private opinion arising from philosophical reflection on the personal experience of marriage. It is substantially in agreement with what many theologians, specialists in other fields, and a great number of Catholic married couples think. Therefore, what has been said is, in its own way, an expression of the life of the Church today. Anyone who shares this point of view, thanks to the bishops' statement, can hope that this conviction will be tolerated in the Church. He must also be ready to respect all those whose consciences lead them to think differently.

Thus the discussion on the encyclical *Humanae Vitae* gives us the opportunity to train ourselves in dialogue on a topic about which so much is being said in the Church. Even in the future, so it seems, we shall have no more effective resource than this.

It is not possible to deny the seriousness and the depth of the subject matter treated by Dr. Scherer. As he notes, what he includes is not just a personal opinion. He has attempted to bring together as closely as possible not just the difficulties that have arisen after the appearance of the encyclical, but also the thinking that had gone before it. This is particularly significant since it gives a clear example of how responsibly some Catholics faced the research and study of the issue. This can also help explain why, in certain cases, the reaction to the encyclical was so strong and critical. It certainly cannot be claimed that *Humanae Vitae* wholly took into consideration the question of which of the philosophical and theological cultural outlooks had most established themselves in the Church. It is true that Dr. Scherer's statement is very much indicative of the German cultural scene, but it must also be kept in mind that in the last twenty years German philosophical and theological thought has had no small influence on practically the entire Church.

The fact that the encyclical seems to have gone against this current of thought could lead one to suggest that it represents a moment of involution or, more simply, a gesture of doctrinal preservation. This is a logical enough question and we shall attempt to answer it. This answer may disclose new elements which are important in the evaluation of *Humanae Vitae*.

Chapter 3 From the Council to *Humanae Vitae*: Continuity, Evolution, or Involution?

The constant and common teaching
Tradition and the magisterium
Fear of the new, restoration, or authoritarianism?
"The anti-council has opened," some say
Has the teaching been revived or repudiated?
The references of the encyclical
Texts utilized by *Humanae Vitae* from *Gaudium et Spes*
The "silent passages" of *Humanae Vitae*
The method of the encyclical
The moral criterion of marriage acts
Responsible parenthood
The judgment of conscience
Married love
"The Council must be quoted, but quoted correctly"
An unavoidable problem

Evolution? Involution? Preservation? Restoration? These are some of the first questions which have arisen after the appearance of the encyclical *Humanae Vitae*. Sparked off by fears that the doctrine would evolve, by hopes that it may evolve, and by a cautious certainty that it has already evolved, these questions have at least one answer in common. All agree that there is no evolution in the proper sense of the word, at least not on the precise issue treated by the encyclical. For some, this lack of evolution means continuity with tradition and with the pure Christian doctrine. For others it means rigidity and the inability to see the direction in which human problems are evolving. For still others it is the spread of the preservation psychosis so typical of the environment that surrounds the Pope. Or else it is a restoration maneuver, almost a kind of symbol raised up against the attacks of the "progressives" in the fields of teaching and discipline. Some even go so far as to suggest an "involution" now under way in the Church after the first dizzy "evolutions" started appearing ominous.

Probably each one of these theories can find arguments in its favor. The most important thing, however, is to see whether in relation to the doctrinal evolution of the last few years and, above all, from the Council onward (taking into account, first, the Council documents), there has been some kind of trend emerging of either a return to the classical teaching, or an evolution, or a period of standstill and reflection.

The Constant and Common Teaching

On March 27, 1965 when receiving the members of the Papal Commission for the Family and Birth, Paul VI affirmed that "the Church, like an attentive mother, has at all times an interest and concern about supplying an answer that is adapted to the great problems posed by men. In keeping with the counsel of the Lord, and with this aim in mind, she welcomes *nova et vetera*. . . ." The declaration, then, shows the Pope disposed toward accepting "new things" as well as keeping the "old things." On October 29, 1966, speaking to the participants of the 52d National Congress of the Italian Society of Obstetrics and Gynecology, Paul VI clarified the sense of this *nova et vetera:*

The thought and the norm of the Church are not changed; they are those in force in the traditional teaching of the Church. The ecumenical Council recently held, brought out certain elements of judgment which are most useful for the integration of Catholic doctrine on this most important subject. But they were not such as to change its substantial elements.

On August 1, 1968, in the first general audience at Castel Gandolfo after the promulgation of the encyclical, Paul VI recalled:

We have reflected on the stable elements of the traditional and binding teaching of the Church, and then especially on the teachings of the recent Council. We have pondered over the consequences of one and then the other decision, and we have had no doubt about our duty to pronounce our judgment in the terms expressed by the present encyclical.

Other statements of Paul VI have underlined his intention of remaining in the line of the "constant and common teaching" of the Church on this matter, even though he has studied all the most recent formulations of the problem and the new difficulties which have arisen as well as having kept in mind the serious problems and hardships of couples and families and the difficulties these give rise to on a world scale.

The encyclical, then, is written in the framework of fidelity to divine revelation and to the teaching tradition of the Church. In his speech to the cardinals and the Roman Curia of December 23, 1968, Paul VI, after speaking of his "firm solicitude for the preservation and defense of the truth," restated his position of fidelity to the truth. He himself, moreover, drew a parallel, later to be taken up on several occasions by theological commentators, between the Credo pronounced by him on June 29 and the encyclical of July 29:

In fact, it is evident that the Church will be fully able to exercise its mission of light and sanctification among men only if it can remain in this a lover of the truth and be as united and solid as its Divine Founder wishes it to be. And it will be able to offer the world a more valuable collaboration in the work of peace, human elevation, and progress, to which, by its very nature as a society of love, it seems to be called. For these reasons we have not been able to withdraw from the duty of reaffirming, before and in the name of the entire Church, as a solemn *Amen* at the conclusion of the Year of Faith, the Credo, ours as well as that of the people of God. For the same reasons again, and in order not to delude the invocation, the expectation, the need of the people of God, we have had to give our reply as pastor of the entire Church to the questions put before the man, the Christian of today, on the age-old problem of responsible parenthood and honest birth regulation. It is a reply meditated for a long time because we wanted a scrupulous examination of the new arguments and objections brought against the constant and common teaching of the Church, which has once again appeared in its severe but at the same time serene certitude.

In fact, the position that the Pontiff had taken a stand on had a dramatic quality about it. This is recognized by the theologian Ferdinando Lambruschini who presented the encyclical to the press. In *L'Osservatore della Domenica* of August 11, 1968 he states that

the position in which the Sovereign Pontiff found himself was like that of being in the viselike grip of a dilemma, not without its dramatic notes. He was confronted both by a continuous ecclesiastical magisterium which has imposed a continuous peremptory condemnation on every kind of contraception without exception unless clearly on therapeutic grounds, and by the push for an opening which ended toward overturning this continuous magisterium. This was not all. There was no shortage of pressure on both sides, on the one hand to phrase this condemnation as a formula of faith and hence make it an irreformable judgment, and on the other hand to follow the widespread trends, disseminated even farther by modern means of propaganda and already strongly promoted among the Protestant Churches.

Amid such a complexity of viewpoints it seems more logical to me to speak of meditation and study than of hesitation. It was not even possible to take a middle course and to look for a tactical solution. A clear decision was called for in order to put an end to all ambiguity. The pressure for a dogmatic definition must have been particularly strong. The whole issue would have been made so much simpler. It would have been enough to declare that such a definition was already contained in the strong expressions of the encyclical *Casti Connubii,* the document of the extraordinary magisterium of Pius XI, or else sufficiently expressed in the ordinary magisterium of the whole episcopate, unanimous and constant in its condemnation of contraception. The Holy Father reaffirmed the continuity of the magisterium, firmly supporting the condemnation.

The Roman theologian sees it, then, as loyalty and continuity on the part of the magisterium, and not as a yielding backward (under pressure for a definition de fide), or forward (under pressure for an updating), or even as a staying in the middle (a via media, a tactical solution).

Therefore, as R. Orfei states in *Settegiorni* of August 4, 1968, "The encyclical brings in no innovations. Possibly its novelty consists precisely in the fact that it says nothing new on an old, controversial problem." After summing up the previous research and the work done by the Papal Commission, the majority of which were found to be "in favor of change," Orfei continues:

And yet, as Msgr. Lambruschini has explained, they—the commission majority—were not agreed on how far the renewal or the magisterium could go before its continuity was compromised. It was not just a question of nuances, but of quite serious disagreement. This fact revealed an uncertainty and an ambiguous openness which in turn revealed the various leanings among Catholics of different countries. . . . In this way a trend was being created. Here was a concrete situation which was also a solution on the practical level to a problem that theology and the supreme authority of the Church held to be not only unresolved, but also containing many elements militating against a new solution.

Today the Pope's encyclical has intervened to block—to the extent that it succeeds in doing so—a move already under way among Catholics, not only among lay people but also among those of the clergy who are their moral guide in the matter. . . . Several sources have raised the question of why the Pope ever published an encyclical just to confirm the strength of the traditional position and the certitude of facts already known, instead of seriously considering the real possibilities for renewal as the study commission had done from the moment it had begun working. It may be presumed that the members of the majority of the study commission in favor of renewal are still in favor and will continue going deeper into the question so as to find a satisfactory answer. In a word, they will attempt to go beyond the Pope's decision which seems to have closed a still open question.

Naturally, on the practical level, discipline will have a certain effect but at the same time will embarrass many people both high and low. When an issue like the present one finally explodes, it will be difficult to keep it under control either by insisting on the traditional viewpoint or by taking action against all the innovations in the air.

Tradition and the Magisterium

The move, then, is toward a traditional position. But to put it in this way is not to say everything. The very fact of linking up with tradition raises other delicate problems as, for example, what this continuous "link" with tradition and with the magisterium is, and whether the magisterium is in perfect agreement with tradition on this point. Ordinarily, when the encyclical's "traditional" outlook is mentioned, the reference very rarely goes any farther back, with any precision, than to Pius XI, or at the most to the declarations of the Sacred Penitentiary in the nineteenth century. The encyclical alludes to "the constant theological and patristic tradition" in only a general way. Cardinal A. G. Renard, for example, in *La Croix* of August 2, 1968 observes:

Paul VI is clearly following the line not only of Pius XI, Pius XII, and John XXIII but above all of Vatican Council II. The often-quoted *Gaudium et Spes* has inspired Paul VI's statements on both "responsible parenthood" and the need for couples to have their consciences enlightened by the continuous teaching of the Church on both the natural meaning of marriage and the marriage act. Paul VI had already summed up the fundamental thought of *Gaudium et Spes* in the document *Populorum Progressio*.

At the same time it must be kept in mind that if tradition can also be understood as a new, strong movement of opinion inside the Church tending toward a given interpretation of the truth, then the situation as regards the contraception issue on the eve of the encyclical was far from clear-cut. The Latin-American theologian Jorge Mejia in the Argentine periodical *Criterio* of August 22, 1968 notes this fact:

Those who protest against a pontifical decision which so deeply touches the individual conscience would be justified if it had been made without taking into consideration the opinion of the episcopate, the thought of theologians, and the opinion of the Christian people, or the *sensus fidelium;* as it is technically known. In my opinion, it cannot be categorically stated that the Pope went on alone without paying any attention to the *consensus Ecclesiae*. . . . On the contrary, it is probable that if the bishops of the world had been interviewed previously they would have given a negative answer to the question put by the encyclical, and maybe to such an extent that the balance would have swung in favor of the encyclical in spite of the majority formed in the now-famous commission. That is why it can be said that the adhesions now being shown are sincere in spite of the haste which at times appeared excessive and the not always happy methods used.

At the end of the Council one had the impression that if the opinion contrary to that of the encyclical had been put to the vote, the bishops would have rejected it. It was really a miracle, considering the pressure which was exerted and the campaigns which were organized, that *Gaudium et Spes* did not close the doors once and for all. . . . Outside of the Council the question could not have been resolved by means of a majority vote. I believe that if the Pope had decided on this procedure he certainly would not have thought of going against the majority. But the dangers in that case would have been greater.

What, then, was to be done in such circumstances? There were two possibilities open for him. The first, which he followed up to a point, was to postpone the decision to an indefinite future date while allowing the new trends to continue with more or less a free hand along with the research. The second possibility open to him was to reaffirm the ordinary teaching at the risk of appearing reactionary and setting off a storm in the Church. The first way had the value of recognizing the real immaturity, at least on the social level, of a new teaching and hence of letting it develop. The second had the definite advantage of being based on the Church's teaching tradition. There is no need to labor the point that both these ways had their share of difficulties.

The fact that the second way was the one chosen does not necessarily condemn the first, in spite of the difficulties which it could have led to. What the most vigorous defenders of the "open-ended" position desired above all was that no premature decision be made. Even though it is possible to think that the present decision is also premature, at the same time it must be recognized that there were reasons for making it.

But what could these reasons possibly have been? In any kind of decision on issues not connected at least in some way with faith and revelation, it is possible to talk of a "preservation," a "progression," a "withdrawal," or an "opening-up." This cannot be said of the encyclical with the same ease, seeing that it is connected with an area of religious doctrine. The only way to talk of it is with reference to the concept of "tradition." In this case, tradition is not synonymous with preservation or withdrawal or involution. For at times, theological research reveals that *the* tradition may be far more "modern" and more developed than a recent opinion.

Jorge Mejia, also an expert at the Council, reexamines the remaining possible reasons for making a doctrinal decision. The one possible reason, of course, was that of tradition; but understood in its theological sense—quite different from the normal use of the word. Mejia says:

Therefore the foundation of the teaching is tradition. The way the encyclical is constructed may conceal this fact for it begins by talking of the natural law and the Church's right to interpret it (No. 4). When the encyclical arrives at the statement of the thesis (No. 14), however, it refers continually to the teaching of the magisterium. The footnotes quote a series of encyclicals and papal speeches which had become more and more frequent from Pius XII onward. The only quotations from previous centuries are those of the Catechism of the Council of Trent which contains, as is known, the theological thought of the years following that Council. On the other hand, there is reason to be grateful that no mention is made of the series of decisions by the Holy Office, collected by Batzill, on the casuistry of the issue, or of the doctrinal condemnation by the same Holy Office pronounced on May 21, 1851 which grades the opinion to the contrary as "scandalous." No reference is made here, either, to a consensus of bishops, and there is no episcopal document quoted, easy as it would have been to find one.

Whenever anyone thinks of tradition, the documents of Vatican Council II or at least of something mysteriously but surely transmitted right from the apostolic era come to mind. Here it is neither of these. It is simply that the Pope, to justify the continuity of a doctrine he pronounced, refers to the constant teaching, recent as it is, of the See of Rome. In other words, in the present circumstances, despite the contrary opinions of a considerable number of theologians as well as important appeals by lay people (like that of the Second Congress of the Apostolate of the Laity), the Pope does not feel authorized to change the teaching of his predecessors. There is no question here of the revealed nature of the teaching or, consequently, of its absolute immutability.

What has just been said reveals an interesting fact. There is a continuity of the magisterium on the issue, but of a rather recent magisterium. On the other hand, as Mejia himself clarifies, seeing that the magisterium must, after the publication of the encyclical, now rely more on tradition than philosophical reasoning on natural law, then a certain perplexity over the "traditional basis" of the encyclical's teaching is inevitable. If there is a teaching, it is quite recent. Moreover, this recent tradition created by the opinion of the magisterium, whether of the Pope or of the bishops, seems to be in favor of the encyclical's teaching.

Not everyone, however, has the same opinion regarding this "consensus," seeing that it is not openly evident. The editorial in *The Times* of July 30, 1968 voices a doubt which was then repeated in other Catholic circles: The question of birth control was removed from the purview of Vatican Council II by Pope John XXIII and referred to a Pontifical Commission. His successor having enlarged the commission and received its divided report, reserved the question to himself. Had the Council been permitted to review it, or had it been committed to the episcopal college as refurbished since the Council, the answer would probably have been different from the stark restatement of the traditional prohibitions contained in the Pope's encyclical.

Fear of the New, Restoration, or Authoritarianism?

The editorial of *The Times* continues:

The reformism and humanism of the Vatican Council survives only in the encyclical's statement of the problems. In his answers to them, the Pope stands pat on the deliverances of his predecessors. Against the prevalence of overpopulation as a contributory cause of miserable living standards if not of famine, against a much more comprehensive understanding by theologians—Roman Catholic as well as others—

of human sexuality, and against the nonconforming practice of many Catholics and the troubled consciences of many more, the Pope has reaffirmed the Roman rigor. The Pope's uncompromising attitude will be greeted with relief by Catholics who feel that the spirit of *aggiornamento* which got loose at the Vatican Council is beginning to erode the fabric of the faith, and who feel robbed of many of the old certainties. But quite as many of them, at least in countries of plural religion, and many more Christians belonging to other Churches, will think his pronouncement as injudicious and ultimately ineffectual as Pio Nono's *Syllabus of Errors.*

Do Catholics really think of *Humanae Vitae* as a new *Syllabus?* Do they see it, that is, as a "restoration," adopting the old for fear of the new?

There are those who think this way. They refer to the encyclical as a sign of the "restoration in neutral gear" now under way for some time. In *Questitalia* of July 1968, an editorial by the director (Vladimir Dorigo) tackles this issue with particular vehemence, giving an interpretation which is at the opposite extreme to preservation—which, after all, may also be taken in a positive way. This preservation and "fidelity and continuity" of the magisterium are now seen in terms of restoration. After recalling that the periodical had already foreseen that there would be a particular "solution" to the problem, the writer notes:

We must once again recognize, as has become the sad tradition of our times, that reality has turned out worse than fantasy. It must be admitted still once again that what is often pictured as our radically incorrigible pessimism is instead, as also in this case, nothing but baseless optimism. The delusion, the astonishment, the wrath that *Humanae Vitae* stirred up throughout the world, more so than any other document of our time, papal or otherwise . . . show that the "updating restoration" stubbornly pursued by the present Pope has reached such extremes as to create an unimaginably deep break between the more recent magisterium and the consciousness not only of mankind in general, not only of believers or even Catholics, but even of a great number of priests, theologians, and bishops. It took only one day for rapid teletype, radio, and television transmitters to shock the world into learning what distance separates the belief and practices of the Vatican from those of hundreds of millions of sensible

99

men of goodwill. So great is the gap that to find another parallel even remotely comparable in the history of the Church, it would be necessary to go back to the Reformation.

This would mean, as well, leaving out of consideration the fact that the events of the Reformation—difficult, violent, and blood-stained as they were—took place in between pauses, negotiations, and attempts at dialogue for several decades. During this period of time people's consciences were developing and widening the content of *los von Rom,* beginning with the ninety-five theses of Wittenburg as the core. Today, however, after allowing Catholics, confessors, bishops, and theologians for years to practice in private, support in public, and quietly authorize the new theses (that would have become part of the patrimony of Vatican II if not for a stroke of the pen of the Pope and the Curia), . . . the papal magisterium has now suddenly burst on the scene declaring all to be in error and in sin.

After a long criticism of the encyclical, the writer returns to the question of what significance it has as a moment in the general "restoration process":

It is certain that Paul VI's updating restoration in its attempts at imposing on the Church a new theological, moral, and political straitjacket, risks jeopardizing even more seriously the outcome of his preservation already showing signs of failing health. The Pontiff, to oppose a theological research felt to be dangerous, had no qualms in inventing a new Credo—"simply a paraphrase of the symbol of Nicaea," he then stated—where there is even a paragraph dedicated to warning Dutch theologians experimenting with the eucharistic concept of "transignification." He would not permit Catholics that same freedom of action in the marriage bed which they were also demanding in the election booth, in the classroom, and in Parliament. The encyclical, as the Vatican theologian Msgr. Lambruschini explained, "is the logical conclusion of the profession of faith solemnly made by Paul VI on June 30." No one doubts this. . . .

To avoid having to grant what common opinion holds just and necessary in order to maintain a level of control over consciences which is more and more today felt to be intolerable, the managing directors of the updating restoration were setting into action a general reverse movement on an issue most felt by and most common to, hundreds of millions of people. They were launching an attack on all the institutional machinery promoting spiritual violence. They were giving

consciences their true autonomy. They were once again setting believers free from the pressures and temptations which were oppressing
their liberty.

Was the hope, then, that the deeper study would have led
to an "opening" merely "baseless optimism"? Was the general
reaction caused by the delusion, arising from the fact that certain values by now deeply assimilated by many believers had
been lost sight of or not recognized in the encyclical? Was it
a disillusion for those who had pinned their empty hopes on
a pontificate like that of Pope John? Was it a new victory for
those who had feared and criticized that period in the life of
the Church—a Church which appeared so unexpectedly alive
under the guiding hand of an old, country pope?

Here and there people have begun admitting this, even
though any appeals to return to wiser, surer positions like those
which appeared at the time of Pope John, always seem to be
alluded to rather than expressed openly. In some cases, however, they are expressed, even if in no other way than to
challenge a fact. This Henry Duquaire does in *Le Figaro* of
July 31, 1968 where he states plainly:

It seems that public opinion was deceived by the good nature of John
XXIII, by the openness to the world that the Council showed, by the
faithfulness with which Paul VI always put himself in the line of
John XXIII and the Council. This opinion had a wrong idea of the
Papacy. The Papacy was seen as a democracy extremely sensitive to
the currents of thought circulating throughout the globe and anxious
not to cause disappointment. It is nothing like this. I know that words
like democracy and monarchy are given a very poor reception in an
institution like the Papacy which is "in the world" without "belonging"
to the world. If this is clearly understood, then it is very easy to see
how the Pope could have made his decision independently of the
public opinion of the world, independently of the majority of the
commission members and also independently of the reservations expressed by the hierarchy and the clergy of many countries. In any case,
if this characteristic of the Papacy had been lost sight of, then Paul VI
brought it back to mind in terms which are as firm as they are benign.
One has just to read his text fully. The encyclical, then, amounts to
awakening believers from their wonderful dream of a "Johannine
Church" and reaffirming "the marks of the true Papacy."

There seems to be, then, a reaffirming of authority, a strong and sure as well as quiet and paternal return to a rigid, traditional orthodoxy, a "fear of the new" as Luciana Castellina put it in *L'Unità* of July 31, 1968. After quoting as particularly observant the famous intervention of Patriarch Maximos IV Saigh in the Council, she goes on to say that

the encyclical does more than just give a negative decision on birth control. It marks a clear backward step on what was the most fruitful and newest terrain discovered by the Council: its condemnation of a casuistic, external morality, and its outline of a morality that is the fruit of continually renewed decisions of the Christian conscience. Why this involution? Why is the conservative wing of the Church, in spite of the present ferment of innovations, making itself felt more and more in the Catholic world?

It seems that once the Church hierarchy had started taking the road laid down by the Council, once man had been freed from the "maze of laws and commands" with which he had been burdened for centuries, then man was destined to become aware of many new problems and to begin attempting personally to reconcile Christian principles with the practice of the Church, in spite of all the risks which this entailed for the Church as an institution, as a social and political reality, and even as a religious body. The Pope, when faced with the risks of a renewal that cannot seem to be contained by the cautious limits of his political and doctrinal reform, has preferred to give a direct No to the renewalists and has imposed a return to rigid doctrinal orthodoxy. He has had second thoughts on "riding on the tiger's back."

When faced with the risks of renewal, authority thought it better to beat a hasty retreat or let involution set in or fall back on a general restoration—anything, before it was too late. It must be admitted, however, that Luciana Castellina's reflections betray a hint of what is a typically Marxist judgment on the phenomenology and etiology of religion. Still, there are Catholics who, although wanting to remain Catholics, have no hesitation in criticizing the encyclical precisely on the issue of freedom of conscience and scientific freedom. Seemingly they have no fear that commitment to a necessary evolution could lead to the self-destruction of the Church or even of Christianity.

The president of the Association of Dutch Catholic Physicians, Dr. Frans Saes, made a declaration along these lines, bordering on both the indignant and the humorous, which highlighted the strange state of affairs that arose during the last few days of July, characterized as they were by a varied ideological show of force. This is how Dr. Saes's words were reported by *De Volkskrant*, Holland's largest Catholic daily, of July 31, 1968: "We Catholics, like the Czechs, are all agreed that the time has come to have a little more liberty. But Rome and the Kremlin say that it cannot be allowed. The clock has been turned back fifteen years; it is incomprehensible. I cannot foresee, either, any change of attitude on the part of the doctors or of the patients." After giving a judgment from the medical point of view Dr. Saes continues: "It seems like a Galileo case: 'No reasonable man could ever separate sexuality from procreation and consider sexuality as a great good in itself!' In Rome the sun still rotates around the earth."

"The Anti-council Has Opened," Some Say

Those who consider the real issue at stake to be continuity of doctrine would not be very shaken by the Dutch gynecologist's remark that in Rome the sun still rotates around the earth. If this is what fidelity to the true doctrine means, then they are quite ready to be accused of being behind the times. If a Catholic, however, thinks that the doctrine of the encyclical was a turning point in relation to the stage that conciliar and post-conciliar thought had reached, then for him the question is no longer of being a progressive or of being behind the times. His problem will be precisely that of the "continuity" of doctrine which is the focal point of concern both of the encyclical and of all Catholics. The point at issue here is no longer "conservatism or progressivism," but that of "fidelity." In this case, fidelity certainly also means "evolution." Evolution, however, can never oppose continuity of doctrine since it is typical of truth to evolve, in a manner which is being continually better understood. It is the old problem of the evolution of dogma, but no longer associated with those neurotic fears of the time of Loisy and the encyclical *Pascendi*.

The evolution-involution-restoration issue could well have been the sign under which the encyclical was born. The issue has now become, instead, one involving the Council, the post-conciliar period, fidelity to the Council, and post-conciliar involution. This has given rise to the hypothesis of the opening of the "counter-council" whose "Magna Chartas" have been the Credo of June 30 and the encyclical of July 29, 1968.

Carlo Falconi, for example, in *Espresso* of August 4, 1968 speaks of the "first serious repudiation of Vatican II" and sketches the outlines of this counter-council as:

A clear-cut, unmitigated No but above all an unjustifiable No—a No that has provoked mass disbelief among Christians and bitter delusion among those of other faiths who had believed that the Church of Rome was undergoing an authentic reawakening. Amid the astonishment and disbelief of millions of people, the Pill affair thus came to a close as far as those who walked within the shadows of the Vatican palaces were concerned. Outside these shadows, however, the trial of Paul VI's decision had only begun. Inquiries had already started into the connection between the condemnation of the Pill and the last few years of Vatican politics, for both have mutilated the spiritual inheritance of Vatican II. After the reform of the Curia (already half neutralized and, in any case, inadequate), after the muzzling of the authority of the bishops and of their Synod, and after the proclamation of the new Credo, the temptation is to ask if the post-conciliar era has not been officially inaugurated with the intention of stunting and rendering sterile several of the spiritual victories that had seemed assured.

Falconi concludes his article with the following observation:

For the time being, however, Paul VI's strongest blow has been dealt against the myth of the reform of the Catholic Church which the Council had been gradually building up. The proclamation of the new Credo and the imposition of so severe a marriage morality indicate that Paul VI holds out little hope that the reform of his Church, while he is alive, will go far beyond a certain amount of simplification of ceremonies, a cautious abandonment of splendor, and some signs of an uncertain ecumenism.

It is relatively easy to sketch the outlines of a counter-council basing oneself simply on the fact that the encyclical rejected both the majority opinion of the Church which seemed to have been already quite clearly expressed, and also, as a consequence, the attempt at rethinking the ideas at the basis of this established majority. It is also dangerous. It involves the risk of making what is an ecclesial issue into simply an affair of ecclesiastical politics, understandable as this is. The surest as well as the most painstaking procedure is to compare and contrast the Council texts and the direction which their thinking has taken, with the statements of *Humanae Vitae*. This difficult task, only roughly sketched by some, has been taken much farther forward by others. Prof. C. P. Sporken had already alluded to this fact in *De Tijd* of August 3, 1968 when he listed the problems and doubts provoked by the encyclical. When he speaks of the discrepancies he finds with the doctrine that had been developing in the Church during the time of the Council, he says:

On reading it for the first time, one notes that the content of the encyclical is in no way continuous with the evolution of marriage morality being worked out previously, just as it is not continuous with the fundamental ideas of the Council and the report of the Papal Commission. In fact, there is open disagreement. In the face of the old declarations of the magisterium of the Church, the Council document—*Gaudium et Spes*—is outstanding for its new approach to reality and to truth. Its tone is based more on the data of human experience. This is foreign to the new encyclical where the norms are laid down from above by the hierarchy. Moreover, the Council document expressly accepts responsible parenthood and a birth control that is in conformity with human dignity, regulated according to the demands of love under all its aspects. The encyclical, on the other hand, lays down only one norm: the biological law of the sexual, physical organism.

The discontinuity is all the more obvious when the fundamental ideas of the Papal Commission are examined. It is a commission which should not be considered too lightly. Paul VI had very much broadened the existing commission. It seems certain to me that he made sure that this international commission be formed in such a way as to give him correct information on the faith and moral consciousness of the ecclesial community. The great majority of the commission showed itself to be convinced in its report that the objective criteria which morally allow birth control are found in the human dignity of the method used. But it also added that only the couple are in a position to decide what method is most in accord with them.

As the commission states, it is impossible to assess according to general, "a priori" norms, and in an adequate way for every individual couple, exactly what these methods might mean for their married life. The encyclical, on the other hand, puts a categorical prohibition on several methods—a prohibition which has the force of law for all couples, all people, all cultures, and all time. The Pope himself notes a difference that was for him clearly a better reason for his rejection of the report of the commission majority: several of their criteria clash with the teaching consistently proposed by the magisterium of the Church on marriage (No. 6). This is the line of thought which clearly makes itself felt throughout the whole encyclical.

Is the encyclical, then, what has been described as the "anti-council's revenge"? It has been affirmed on different occasions as, for example, by Prof. Sporken. Yet, precisely on the basis of the Council documents, the lecturer in moral theology Enrico Chiavacci, states that "it is futile to imagine a revenge on the Council." In *Rocca* of September 1, 1968 he writes at great length on the different aspects of the encyclical, and examines also the

two strong points which the document is based on; both are typically conciliar. I would say that both, in the history of Christian moral thought on marriage, are as recent or almost as recent as the Council. They are: first, the inseparability of the two elements of value in married relationships, the unitive element and the procreative element; and second, a responsibility for procreation; that is, responsible parenthood. On the first point *Gaudium et Spes* has put forward, in fact, a totally new doctrinal element. . . . The justification for intercourse is not exclusively in its objective of procreation but also, in a coordinated and not subordinate way, in its capacity to express and further total, intimate, and interior union. . . . The earlier view— that is, that which subordinated the unitive element to the procreative element—however, certainly belongs to the official magisterium. *Humanae Vitae* takes up this very issue to such an extent that it is here where the whole problem of the encyclical starts.

Humanae Vitae always sees the two elements as strictly coordinated. Their inseparability does not come from the fact that one is always subordinated to the other, but that they both belong to the nature of the one and the same act. This starting point of our discussion, then, is a conciliar theme and at the same time a new theme in the history of the Church. . . . *Gaudium et Spes* has established and *Humanae Vitae* has confirmed the fact that responsible procreation—that is, bringing a child into the world—must be a deliberation and a choice that is made, keeping in mind certain criteria. Their respective claims to uniqueness lie in the fact that *Gaudium et Spes* saw birth control as always justifiable if responsible parenthood was to have any meaning. The present issue is one of ways, means, and ends in birth control. This is now accepted as the fruit of the Council, and the papal document presents it again not only for individuals but also for countries when it states in No. 23: "Quite different is the way in which public authorities can and must contribute to the solution of the demographic problem." These two ideas are the foundation of *Humanae Vitae,* and it would be incorrect to read the document in any other way.

After making some observations on the tone, form, and some particular aspects of the encyclical that "could bring about perplexities which, however, cannot arise from the teaching of the encyclical itself," the moralist then draws attention to the flood of letters of adherence to the encyclical. He says:

Reading some of these letters, also published in *L'Osservatore Romano,* the temptation would be to say immediately that all the new formulations of the theologians during and after the Council were careless and diabolical attempts to mislead the good people of God who did not want theological opinions but certitudes. As if the magisterium could have gone to the extent of giving certitudes without laborious discussion and effort on the part of theologians! It is futile, then, to imagine an anti-conciliar revenge. The Pope himself states it in the encyclical.

Basing himself on these two hinge concepts of the encyclical, this theologian establishes not only that it cannot in any way be thought of as an anti-conciliar revenge but also that there is continuity in its teaching. Philippe Delhaye, professor at the University of Louvain and member of the Papal Commission, is not exactly of the same view. Whereas Chiavacci has made a comparison between two doctrinal points, Delhaye first makes an accurate analysis of the two texts of *Gaudium et Spes* and *Humanae Vitae* and then compares their contents. Delhaye's analysis, published in *Bijdragen-Tijdschrift voor Filosofie en*

Theologie of October–December 1968, is the first accurate comparative study of two texts that have triggered off what is certainly a large-scale debate.

Has the Teaching Been Revived or Repudiated?

Many who read *Humanae Vitae* ask themselves if the teaching of this document published on July 25, 1968 is in agreement with or has diverged from the teaching of the chapter on "the dignity of marriage and the family" (Nos. 47–52) found in the pastoral constitution *Gaudium et Spes,* promulgated by the Sovereign Pontiff on December 7, 1965.

Some have maintained that they clash with each other so as to be able either to rejoice over a "doctrinal revival" or to bitterly acknowledge a repudiation and a reactionary trend. Some commentators, instead, whether to calm joyous spirits or to soften the blow of defeat, have believed that they could note a similarity of doctrine between the two documents. The historian's attitude is quite different. "Ataraxy," impartiality, and objectivity remain his essential criteria, even though, as philosophy and historical criticism have shown over the past few years, their practical realization is difficult. The historian believes that it is both possible and necessary to prescind from emotional reactions as well as from the concern for giving a "pastoral commentary."

Does this mean that the historian separates himself from the life of the Church and practices "noncommitment" and even "disinterestedness" in the worst sense of the word? No. On the contrary, the concern for objectivity will allow more light to be shed on the factual situation. The theologians and pastors can then use this as the point of departure for their statements.

False agreements are harmful. This was seen thirty years ago when some authors wanted at all costs a synthesis in philosophy and theology between the Neoplatonism of St. Augustine and the Aristotelianism of St. Thomas. When it is a question of papal teaching, no doubt a greater consensus may be expected. This in no way alters the fact that there was an immense distance between Pius VI who condemned the rights of man and Pius XII who became their defender during World War II. *Mirari Vos* and *Quanta Cura* affirm that freedom of conscience, even in the civil sphere, is a *deliramentum.*

Yet John XXIII made freedom of conscience one of the key points of *Pacem in Terris.* At the moment when Paul VI was offering a chalice to the ecumenically minded patriarch in Jerusalem and while he was praying with him in St. Peter's in Rome, it would have been interesting to have reread *Mortalium Animos*, not, let it be said, to act the sceptic or the critic, but to observe that from one age to another different points of view can gradually become complementary and more moderate. Timeless principles are applied differently in varying circumstances. Christian truth is so broad and deep that it can be seen from different points of view without at the same time being betrayed.

Investigabiles divitias Christi: it is in this sense of an open and polyvalent research that many of the Council Fathers, and particularly Cardinal Léger, interpreted this quotation of Ephesians 3:8.

Let us go even farther by placing the drafting of the papal texts in the concrete circumstances of their time as far as present-day history and the press have revealed them. Everyone knows that Pius XII had his dossiers prepared by twenty Jesuits, working as a group under P. Leiber, his old confidant from Munich. The Pope requested his collaborators to work in separate groups and then made a choice of the different reports they had drawn up. It is possible in this way to tell each time which of the different viewpoints and treatments prevailed. When Paul VI published *Populorum Progressio*, the Vatican itself announced that Fr. Lebret had had an important part to play in the preparation of the document. In this way a different vision is evident when it is contrasted with those pages of *Pacem in Terris* which deal with similar ideas because this document had been drawn up by Msgr. Pavan. In particular, the role given to natural law in the two encyclicals varied considerably.

In the present case, the differences visible between *Humanae Vitae* and *Gaudium et Spes* may be attributed to different work groups. In both cases their conclusions received papal approval. The theologians will attempt a doctrinal synthesis and the historians of Catholic morality will in no way be surprised at seeing two work groups structured in completely different ways presenting reports that at first sight seem to diverge. The different groups which had prepared the chapter of *Gaudium et Spes* devoted to marriage are now a well-known part of the long, tormented history of this document. They had nothing in common with the writers of *Humanae Vitae* whose names circulate through the streets of Rome and may be read between the lines of *L'Osservatore Romano*. Moreover, the Vatican seems to have reserved to them the joy and honor of announcing the "good news" in the press conferences especially organized in Rome and Paris.

There is no need to think, then, that historical research will be prejudiced by an objection raised in the doctrinal and canonical sphere. Two documents published by the same authority but prepared by different centers of thinking certainly can have very little in common. In limited cases they may appear to be juxtaposed or even to contradict each other. The method which shall follow is quite simple. *Humanae Vitae* quotes and mentions *Gaudium et Spes* on nine occasions. It is important to see whether these instances refer to doctrines pertaining only to *Gaudium et Spes* or to doctrines that belong to the common store of Catholic teaching. Also, if *Gaudium et Spes* is quoted with reference to specific texts and terms, it is then possible to examine *Humanae Vitae* to see if it takes up again these same terms of the conciliar document or if it limits, softens, or modifies them. Finally, as well as the explicit references there are some themes common to both texts which will be examined. Care will be given in ascertaining if there are significant omissions, as well as in comparing them.

The research plan, then, is as follows:

1. Initially we shall attempt to lay out the general plan of citations and references made by *Humanae Vitae* to *Gaudium et Spes* in order to gauge what importance is given to *Gaudium et Spes* and to compare it in this respect to other documents.

2. We shall then undertake a study of the points in *Humanae Vitae* which coincide with *Gaudium et Spes*. We shall study, initially, those quotations touching on doctrinal points which are not the private teaching either of *Humanae Vitae* or of *Gaudium et Spes* but which represent "Catholic doctrine," or "the common teaching."

3. We shall next deal with the controversial points of doctrine in *Humanae Vitae* which seem to contradict the new teaching of *Gaudium et Spes*. Does *Humanae Vitae* refer to *Gaudium et Spes* in these questions? If so, in what sense?

4. Finally, this stage of purely textual analysis will open the doors to a historical and doctrinal analysis. Does *Humanae Vitae* take up the broad themes of *Gaudium et Spes*? Does it interpret them in the same way or is it silent on these matters?

The References of the Encyclical

Humanae Vitae refers to more than 70 biblical, conciliar, papal, and juridical texts. Except for notes Nos. 11, 13, 33, and 37, all these references are preceded by the abbreviation "cf.," which permits a wider adaptation of the text. Some documents receive a vague mention as, for example, in the block of citations in note No. 4, which shows that the Church has always had an interest in the doctrine of marriage.

The temptation, initially, is to immediately begin a statistical analysis of the texts. This, however, would be particularly difficult to interpret. For example, there are 16 references made to biblical texts. The tendency would be to think, then, that the encyclical was written from a biblical point of view. As Msgr. Lambruschini noted, however, when he presented *Humanae Vitae* to the journalists in Rome, this is far from the truth. The encyclical is largely on the level of natural law. It even omits altogether the mention made of Onan's condemnation by *Casti Connubii* (Denzinger, No. 3716). The scriptural texts employed here refer to general features of Christian living. Thus, for example, *Humanae Vitae* encourages Christian couples not to despair and quotes Romans 5:5: "This hope is not deceptive because the love of God has been poured into our hearts by the Holy Spirit which has been given us."

No further useful information is obtained, either, by comparing the number of citations taken from one document with the number of those taken from another. *Mater et Magistra* is quoted five times in the notes whereas *Casti Connubii* barely rates a mention. Yet it is quite evident that the influence of Pius XI had far more weight in the encyclical than that of John XXIII. It does well to note, moreover, that the manner in which *Humanae Vitae* utilizes these texts often varies. Note 28 corresponds to a text which itself is a quotation. Note 38 refers back to three texts without clearly specifying which was the one intended. Note 1, we find, refers only to a general statement.

Let us take a rapid glance, then, at the list of quotations drawn up below, after which we shall examine the quotations themselves:

Scripture: 16 texts from the New Testament. Notes 2, 3, 6, 7, 18, 22, 24, 31, 32, 34, 35, 36, 37, 40, 41.

Codex Juris Canonici: 3 canons in a single reference. Note 4.

Catechismus Romanus Concilii Tridentini: Part Two, chap. VIII: 2 references. Notes 14, 16.

Vatican II:

   Lumen Gentium: 3 texts. Notes 32, 38, 39.

   Apostolicam Actuositatem: once. Note 38.

   Inter Mirifica (decree on communications media): once. Note 25.

   Gaudium et Spes (De dignitate matrimonii . . .): nine times. Notes 4, 8, 10, 11, 14, 28, 30, 32, 38.

Pius IX:

   Qui Pluribus: once. Note 1.

Leo XIII:

   Arcanum: once. Note 4.

Pius X:

   Singulari: once. Note 1.

111

Pius XI:

    Casti Connubii: six times. Notes 1, 4, 12, 14, 15, 16.

    Divini Illius Magistri: once. Note 4.

Pius XII:

    To the Union of St. Luke, 1944: twice. Notes 4, 14.

    To the obstetricians, October 29, 1951: six times. Notes 4, 12, 15, 16, 20, 29.

    To large families, November 28, 1951: once. Note 4.

    To the members of the Congress of Urology, October 8, 1953: twice. Notes 19, 21.

    To cornea donors, October 8, 1953: once. Note 21.

    To jurists, December 6, 1953: once. Note 17.

    To the Catholic episcopate, November 2, 1954: once. Note 1.

    To hematologists, September 12, 1958: three times. Notes 4, 15, 19.

John XXIII:

    Mater et Magistra: five times. Notes 1, 4, 13, 16, 26.

    Pacem in Terris: once. Note 4.

Paul VI:

    Allocution to the Sacred College, June 23, 1964: once. Note 5.

    To the Papal Commission: once. Note 5.

    To the Congress of Gynecologists: once. Note 5.

    Populorum Progressio: twice. Notes 23, 27.

St. Thomas: once. Note 9.

Holy Office: once. Note 15.

Texts Utilized by Humanae Vitae *from* Gaudium et Spes

1. First, in No. 4 of *Humanae Vitae*, mention is made of *Gaudium et Spes* along with ten other documents to support the following statement, "Conformably to this mission of hers, the Church has always provided—and even more amply in recent times—a coherent teaching concerning both the nature of marriage and the correct use of conjugal rights and duties of husband and wife." The pastoral constitution and the Council itself do not receive special mention. They are quoted under the same heading as the Roman Catechism, the speech to obstetricians in 1951, and the *Codex of Canon Law*.

2. *Humanae Vitae* refers, this time explicitly, to the Council to declare that the use of marriage is good in itself (No. 11): "These acts, by which husband and wife are united in chaste intimacy, and by means of which human life is transmitted, are, as the Council re-

called, 'noble and worthy,' and they do not cease to be lawful if, for causes independent of the will of husband and wife, they are foreseen to be infecund, since they always remain ordained toward expressing and consolidating their union." The terms "noble" and "worthy" are certainly to be found in *Gaudium et Spes* (No. 49, sec. 2) but in a completely different context, because there they refer only to married love itself: "This love is uniquely expressed and perfected through the marital act. The actions within marriage by which the couple are united intimately and chastely are noble and worthy ones. Expressed in a manner which is truly human, these actions signify and promote that mutual self-giving by which spouses enrich each other with a joyful and thankful will." It is evident that the reference has passed from sexuality to procreation.

Already here we may detect one factor which will influence all the references made to *Gaudium et Spes* in *Humanae Vitae*: the hand of the Pope's own theologian. The text as prepared at Ariccia (No. 62) stated: "Actus proinde, quibus coniuges intime et ordinatim inter se uniuntur . . ." In the subsequent draft "ordinatim" was replaced by "caste" and was defended in the following way (p. 17): "Proponitur ut loco ordinatim dicatur caste ut ordo moralis hac in re indicetur secundum propriam virtutem." No speeches of the Council Fathers supported such a proposal. The motive behind this change is to be found in an oral intervention made by the Pope's theologian who acted to some extent as unofficial Papal Commissioner in the subcommission. This theologian observed that too little reference to chastity had been made in the text, and demanded that this virtue be mentioned here.

3. There is an appeal made to "men of science" in *Humanae Vitae*, No. 24, which refers to *Gaudium et Spes*, No. 52, sec. 4, and to the Pope's speech to obstetricians (notes 28–29). A slight difference between the two documents may be observed in passing. *Gaudium et Spes* hopes that doctors "labor to explain more thoroughly the various conditions favoring a proper regulation of births," whereas Pius XII, as *Humanae Vitae* mentions, held the hope dear to his heart that "medical science succeed in giving a sufficiently secure basis for birth regulation which is founded on the observance of the natural rhythms."

4. A new reference to *Gaudium et Spes* and also to *Lumen Gentium* is seen in *Humanae Vitae*, No. 25: "By it (the sacrament of marriage) husband and wife are strengthened and as it were, consecrated for the faithful accomplishment of their proper duties, for the carrying out of their proper vocation even to perfection, and the Christian witness which is proper to them before the whole world." Note 32 quotes *Gaudium et Spes*, No. 48 and *Lumen Gentium*, No. 35.

Gaudium et Spes, in fact, mentions part of this phrase, *"peculiari sacramento roborantur et quasi consecrantur,"* which utilizes again a text from Pius XI: "magis ac magis ad propriam suam perfectionem mutuamque sanctificationem . . . accedunt . . . (sec. 2). Familia christiana . . . vivam Salvatoris in mundo praesentiam patefaciet" (sec. 3). *Humanae Vitae* does not say in what this witness consists. *Gaudium et Spes* does, however: "This the family will do by the mutual love of the spouses, by their generous fruitfulness, their solidarity and faithfulness, and by the loving way in which all members of the family work together."

5. *Gaudium et Spes,* together with the decree on the laity (No. 11) and the Constitution on the Church (Nos. 35, 41), is once again quoted in the footnotes on the subject of the family apostolate which *Humanae Vitae* praises in No. 26. Here again we notice that it is a general reference and includes other references. This block reference to *Gaudium et Spes,* Nos. 48 and 49 offers a large number of texts which may be quoted. It expresses, in fact, ideas similar to those of *Humanae Vitae:* "Families will share their spiritual riches with other families too" (No. 48, sec. 4) . . . "Authentic conjugal love will be more highly prized, and wholesome public opinion created regarding it, if Christian couples give outstanding witness to faithfulness and harmony in that same love, and to their concern for educating their children" (No. 49, sec. 3). This text of No. 49 could possibly be more suitably applied to note 48 on witness, but *Humanae Vitae* did not look at it from this point of view. In any case, of the 9 citations or mentions made by *Humanae Vitae* of *Gaudium et Spes,* it can be seen that 5 are on the level of general principles and may be found in past ecclesiastical documents.

We shall now review the 4 passages from *Gaudium et Spes* that *Humanae Vitae* either quoted or utilized in some way. In these texts the Council Fathers wanted to express their positions on several present-day issues: procreation as an objective in marriage, abortion, conflicting values, the authority of the Church hierarchy in matters of this nature. We shall continue our strictly textual analysis and follow the order of the texts as given in the document published on July 29, 1968.

1. In paragraph 9, dedicated to the characteristic qualities of married love, there appears a quotation from *Gaudium et Spes:* "Marriage and conjugal love are by their nature ordained toward the begetting and educating of children. Children are really the supreme gift of marriage and contribute very substantially to the welfare of their parents." Exception can be taken to the fact that the French text

114

of the encyclical states "of their nature" where the Latin text is *"indole sua"* and the official translation of *Gaudium et Spes* in Italian reads "are of themselves ordered." It is sufficient to note here that these words are the end result of a dispute which took place four years before. Those who drafted the conciliar text had avoided as far as possible the word nature on account of its ambiguous connotations. *Humanae Vitae,* on the other hand, finds it a very attractive word. Let us leave aside, however, this minor detail found in the French text, and return to No. 50 of *Gaudium et Spes.* If we read the complete text, we notice that the first two phrases, in the way that *Humanae Vitae* uses them, are taken out of their context and deprived of that complementary viewpoint essential to *Gaudium et Spes.*

The text of Schema XIII that the Council debated in October 1965 clearly affirmed the importance of procreation but immediately included the other essential element and stated that marriage is not just a means for assuring fertility. The text is as follows: "Talis est matrimonii et amoris conjugalis indoles ut, ex semetipsis, ad prolem procreandam simul et educandam ordinentur. Unde verus amoris conjugalis cultus totaque vitae familiaris ratio inde oriens eo tendit ut conjuges forti animo dispositi sint ad cooperandam cum amore Creatoris et Salvatoris, qui per eos suam familiam in dies dilatas et ditat.

"Matrimonium autem, licet in prolem ordinetur, non est merum procreationis institutum; sed natura foederis indissolubilis inter personas bonumque prolis exigunt ut mutuus etiam conjugum amor recto ordine proficiat et maturescat."

As may be seen, the text centers around two ideas: "marriage is bound up with procreation" but "it is not solely this; it is also love." This balance was destroyed when as a result of the efforts of some and the lack of attention of others the second statement was put much farther back in the text. In the final text one must read through two pages before the second part of the affirmation is found in sec. 3: "Marriage to be sure is not instituted solely for procreation. Rather, its very nature as an unbreakable compact between persons, and the welfare of the children, both demand that the mutual love of the spouses, too, be embodied in a rightly ordered manner, that it grow and ripen."

On the other hand, some Fathers, during the discussions of October 1965, found that this text insisted excessively on fertility. Hence the subcommission introduced the word *etiam* to highlight a subtle but important point. The text then becomes: "Unde verus amoris conjugalis cultus totaque vitae familiaris ratio inde oriens etiam eo tendunt ut conjuges."

The *Relatio* defended this modification of the text by stating: "Proponitur ut addatur 'etiam,' ne, uti quidam Patres timent (E 5614, E 5648) nimis matrimonium unilateraliter ut procreativum habeatur." The insertion of this *etiam*, however, provoked a strong reaction on the part of some bishops and experts of the minority who took the matter to the Pope. One of the four *modi* issued by the Secretariat of State informed the commission that it approved the following text: "Omittatur verbum etiam atque brevis haec enuntiatio in extremum periodum addatur, ad lineam 13: 'Filii sunt praestantissimum matrimonii donum et ad ipsorum parentum bonum maxime conferunt.'"

The subcommission then managed to have *etiam* replaced by *non posthabitis ceteris matrimonii finibus*. This formulation was to remain in spite of a last-moment attempt to weaken its effect with *non neglectis ceteris matrimonii finibus*.

The phrase *"Filii . . ."* had already been imposed on the subcommission by the papal commentary several days before the appearance of the modus. The Pope's theologian had gone even farther. He spoke of "praestantissimum bonum," which amounted to calling it the *"finis primarius"* since what is good is also a goal to be aimed at. Bonum est quod omnia appetunt. On this point, however, Msgr. Ruess reacted with astonishing vigor: "Non bonum sed donum." The victory was eventually his.

In order to have a clear idea of each of the phrases in this first paragraph, the origins of the phrase *"Ipse Deus . . ."* remain to be shown. This modification had been put forward in November by the German episcopate in order to retain the two perspectives as given in scripture: on the one hand, union and love (*non est bonum hominem esse solum*), and on the other, fertility (*crescite et multiplicamini*). A phrase in the commentary explained the authors' intentions: "Intima ab initio ordinatio viri mulierisque ad invicem ut mutue se compleant, coniungitur cum humani generis procreatione." It was not included in the text so as not to disturb this fine network of texts that seemed to adequately express the two themes. After the smoke had finally risen from the battlefield, it became clear that both aspects of married love had been affirmed:

Procreation	Love
Matrimonium . . .	
Filii . . . (papal *modus*).	Ipse Deus qui dixit; non est bonum hominem esse solum.
Crescite et multiplicamini.	Non posthabitis ceteris matrimonii finibus.

It is evident, then, that this text of *Gaudium et Spes* as quoted by *Humanae Vitae* would take on a different shade of meaning if taken by itself or if put in its context so that its true meaning could be revealed from its "redaction history." In *Humanae Vitae* the two phrases are deprived of that complementary character which *Gaudium et Spes* wanted to give them.

2. Still farther on, in No. 10, note 10 refers once again to the conciliar document: the pastoral constitution *Gaudium et Spes,* Nos. 50 and 51. The note comes at the end of the following passage: "In the task of transmitting life, therefore, they (Catholics) are not free to proceed completely at will, as if they could determine in a wholly autonomous way the honest path to follow; but they must conform their activity to the creative intention of God, expressed in the very nature of marriage and of its acts, and manifested by the constant teaching of the Church."

In Nos. 50 and 51 in fact, several phrases from *Humanae Vitae* are to be found, for example: "In officio humanam vitam transmittendi (the encyclical omitted *educandi*, No. 50, sec. 2) . . . in sua vero agendi ratione conjuges christiani conscii sint se non ad arbitrium suum procedere posse." What follows in the text, however, is so completely different that we are forced to give it fuller treatment, noting especially the "silent passages" in *Humanae Vitae.* Let it be said immediately that it is not possible as may be observed in the comparison drawn below, to apply the same criteria to *Gaudium et Spes* which were used in *Humanae Vitae.*

Humanae Vitae (No. 10)	*Gaudium et Spes* (No. 51, sec. 3)
Conform their activity to the creative intention of God, expressed in the very nature of marriage and of its acts. ". . . Ipsa matrimonii eiusque actuum natura."	Objective standards based on the nature of the human person and his acts. ". . . Personae eiusdemque actuum natura."

For *Gaudium et Spes* the criterion of morality is held to be in the person; for *Humanae Vitae,* in marriage. The word acts is the same in both cases, but *Gaudium et Spes* understands it as acts of the person whereas for *Humanae Vitae* it means acts of marriage considered in their biological sense.

On the other hand, we see a certain similarity in the meaning given to the last few words in *Humanae Vitae,* No. 10, and in *Gaudium et Spes,* No. 51, sec. 3.

Humanae Vitae (No. 10)	*Gaudium et Spes* (No. 51, sec. 3)
Manifested by the constant teaching of the Church.	Relying on these principles, sons of the Church may not undertake methods of regulating procreation which are found blameworthy by the teaching authority of the Church in its unfolding of the divine law.

This similarity is easily explained by the fact that the phrase in *Gaudium et Spes* is, for all practical purposes, Modus 4 which the Pope sent the commission. The document was worded as follows:

"Haec dicantur:

"Quibus principiis innixi, (docemus) filiis Ecclesiae in procreatione regulanda vias inire non licere, quae a Magisterio improbatae sunt vel improbentur; vel

"Quibus principiis innixis, filiis Ecclesiae in procreatione regulanda vias inire non licet, quae a Magisterio improbatae sunt vel improbentur.

"Praeterea in annotatione de duobus praestantissimis de hac materia documentis mentio fiat, scilicet: de Encyclicis Litteris *Casti Connubii* AAS 22 (1930): cfr locos in Denz.-Schon. 3716–18; ac de oratione a Pio XII ad Obstretices habita: AAS 43 (1951)."

In spite of the astonishment which this document produced when it was read, the *improbentur* still gave the vanquished a reason to smile. A secretary let it be known that it was a grammatical error and should have been *improbuntur*. The blush which then lighted up the face of one of the theologians, betrayed if not the author at least the secretariat from whose pen it came. After much talk these uncertain Latin grammatical variations were finally reduced to the more suitable *improbantur*. The citations formed the famous note 14 in which it was not permitted to give the corresponding Denzinger references for the pages of the *Acta Apostolicae Sedis*. (Those drafting the encyclical had greater freedom.)

Msgr. Garrone succeeded in having the speech that Paul VI had given to the cardinals several months before included along with the two citations from Pius XI and Pius XII. Seeing that the Pope had officially announced the existence of the Papal Commission charged with revising the problem of contraception, it appeared that his opinion on the issue was not fixed and that he was searching for new insights. The struggle which certain experts of the minority put up against the inclusion, of a speech that was so unfavorable to them, showed that some of them feared the door was now being left open.

To conclude the study of this reference to *Gaudium et Spes*, then, we once again recall that it refers us to a passage which the Sovereign Pontiff had modified. The passage modifies above all the text treating of the moral criteria in questions of marital relations.

3. A third doctrinal reference to *Gaudium et Spes* appears in the first paragraph of No. 14 regarding "the direct interruption of the generative process" and abortion. It reads: "We must once again declare that the direct interruption of the generative process already begun, and above all, directly willed and procured abortion, even if for therapeutic reasons, are absolutely to be excluded as licit means of regulating birth." Note 14 of *Humanae Vitae* refers back to five documents in the midst of which is found, "*Gaudium et Spes*, No. 51."

There is no doubt that *Humanae Vitae* was referring to the following phrases: "Sunt qui hic problematibus solutiones inhonestas afferre praesumunt, immo ab occissione non abhorrent . . . (No. 51, sec. 2). Vita igitur inde a conceptione, maxima cura tuenda est; abortus necnon infanticidium nefanda sunt crimina" (No. 51, sec. 3). The earlier conciliar text spoke of "*vita in utero iam concepta*," but some Fathers thought that this left out of consideration the fertilized ovum not yet implanted in the womb. It was thus decided that the best solution would be to use the expression "*inde a conceptione*" which let it be understood that the Council was not in a position for the moment to give a solution to the problem of ensoulment "*quin tempus animationis tangatur*" (Modus 101, p. 36). Does *Humanae Vitae* add anything new to these considerations? To answer this question, it would be necessary to know precisely what the document means by "*directa generationis iam coeptae interruptio*." Taken strictly, it could be interpreted as saying that coitus is the starting point of the process of generation. Possibly the exegetes of *Humanae Vitae* will be able to shed further light on it. The historian contents himself with noticing once again that the references in *Gaudium et Spes* do not fully correspond to what is affirmed in *Humanae Vitae*.

4. This leaves us with the last citation of *Gaudium et Spes* found in No. 24 under note 30: "A true contradiction cannot exist between the divine laws pertaining to the transmission of life and those pertaining to the fostering of authentic conjugal love."

This text is to be found in *Gaudium et Spes*, No. 51, sec. 2. However, let it be noted once again that it would be futile to search for this passage in the text discussed at Ariccia in October 1965. It is not until after the modifications were made in November by the subcommission that it made its appearance with the following commentary added: "Altera additio proponitur, in qua affirmatur veras exigentias vitae nunquam leges divinas vere contradicere" (p. 20).

As before, the subcommission had no recourse to speeches by Council Fathers requesting an addition of this kind. Its source is to be found, rather, in the work of the Papal Commissioner. This prelate wanted to suppress objective sec. 1, which recognized the relative necessity of marital relations. Reserved as the subcommission normally was, this time the Papal Commissioner's proposal collided with its statement of everyday experience given by Mr. and Mrs. Alvarez, two Mexican lay members of the subcommission: "It was simply a matter," they stated, "of recognizing a fact of experience. Whether you like it or not, the fact exists." After this setback, the prelate demanded that the phrase as now found in *Humanae Vitae* be inserted. Once again, we may observe the same fact: *Humanae Vitae* quotes a text introduced at the last moment, without taking any other factors into consideration, as a countermeasure to a statement of *Gaudium et Spes*.

The uneasiness we feel after this investigation seems to be suggesting certain conclusions.

1. Of the 9 citations and references that *Humanae Vitae* makes to *Gaudium et Spes*, only 4 are anything other than general principles.

2. In two cases (9 and 24) the citations are repeated *ad literam*, but are taken out of their context where a complementary viewpoint was also expressed.

3. In the other two cases (10 and 14) *Humanae Vitae*'s citations are superficial, and modify the thought of *Gaudium et Spes* on the moral criteria in marriage relations (No. 10) as well as on its condemnation of abortion with "the direct interruption of the generative process" (No. 14).

4. If we return to the origins of the doctrinal texts of *Gaudium et Spes* as quoted by *Humanae Vitae*, we notice that only one (the condemnation of abortion) belongs to the text as composed by the Council. The other three (9, 10, and 24) are the result of interventions by authority.

5. The purpose of these interventions was to bring a countermeasure to bear against those statements in *Gaudium et Spes* which to the minority appeared too audacious. They were included in the Council text in order that all tendencies be given a voice. In *Humanae Vitae*, however, only these positions of the minority are quoted and

at the same time the appearance is given that the whole of *Gaudium et Spes* is being quoted.

The equilibrium that the Council majority had arrived at was thus upset in order to give added weight to the ideas of the minority.

This impression will be confirmed when we continue our inquiry. We shall examine what type of viewpoint *Humanae Vitae* adopted on the basic themes of *Gaudium et Spes*, and in general the whole issue of marriage as proposed by this document of the Church.

The *"Silent Passages"* of Humanae Vitae

The influence of one text on another cannot be calculated simply from the quotations made from it. Many ideas of the former may be included in the latter without their being immediately identifiable.

Likewise, after having studied the explicit references and citations from *Gaudium et Spes* that we have found in *Humanae Vitae*, we now face a further historical problem. Do the main themes of *Gaudium et Spes* on marriage, particularly on married love, reappear in *Humanae Vitae*? Can one speak of a common thought inspiring the two documents, or do they instead complement each other, or is there simply no connection between them?

It seems important that this third possibility be fully considered, for it is not immediately evident how *Humanae Vitae* and *Gaudium et Spes* agree on matters of importance.

The problem is considered here with reference to marriage. The inquiry, however, could be widened to include the whole line of thinking of *Gaudium et Spes*, especially on what it states of man's powers over nature and his right to assume his responsibility. *Humanae Vitae* takes nature and the natural law in the sense that the jurisconsult Ulpianus used the term. For him, natural law is a primitive, moral instinct common to men and animals particularly in the sphere of sexuality and childbearing:

"Ius naturale est quod natura omnia animalia docuit. Nam ius istud non humani generis proprium sed omnium animalium quae in terra, quae in mari nascuntur, avium quoque commune est. Hinc descendit maris atque foeminae coniunctio quam nos matrimonium appellamus; hinc liberorum procreatio, hinc educatio" (*Digest.*, lib. 1, t. 1, num. 1, secs. 2–4).

Gaudium et Spes, instead, bases itself on the definition of Gaius, the Scholastics, and especially St. Albert the Great, who contrasted animal nature with human reason. This is apparent in the chapter dedicated to culture (No. 53, secs. 1–2):

"It is a fact bearing on the very person of man that he can come

121

to an authentic and full humanity only through culture; that is, through the cultivation of natural goods and values. Wherever human life is involved, therefore, nature and culture are quite intimately connected.

"The word culture in its general sense indicates all those factors by which man refines and unfolds his manifold spiritual and bodily qualities. It means his effort to bring the world itself under his control by his knowledge and labor. It includes the fact that by improving customs and institutions he renders social life more human both within the family and in the civic community."

A wider comparison of this kind cannot be avoided. Too many Catholics who have put their confidence in the Council are now shocked when they read this document with its totally different theology and anthropology. We must limit ourselves, however. *Non omnia possumus omnes.* Simply comparing the thought of the two documents on marriage is already a formidable task.

The Method of the Encyclical

Gaudium et Spes was written from the standpoint of a biblical renewal of Christian morality expressly demanded by the Council itself (Decree on Priestly Formation, No. 16). This does not mean searching revelation and especially scripture for concrete solutions to all modern problems. How could the Gospels have spoken of the rights of man if this was a later development in man's moral awareness? In the revelation of Christ there may be found and must be found, however, light which illuminates even these problems by establishing the dignity of man and by laying down what the demands of charity and universal justice are (*Gaudium et Spes*, Nos. 29, 41). When it is a question of marriage, a biblical treatment is all the more called for, seeing that marriage is fully developed in Genesis, the Prophets, the Gospels, St. Paul, etc. There also is reason in the light of revelation that *Gaudium et Spes* presents marriage (Nos. 48–49) as well as procreation (No. 50, sec. 1): "God himself said: 'it is not good that man be alone (Gen. 2:18),' and 'that he created man in the beginning both male and female (Matt. 19:4),' and wishing to offer man a special participation in his creative work, he blessed the man and the woman, telling them to 'grow and multiply (Gen. 1:28).'"

Humanae Vitae sees things in a different light. It remains on the level of natural law. This point of reference is very clearly seen from No. 4 onward: "It is in fact indisputable, as our predecessors have many times declared, that Jesus Christ, when communicating to Peter and to the apostles his divine authority and sending them to teach all nations his commandments (Matthew 28:18–19), constituted them as guardians and authentic interpreters of all the moral law; not only, that is, of the law of the gospel, but also of the natural law, which is also an expression of the will of God, the faithful fulfillment of which is equally necessary for salvation" (Matthew 7:21).

The historian logically asks the exegete if the interpretations of Matthew 28 and Matthew 7 are those commonly agreed upon by all exegetes or whether they have been just accepted traditionally. It is not astonishing to see a pope claim jurisdiction over the natural law. Many medieval popes spoke in the same way. Paul VI will not be able to avoid, however, the accusation of being outdated. When the medieval popes claimed the right of judging and even modifying the natural law they were employing Gratian's hypothesis which identified natural law and evangelical law: "Humanum genus duobus regitur, naturali videlicet iure et moribus. Ius naturale est quod in lege et evangelio continetur . . ." (*Decretum Gratianum*, (dist. 1st ed., Freiburg, col. 1).

From the time when natural law became, in a pluralistic society, what it was in the mind of Aristotle and the Stoics—that is, moral philosophy—it has become far less clear how a pope could bracket it under the same heading as the precepts left by the Lord. It is evident that ecclesiastical authority may and should make use of reason in presenting the divine message, but can it authoritatively substitute a philosophy for a theology? It is doubtful to say the least. Even if ecclesiastical authority were to have the right to authoritatively interpret the indications given by nature, this would still leave many problems. Science and philosophy have their word to say also. It is medical science which must determine whether intercourse is always connected with procreation. If pregnancy occurs only once in a possible two hundred times and if the creation of new life is closely linked with a series of acts where nature wastes the germinal cells, should not one keep this in mind when formulating the moral norm?

No one will be astounded if ecclesiastical authority confirms the obvious fact of the link between sexuality and genitality. But maybe the precise nature of this link depends more on the competence of science than that of ecclesiastical authority. The farther one goes from the center of affirmations formulated by reason toward detailed clarifications, the weaker becomes the argument from authority.

At the risk of being tiresome, the historian must also ask, moreover, other questions that can only be alluded to here:

How is it that a truth of natural law is perceived as such only by Catholics or, to be more exact, only by a privileged few of them?

Can a papal proclamation be considered as a revelation of natural truth—for example, the existence of God or human liberty? Some apologetes have in the past presented it in this way. Does not this, however, put revelation and the magisterium on the same level? Scripture and tradition teach the existence of God. An encyclical condemns contraception. Is it the same?

When the history and motivations behind the encyclical become better known, will it be possible to justify the triumphalism of the natural law school? Is it, in fact, as some say, the revenge of the "natural law school" on the "charity school"?

The Moral Criterion of Marriage Acts

Humanae Vitae affirms that the criterion of morality is nature taken in the biological sense; as we note, for example, in No. 13: "To use this divine gift destroying, even if only partially, its meaning and its purpose is to contradict the nature both of man and of woman, and of their most intimate relationship, and therefore it is to contradict also the plan of God and his will. On the other hand, to make use of the gift of conjugal love while respecting the laws of the generative process means to acknowledge oneself not to be the arbiter of the sources of human life, but rather the minister of the design established by the Creator." On account of this, *Humanae Vitae* contradicts the insistence of *Gaudium et Spes* (No. 51, sec. 3) on the personalistic criterion of intersubjectivity: "(The transmission of life) must be determined by objective standards. These, based on the nature of the human person and his acts, preserve the full sense of mutual self-giving and human procreation in the context of true love. Such a goal cannot be achieved unless the virtue of conjugal chastity is sincerely practiced."

The personalistic perspective in the drafting of *Gaudium et Spes* is brought very clearly into light by the history of the texts. In November 1965, the text reads: "Obiectivis criteriis, in eadem personae humanae dignitate fundatis, determinari debet, quae integrum sensum mutuae donationis ac humanae procreationis in contextu veri amoris observant (p. 9)." The subcommission comments: "Criteria enim obiectiva adhibenda sunt, quibus intrinsecus sensus donationis mutuae in actu humanae procreationis servetur, in contextu quidem veri amoris at verus amor recte exprimatur." This is not a falling into subjectivism. It is a substituting of interpersonal criteria for biological criteria. Every dehumanizing gesture, every method that depreciates a partner, must be rejected.

When this text was put to the Council Fathers for voting there were found to be a sizable number of proposals of amendment. It was revised by a commission now increased in size. The influence of Cardinal Ottaviani was such as to allow a certain number of theologians chosen by him to be included. These scholars were to have devoted their efforts to having the word nature introduced. In this way, if a biological orientation would not have supplanted the personalistic orientation, it would at least have been included together with it.

In this way, therefore, after the *expensio modorum*—a poor phrase for expressing what actually happened—various formulations were proposed: "In eadem personae humanae dignitate atque iusta naturam ipsorum (actuum)." This was rejected. After a fiery struggle in which one of the more observant experts warned his collaborators in the majority against what was in his eyes obviously a subtle maneuver on the part of the minority, the following text was accepted: "Ex personae eiusdemque actuum natura desumptis." In the commentary it is clearly shown that the intention was to reject the biological standpoint: "Quibus verbis asseritur etiam actus jiudicandos esse non secundum aspectum merum biologicum sed quatenus illi ad personam humanam integre et adaequate considerandum pertinent" (Modus 104, p. 37).

Responsible Parenthood

In one sense there is a certain agreement between *Humanae Vitae*, No. 10 and *Gaudium et Spes*, No. 50. Both refer to the speech of Pius XII in 1951. On the other hand, it is doubtful whether *Humanae Vitae* uses the term "responsible parenthood" in the sense that it is used in *Gaudium et Spes* and in everyday language. *Humanae Vitae* does not view it as the responsibility of parents for their present and future children but sees it rather in relation to physiology—a physiology promoted both by God and by the presumed supreme interpreter of his will. Thus we read: "In relation to the biological processes, responsible parenthood means the knowledge and respect of their functions; human intellect discovers in the power of giving life biological laws which are part of the human person. . . .

"Responsible parenthood also and above all implies a more profound relationship to the objective moral order established by God, of which a right conscience is the faithful interpreter" (*Humanae Vitae*, No. 10).

It is not certain at all that everyone will accept without question the principle that man is responsible before his physiology. That man is responsible before God is far more easily granted.

The Judgment of Conscience

Throughout *Gaudium et Spes* as well as in the whole of the conciliar texts, it was evident that Catholics were being continually reminded to accept their responsibilities "in soul and conscience." In particular in No. 43, sec. 2, on lay people one reads that "laymen should also know that it is generally the function of their well-formed Christian conscience to see that the divine law is inscribed in the life of the earthly city." This does not mean that Catholics have to reinvent a whole new morality, outside the revelation transmitted and interpreted by the Church. But it does imply that conscience does not act solely in the application of the law as, for example, in the case of the Catholic who on Sunday asks himself if he is sick enough to be excused from going to Mass.

Christians in conscience, together with the Church and with their spiritual leaders, have to discover the evangelical imperatives and apply them to their lives. This consideration has completely disappeared in *Humanae Vitae*. Only authority's point of view is considered, and Catholics are asked solely to obey. This is true not only for lay people. The bishops expressed their opinions in the Council. This evidently contributed to the uneasiness felt by the Secretariat of State in deciding on the schedule of the Synod, so that everything was carried out as if the bishops were only executives (No. 30). The question of collegiality and corresponsibility, even subordinate corresponsibility, is evidently best solved by rejecting it.

As for the lay people, *Humanae Vitae* does not appeal to their deliberative conscience on this matter. *Gaudium et Spes* (No. 50, sec. 2) asked them to form "a correct judgment" on the issue "in mutual agreement and with a common effort." The conciliar text provided the elements for this judgment: "They—the couple—will thoughtfully take into account both their own welfare and that of their children, those already born and those which may be foreseen. For this accounting they will reckon with both the material and the spiritual conditions of the times as well as of their state of life. Finally, they will consult the interests of the family group, of temporal society, and of the Church herself." The number of "possible" children will be decided upon in this way. In spite of the many hurdles to be leaped, the commission kept at least this judgment the exclusive privilege of lay people: "This judgment must be made, in the long run, before God by the couple themselves." As Mr. and Mrs. Alvarez said, "The issue at stake was the principle of protecting husband and wife against 'clerical paternalism.'" Possibly an affirmation of this kind is implicitly contained in *Humanae Vitae*. Explicitly, certainly, no mention is made of it.

After all the struggles that this text had been through, the silence of *Humanae Vitae* here becomes rather significant.

Married Love

Possibly nowhere else are the two documents farther apart than here. Certainly both affirm that marriage is an institution willed by God and that married love comes from God (*Gaudium et Spes*, No. 48; *Humanae Vitae*, No. 8). However, their description of married love as well as their enumeration of the requirements of married love clearly differ.

Gaudium et Spes describes the love of a couple in personalist terms as a mutual giving on all levels of one's individuality: will, affectivity, sentiments, and senses. *Humanae Vitae* makes a hasty mention of "an attempt at communion" in order to insist on its objective: procreation. Vatican II had tried to rehabilitate married love, to show that it finds its raison d'etre in itself not just on the erotic level, but principally as the fulfilling of one's personality. *Humanae Vitae* returns to the Augustinian view and justifies love only by "finalizing" it in procreation. In any case, how else could *Humanae Vitae* have spoken if it wanted to affirm the strict union between every act of love and procreation? *Gaudium et Spes*, on the other hand, considered that this love is generous and creative of itself, and also that it has sufficient value in itself to justify it over and beyond its procreative value. Let us contrast the respective texts:

Humanae Vitae, No. 8 states: "By means of the reciprocal personal gift of self, proper and exclusive to them, husband and wife tend toward the communion of their beings in view of mutual personal perfection, to collaborate with God in the generation and education of new lives."

Gaudium et Spes, No. 49, sec. 1 states: "This love is an eminently human one since it is directed from one person to another through an affection of the will. It involves the good of the whole person. Therefore it can enrich the expressions of body and mind with a unique dignity, ennobling these expressions as special ingredients and signs of friendship distinctive of marriage. This love the Lord has judged worthy of special gifts, healing, perfecting, and exalting gifts of grace and of charity.

"Such love, merging the human with the divine, leads the spouses to a free and mutual gift of themselves—a gift proving itself by gentle affection and by deed. Such love pervades the whole of their lives. Indeed, by its generous activity it grows better and grows greater. Therefore it far excels a more erotic inclination, which, selfishly pursued, soon enough fades wretchedly away."

The line of thought in *Gaudium et Spes* does not find it strange to admit a relative necessity for intimacy in marriage. Persons can very strongly experience the need for union in those moments when they cannot take on the responsibilities of another child. Besides, this act retains its creative quality. Frustrated parents are the worst of teachers, and they also risk having their family life slowly destroyed when they begin looking elsewhere for what has been denied them at home. This is the reason that *Gaudium et Spes* could say (No. 51): "This Council realizes that certain modern conditions often keep couples from arranging their married lives harmoniously, and that they find themselves in circumstances where at least temporarily the size of their families should not be increased. As a result, the faithful exercise of love and the full intimacy of their lives are hard to maintain; but where the intimacy of married life is broken off, it is not rare for its faithfulness to be imperiled and its quality of fruitfulness ruined. For then the upbringing of the children and the courage to accept new ones are both endangered."

In this case there is a real conflict between values and duties. On the one hand, the couple is conscious of the necessity of continuing their intimate relations so as to live out the logic of their mutual gift blessed by God. On the other hand, they have to refuse procreating new life. *Gaudium et Spes*, believing it could resolve the problem by utilizing the personalist criteria mentioned above, would allow this. *Humanae Vitae*, however, would consider any solution along these lines as violating the natural law which requires a direct and immediate link between intercourse and procreation. It is, furthermore, immoral to do an intrinsically evil act to attain a good end. As the encyclical notes (No. 14): "In truth, if it is sometimes licit to tolerate a lesser evil in order to avoid a greater evil or to promote a greater good, it is not licit, even for the gravest reasons, to do evil so that good may follow therefrom; that is, to make into the object of a positive act of the will something which is intrinsically disorder, and hence unworthy of the human person, even when the intention is to safeguard or promote individual, family, or social well-being."

As can be seen, this present investigation is even more negative than the previous one. From the historical point of view it is difficult to avoid the conclusion that *Humanae Vitae* has ignored in a systematic way the Council's broad lines of thought on marriage. Why, then, did the encyclical consider them to be already agreed upon? Why also did it want to disown them? It is clearly impossible to give an answer to such a question purely from the point of view of textual criticism.

Will documents one day—possibly within fifty years!—allow us to get nearer to an answer to these questions? Will it be possible to give an interpretation that does justice to the facts? While the canonists, the theologians, the priests wait, they must still help Catholics to live in a Christian way. The canonists, no doubt, will be the least disorientated. After centuries of toil they have become masters in *concordantia discordantium canonum*. Theologians will be able to put the two teachings side by side and, hopefully, eventually partially integrate them. Priests will follow the orders which their bishops have given them.

"The Council Must Be Quoted, but Quoted Correctly"

Possibly Delhaye's analysis is somewhat tiresome, but it is necessary if all the data required for forming an opinion—a concrete comparison of the respective texts, the doctrinal positions, the psychological positions—is to be at hand. Judging from the ingenious way in which he started his comparison and from the questions that he asks himself at the end, perhaps the Louvain scholar expects further development in the teaching in the future. He is not alone in this opinion. We shall see what real possibilities exist for this in another section.

Delhaye quoted the Council. His intention was to contrast *Humanae Vitae* with the Council, text by text. Did he succeed in his intentions? Certainly not everyone would agree with him, as, for example, Cardinal Pericles Felici who was secretary-general of the Council during the whole conciliar period, having previously been secretary of the Central Preparatory Commission.

It is Cardinal Felici himself who, although writing before Delhaye, seems to take up the discussion with him. In fact, comparisons were already being made on all sides and in a more fragmentary way, as we have seen, between the Council and the encyclical. It is Cardinal Felici who ends his work, *L'enciclica paolina "Humanae Vitae" e la costituzione "Gaudium et Spes"* in *L'Osservatore Romano* of September 7, 1968 with this statement which is at the same time an invitation: "The Council must be quoted, but quoted correctly." The cardinal's work, therefore, is an essay on how to quote the Council in such a way that the logical doctrinal continuity between it and *Humanae Vitae* is brought into evidence. Cardinal Felici observes:

Some maintain in an extremely superficial way that Paul VI's encyclical closed off the broad horizons opened by Vatican II and Pope John—oh, if Pope John could only rise from the grave and give an answer to all those foolish people who abuse his name and authority! Others have asserted that Vatican II did not deal with the specific issue at all. Others finally have said that the teaching of Paul VI is all to be found in Vatican II. I wrote on a previous occasion, interpreting a passage from the Council, "in order to understand what the Council has taught, an exegetical examination of the text will at times be necessary, seen in the context of the *iter* which its formulation underwent. It will also be necessary to be guided by the voice of the magisterium, which is the authentic interpreter of the decrees of the Council" (*Concilio si, Concilio no*, in *L'Osservatore Romano*, April 12, 1968).

The cardinal then passes on to describe the *iter* "of the formulation of the doctrine regarding so-called birth regulation"— "short notes," he says, "that we shall leave for the scholars to deepen."

The cardinal says:

Explicit mention is made on the matter in part two, chapter one of *Gaudium et Spes*. Various schemas and different studies preceded this constitution, from the time of the preparation for the Council. The first really proper Schema on the question was sent to the Fathers on July 3, 1964. It began with the words *Gaudium et Luctus* . . . in this first Schema it was stated that "such is the nature of married love that marriage of its nature is ordained to the bearing and education of offspring." As regards, then, the number of children, it was stated that the couple should not follow blind instinct but should fulfill their duty "with full, conscious responsibility, according to the gifts of God and the law of true love." They should form a judgment on the basis of pedagogical, economic, hygienic, family, public—that is, civil and ecclesiastical—requirements.

In the *Adnexa* the same concepts were more fully developed, but a further clarification was added to the effect that the judgment, as mentioned above, had to be formed "according to the doctrine proposed by the Church." Following the numerous interventions made by the Council Fathers, a new text was drawn up which was then distributed to the Fathers on May 28, 1965. It was a single text with the *Adnexa* included in large part.

On the subject of married fertility, the conciliar commission observed, "Although in each age parents have decided on the number of their children, the matter has become more urgent today since many new elements have entered into this decision. Various opinions have been brought forward in the aula. A great number of Fathers desire that parents, trusting in God's providence, give birth to as many children as God gives them by the workings of nature. But the great majority of the Fathers, in one way or another, hold the opinion of so-called responsible parenthood. Only a few—and two of these with hesitation—exclude the use of contraceptive methods in the gravest cases." The commission had followed on the whole these two opinions shared by so many of the Fathers.

With regard to responsible parenthood, it recalled the words of Pius XII to the Italian obstetricians (October 29, 1951), where "birth regulation" is permitted—but distinct from the so-called *contrôle des naissances*—on medical, eugenic, and social grounds. The text (of the new Schema) clearly states that parents' consciences must be guided by objective laws and by the demands of values of another order than the human. The words used (*conscientia lege Dei recte informata*) clearly highlight the fact that dishonest means are prohibited.

The mind of the commission was clear, and the recalling of the doctrine of Pius XII on a point that could have given rise to misunderstanding—responsible parenthood—was very timely. The text, then translated into various modern languages, faithfully expressed the "mind" of the commission. Moreover, in the paragraph treating of the harmony that should exist between married love and the responsible transmission of life, a very important statement was introduced: "The moral nature of a course of action when harmonizing married love with the responsible transmission of life, depends not only on sincere, cognizant motives, but also on objective criteria, based on the very dignity of the human person. In this way, the whole meaning of reciprocal giving and human procreation in the context of true love will be retained. If brought up with these principles, the sons of the Church, when regulating births, will not take paths criticized by the magisterium."

At the beginning of the fourth session, the discussion on the prepared text took place in the aula. Many Fathers requested that it be clarified even further in order to avoid all hint of subjectivism in so delicate a matter. In the new text that was drawn up, even though it was restated that the judgment of the size of the individual family in the final analysis belonged to the parents, it was also unequivocally clarified that the couple could not proceed arbitrarily but should follow their consciences "illuminated by the same divine law, docile toward the magisterium of the Church which interprets it authentically under the light of the gospel." It is the first time that express mention is made of the magisterium of the Church which interprets the divine law. There was already, however, an indication of it in the *Adnexa* mentioned above.

In the voting that followed on the Schema, numerous modi were put forward. Still further precision of phrase was being demanded. Two Fathers frankly felt the text to be "theologically immature, equivocal, and silent on some essential matters."

The commission replied that it was not its task to solve each and every problem which could have arisen on the matter, all the more since the Pope had established a certain ad hoc commission for this purpose. Nonetheless, the text clearly brought into light the sacred character of marriage, of love (and that in harmony with the encyclical of Pius XI: *Casti Connubii*), and of fertility, not to mention also the many duties and rights inherent in marriage and family life. After the insertion of the accepted modi into the emended text that had been developed earlier, the text was brought back. The expression "*conscientia ab ipsa lege divina illuminando,*" however, was replaced with another more precise expression, "*conscientia ipsi legi divini conformanda.*" In the next paragraph that dealt, as stated above, with the harmony between married love and the responsible transmission of human life, some very valuable expressions were introduced.

The objective criteria determining the morality of intercourse had to be taken from the nature of the person and from the *nature of the acts* of the same person—in the previous text no mention had been made of these acts. The full meaning of giving and procreation could not be understood unless by a sincere esteem for married chastity. For the sons of the Church . . . it was not lawful—and not just advised against as the previous text may have suggested—to take paths criticized by the magisterium in interpreting the divine law—these last words were lacking in the previous text.

Finally, after some Fathers had expressed their concern that the text was open to interpretation in a way differing from the teaching of the previous magisterium, to avoid any further doubt, a note was added in the text which gave the principal proceedings of the previous magisterium. They are the encyclicals of Pius XI, *Casti Connubii,* the allocution of Pius XII to the obstetricians of October 29, 1951, and the speech of Paul VI to the cardinals of June 23, 1964. In the same note it was mentioned that Paul VI had established a special commission "so that after it had finished its work, the Sovereign Pontiff could give his judgment." Thus the text passed into the constitution, approved and promulgated by the Council on December 7, 1965.

Having thus outlined the *iter* of the Council's treatment of the theme, Cardinal Felici continues by showing that there is no discrepancy between the outlook adopted by the Council and that of the encyclical:

It is evident from this brief examination that the Council not only gave an indication of the direction which the Pauline decision would eventually take but also enunciated the principles which inspired it. The continual work of clarification, documentation, and reevaluation of the magisterium in its interpretation of the divine law, all bear unequivocal witness to it. Finally, the Council referred the solution of certain questions to the Holy Father. The supreme personal magisterium bestowed on him by Christ himself was restated and stressed by the Council, especially in the dogmatic Constitution *Lumen Gentium.*

It is very puzzling, therefore, to hear phrases like the following, especially when coming from the lips of responsible people: "The Pope has decided by himself" (after all, he may do so!); "The Pope has gone against the Council"; "The Pope has not taken account of the opinion of the people of God"; and other statements, even less respectful.

As regards the commission itself, of which mention is made in the conciliar document, its sole purpose was to provide information and the elements on which a judgment could be based. This it did. It was up to the Pope then, and only the Pope, to decide. . . . The Pope decided in line with the Council's teaching after having consulted many other qualified, competent persons and bodies, as is stated in the encyclical. Paul VI has been extremely respectful—I would even say scrupulously respectful—toward all. Respect, however, could neither deprive him of that authority which belongs only to him nor keep him from feeling that responsibility, falling on his shoulders, of Supreme Pastor of the Church. Were anyone to hold the opposite opinion, he would immediately be falling into a practical if not theoretical conciliarism. This conciliarism was once again condemned by Vatican Council II when it reaffirmed the supreme personal prerogatives of the Pope.

In this way, the cardinal concluded that there was a perfect concordance between the thought of the Council and that of the "Pauline encyclical." At the end he briefly alluded to the fact that the Council had asked the Pope for the "solution to certain questions." Evidently the certain questions were those questions, or better still, that question, resolved and decided on by the encyclical. In the cardinal's examination not a word is mentioned of the famous incidents of the "pontifical modi"; that is, the corrections which the Pope personally asked to have introduced in the conciliar text. The whole history of it is long and complex. In any case, Delhaye had already spoken of it in his examination of the texts. It was an examination which came to rather different conclusions from those arrived at by Felici. Was it based on a "bad quoting" of the Council? We leave it to the reader to compare and contrast the procedure of Delhaye with that of Felici.

In the meantime, there took place at Amsterdam, on September 18–19, 1968, a convention of twenty European theologians who discussed *Humanae Vitae*. At the end of their convention they issued a bulletin stating their conclusions (the same as quoted in the chapter on theologians). In this bulletin, among other things, it was stated: "We must notice with concern that the encyclical *Humanae Vitae* does not respond to the hopes that the pastoral constitution *Gaudium et Spes* had given rise to."

Was the theologians' concern caused by the fact that the encyclical shows no evolution of the thought of the Council? Was it, rather, the lack of interest which it shows in the present theological development on the issue? Or was this concern evoked by the fear that repeated interventions of teaching authority can slow down and even dry up theological study? Possibly it was all these together. It is well illustrated by a fact which occurred a few days after the proclamation of the Credo on June 30. A commentator on Vatican Radio was heard to state flatly: "We have just witnessed a historic half hour. The Holy Father with this discourse has put an end to the confusion that has been reigning for 5 or 6 years by cutting short all useless theological discussion."

The European theologians' concern lead Cardinal Felici to return in greater detail to the same theme he had already dealt with on September 7. This he did on October 10, once again in *L'Osservatore Romano* under the general heading of "From the Pastoral Constitution *Gaudium et Spes* to the Pauline Encyclical *Humanae Vitae*." His article is entitled, significantly, "Continuity, Coherence, and Solidarity of Doctrine." Felici clearly states that he wishes to reply to the Amsterdam theologians and to develop more fully—that is, by more fully quoting the texts of the various conciliar documents—his previous article. There seem to be no new arguments put forward in this article. His basic theme is still that the principles established in the whole conciliar *iter* are the ones which *Humanae Vitae* has simply reconfirmed. The Pope had given a solution in only one particular instance, that dealing with contraceptives. The cardinal sums up his examination at the end of the article where he lists the principles that resulted from the conciliar discussion and compares them with the thought of *Humanae Vitae*:

On the question of fertility in marriage the *iter* of the constitution *Gaudium et Spes* clearly shows that the following principles have constantly been affirmed:
1. Marriage and married love tend of their nature toward procreation and to the education of offspring who are the greatest gift of God and the highest fulfillment in the union of marriage.
2. It is the couple's conscience that must make the final decision as to the number of offspring.
3. The couple's conscience must be formed according to the objective norm of morality.
4. In the moral evaluation of the act of procreation the nature of the act itself as well as its intrinsic finalities must be kept in mind.
5. The objective norm of morality is constituted by the law of God. The magisterium of the Church, at the head of which Christ places the Sovereign Pontiff, is the authentic interpreter of this law.
6. On this matter the magisterium of the Church is expounded in the principal documents of Pius XI, Pius XII, and Paul VI.

These are precisely the principles which the encyclical *Humanae Vitae* restates. Not only, then, does the encyclical not delude the hopes that *Gaudium et Spes* inspired; it is also in perfect agreement with the doctrine expounded in the constitution. This doctrine has been authentically clarified and deepened by the Sovereign Pontiff who has followed the majority votes and desires of the Council Fathers.

The theologians, then, should not feel themselves "deluded." As for the "majority votes and desires of the Council Fathers," the history of the issue may be read in Jan Grootaer's essay *Il Concilio di fronte ai problemi del matrimonio e della famiglia,* in the volume *Diritti del sesso e matrimonio,* Milan, 1968, especially pages 146 to 167.

It will be observed in passing that Delhaye's and Felici's respective methods differ in no small way. Possibly the differences in the conclusions arise from this fact.

An Unavoidable Problem

Still, there are other theologians who, even though following Felici's method rather than Delhaye's, arrive at conclusions which are not exactly those of Felici. One example is the noted moral theologian Bernard Häring, well-known for his numerous works which have profoundly renewed the teaching of moral theology in the past few years.

Häring wrote an extremely clear and direct article in the American periodical *Commonweal* of September 6, 1968. In it the theologian gives proof of a faithfulness and clarity that is truly enviable in expressing his opinion. Among other things he makes a general observation on the method and on the themes of the Council:

Vatican Council II, following scientific developments in the field of moral theology, strongly developed the issue of responsible parenthood. There it is clear that birth control is evaluated quite differently in different circumstances. It is one thing if it is practiced as the result of a conscientious decision that new life cannot responsibly be brought into being here and now; it is quite another if it is a simple rejection of the parental vocation. Since Pope Paul makes the analysis of the act his starting point, this fundamental distinction does not appear. The evil seems to consist exclusively, or at least principally, in the violation of sacred biological functions. The encyclical also fails to see that abortion is a much greater problem than the methods of birth control. In the encyclical, abortion is rejected only in passing; the Council put its principal emphasis on a condemnation of abortion. So the encyclical, from a pedagogical standpoint, is rather confusing.

Going into greater detail in his comparison, Häring quotes a biblical text that, as he observes, had often been quoted in previous years and was even referred to in the Papal Commission; it is in the text of 1 Corinthians 7:1–5: "The husband must give the wife what is due to her, and the wife must give the husband his due. . . . Do not deny yourselves to one another, except when you agree upon a temporary abstinence in order to devote yourselves to prayer." Häring relates this sole biblical text (not quoted by the encyclical) which has the least connection with the problem to the psychological phenomenon of periodic continence that couples are forced to undergo over a long period. He continues:

Relying on this psychological knowledge, and following Paul's line of thinking in 1 Corinthians 7, the Council gave this warning: "Where the intimacy of married life is broken off, it is not rare for its faithfulness to be imperiled and its quality of fruitfulness ruined. For then the upbringing of children and the courage to accept new ones are both endangered" (*Constitution on the Church in the Modern World*, No. 51). The failure of the encyclical to use either of these texts is indeed one of its gravest defects.

The moral theologian then finally asks himself what he calls an "unavoidable question": "Can the encyclical *Humanae Vitae* be reconciled with the teaching of Vatican II?" Häring gives his reply, not without mentioning his own personal position, highly significant for a theologian who is among the most important and creative of our time. He says:

This is a particularly acute question for the present writer. In January of 1967 I received, by word of mouth, a very precise warning from the Holy Office because of what I had said in an interview for *La Rocca*, an Italian Catholic magazine. The remark which was found objectionable was my statement that the awaited statement of the Pope would obviously have to be based on the criteria which had been worked out in the Council document *The Church in the Modern World*, and could not be a simple return to *Casti Connubii*.

I was instructed that this was theologically incorrect: the Pope was not bound by the Council document. Later, for my further instruction, I received two memoranda (*monita*) of Vatican theologians; one of them said that the two documents, *Casti Connubii* and the Council document (*The Church in the Modern World*), could not be set in opposition to each other—it was simply a matter of one complementing the other. The other memorandum (*monitum*) instructed me that the doctrine in this matter was to be drawn from the encyclical (*Casti Connubii*), and that the Council constitution was only "pastoral." This remark disregarded Pope John XXIII's opening speech of the Council in which he said that the teaching office of the Church was in its entirety pastoral.

The two facts, which Häring does not comment on, clearly give a better idea of the issue than would a long article. Häring, in any case, immediately follows with his personal opinion:

In my opinion it is harder to reconcile *Humanae Vitae* with the Council constitution on *The Church in the Modern World* than it is to reconcile the *Declaration on Religious Freedom* with the *Syllabus* of Pius IX, or at least no less difficult. This assertion is based especially on the fact (1) that the question just mentioned from the Council constitution and the text of 1 Corinthians 7 are simply not taken seriously, (2) that the conception of natural law of the whole pastoral constitution of the Council has simply not been incorporated into *Humanae Vitae*, and (3) that the criteria worked out in the constitution for the acceptability of methods of birth control are not even mentioned, and simply replaced by biological "laws."

Häring then advances some practical conclusions regarding the actual course of action which Catholics, priests and theologians, should take. Like a good moralist, he has become aware that here, too, the problem has become just as "unavoidable."

The problem is even unavoidable for many other Christians; for example, for the group that heads *La Lettre* in Paris. In the November 1968 issue of this periodical, Jacques Chatagner, in the name of the group, after calling the speech and the Credo of June 30 "an act of the magisterium that clearly contradicts the conciliar spirit," goes on to say that

the second act of the magisterium which contradicts this spirit is the promulgation of *Humanae Vitae*. It is difficult, to say the least, to find in the text of the encyclical the same theology which inspired the

138

authors of Vatican II on this issue. In fact, as our friends from *La Vie Nouvelle* note, "The encyclical poses the question in terms of the constitution *Gaudium et Spes* and answers it in terms of a preconciliar theology." In any case, it is impossible not to see in *Humanae Vitae* a typical example of what Vatican II seemed to have by now rejected.

Marie-Claude Betbeder in turn, in the October 1968 issue of *La Lettre,* treating the "Meaning of the Present Evolution of the Church," takes up our theme:

Even if it makes an effort not to directly contradict the Council texts, the encyclical all the same returns to the religious world before John XXIII. It never stops speaking of the moral order but not once is the gospel quoted on it. It is a world of unchanging laws and rigid prohibitions somehow lacking the breath of life. So many steps backward! The genuineness of Paul VI's intentions is beyond question. He is conditioned, however, right to his innermost self by a Roman *appareil* more efficient than even the walls of a prison for cutting a man off from others. In the face of the upheavals that Vatican II provoked in the Church, fear and incomprehension have prevailed over trust. The Church is bending back on itself and is beginning to close itself up in its ivory tower. We even feel it in the way we have been told to bow our heads to it.

Betbeder then quotes the words with which Msgr. Lambruschini presented the encyclical to the press: "A Catholic who does not understand the reasoning of the papal declaration . . . cannot demand the right to challenge the decision. On the contrary, he must humbly accept it."

There can be no doubt that whoever studies the encyclical in the light of the Council and all the theological discussion of the past few years, and whoever even studies it to observe its remoteness from today's concerns and even its "involution," does so "humbly." Humility is, in fact, the scholar's first virtue. Humility of itself, however, cannot convince him that *Humanae Vitae* is clearly following the guidelines of the Council. A conclusion of this kind can only be the fruit of an accurate, scientific examination. That is not all; a comparison of the encyclical's teaching with the real life of believers and all men of goodwill will also be necessary. The future of the problem that *Humanae*

Vitae has tackled cannot be kept simply within the framework of an evolution of the *iter* of the Council documents. As for all the great problems of mankind, its future is inscribed in the future of humanity itself.

Chapter 4   A Grave Question for Ecumenism

The most profound laws of life

In consonance with scripture and the gospel

A danger for ecumenism?

Speaking the same language

The language of theology and of the Bible

Buttress the edifice of ecclesiastical authority or defend
conscience?

The authority of the magisterium and that of conscience:
an irremediable dissension?

All in search of the same truth but along different paths

Natural law and sexuality: Manichaeism or the law of the
gospel?

Let us thank the Bishop of Rome

Following a custom introduced by Pope John XXIII, *Humanae Vitae* is addressed to "all men of goodwill" as well as to the hierarchy and those Catholics "who are in peace and communion with the Apostolic See." Was the purpose of this gesture by Paul VI to extend his magisterium also to non-Catholics; that is, to the other Christian churches or to the Jews or to nonbelievers in general? Certainly he had no intention of imposing a teaching on them and much less of claiming a right to teach those who do not accept the authority of the Catholic magisterium. The fact that the encyclical was addressed to all men of goodwill more likely means that it intends addressing all men on the statements contained in No. 18 of the text. This paragraph, in the official Italian translation, has the heading "The Church as Guarantor of Authentic Human Values."

The Most Profound Laws of Life

The fundamental problem of the encyclical is seen by the encyclical itself on two levels: "to proclaim . . . all the moral law, both *natural* and *evangelical*" (No. 18). It is a problem, therefore, which affects all those who accept and believe in the moral, evangelical law, and in a more general sense, those who follow the dictates of the natural moral law. Seen in this light, the encyclical can be of interest to non-Catholics or even non-Christians to the extent that they accept a magisterium on this law or according to the doctrinal principles which guide them in their interpretation of it. It is along these lines that Louis Salleron, in *Le Monde* of August 6, 1968, after having discussed the reactions of Catholics, especially of theologians, asks the question of Protestants and nonbelievers:

There is still the world—the world of Protestants and nonbelievers. This world is not obliged to obey the Pope and hence is free to reject the encyclical. It seems probable, however, that all those who reflect on the problems of humanity and its future, will be led to ask what the significance of the papal teaching is, seeing that, all things considered, this teaching is characteristic of the highest humanism. By affirming together the two principles that man must subject himself to the laws of life and that he must subject these in turn to himself by means of his reason and his will, the encyclical is affirming man's

142

preeminence over nature and is making an absolute act of faith in his capacity to take on his own future. Science has shown itself powerless up to now in adequately explaining population trends, and the demographic explosion gives cause for concern. Lewis Mumford sees it as a provision against the aftermaths of the atomic bomb! No doubt the phenomenon of sterility is preferable to that of the bomb. But who knows what collective traumas we shall be menaced by?

On the other hand, who knows how humanity even now will be able to find a solution to the problems of China and Biafra or those of India and Latin America? The Pope is clearly worried about the biological manipulations that tomorrow's leviathan will have in store for us. It is the sacredness of life which he wants to defend. *Humanae Vitae,* as its title itself indicates, is an encyclical about the most profound laws of human life. Paradoxically, in order to indicate the guidelines for a universal, demographic regulation, the Pope simply reaffirms the right to life and love. He does it, however, by referring to the highest concept of life and love.

The reactions of non-Catholics and non-Christians have centered around these two issues of safeguarding the basic laws of life and fidelity to the divine evangelical law. On both counts the reactions have been ones of either complete agreement, critical agreement, or complete disagreement. Generally the full agreement results precisely from a desire to defend the laws and basic values of human life.

The Protestant Dr. Siegfried Ernst, a councillor of the Commune of Ulm and a lector of the Protestant ecclesiastical community (Lutheran) sent the Pope a letter, also in the name of four other Protestant doctors, in which he expresses his profound gratitude to Paul VI for the clear and courageous stand adopted by him. He stresses

the great moral value of this document for the present time which is so amenable to a decline in moral standards. The Holy Father must not become too concerned over the numerous negative reactions which clearly show that many are not really interested at all in the situation in developing countries, but just want to justify their own attitude and decide on their own idea of sin. None of these voices raised in criticism have taken into consideration the repercussions that contraceptive methods can have on the spiritual life of the human person and on his relationship with God. Those who think only in scientific categories show a certain amount of infantilism. . . .

The clear position that the Holy Father has adopted is leading many of the faithful to a new awareness of the vital necessity of fighting against what is a systematic destruction of the divine ordering of marriage and the family. For many non-Catholics the Pope's document is a clear testimony of the Lord's promise, given to Peter, that the gates of hell will not prevail against the Church. Paul VI's encyclical is no doubt a great "provocation." People should understand, however, that it is not to be seen as a harsh law but rather as a most eminent occasion for them to acquire freedom and a call to the highest creative activity.

There is an evident concern here that the values of life, procreation, and love be saved and, as well, be preserved in line with God's design. This same idea recurs in a letter sent to the Pope through the late Cardinal Augustine Bea from the Lutheran association *Bund für evangelisch-katholische Wiedervereinigung* ("For the Reunification of Protestants with Catholics"). As well as giving a "vote of thanks for the clear and helpful guidelines indicated by the encyclical" it says: "We pray that the consciences of all Christians be illuminated in order to understand that we humans are not the masters but the servants of the divine mystery of both the earthly and the eternal life we have received from the hand of God."

The Anglican Dr. F. King from Middlesex and now living in Africa, praises "the courageous and wise teaching of the encyclical, which summons man to respond with genuine action."

In the Hindu world it is interesting to note the full adhesion given by the grandson of Gandhi, Rajmoham Gandhi, who in the Indian weekly *Himmat* of August 1968 states:

There is another man who has shown courage, and this man is Pope Paul VI. When the pontifical encyclical which confirms the disapproval of any means of artificial contraception was presented to the journalists by Msgr. Lambruschini, the latter said: "The Holy Father's decision, which makes no concession to popularity, is a great act of courage and perfect serenity." Msgr. Lambruschini is right. Placing conscience above an immediate popularity among men, the Pope has given an example to both politicians and churchmen. Moreover, the Pope's point of view may not be as unpopular as some loud voices expressing their opposition are trying to suggest. A certain number of people who do not follow the directives imparted by the Pope are nevertheless conscious of the fact that these directives are right. It may well be that they feel a sense of guilt in not following them, but quite a few prefer an honest sense of guilt to the uncertainty of a moral desert without norms. In an epoch in which ambiguity constitutes an art, in which a straightforward line is considered with suspicion, where black and white are always unpleasant and the shades of gray always beautiful, in which ambiguity is elegant and precision something that is heavy, Paul VI has traced a clear and precise line. Although it is intended for the guidance of the Catholics, his encyclical will reward anyone who reads it without prejudice.

Next, a Muslim living in France, Mr. Mohammed Chérif Zeghoudi, wrote to the cardinal Secretary of State in September 1968:

After Paul VI's strong stand on the birth-control issue, I feel bound to write to you and declare that I accept this supreme decision with profound respect and humility. I have wanted to tell you how inwardly happy I, a believer of the Islam religion, am for this stand which has been adopted and also that I am now honored to interpret the concept of the marriage bond in the sense intended by His Holiness.

This complete acceptance on the part of Hindu and Muslim believers is very interesting, not least because of the ease with which it can be noticed that these views reflect ideas on marriage, divine providence, and trust in God which are typical of these religions and which are felt to have been almost reechoed in the voice of the Christian magisterium.

Among the Protestant reactions, almost all of which have been rather critical and have expressed disappointment, the adhesion of Bishop Fred Corson, former president of the World Methodist Council, is important. He tells Paul VI: "We are grateful for your courage and your resistance to every conformist compromise between spirit and matter. You remind the world of its religious, moral, and doctrinal heritage."

Bishop Corson's declaration is all the more interesting because the Protestant criticism and disagreement is based above all on the notion of "natural law," a notion which is foreign to Reformed thinking. Also, as a result of these doctrinal tenets, the division between spirit and matter in sexual matters is not

145

nearly so pronounced in more recent Protestant thought as it was in the past.

In Consonance with Scripture and the Gospel

One sector of the non-Catholic world which deserves careful attention for the adhesion it has given to the encyclical is that of the Eastern Orthodox Churches. The reactions are not numerous but yet significant because they highlight an outlook typical of the Eastern Church. The ecumenical review *Irénikon,* No. 3, of 1968 observes that

the Orthodox adopt this position on account of the evangelical principle of Christian ascesis so dear to them, while recognizing at the same time the legitimacy of the *oikonomia* [the historical intervention of divine salvation—EDITOR], which permits a certain amount of attenuation of the general law.

Already during the World Assembly of the Ecumenical Council of Churches held at Uppsala on July 4–20, the Metropolitan Nikidim of Leningrad was found in an interview to be vigorously in opposition to birth limitation and birth control.

The first position to be stated in the Orthodox world, as early as July 29, 1968, was that of the Greek Orthodox Church, which declared itself to be fully in favor of the encyclical. The Greek bishops state in a letter to their people that the reason for their attitude lies "in the national interest. A greater number of children is necessary." The letter makes no reference to any ethical and pastoral considerations, and was hence bitterly criticized by many priests and members of the Greek Orthodox Church. This sole reaction of an entire "autocephalous"—that is, independent—Church is all the more significant since it was the Greek Church which showed so much concern over Patriarch Athenagoras I's rapprochement with Rome. On the other hand, the bitter reactions of theologians, priests, and laity on this issue were not motivated so much by concurrence with the Catholic magisterium on this issue but rather because the letter seemed too orientated around patriotic and political motives. In any case, there are no reasons in the Greek Church's letter for qualifying this Church's concurrence as based on an Orthodox understanding of the moral law, the Church, and authority.

146

All this, however, is also contained in the short interventions of the patriarch of Constantinople, Athenagoras I. Very close to Paul VI and committed to the search for union and comprehension between the Eastern and Western Churches, his declarations are stamped with this spirit as well as the Orthodox tradition. Replying to Paul VI's message on the anniversary of his visit to Istanbul, Athenagoras states: "We remain close to you, especially in these last few days during which you did well to publish the encyclical *Humanae Vitae*. We are completely in agreement with you and we invoke the full assistance of God to allow your mission in the world to continue."

A few days later in a statement to the agency *France-Presse*, Athenagoras said: "I am completely in agreement with the Pope. Paul VI could not have expressed himself in any other way. The interests and the survival of the family and of entire nations are at stake."

Associated Press reported another statement of the patriarch in which the basic reason for his agreement with the encyclical is brought out more clearly:

The Pope's encyclical is coherent with the doctrine of the Bible. All the religious books, including the Bible and the Koran, favor the safeguarding of the family, and in his encyclical the Pope has followed the line laid down in the Bible. It was not possible to expect that a different position might be taken.

Athenagoras stated as well that preparations were under way for a conference of the Holy Synod of all the Orthodox Churches of the world, during the course of which the encyclical could be examined. Such a conference is a dream very close to Athenagoras' heart because it would create a certain unity between all the autocephalous Orthodox Churches. It has been indicated by some, however, that the introduction of an examination of *Humanae Vitae* into the conference proceedings could prejudice the serenity of the mutual understanding and result of the conference.

Almost as if he had foreseen this difficulty, which is also present in other ecumenical circles as we shall see later, Athenagoras declared: "The Pope had to issue that encyclical. He has to follow the gospel. I do not believe that this encyclical will harm the ecumenical movement. It will, rather, help to bring the different faiths even closer together." After stating that there already exists a rapprochement if not a union between the Orthodox and Catholic Churches (he gives a case of this in the possibility of an Orthodox participating in a liturgy in a Catholic Church, and vice versa for a Catholic), Athenagoras expresses the hope that a similar agreement be found with all the other Churches and concludes: "The Pope is learned, wise, and diplomatic: he is a pastor. I have read his sermons and I see it in this encyclical. He is keeping his Church united and is bringing about a religious revolution." These statements by Athenagoras have clarified two points: in the eyes of the patriarch the encyclical is also a move by the Pope to keep the Church united; and it is neither a hardening of positions nor a step backward, since the Pope "is bringing about a revolution."

A Danger for Ecumenism?

In many sectors of the ecumenical world the fear has been voiced that a unilateral decision made on the Catholic side without consulting the feeling of the other Churches, may be equivalent to a totalitarian affirmation that only the Roman Catholic Church possesses the teaching in its fullness. This would be tantamount to breaking off the relationship at the very moment when the efforts at interconfessional dialogue are being stepped up.

It is a particularly obvious fact that the World Assembly of the Ecumenical Council of Churches held at Uppsala closed on July 24, 1968 and on July 25 the Pope signed the encyclical which was then released on July 29. Fr. Tucci had just spoken at Uppsala in a tone and outlook so open on the Catholic side that it gave rise to a wide consensus and to no small amount of emotion.

The person most qualified to give the tone of the reply on behalf of the non-Catholic Churches—with a reservation for the Orthodox, as we have seen, though they are still in the World Council—was certainly the pastor Dr. Eugene Carson Blake, general secretary of the World Council of Churches. Dr. Blake stated from Geneva, where the World Council of Churches has its headquarters:

148

I regret that the search begun in 1964 has been cut short so quickly, notwithstanding a long and minute study. Some Churches, members of the World Council of Churches, and particularly some Orthodox theologians, have adopted a position very close to that taken up by Paul VI. But it is nevertheless disappointing for numerous Christians in all the member Churches of the World Council, just as it is for numerous Roman Catholics, that one cannot see any progress toward an early solution of this problem of conscience. After reading the principal passages of the encyclical, my personal reaction is that one will have to make a more complete examination of the distinction between artificial and natural methods of birth control. It would also seem that the Roman Catholic position, such as has once again been expressed, is too dependent on an old conception of natural law for it to have any persuasive effect on twentieth-century man.

Carson Blake, then, presents the objections of the greater part of the Churches belonging to the World Council, and makes mention as well of his own private objections which happen to coincide with those of almost all the theologians of the Reformed Churches.

The Information Office of the Protestant Federation of France, in its July 30, 1968 bulletin, made the following comment:

The encyclical has appeared not long after the publication of what has been called "the Pope's Credo" which had already provoked a certain amount of astonishment in non-Catholic spheres. The encyclical of July 29 was no less provocative. . . . All the well-known Protestant figures who were consulted made no show of hiding their surprise at this text which no doubt merits attentive reading but which seems to be opposed to the view which the overwhelming majority of Protestant Churches and numerous Orthodox theologians have expressed on more than one occasion. The astonishment has been increased by the fact that the document of Session VI of the Fourth General Assembly of the World Council at Uppsala took up a position totally opposed to that adopted by the encyclical.

While it is true that the standpoint of the encyclical has not been accepted by the larger number of the Churches, it is not exactly true, however, to say that it has not been accepted by many Orthodox theologians. The same applies to the statement that the definitive Uppsala text is completely opposed to the

149

encyclical. It is true that the positions are notably distant from each other, but there still exists some room for discussion.

The blow which the encyclical delivered to the Reformed world was particularly felt at the conference of the Anglican Communion at Lambeth Palace, London. At that very time the Anglican Communion—the union of all the Anglican Churches —was holding its important conference. One of the most alive to date, it was open to all today's world problems owing to the presence of some new, autonomous Anglican Churches situated in the Third World as, for example, the Anglican Church of India and the Anglican Church of Africa. The Anglican Church has long been aware of the problem which the encyclical had faced. It has studied the problem at great length and in great depth. Already in the 1930 Lambeth Conference it had taken up a position in favor of limiting births. Several months later—December 31—there appeared Pius XI's encyclical, *Casti Connubii*, which strongly condemned the solution proposed at Lambeth and, what is more, left a very unpleasant impression on the conference.

A certain number of Catholic theologians considered this encyclical to be an *ex cathedra* document, given its solemn tone. The commentaries on the present encyclical—for example, the "unofficial" one of Msgr. Lambruschini—exclude the possibility that *Humanae Vitae* be interpreted in this way. It was an astonishing fact that the opening of the Lambeth Conference coincided with the day the encyclical was signed. It is all the more disquieting since Msgr. Willebrands of the Roman Secretariat for Unity had come to Lambeth as the bearer of Paul VI's message which he read before the assembly on July 27. The text of the encyclical was brought to the assembly's knowledge the following day. The ecumenical news commentator of *Irénikon*, No. 3, 1968 noted with regard to this fact:

The various different commissions which were created before and after the Council to study this issue certainly spared no effort in devoting all their care and attention to the work. There seems to have been less care taken, however, over the choice of the date for the encyclical's promulgation, which unfortunately coincided exactly with the Lambeth Conference.

On July 31, the Archbishop of Canterbury himself, Dr. Michael Ramsey, made a declaration which was then published on August 2, 1968 by the *Church Times.* Dr. Ramsey says:

I certainly have not yet had the chance of making a really detailed study of this important encyclical issued by the Pope. But I can already say that the moral teaching it contains about the "artificial" means of birth control is very different from that given by the Anglican Communion. The judgment of the Anglican Communion was adopted by the Lambeth Conference of 1958 and is expressed in Resolution No. 115. This resolution is based on the doctrinal position explained in the report of the Commission for the Family in Present-day Society, and can be summarized as follows: the parents have the serious responsibility of deciding the number of their children and the intervals at which they are to be born. Numerous elements must be taken into consideration before this decision can be made. The means to be adopted for limiting the number of children in a family is a matter for the conscience of each married couple. The use of "artificial" means of birth control is not excluded.

It seems to me that the changes which have occurred in human society and in the world population since 1958, as well as in the means of birth control themselves, strengthen rather than weaken the arguments and the conclusions of the Lambeth Conference of 1958.

It was only logical for the conference to discuss the encyclical. This was done by the 460 Anglican bishops under the form of a resolution presented by the bishop of Central Brazil, Rev. Edmund Knox Sherill. The resolution presented to the assembly stated:

The bishops representing the Anglican Communion, assembled in plenary conference, render homage to the Pope's profound preoccupation with the institution of marriage and the integrity of married life. Nevertheless, the conference was not able to agree with the Pope's conclusion according to which all the methods for the control of conception, with the exception of abstinence or recourse to the periods of infecundity, are contrary to the order established by God.

They therefore reaffirm the doctrine about marriage which was proposed by the conference in 1958:

1. The idea of the human family has its roots in God, and consequently all the problems of sexual relations, of procreation and the organization of family life must be consciously and directly linked to the creative, redeeming, and sanctifying power of God.

151

2. Marriage is a vocation to sanctity by means of which men and woman participate in love and in the creative design of God. The sins of gratification and sensuality, which arise from egoism and a refusal to accept marriage as a divine vocation, destroy the true nature and the profundity of marriage, as well as the legitimacy and the equilibrium of the relations between men and women. Christians must always remember that sexual love is neither an end in itself nor a means of pleasure, and that self-discipline and control are essential conditions of the responsible liberty of marriage and family planning.

3. God has everywhere left the responsibility of deciding the number of children and the frequency of their birth to the conscience of the parents. This responsible parenthood, based on the acceptance of all the duties of marriage, requires an intelligent utilization of all the resources and possibilities of the family, as well as reflection about the variable needs of the population and the problems of society, and also about the needs of future generations.

The bishops participating at the conference then voted, after the discussion on the motion relating directly to the doctrine on birth control and indirectly to the teaching contained in the papal encyclical. The motion states:

This conference has taken note of the papal encyclical letter *Humanae Vitae* recently issued by His Holiness Pope Paul VI. The conference records its appreciation of the Pope's deep concern for the institution of marriage and the integrity of married life.

Nevertheless, the conference finds itself unable to agree with the Pope's conclusion that all methods of conception control other than abstinence from sexual intercourse or its confinement to the periods of infecundity are contrary to the "order established by God." It reaffirms the finds of the Lambeth Conference of 1958 contained in resolutions 112, 113, and 115, which are as follows:

"112. The conference records its profound conviction that the idea of the human family is rooted in the God-head and that consequently all problems of sex relations, the procreation of children, and the organization of family life must be related, consciously and directly, to the creative, redemptive, and sanctifying power of God.

"113. The conference affirms that marriage is a vocation to holiness, through which men and women may share in the love and creative purpose of God. The sins of self-indulgence and sensuality, born of selfishness and a refusal to accept marriage as a divine vocation, destroy its true nature and depth and the right fullness and balance of the relationship between men and women. Christians

152

need always to remember that sexual love is neither an end in itself nor a means to self-gratification, and that self-discipline and restraint are essential conditions of the responsible freedom of marriage and family planning.

"115. The conference believes that the responsibility for deciding upon the number and frequency of children has been laid by God upon the consciences of parents everywhere. . . . Such responsible parenthood, built on obedience to all the duties of marriage, requires a wise stewardship of the resources and abilities of the family as well as a thoughtful consideration of the varying population needs and problems of society and the claims of future generations."

There is a noticeable absence of a detail in the Lambeth resolution which was present in Bishop Edmund Knox Sherill's motion: the statement on the positive value of contraceptive methods for couples' growth in maturity. This statement was excluded following a request for an amendment, and was seen as a desire for dialogue with the Catholic Church, though also a desire to remain firm on those positions which the Anglican Commission had already adopted. Moreover, in comparing the 1968 Lambeth resolution with that of ten years before, it is noticeable that the theology of the family and of sexual relationships has been deepened in an extremely sober way. Two important representatives of Anglican theology, both bishops, have written particularly important works in this field. One, the Archbishop of Canterbury himself, Dr. Ramsey, has written a book on the resurrection and the transfiguration of Christ in which he outlines his understanding of the body and its meaning in relation to the central mystery of the redemption of bodily reality through the resurrection. The other, the famous author of *Honest to God*, the bishop of Woolwich, J. Robinson, wrote a penetrating book on the theology of the body and sexuality in St. Paul.

The Anglicans, in any case, because of their previous activity in theological reflection and sociological study on this issue, felt very strongly the shock which the encyclical produced. The Canadian Anglican Bishop Ralph Dean declared: "The Anglicans are not surprised by the encyclical, but they are profoundly disappointed. I do not think that the encyclical makes the ecumenical dialogue more difficult, but I must admit that the difficulties in connection with mixed marriages have undoubtedly been increased."

If, in the Protestant world generally, there has been no desire to dramatize the difficulties the encyclical could create for ecumenical dialogue, it has nevertheless been predicted that the encyclical will experience a setback, especially on the very practical level of mixed marriages because of the moral problems and the conflicts of conscience which can develop from it. Pastor Albert Finet in *Réforme* of August 10–17, 1968 has given some reflections on the ecumenical problem which the encyclical has produced:

There is finally the ecumenical problem that the encyclical has provoked. How can we possibly work together and all go ahead at the same speed when there are divergencies over the conclusions we believe we can deduce from faith in Jesus Christ? Moreover, even before publishing this document Pope Paul VI had expressed a "Credo" which had put the same question to the Churches sprung from the Reformation. It is in no way certain that Taine's prediction that Protestantism will disappear but the Catholic Church will have become Protestant, will come true. It will certainly not happen in the foreseeable future. But I calculate this without any bitterness or sadness, and I feel that God . . . gets a certain amount of amusement from all our differences and looks *first of all* at the heart.

Even from the ecumenical point of view, then, criticisms are voiced but in the light of a hope that surpasses differences over interpretations of the law of the gospel. It is all seen from the point of view of providence in spite of all the undeniable perturbations that it has produced, above all in the Churches of the Reformation.

The same again is said but in a more concrete way by Dr. Richard M. Fagley of New York, who was previously connected with F.A.O. but is now consultant for the Church Commission on International Affairs and a well-known specialist in demographic questions relating to religious faith (cf. Richard M. Fagley, *Le religioni di fronte al problema di controllo delle nascite*, in *Diritti del sesso e matrimonio*, IDO-C-*Documentinuovi* 6, pp. 101–19, Milan, 1968). On August 2, 1968 he had a long interview with the Religious News Service (RNS) in the United States in New York. Among other things he said:

Although one may consider the Pope's encyclical on birth control to be a backward step, it may also have some positive consequences as a result of a more thorough interconfessional dialogue about the significance of marriage and about responsible parenthood. By virtue of the very fact that the Pope has assumed such an expressly conservative position there will have to be a discussion between the confessions, and valid positions will undoubtedly be attained. All the Churches find themselves faced with the task of examining with Christian responsibility those parts of the biblical principles which are no longer applicable to marriage; however, the problem is whether this must be done unconditionally on the basis of natural law as is claimed by the Roman Catholic Church. The fundamental weakness of the position taken up by the Pope lies in the request made to the state authorities to prevent transgressions against divine and natural law through contraceptive practices being used in marriage. Because this cell of human life must remain reserved to such decision as may be dictated by the conscience of the married couple, there must be no appeal for any help that may come from without the Church, but one must do everything possible to defend the domain of religious liberty and of conscience against all outside influence.

Dr. Richard Fagley, also a minister of the United Church of Christ in the U.S.A. (who has also written an important book: *The Demographic Explosion and Christians*), first shows the possibility of a positive outcome from the encyclical as a result of the dialogue desired and initiated by the Council. Dr. Fagley says:

There remains, however, the fact that the greater part of the scholars in this field, including a certain number of Roman Catholics, do not find the old arguments that insist on the procreative function of every single conjugal act very convincing. . . . In view of the fact that millions of married couples find that in certain circumstances family planning with the help of mutually acceptable scientific means becomes a duty to their conscience, a complete application of the principle upheld by the encyclical would violate the basic principles of religious liberty and the rights of man.

Fagley, then, has objections to the encyclical's teaching, both as a research-worker on demographic problems and as a Christian who holds the principle of freedom of conscience. However, he admits that the very objections which have been leveled at the encyclical result in a greater impetus being given to inter-faith dialogue.

Cardinal Ottaviani, who is not exactly of the same opinion, in an interview with the *Katholiek Nederlands Persbureau* of July 28, 1968 distinguishes between ecumenical dialogue and fidelity to the truth, which at least in this case is evidently the possession of the Catholic Church and, in part, of the Eastern Orthodox Church. The cardinal stated:

I do not think that ecumenism can suffer as a result of the encyclical. The Orthodox have the same idea as the Pope on birth regulation. The Anglicans are not very happy with the encyclical, but it must be remembered that the Pope of Rome cannot favor ecumenism at the expense of truth.

Speaking the Same Language

Possibly this last statement of Cardinal Ottaviani sheds some light on the real problem which the encyclical has produced in the ecumenical world. It is precisely the question of a common search for the truth, for not even among Catholics today is the attitude one of insisting on an "ecumenism of return to the Father's house." Fr. Tucci's speech at Uppsala is extremely indicative of this. Even if this Jesuit priest later stated in a press conference that it was not the official thought of the Catholic Church as such, it is still clear that he was not just speaking in the name of himself or of any small and very progressive ecumenical group.

The problem is also, however, one of finding a common language and yet this, evidently, is not even a starting point for reaching a possible solution. It is clear that these are not problems concerning ecumenical dialogue as such, but only methodological considerations prior to the actual dialogue.

Along these lines, too, the Anglican *Church Times* of August 7, 1968 states:

Paul VI has gone back to maximalism, and he has therefore aroused the old suspicions and long-standing contrasts. . . . If the encyclical had been published as little as five years ago, when the problem of birth control was only just beginning to be examined in the Catholic Church, there would have been a very limited reaction. . . . At this point, however, the exercise of the pontifical prerogatives as expressed in the encyclical will have a negative effect on the ecumenical movement.

Among these "prerogatives," which are some of the critical points of ecumenical dialogue, it is evident that "infallibility" and the papal magisterium are of primary importance, even if in this particular case authority has not been exercised on its highest level.

The Churches of the Reformation feel that the reaffirmation of these prerogatives on the Catholic side would be an obstacle to dialogue, and now a trend to their reaffirmation has been initiated by the encyclical. This has become all the more necessary due to the fact that the intrinsic value of the arguments contained in the encyclical leaves many Catholics perplexed. They accept the encyclical only because it is based on the authority of the papal magisterium.

This explains why *The Universe* of August 9, 1968, almost as if answering the *Church Times,* stated that *The Universe* affirms that

where the prerogative of infallibility is not exercised there is no certainty, and in the absence of certainty there is room for discussion. Our role in the Church is not a passive but an active one, and it becomes a basic imperative when the problems under examination are of universal importance as in the case of the means of contraception.

Here also, then, in spite of the seemingly greater insistence on infallibility, a possible area for discussion has been disclosed on a theme which directly interests all Churches seeing that it is not a specially confessional issue.

Other Protestants, instead, feel that Rome is tending to accept the Orthodox positions to some extent, rather than the Reformed positions—a kind of "ecumenical policy" useful in this happy moment when the gap is being bridged with the Eastern Orthodox. Thus the Protestant *Christ und Welt* of Stuttgart of August 7, 1968 writes:

From the ecumenical point of view the encyclical once again reveals the tendency during the present Pontificate to give preference to the theology of the Orthodox Church to the detriment of the Protestant

Church. It is possible to detect the Soviet demographic policy behind Metropolitan Nikodim's firm rejection of the Pill.

As well as this reference to "ecumenical policy," the Protestant newspaper makes two others, one to "ecclesiastical politics" and the other to "general policy":

Like the Pope's Credo, *Humanae Vitae* takes up a stand against the new "modernism" which is the Church's serious sickness today, according to Maritain who immediately sent a telegram of adhesion. . . . The French conservative groups have found strong support in Rome after the participation of many of the "progressive" priests in the May revolution. It is also possible that the trends toward conservatism can be explained, among other things, by the conviction that de Gaulle's victory signifies a world-scale turning to the right and that the Church will benefit by ensuring absolute values in our disorientated world.

The ecumenical problems which arise from differences in the language and in the judgments of the points involved in the encyclical's teaching clearly come to the fore in the communiqué of the Synodal Council of Wallis (Switzerland), as relayed by the *Schweizerische Evangelischer Pressedienst* of August 14, 1968. This communiqué not only touches on issues of doctrine and hence problems of interest in ecumenical dialogue but also clearly reveals its ecumenical concern over mixed marriages and the connected problems dealing with conscience and ecumenical relations. The communiqué states:

1. Even though the encyclical is written primarily for Roman Catholics, "all men of goodwill" are also mentioned as well as "state authorities." The encyclical recalls the unquestionable right of the ecclesiastical magisterium to interpret not only the law of the gospel but also the natural law. Consequently, its claims go beyond the boundaries of the Roman Catholic Church. Moreover, in a period of ecumenical dialogue, the encyclical affects, whether one likes it or not, even Christians of non-Roman Catholic confessions. First, it affects Reformed Christian husbands or wives who are in mixed marriages, and especially those who in the last few years took the risk of taking this path in the hope that these changes which everyone was demanding and which had already been mentioned by the Roman Catholic Church, would materialize. The encyclical's conse-

quences will now burden couples of differing faiths with yet another problem.

2. The Pope's encyclical certainly has the intention of promoting reciprocal esteem and love in the couple's sexual life. Since it leaves them no other choice, however, outside of submission or disobedience, it limits their responsibility to such an extent that the very realization of this noble aim is endangered. If the encyclical urges couples to dominate their instinctive impulses and passions, then it should also give them the possibility of exercising their domination of "technical means."

3. The meaning given to the natural law by Roman Catholic theology is always a debatable point. Once again, in the papal encyclical, the respective, radically different positions are clearly highlighted. Reformed Christians do not believe in the divine character of the natural law but rather in the power that the Christian exercises over nature. If man is called to "subject the earth to himself" —that is, to exercise his dominion over nature—he must and can discover its secrets and give them value, making himself responsible before God his creator. This applies to the secrets of the sea, of the cosmos, of the atom, of life, and hence of sexuality and the transmission of life.

4. Being convinced of our fidelity to the gospel, let us give couples the freedom to choose their own way of acting in relation to the procreation of children. The choice of methods is less a moral problem than one of mutual agreement and of bodily and spiritual health. A suitable legislation should help to keep in check the danger of abuses which the encyclical mentions.

The whole question, then, is one of finding a language which will correctly interpret the divine law and the law of nature. There are statements to this effect in the encyclical, insistently repeated by the Pope himself, by theologians, and by Catholics who accept the encyclical without reservation. The question of language is not just a question of words; it is a "hermeneutical" question in the most specific sense of the word—it is a question of interpreting the divine message. This is the reason that some Protestants felt slighted, since to them it appeared that the Pope, by making this decision, has not recognized or doubts the efficacy of a "language" interpreting the Word of God as used by non-Catholics. A criticism along these lines and an explanation of the controversial doctrinal elements has been fully treated by

Hessischen Rundfunks of August 13, 1968 in a transmission carrying the title "The Language of the Pope." Here is the extremely interesting text in the redaction provided by *Evangelischer Pressedienst Zentralredaktion* of Frankfurt:

When Pope Paul VI finishes the encyclical by expressing his hopes for "peace of consciences and the unity of the Christian people . . . that all should speak the same language," he means the papal language which he holds as the saving teaching of Christ. This means, then, that everyone must submit to the Pope's verdict in his thoughts, words, and actions. We here wish to discuss the problem of whether the Pope is exceeding his competence and by what right he identifies his interpretation of the natural law with the will of God and with Christ's commands. We would like to give a small contribution to an analysis of his style and to a search for some basic element in his language. In this process we seem to come across a series of clichés, the use of which is always dangerous and immediately arouses opposition in anyone who reflects on them.

By "cliché" we mean an object or a series of useful and used products which suggest an association with high values and ideas and give the impression, or at least intend to give the impression, that what is presented is obvious and generally recognized for its authenticity. On deeper examination, however, it begins to be noticed that the idea is really vague, no matter how clearly it has been presented, and above all it is noticed that it corresponds only approximately to the topic under discussion.

The stereotyped concept is not a word-covering or a word having an exact content; it is a word that covers only part of the truth but which pretends to be the key to the whole of the truth. By this it becomes more, therefore, than just a comfortable way of saving effort in thinking (since usually when an idea is lacking, the word comes at the right moment); it also applies pressure and simultaneously leads the person hearing it to believe that the question he has asked has already been answered for a considerable time or that the difficulty he is being besieged with has already been solved long ago (reading between the lines the message is: "Agree with this venerable word produced in the factory of centuries, and adhere to it!"). For this reason we would like to single out some of the basic concepts contained in the encyclical which have been used precisely in this stereotyped way as if possessing the very solution to the problems raised by these concepts:

1. *Truth.* In the encyclical truth is held to be unchangeable, es-

pecially when it is proclaimed by the Church, an edifice built on a rock. Truth is the reflection of the divine thought. It always remains solid—how can it possibly waver? The encyclical ignores the fact that the search for truth is a living process which must be continually recommencing, that a statement of its truth content can only be approximate and must be compared with other ways of looking at it lest the statement unexpectedly change into falsehood because of its one-sidedness. Truth, at least in the way the concept is used in the encyclical, gives the impression of being a formula simply to be repeated again and again. Why, then, are there people who repeatedly keep asking the same questions and continually seek to restate the formulas? It is from these that the divine truth and, consequently, God himself seemingly are to be discovered.

2. *Nature*. Here, too, something happens as for truth. Nature is the *"Magna Mater,"* God's marvelous creature in which all his ideas and plans can be read. The person acting in accordance with nature is he who submits to her and follows her laws. In this way the concept is drawn up into the sphere of divinity, and from the very beginning is safeguarded by being surrounded with a region which is taboo. The encyclical, however, does not consider the fact that nature is the raw matter which must take on a definite form. Above all it is unaware of the fact that man is lord of the nature which surrounds him and not vice versa, and that he has the task of giving nature this form, ordering it, directing it, changing it. In addition, the directives for ethical behavior which have been laid down are taken from a preconceived concept of nature which is basically pre-Christian, while the physical order unquestioningly remains below and not above the ethical order.

3. *Church*. Here, also, the Church has been presented as unchangeable and always faithful to herself in doctrine and in discipline. Moreover, she is the "Mother and teacher" of all people. Therefore, why should she not know, and in an exact and immutable way, what the plan and the will of God are for them? Here again the human element in the Church has been forgotten, and this can lead to serious mistakes. However, by means of an extreme simplification, this image of the Church has been couched with the image of the pilgrim Church and hence the community of sinners.

How could the Church presented in such a simplistic and stereotyped manner, possibly admit a mistake on the Pope's part or even a simple deficiency in her doctrinal tradition? *Errare humanum est*, but this is not allowable in the scheme put forward here. Above all, it must be noted that the Church is being continually, even though

161

tacitly, identified with the hierarchy. It is exactly this continuous contrasting of the "provident mother," "teacher," "guide," with the "docile children" which reveals the fundamental misunderstanding. The result is that the authentic Church, the fullness of the Church, does not consist of the community of the faithful but of individual persons, especially of the highest person in the hierarchical order.

4. *Family.* This is another cliché which harks back to a more ancient cliché formed in patriarchal times, that of "the family of the sons of God" whose father is the Pope who rules in a gentle and yet severe manner (as head, as the representative of God on earth) and whose provident mother is the Church (that is, the hierarchy, and thus the ministerial Church). In this way an identification is set up between God the Father, and the Pope (father-figure), and as we have observed, between the mother-figure and the official Church (or also Mary, "the 'type' of the Church").

The end result, which lends itself to some degree of corruption, springs immediately to mind: the other members of the people of God (above all the laity) are children who must listen attentively and obey. All this is reinforced by the archetypal image of the pastor and the flock. If the hierarchy is enrobed in the splendor and impregnability of the heavenly Father, any opposition can only be considered as rebellion and moreover as a crime against God. If the Church is portrayed as a loving mother, criticism against it becomes the act of a cruel and ungrateful son. The image of the family would not be so bad if it intended only familial relationships, especially those pertaining to the growth of children in the sense of the family of today. But as a cliché drawn from the age of paternalism, this image is highly dangerous.

5. *The world.* It is true that a New Testament expression found principally in Paul and John, can be referred to here. Not enough care is taken, however, to not go beyond what this New Testament expression signifies. Along with the cliché of the Church-world Schema there are also the good-evil, superior-inferior, and Christ-antichrist schemas. It is well-known that a Church pushed to the outskirts or into a ghetto will isolate itself all the more and with its "ghetto mentality" begin judging everything which goes on outside it negatively, or see everything as an attack on its own position, or at least look at everything with considerable suspicion.

The "spirit of the world" or "the spirit of the times" is presented in this encyclical too much in the light of the decadence, the trend toward barbaric customs, and the new paganism which has become the rage. Consequently it is quite easy for the new ideas being advanced, and hence the new criteria being put forward and the concrete problems arising, to be rejected as something contradicting the spirit of the Church. The warning toward the end of the encyclical to be on the watch against the evil spirit who evidently has now also hit Christian marriages, takes on the pathetic tone of an exorcism.

6. *Sex.* From the time of Augustine onward, in fact much earlier, the body was judged as the inferior part of man, as the soul's earthly "prison" or "tomb," or as a burden for the spirit. This is no longer being said today in the same, strong words but the old, stereotyped outlook still predominates in many parts of the encyclical. Even though it stresses the totality of the communion between body and spirit, it still speaks of the realm of instincts, passion, disordinate enjoyment of life, and the pleasure of the senses. The price that the body must pay for its enjoyment of marriage and with which it must justify itself before the spirit, and hence before conscience, is "shame," "self-dominion," and "chastity." These values are seen in a false light so that the couple is given the impression that they are unfortunately too much inclined toward dissoluteness, and hence are urged to continual renunciations. In other words, the joys of marriage are made lawful within the demands of periodic continence only if these joys are renounced at regular intervals. And whoever wants to accommodate himself in any other way must be able to settle accounts with his own conscience.

7. *Woman.* The fear that man, by using forbidden contraceptive methods, will come to the stage of losing respect for the woman and consider her as an "instrument of egoistic enjoyment" and no longer as his respected and beloved companion, can only be envisaged if the man has a strictly carnal view of marriage. From this it is easy to understand how a consequent attempt can be made with the best of intentions, but which particularly affects the woman, to protect the weaker sex against what can be called a morality of exploitation. In the first place, both husband and wife have equal right to satisfy their desires. Second, the dignity could be defended only by the wife herself and not from outside if this dignity were to be harmed by the husband. Third, what has been said above seems to suggest that there is only one, single method by which we assure the woman her respect, whereas it can be assured only by true love. In fact, the very necessity of fixing a set date for intercourse injures not a few women's sentiments.

For these Reformed Christians, then, the encyclical's language is one which is too much imbued with the old stereotypes still very much in vogue in religious spheres and especially in the Catholic world. When alternative interpretations of these stereotyped words are given, they are found to be in opposition to the encyclical's reasoning rather than in support of it.

The Language of Theology and of the Bible

As soon as the debate descends into the field of theological and biblical language the criticisms become more precise and direct. Once again it is a question of the meaning and content of the language; that is, of the worth of the words expressing the themes touched by the encyclical. The problem becomes even more acute in its ecumenical implications since it is precisely here that theological reflection, insofar as it is theological interpretation of the Word of God, and of the Word of God as contained in scripture itself, is vitally important. Several serious controversies which have not yet been settled by the only recently begun ecumenical dialogue have been hauled back into the spotlight. On the Protestant side the criticism is aimed at the very foundation of the encyclical which betrays a lack of biblical doctrine, and at the incongruous nature of a theological reflection which is carried on without this biblical basis.

The Waldensian theologian, George Girardet, in the Evangelical weekly *Nuovi Tempi* of August 11, 1968, has given one of the most significant criticisms of the encyclical on the basis of its biblical and theological language and has, at the same time, put this fundamental criticism by Evangelical Christians in correct perspective. Naturally the criticism of the worth of the encyclical immediately becomes a criticism of the Catholic Church in the name of a "new and authentic fidelity to the Word of God." It must also be noted that in this Protestant theologian's reactions many elements of the discussion and many of the reactions to the encyclical, both positive and negative, can be seen converging. Note, for example, the judgment on the "unpopularity" of the encyclical which was very quickly adopted as the *leitmotiv* in one area of Catholic apologetics that sprang up immediately after the encyclical's promulgation. These, then, are the comments of the Waldensian theologian, under a title which is already significant: "A Theologically Unfounded Document Which Replaces the Gospel Message with Legalism." Girardet says:

It is difficult to find any elements for a positive evaluation when faced with an encyclical like *Humanae Vitae*. On the human level one can appreciate, naturally, Paul VI's courage in going against the stream and knowing that it would make him unpopular. Courage, however, is not enough; for a document which is presented as having binding authority on Catholics it is expected, above all, that it be profoundly true and theologically well-founded, that it take into account, that is, the situation of the man to whom it is directed, and that it not create more problems than it intends to solve. On all these points, however, Paul VI's latest encyclical seems sadly deficient. In fact, it is not so much the encyclical's central teaching—the No to all types of contraceptive methods—which leaves us perplexed.

Let us remember that until several decades ago it was the prevailing opinion among Christians of all confessions, and we are also convinced that what is true must be stated and taught even if it is unpopular. But this is not the point at issue here. Christians' reflection and experience over the last generation have led them to a deepening and a rediscovery of the profound significance of marriage and of love so that these are no longer seen under a predominantly "sexual" light. This has led also to a new evaluation of what are called "contraceptive" methods in the framework of an ethics of the husband's and wife's responsibility to each other and to their offspring, both present and to come. This has not been opposed at all by the encyclical; it has simply been ignored.

In the name of the traditional teaching based on St. Augustine and St. Thomas, a teaching has been given which is deeply anti-evangelical because it is both nonbiblical and legalistic. In other words, all the more recent theological research, based precisely on a clearer understanding of the teaching of the Old and New Testaments, and which has reevaluated in an entirely new way man's—and woman's— dignity in the totality of his person and hence also in the sphere of his sexuality, has all been ignored. Appealing to a legalistic view of the Christian life, inherited from Counter-Reformation times, the encyclical presents the order of creation as a law, with all its casuistic distinctions, imposed on man, and so denies the gospel's call to liberty and responsibility, thus transforming the gift of marriage and sexuality into a chain, a weight, and an exhortation to renunciation. On what is one of the most positive aspects of human life which has been opened by the discoveries of science to a liberation and new, constructive possibilities (obviously to be used in a responsible way), the encyclical gives the appearance of being negative, gloomy, and riddled with complexes.

The main line of reasoning in *Humanae Vitae* is as follows: according to the natural law, the sexual act cannot be separated from procreation in any precise, direct way. Every sexual act must be in a positive relationship to the possibility of procreation. Every form of interference is an act against nature and hence against the will of God while it is permissible—illogically, in a way—to make use of the naturally infertile periods. This type of discipline corresponds very closely to the requirements of a naturist religion which sees in sex a sacred power, more mysterious and dangerous than any other area of human life and hence to be regulated, exorcised, and channeled toward procreative goals.

This view has nothing in common, however, with the biblical message, in which sex is neither more nor less sinful than other aspects of human life and in which procreation is not mythologized. It is not simply by chance that the passage in Genesis which speaks of the union of the first couple (Genesis 2:21–24) makes no reference to procreation. Procreation is recalled in another context as an exhortation that again takes up the command "Be fruitful and multiply," which had already been given to animals. Biblically speaking, it seems that the affirmation can be made that while "procreation" belongs to the nature of all living beings, "love" is typical of man and belongs, to use the language of the encyclical, to his "nature." The rediscovery of the biblical message of the value of man-woman relationships corresponds also to the direction that thinking has been taking during the last generation which, in its turn, has helped purify and deepen the understanding of the significance of the human couple.

Paul VI, however, did not take these things into account, in contrast with many Catholic biblical scholars and Catholic theologians and even the majority of the commission nominated to study the question. In fact, he shows a complete lack of understanding of this line of thought.

Thus it is a painful and downright offensive insinuation that the use of contraceptive methods in itself, degrades marriage and puts women in an inferior position. It is precisely the opposite that happens —and the Anglican bishops have recalled this—when a responsible, Christian use is made of these means. There is no need to mention, either, the dramas of overpopulation, infant mortality, and food shortages in many parts of the world, which are not solved by referring back to *Populorum Progressio* or by an appeal to governments.

166

As for possible abuses, Paul VI certainly knows that *abusus non tollit usum*. It would have been far more constructive to have investigated and to have given instruction on the new marriage ethics and social ethics, once the freedom of procreating or not procreating had been recognized. In any case, it is a freedom of which the contemporary masses and also Catholics had in fact availed themselves, and now they find themselves faced with a general condemnation and a perpetually bad conscience. Or else, tacitly or openly, they are rejecting an authority which is no longer capable of grasping the truth about the man of today and his problems.

Basically it can be asked whether the full procreation plan which Roman Catholicism has been prescribing for a century as the keystone of "Catholic morality," instead of responding to a supposed natural law, does not in reality constitute a kind of sacral sanctioning of rural and bourgeois familial morality which from time immemorial has been sacrificing the woman to the necessities of perpetuating the family line and thus condemning her to one pregnancy after another as the will of God. Moreover, for man's pleasure solutions have always been found toward which, and let us not forget it, Catholic morality has shown itself very understanding on the practical level. By renewing the ban on contraceptives Paul VI has, in a way, confirmed this social structure and mentality. It only leaves us deeply perplexed.

At this point, however, we must ask ourselves why Paul VI made this choice which he knew to be unpopular and which, even from the point of view of Catholic theology, was not absolutely necessary. Why did he make this effort, as we have seen above, to turn back the clock of history?

Probably the closest we can come to answering this question is by seeing it as a defensive move imposed on him by the very logic of the Catholic system, so that he was almost forced to take the step. To legitimize birth limitation would mean bringing into the Catholic world and into the very center of every practicing family, the distinct sensation that change is possible, that what was forbidden yesterday and was practiced with a bad conscience, may be allowed tomorrow, that Catholic morality may evolve and follow the times, that the teaching of the previous Popes was mistaken or unnecessarily severe, to say the least, and that those Anglican bishops against whom Pius XI in 1930 had hurled *Casti Connubii* were right after all. Once the adaptation had begun with birth limitation, would not new demands have arisen, for example, for married priests? A system which declares itself immutable and infallible cannot adapt itself to the times or admit having made a mistake in the past without undergoing a crisis, the outcome of which would be difficult to foresee.

Thus, Paul VI and his conservative counselors did the one thing possible if they were to remain within the system: cling to the tradition and renew the ban. The birth-control issue marks the end of the post-conciliar updating process. Rome's teaching cannot go against itself. To go outside it would be to leap into the dark, the very negation of the Catholic system and of the premises for a true reform of the Church.

Naturally this is not to say that the solution dictated by prudence has been the wisest. In fact, instead of ending the controversy, the encyclical seems to have started it again, with the difference that now the debate has extended to include the value of encyclicals and the infallibility of the papal magisterium. The violence of the reaction has stunned the Vatican, accustomed as it has been in the past to seeing the encyclicals received "with gratitude" as infallible oracles. This time again there was certainly no shortage of statements of approval in which there can almost always be detected a tone of submission. The voices of protest we have heard indicate that possibly the most serious crisis which contemporary Catholicism has known to date is under way.

On the ecumenical level, at least for those who had great hopes that Catholicism "en bloc" would be able to reform itself, the encyclical has created deep disillusionment. The Council era is over. Some will leave the Catholic Church, not in order to follow the "easy way out," but to retain a coherent faith. Others in greater numbers will find refuge in semi-clandestine, dissenting groups, once again only formally Catholic. All this cannot but pose new problems for classical ecumenism. The great mass of Catholics and non-Catholics, however, will remain disorientated by a great Church which puts herself forward as the mother and teacher of peoples and who then shows that she has a greater love for herself and the continuity of her formal teaching and cultural supports than for the man who, faced with a new situation, does not always know how to act with sufficient responsibility to retain a new but authentic fidelity to the Word of God before ethical choices unknown to previous generations.

Buttress the Edifice of Ecclesiastical Authority or Defend Conscience?

The criticism, then, has been directed at the theological and biblical foundations of the encyclical, but also at the immediate motives that the promulgation of the encyclical suggested. The Waldensian theologian clearly insists on this point and mentions some basic problems really present in the troubled post-conciliar period. The theme of a Church concerned with fidelity to herself and with the problems that are today connected with this self-understanding, reappear, along with comments on the encyclical's subject matter, in other Protestant reactions. The issue of ecclesiastical authority is another theme to which the Protestant spirit is particularly sensitive. It must be noted, however, that it concerns Catholics also, and has been resurrected by the fact of the encyclical. The *Evangelischer Pressedienst* broadcast on August 21, 1968 a synthesis of a discussion between Protestants and Catholics, put on the air on the evening of July 31. The communiqué from the *Evangelischer Pressedienst* states:

In the transmission the Protestant contributor, Pastor Ebhard Stammler of Stuttgart, said that Paul VI has put the authority of the ecclesiastical magisterium along with that of his encyclical in a position which is no longer basically tenable. On this point he was found to be in agreement with the Catholic members of the panel. Together with Prof. Eugen Kogon as well as the Catholic journalist Katerin Burger from Frankfurt and the Catholic priest Dr. Alfons Kirchgaessner, well-known as an expert on questions of sexual ethics, they all expressed their disappointment over the papal declaration which did not take into consideration the more recent knowledge and developments, and which could only be interpreted as a relapse by the Church into its habitual enmity toward the body.

Pastor Stammler shared the suspicion with the Catholic members that the Pope not only had the intention of erecting a bulwark against the sexual revolution but at the same time wanted to preserve the tradition of the ecclesiastical doctrine valid up to now, and hence to reinforce his crumbling authority. Pastor Stammler, however, stated that he feared the edifice of formal ecclesiastical authority has now been put in question more than ever. Protestants had followed the transformation process under way in the Roman Catholic Church during the past few years and were therefore disappointed by the sad countermove begun by this encyclical, and feared it could lead to a strengthening of the forces of restoration. In turn, the Catholic priest Fr. Kirchgaessner called it "a tragic development" since the new papal directives for married life could lead to the relationships of mixed marriages taking a turn for the worse. Pastor Stammler observed that the encyclical also brought problems for militant Catholics and unease into Catholic marriage itself.

The edifice of ecclesiastical authority, now in crisis because it has entered into a problem which nearly all Reformed Christians maintain belongs to the consciences of individual couples, is a topic which also interests André Dumas, professor of ethics with the faculty of Protestant theology at the University of Paris and the author of a work fundamental to the understanding of Reformed thought on birth control (André Dumas, *Il controllo delle nascite nel pensiero protestante,* Turin, 1967). Dumas states, in *La Vie Protestante* of August 30, 1968, that along with the encyclical there occurred an "authority wastage." He continues:

The Pope is not wrong in being concerned over the authority of service in the Church in the name of the gospel and for the good of all men. Likewise, he is not wrong in teaching a doctrine instead of referring everyone back to freedom and secrecy; that is, the solitude of their consciences. Precisely because he is not wrong, however, in courageously calling our disorientated society back to norms, he then risks wasting the authority, which is not his but belongs to the entire Church endeavoring to be attentive to Christ, by means of a fallible authoritarianism. Doubtless it would have been better to have no encyclical rather than this encyclical. In it all the possible objections are mentioned in the beginning but none of them are answered in the course of its exposition.

Thus it concludes by putting its very authority in question. The only solution which the Pope put forward was that science get a better understanding of the natural cycles. The Pope is not a biologist. A biologist will never be, of himself, a moralist, and a moralist will never be able to take the place of lovers themselves! And while we are waiting for science to travel this long uncertain road, who is going to believe a pope with such diminished authority, when reason and faith reveal a completely different outlook on how to love with responsibility and spontaneity—an outlook which is certainly not ideal nor culpable?

The continually recurring problem, then, is one of authority, already debatable for Reformed Christians and now being debated even by Catholics. This problem, however, refers back to the more basic one; that is, that of the authority of conscience

170

or of an authority capable of interpreting the data of the individual conscience directly before God.

In this way the Synod of the Reformed Waldensian Church on August 14, 1968 judged that "the Pope's encyclical leaves only the choice of submission or disobedience for the couple. Their personal responsibility is strongly limited. While the scope of the encyclical is to favor the mutual esteem and the love in the couple's sexual life, this esteem and love are, in fact, put in danger." In order to break the couple's dilemma of either pure submission or disobedience to the law, the Protestant Synod, after observing that "the encyclical's subject matter also affects those Christians of different faiths from the Roman Catholic when they are living in a mixed marriage," then intends confronting the Christian with his responsibilities in conscience and hence states:

In the conviction that we are faithful to the gospel we leave the couple the freedom of choosing for themselves their course of action with regard to procreating children. The choice of means, or rejection of them, is less a question of morality than one of mutual agreement and the health of both body and soul. If necessary, a suitable legislation should help limit the danger of the abuses mentioned in the encyclical.

The question of whether to safeguard ecclesiastical authority or to defend the authority of conscience comes to the fore in the ecumenical meetings already initiated on the concrete, deep basis of a recognition of the convictions and sensibilities of the Reformed brethren. This aspect of the problem which has been acutely posed again by the encyclical has been very quickly faced by ecumenical groups, especially by those groups interested in mixed marriage questions as in Belgium or Holland, where already numerous meetings have taken place in steadily increasing numbers from the beginning of August 1968 onward. In these group discussions the difficulty faced by a couple united in a mixed marriage in which the partners have different views on authority has been felt in a very real way, and concern has been shown for specific pastoral care regarding this situation. On his side, the delegate for the Protestant Churches at the

Dutch Pastoral Council, Prof. A. J. Bronkhorst of Utrecht, says in a statement he gave at the beginning of August that

the attitude of the Catholic bishops after the encyclical must reveal their pastoral care toward their own faithful, also their ecumenical responsibilities. The encyclical, thanks to the ecumenical contacts which have developed in the last few years with a large circle of Catholics, will be rejected without too much ado, and it is likely that it will be considered erroneous given the regained sense of maturity of conscience on the part of the faithful. . . . For a humanity already mature, such an encyclical appears rather irrational.

The force of the criticism is explainable here precisely by the concern for safeguarding the maturity and responsibility of the individual conscience, a value to which the Reformed Christians are extremely sensitive.

The Authority of the Magisterium and That of Conscience: An Irremediable Dissension?

The Reformed Christians, however, perceive that in the encyclical there are also expressions of deep concern as, for example, in foreseeing abuses which will harm married life and in awakening a sense of responsibility rather than almost mechanically solving the problem of limiting births. But how this is to come about is another question. In the last analysis, the decision must always be referred back to conscience, and this may never be suppressed. For this reason, a considerable number of Protestant reactions are simultaneously understanding toward the Pope's concern and yet critical of the solutions which he has chosen. They admit certain values in the encyclical but reaffirm the fundamental value of conscience. Hence, the whole issue centers around both the possibility of limiting births and the individual decision of conscience as to which method is to be followed. For example, both understanding and criticism, as mentioned above, appear in the statements of Dr. Hermann Dietzfelbinger of Monaco, superintendent of the Lutheran Church. He observes that "the seriousness with which the encyclical speaks of marriage and the sanctity of life must be taken into account. And yet, many Christians are irritated by the Pope's encyclical, including many Evangelicals. Prayer and dialogue with God make

Christians free and bind them at the same time, even on such debated questions."

The theologian Reinhard Henkys develops the theme of the Protestant's perplexity when having to face both birth regulation as proposed by an authoritative law and the individual responsibility of conscience. He also outlines some of the encyclical's positive aspects without, however, seeing this as a reason for not criticizing it. In his statement of July 31 as given by the *Evangelischer Pressedienst,* he says among other things:

Rarely has an ecclesiastical doctrinal document aroused so much and so wide attention but at the same time caused such a vast amount of consternation and provoked such severe, immediate criticism by public opinion. The head of the Roman Church has reconfirmed the teaching developed by his predecessors with great forcefulness: all forms of birth regulation are morally prohibited except for sexual continence and the use of the woman's infertile days. A reading of the document poses the Protestant with such a great number of problems and evokes so many critical objections that he, even though respecting the serious intentions which led the Pope to take this position, cannot envisage it as a helpful contribution to either humanity as a whole or to the individual toward solving the problem. In the first place, it is surprising that the Pope should entrust himself with defending an order of moral values considered to be irrevocably fixed and that he should base his reasoning in this matter less on sacred scripture than on philosophical, moral principles.

All this is alarming for Evangelical Christians. Love of one's neighbor which relativizes every principle does not seem to have been taken very much into consideration. Likewise, it does not seem that much account has been taken of either man's participation in the process of creation which arises from his likeness to God, or man's task of creating life on earth which is his immediate responsibility before the Creator. The traditional papal teaching which authorized only the so-called natural methods of birth regulation and, correspondingly, rejected every other method—now including the Pill—is certainly not presented in this encyclical in an anymore convincing way than before. If a couple is really allowed to come together without necessarily having the intention of generating a child every time (and this the Pope recognizes), then the method they use is not something which can be decided once and for all by applying principles and reasoning theologically.

However, and it is precisely here that we agree with the encyclical, it must be said that abortion—that is, the killing of life which has already been conceived—cannot be considered as one of the methods allowable for responsible family planning. This presents the Pope's document with a pastoral problem: Is it just to restrain practicing Christians from a suitable, responsible regulation of births, with the subsequent danger of forcing them, when it is too late, to resort to the killing of the fetus as the last means? It cannot be denied that today the interruption of maternity is striking like an epidemic. And this cannot be underestimated and laughed off for the sake of a principle.

These are some of the objections and some of the problems. They have not been presented just by Protestants and by those who are indifferent to the issues involved, but also by Catholics, lay people, priests, and bishops. Alongside this criticism there is a positive element deriving from the encyclical which must be clearly brought out in the Protestant reaction: within the Catholic hierarchy itself the Pope's stand has received an extremely varied response.

All the signs point to the fact that the papal encyclical has not by its authority put an end to the discussion inside the Catholic Church. If anything, it has increased the discussion. After the Council, the Catholic Church has evidently fallen into what is a "Protestant situation." The Pope's word does not take away from Catholics their responsibility but induces them to a personal decision of conscience which can be consciously different from that given in the Pope's directives.

This last judgment is extremely interesting seeing that Henkys' contribution has as its title, "A Document Nobody Finds Useful." In fact, the papal document has a positive value, but only because it evokes a process of reflection and thus leads to a maturation of conscience and responsibility on the part of Catholics. Even though it is not stated as clearly and decisively as by the Protestant theologian, this idea nevertheless returns again and again in a considerable number of episcopal statements on the encyclical.

The position in which the faithful will find themselves has also been mentioned by Bishop May of Vienna in a letter of August 14, 1968. Initially, he recognizes the positive aspects of the encyclical as regards the sense of individual responsibility, but maintains that the direction which conscience is to follow is not, of itself, in the Church's competence to decide. He then faces the fundamental issue of the role of ecclesiastical authority in the realm of conscience. The Lutheran Bishop May states:

The Evangelical [Protestant] attitude toward family planning and contraceptives, or preservatives, is not a negative one toward "birth control" but a positive one of "responsible parenthood." The Church must quite clearly tell all parents: "You are sinning against the will of God if you arbitrarily and for self-centered reasons set yourselves against the gift of a child. You are serving the will of God if you exercise a responsible parenthood in choosing the number of children you want." But it is not for the Church to decide whether periodic continence, the Pill, or other contraceptive methods are suitable. The conscientious doctor is the expert in these matters. With the papal encyclical dissension has now appeared within Catholicism in a more evident way. It is in itself a contradiction when the Pope allows the Ogino-Knaus method, which is basically a preservative method, and then rejects all other methods.

Another contradiction has arisen between the solemn proclamation made by the Council on human liberty favoring the personal decision of conscience, personal responsibility, and Christian maturity, and the encyclical, which once again does not recognize any of this in fundamental areas of private life and marriage and, what is more, would like to invoke the assistance of the state on this issue—the same thing has happened with the statements on mixed marriages. An even more evident dissension is apparent in the contradiction between the practice of the majority of Catholics and the new encyclical. From now on the fervent Catholic will be overburdened with a bad conscience or will not recognize the Pope's authority in practice. From the Evangelical point of view, does this not favor the spread of insincerity and hypocrisy? Will Catholics allow themselves to be once again surrounded by prohibitions after the Council had given them such great freedom? Once again, under the form of many dogmatic and moral statements, the Catholic Church's claim to power and dominion over souls and consciences is revealing itself.

Bishop May's judgment becomes rather severe toward the end of his statement when he highlights those interior dissensions which the encyclical has provoked inside Catholicism and in the depths of people's consciences. Obedience to the authority of the Pope or the authority of conscience—this is the problem which Protestants see as the cause of the "dissension," and related to the further problems of birth limitations, the methods employed, and hence personal responsibility.

The problem is taken up again more specifically by the Evangelical Community of Action for Family Questions (Lutheran) in a text published on August 29, 1968 and entitled precisely, *The Papal Encyclical Has Brought an Irremediable Dissension*. The position of the Evangelical Community of Action for Family Questions, with its headquarters in Bonn, has been expressed by its president, Dr. Cornelius A. von Heyl, who is also a member of the Supreme Consistory of the Lutheran Church. He states:

The Pope's attitudes on birth regulation as contained in the encyclical are neither new nor unusual. The Protestant is surprised by, and seeks a reason for, the violence of the criticism which has now flared up against this new statement of what is an old opinion. The irremediable dissension which many Catholics have adopted has been sparked off by the demand for obedience to the magisterium. This obedience is easy for the Catholic in cases where the ecclesiastical magisterium is infallibly assisted by the Holy Spirit and therefore in the Pope's doctrinal decisions "ex cathedra." But a doctrinal decision contained in an encyclical is not held to be infallible for Catholic faith. A Catholic Christian, therefore, can be convinced that the Pope is mistaken in saying that some particular contraceptive methods are incompatible with the will of God. The real question posed by the encyclical is, If the Pope may have made a mistake, if the will of God is not as univocal as the Pope claims, what right then has he to demand obedience? The answer to this question is very important for the future development of Catholicism.

An issue which has been left so open-ended on a question which concerns the very future of Catholicism has been taken up again by *Népszabadság* of Budapest on August 11, 1968 where it is formulated far more negatively:

Pope Paul VI's No hinders the modernization of the Catholic Church and the process of mutual rapprochement between the Churches. The problem cannot be solved by appealing to the human element, to a person's well-intentioned state of mind. The true, definitive solution comes from creating in every part of the world a society which puts every conquest of technology and science to the service of the material and cultural improvement of millions of active people. But as long as we remain at the present stage and as long as the backwardness inherited from the past is not overcome once and for all even in socialist countries, and the widest possible abundance of material goods is not created, the regulation of births is solely a means, but not an unimportant means, to calm the anxieties weighing on so many countries in the world. That the problems precipitated by the encyclical are not over and done with for Catholic Christians is proved by the debates which have arisen among them and by the contradictions which the Church, sooner or later, must fully incur.

Possibly the real problem is not one along the lines of a kind of "politics" of the future of Catholicism. It is certain, however, that the questions raised by non-Catholics are questions which now even Catholics themselves are asking: Can the encyclical become a new factor leading to a process of rethinking in the Church or an opportunity for rediscovering dimensions in Catholicism which had slowly become covered over? The fact that the discussion on the authority of the magisterium, the hierarchy, conscience, obedience, and personal responsibility was occasioned by an encyclical is fundamentally something positive since it shows Catholicism's vital capacity for conscientiously coming to grips with the divine Word and that this process occurs through the normal channels of understanding, language, and human experience. Through these channels Catholics are also forced, up to a point, to put themselves before the same Word together with their brothers of the Reformation and with the "sons of the promise"; that is, the Jews.

All in Search of the Same Truth but Along Different Paths

It appears, in fact, that the problems exist for all Christians. It cannot be said, and we have seen it ourselves, that the basic problems of responsibility, conscience, and fidelity to the divine law do not exist for Protestants. The same must be said of the Jews, whose reactions are just as indicative on account of the motivations as well as the conditioning factors which influence them.

The Grand Rabbi of Jerusalem, Yotshak Nizzim, on July 30, 1968 immediately took up a favorable position toward the encyclical and stated to the press: "Artificial birth regulation is immoral and contrary to the principles of Judaism. I am making an appeal that the laws against abortions, which have reached disquieting figures in Israel, be made more operative and be more respected." Apart from the statement that every form of contraception is contrary to the principles of Judaism, it appears that the Grand Rabbi of Jerusalem may have interpreted the encyclical's teaching as primarily directed against abortion or else he wanted to extend the ban on contraceptives to include methods which interrupt maternity because of his preoccupation with the problem in Israel. He has, then, in a certain sense, instrumentalized the encyclical without, however, falsifying it in the process, since it is clear that the reasons for excluding contraceptives apply all the more to the exclusion of abortion.

However, alongside Grand Rabbi Nizzim's statement that artificial regulation of births is contrary to the principles of Judaism, some maintain that Judaism cannot be opposed to it. The director of the Center of Jewish Studies in Paris, Léon Askenazi, in *Information Juive* of September 1968 strongly opposes the quite widespread opinion that Judaism has the same idea as Catholicism on birth control, and above all, on contraception. Consequently, Askenazi treats this issue at great length by referring to the Bible and the Jewish law. He says that according to the Jewish law, "the legal obligation to procreation ceases the moment when the couple have brought two children, a son and a daughter, into the world." Besides,

the resultant stop to procreation does not in any a priori way annul the moral and religious duty of sexual satisfaction which the Talmud calls the "joy par excellence" (*Ein Simha Elah Simha chel Houppa*). . . . When for medical, psychical, and psychosocial reasons it is advised to provisionally or definitively suspend the fertility of sexual acts, then contraception becomes possible and not as if it were something just tolerated, but is a fact written into the Law itself.

As for the practical contraceptive methods,

only the woman is authorized in employing contraceptives, but they must not put her psychic and physical health in danger. The Pill must be judged according to these criteria. The drama of conscience which is the real, deep-down tragedy of couples faced with this problem on the level of principles, does not in itself exist in Judaism.

178

The same position centering around the duties of procreation and intercourse understood as religious duties and taking into consideration the concept of psychic and physical health, has been expressed in the *Jewish Chronicle* of September 1968 in an article by Rabbi David M. Feldmann. He had published in that same month *Birth Regulation and Jewish Laws,* a book in which he fully explains the Jewish attitude which he sums up in the following article. Rabbi Feldmann states that

procreation is an imperative which must be obeyed; certain contraceptives are to be rejected, but birth control practiced with suitable means and for valid reasons is permissible. The preservation of health is a commandment for Jews and it takes precedence over all other considerations. Contraception is therefore permitted, or rather, required, whenever the health of the woman is in danger. Procreation is a religious commandment; but conjugal sexual relations, quite independently of procreation, constitute another religious commandment. Historically, conjugal love has been held in sufficiently high consideration by Jews for them to be able to reject the fundamental objections against certain means of birth control.

The topic of the ethical duty of the individual when facing the problems of personal health and the wider, social problems which this brings, has also been included in the communiqué issued at the end of a session held at Geneva in September 1968 by the Commission for Medicine of the World Council of Churches. After having declared itself in favor of the personal decision of conscience in the choice of contraceptive methods, the commission stated that

few world problems are as important and at the same time have as yet been as insufficiently studied as the one of the unprecedented increase of the population. By virtue of the ethical consequences that the vast effects may have on family health, and above all by virtue of their preoccupation with the well-being of the children, Christians are particularly obliged to proceed in a constructive manner in the search for solutions.

Furthermore, the commission declared that it would dedicate itself to ensuring that the "programs of medicine practiced in a Christian sense would assume a paramount importance in the development of new ways for responsibly overcoming this vast problem."

The Christian's ethical responsibilities in relation to the vast world-scale problems of birth and procreation have also been studied by the executive committee of the World Council of Methodist Churches in the September 1968 session held at Helsinki. The Council reiterated "the already accepted principle of planned parenthood, and in addition urged the Churches to undertake a new activity for resolving the great problems of the world, such as hunger, injustice, and demographic increase." The same communiqué went on to say that "side by side with the traditional work of evangelization and the medical services, the responsibility of the constituted Council for Rural Problems and Development, as well as education for planned parenthood, form part of the mission of the Church." It was then decided that these topics would be discussed further in a world conference to take place in July 1972.

Natural Law and Sexuality: Manichaeism or the Law of the Gospel?

A further aspect of the Protestant reaction to the encyclical was revealed on the topic of sexuality, rights, and natural law. The encyclical was contrasted with the law of the gospel and, in any case, with the data given by the Bible on this issue. It is natural, therefore, after giving a judgment on the manner and the criteria with which the encyclical faces these issues, to go on and give a more straightforward judgment regarding the Church's authority in this field and on Catholic opinion on the topics the encyclical has raised. Thus Prof. André Dumas, already quoted in *La Vie Protestante* of August 30, 1968, in an article bearing the title "Better No Encyclical than This Encyclical," observes that the Pope "has decided to reaffirm the continuity of Catholic teaching both *in spite of* and *with* the Council, according to how one wants to interpret it." He then says that "in fact, the doctrinal position and even more so the pastoral position had become ambiguous."

After summarizing the teaching of *Casti Connubii*, Dumas notes that "for some time it was no longer certain that *Casti Connubii* was the Roman Catholic Church's last word on the matter." After describing the progress made by Catholic moral theology, especially as regards its acceptance of the temperature method which perfected that of Ogino-Knaus and noting how even this had given Catholic moralists headaches, Dumas summarizes the positions which have been making headway in recent Catholic theological thought. After this, he continues:

Paul VI unambiguously repeated Pius XI's position which had been given its final touches by Pius XII. He has given back to the concepts of nature and natural law, concepts which the texts of Vatican II had almost completely omitted mentioning by name, a vital importance. Hence, diverging from the Council, he has restored both the Aristotelian and the neo-Thomistic influences in the Catholic Church's teaching as well as the concept of the supreme authority of the papal magisterium which can exercise the mandate given by Christ to Peter against the majority opinion of the commissions called together by the same magisterium and probably against what would have been a majority of the episcopal college. All this is strictly in line with Catholic teaching. The fact is that the frequent use of scriptural arguments (there is no shortage of them in *Humanae Vitae*, as some have wrongly claimed; they never refer, however, to what is being taught), the experience of collegiality within the Church, and the experience of dialogue with the outside world had led us to forget this untouchable central core.

Here, in my opinion, are the three weak points of this encyclical which courageously wanted to bring the contradiction of the gospel to a slowly declining, modern morality but which has left us quite unconvinced that it has taken the contradiction to the right place.

The whole notion of natural law as the guarantee for human respect and as fidelity to the design of God the creator is quite shaky. Would it not be necessary, for example, to respect infant mortality as a natural law, especially seeing that its progressive eradication has provoked the new problem of birth control? Paul VI would answer No. How, then, are we to determine what in nature is a beneficial order which must be respected and what is a destructive force and must itself be destroyed? What aids do we have in this choice if not that of reason which teaches us to dominate nature, and faith which teaches us to love our neighbor as ourselves? Is not possibly the most serious danger to which the encyclical exposes us that of substituting natural law for man's reasoning powers and his decision of faith? It has done a very bad job of distinguishing between Aristotle's and the Stoics' dictum "Follow nature," and the "Follow me" of the liberation of the gospel.

In the present context, is it not possibly one and the same thing to legitimize the sexual relationship by means of procreation and to declare that the duty of perpetuating the human species predominates over all the other values which have been found in sexuality today— those of affection and peacefulness as opposed to mutual injury and anxiety and aggression? In this way we are being treated like potential libertines who are to be judged only on their parenthood. This is certainly the classical view of the time of St. Augustine, but its depressing Manichaeism has forgotten everything about what the Bible itself calls sexual "knowledge," this no-doubt unique area in human nature where instinct and intelligence learn to reciprocally fructify each other.

Dumas then develops the third point of his criticism which he calls "authority wastage" and which we have already quoted.

The law of nature, sexuality as a gift and as a danger, the philosophical and biblical justification of the papal choice, human, rational intervention into the process of intercourse— these are the topics that the pastor Prof. Albert Finet of the Reformed Federation of France treats in *Réforme* of August 10–17, 1968. After observing and giving the relevant quotations to show that the Churches which have sprung from the Reformation limit themselves in this field to proposing, counseling, and noting, but not to legislating, Prof. Finet states that the problem which the encyclical has precipitated interests him on the ecumenical level, since, as he says: "I often feel close to Catholics in both mind and heart while remaining very much a Protestant, since I think that this (ecumenical) dialogue is essential for the witness we give to Jesus Christ. It is necessary, then, to give considerable attention to this encyclical." Prof. Finet continues:

I must admit that this document (the encyclical) is more elaborate than the greater part of the declarations of our Reformed Churches or of the World Council of Churches, that its subtlety requires attentive reading, and that it would be thoughtless to reject it en bloc protesting that it reflects a solid perpetuity of Catholic theology bound to the Middle Ages and even farther back to Aristotle. It would be equally thoughtless to accept it en bloc for the sake of defending free-thinking morality. It is useful, moreover, to seriously consider the warnings it expresses, for it denounces dangers which are not altogether illusory.

It is correct to say that a gradually more widespread use of contraceptives can favor a materialistic outlook on love, a "radical" separation of love from procreation, and eventually a sexual liberty where the physical relationship would get the upper hand over (forgive the big words) that communion which is at the same time physical and spiritual and which, by grace, a man and a woman create in marriage.

It is also correct to say that contraception and demographic planning can become a dangerous and diabolical weapon in the hands of a totalitarian power. Simply recall the laws and the sterilization centers in Hitler's time.

Finally, the Pope cannot be rebuked for adopting an attitude in opposition to conformity to the world. Christians' "presence in the world" leads them to say terrible things at times and commits them to an active sharing in men's sorrows. But it can also lead to an easy acceptance of political and economic commitments which lose sight of that fundamental contradiction to the "world" which was Jesus. As for knowing whether the Catholic Church through the lips of Paul VI is really the sign of contradiction which the gospel speaks of, that is another matter altogether.

Even admitting all this, the papal encyclical, on account of the basis for its dialectics and the justification it gives for its purpose, still strikes against deep sentiments within me which I believe are connected with the gospel.

The Pope's proof is based on nature, or natural law (enriched by revelation—thanks for this contribution!). I confess, but perhaps it is a confession of ignorance, that I do not succeed in understanding very well what "natural law" means and represents to the pardoned sinner who I am. When I take life on its humblest level, for example, if I let "nature" do everything, then I am certain that I shall find weeds growing in my garden. When I think of life on the animal level, then natural law becomes the relationship between the wolf and the antelope or, in our part of the world, between the hare and the rabbit.

When I reflect on the human condition, I find that the natural law seems to me to have been very well stated by Plato and taken up again by Bacon and Hobbes: "Man is a wolf to man." Even Sartre does not contradict this. If natural law controls and determines our attitude toward procreation, then we must also, as a just countermeasure, respect "natural selection" and hence rigorously condemn medical science for prolonging the life of those who, "naturally," should already be dead, as in the case of the heart transplant performed on the Catholic priest. Excuse me. [The author is referring here to the Dominican Fr. Boulogne who underwent the first successful heart transplant in France, who defended both the morality and the Christian understanding of these transplants, and who when interviewed in the hospital, energetically defended *Humanae Vitae.*—EDITOR]

Maybe I am writing nonsense. But I am writing it to try and show just how questionable the evolution of the natural law is, and how it must be questioned when applied to marriage and procreation.

If it is recognized, as I myself recognize, that medical science is correct, just, and good when it seeks to correct nature and prolong life, I do not see any reason to stop it from using methods for limiting the appearance of life when this life has not yet begun. In the one case as in the other, it corrects "nature."

True, Paul VI has provided a "natural method," if one may call it that, which limits the risk of procreation: the thermometer. The Ogino method, however, has produced as many children as it has avoided unwanted births, in fact to such an extent that Paul VI had to appeal to experts to go deeper into the matter. No, I believe that the encyclical's starting point itself is mistaken and it must be said fearlessly. It is not the sign of contradiction spoken of by the gospel. It is not by referring back to natural law that a helpful solution will be given to the problems of marriage, contraception, and procreation. I am loath to use these abstract terms in order to technically qualify what in reality is the happiness or unhappiness, joy or torment, of the men and women of our time and of all time. To find an answer to this we must not go searching on the side of "nature" or the natural law, but on the side of the vocation which has been addressed to us. We shall never go deep enough into Jesus' saying, "The sabbath has been made for man and not man for the sabbath."

I know that by this I am indicating a path which entails many more risks since it implies responsibility lived in freedom. It is more comfortable, but also more alienating, to be always referring back to a legalism sanctioned by high and holy authorities. It is in this way that man and woman, in order to have a relative amount of security, lose their liberty. It may well be feared that a love which eliminates its procreative side is, in a way, incomplete. On the other hand, when a man and a woman come to a well-thought-out agreement on the size of their family, this exercise of their responsibility cannot but be respected.

Farther onward, Finet allows himself an "impertinence," as he calls it:

Paul VI does not know how to speak about women. He traces out a stereotyped image of them and assigns them a traditional position which very well shows how he has not had the experience of married life and of this relationship with another which is so close and so secret at the same time. Supervielle has said some wonderful things on all this, but he is a poet. Jesus too, we know full well, was not married, and yet every time he met a woman he gave her a dignity, responsibility, and liberty which the encyclical does not even faintly reflect.

At this point, Prof. Finet takes up the problem of ecumenism, which we have already mentioned.

Does the choice the encyclical made really assist the high vocation of married love and does it really oppose the dangers to fidelity in marriage, and the general decline in morality as well as the loss of respect for the woman? Is the notion of sexuality at the basis of the encyclical really biblical and Christian or does it, rather, show the effects of other eras and traditions? Besides, if the encyclical were to fully reaccept these positions, would it not risk closing the doors on the present-day research on so many values in the Church by simply exercising its authority? These are questions which easily come to Protestants' minds and to which Prof. André Dumas in *Réforme* of August 10–17, 1968 attempts to give some answers or at least show the general Reformed understanding of them. He notices that the Pope's reply came after years of hesitation and that the Pope himself expected a strong reaction to it. For this reason, Dumas says that

recognition must be shown for his courage in provoking unpopularity, for the solitude which he now intends facing for the future good, as he thinks, of humanity. I say this even though I shall later state why the encyclical, in my opinion, is a disaster. It must also be recognized that Paul VI's position follows a fearsome logic. From the simple fact that he insists on saying "a marriage act voluntarily made infertile is consequently intrinsically evil" it quite logically follows that all artificial methods of contraception are to be condemned and that the Pope cannot share the commission majority's conciliatory attitude. This commission worked toward an evolution of the Catholic teaching on two points but without clearly stating that the teaching would also change.

The first change was that of extending the procreative purpose in marriage to the whole of married life and without necessarily applying it to every act of intercourse. The second was to demonstrate a legitimate use of the Pill by means of the concept of regularization, or of restoration of the "natural state" in which the Pill is used, to ensure a momentary suspension of ovulation similar to that observable after gestation.

The Pope has rejected these makeshift devices which would be called pastoral by some and casuistic by others. He reaffirms the doctrine of *Casti Connubii* in all its intransigence and purity. . . . Reflecting on the fact that *Casti Connubii* was written against the Conference of Bishops of the Anglican Church meeting at Lambeth in 1930, and noting that *Humanae Vitae* was promulgated thirty years later at the very moment when another Lambeth Conference was meeting, it is easy to see how wide the gap still is which separates the attitude of the Catholic magisterium from that adopted by the majority of Christian faiths on this new area of human self-understanding which the technical possibility of contraception has made possible.

Respect must be shown the Pope for the logical way in which he follows out his principles; but at the same time it must be asked how Paul VI, confirming Pius XII's further stand adopted in 1951, can possibly admit that "a marriage act made voluntarily infertile" does not just as much apply to those acts done using the so-called natural methods of birth control. It is quite evident that these also allow the intention of having intercourse in moments which biological nature indicates are not suitable for procreation. Is not the only true logical outcome of a position which does not allow honest married relationships unless united with the intention of procreating, that of sexual abstinence? Can these natural rhythms, also, be assigned the character of a law given by the Creator when we know that our knowledge of these rhythms is the result of modern scientific discovery and therefore that the so-called natural methods are, like all other methods, the result of man's handiwork?

Let us now examine, however, some of the basic issues of the encyclical.

First, Paul VI fears that contraception will encourage license, "a broad and easy" path to unfaithfulness in marriage, a general decline in morality, and a "loss of respect for the woman." He urges the "victory of healthy liberty over license by means of respect for the moral order."

It seems strange to me that the encyclical should see everything so much through the fearful eyes of the child, that morality is spoken of as if it were a police officer and contraception as if it were the open door leading to adultery. Consequently, the name "healthy liberty" is given to what will later become a multitude of guilt-ridden consciences, not sufficiently formed to use the progress of science in the field of contraceptives as legitimate aids for the exercise of responsible parenthood.

Is human sexuality then, in the time of Paul VI as in the time of Augustine, still something licentious whenever it expresses interpersonal affection between couples who have the free, mutual intention of not willing, if possible, the continual procreation of children?

I quote St. Augustine who is unfortunately still so much the order of the day: "It is a good thing to get married because it is a good thing to bring children into the world and become the mother of a large family. . . . Marriage does not allow embraces whose sole object is not procreation, but it closes its eyes and excuses these embraces on the condition that they are not too frequent, that they are not to the detriment of time given over to prayer, and that they do not degenerate into unnatural practices. . . . Those who practice embraces in which there is anything less than the patriarchal desire for descendants, are living in a union which misunderstands the spirit of marriage."

What I have called intransigence, the logical purity of Paul VI, obliges us, possibly even more than the positive majority view defended by Cardinal Döpfner does, to ask the fundamental question: Is the Roman Catholic Church, casuistry aside, still ready to judge married relationships not having a procreative intention as guilty and hence condemnable?

We are here at the root of the problem. It is important to know if patristic teaching is unanimous in this direction, if it is faithful to the Bible or not, and if Christian witness must really decree that bodily affections are sinful when they truly witness to the togetherness of two hearts who are not consequently going to "fill the world with their descendants."

Prof. Dumas then examines the question of a magisterium which seems to be opposing the opinions of the majority of the faithful and even the representatives themselves of the faithful who were brought together and questioned by the same magisterium. Dumas' concern is the following:

Is it fear, then—fear of a lowering of the value and prestige of the magisterium—which led Paul VI to follow the indications given by the ministry? I do not think so because the courageous way in which the Pope took on unpopularity seems to me to reveal a very deep conviction on his part. But if there was reason for fear, cannot we also humbly admit on the other hand, that nothing would have benefited the Catholic Church more than for her to have recognized the fact that even she does not have infallibility unless she gropes and searches in order to be faithful, which may mean reforming her teaching? The Council certainly could have been clearer on contraception, but in any case it opened the doors. Speaking quite directly, is it not possible that *Humanae Vitae* marks the end of the search begun by the Council? We outside Catholicism, and doubtless even millions of people inside Catholicism, bitterly deplore this fact.

Dumas' questions are serious and certainly cover the whole spectrum of ecumenical issues, and these have now bounced back into Catholicism's court. It is quite clear that the problem at this stage is no longer one of the Pill but of the Church, truth, freedom, and growth. The encyclical has precipitated them, and this is by no means the smallest point in its favor.

Let Us Thank the Bishop of Rome

The problem, over and beyond the strong and even radical dissensions and criticisms it has raised, seems to be basically positive and constructive. It is a problem which coincides with the enormous efforts being made at rethinking and discussion. The broad lines of ecclesiology, conscience, and anthropology are once again being exposed to their influence. If this produces a crisis, it is a crisis of growth which is both necessary and creative. The only person who trembles with fear today is the one who is without faith. That is why an overall view of the reactions to *Humanae Vitae* in the ecumenical field cannot but leave an extremely positive impression. The deep-down problems which the encyclical has evoked in fact go beyond those mentioned in its pages, and even some of the Protestant reactions have clearly grasped this. Finet and Dumas have already made various references to this when the positive side of the encyclical's picture appears in issues not really mentioned by it.

Even the undeniable crisis of teaching authority which could easily have become a motive for interconfessional enmity is normally seen in a far deeper and more thought-out perspective. The problems which the encyclical has raised are seen as common problems even though they are confronted in different ways.

In this sense the statement of the bishops of the "Old Catholics" of Switzerland issued on September 20, 1968 is quite positive. It declares that

the Christian Catholic Church (of Old Catholics) of Switzerland remains favorable to family planning and birth regulation. Family planning is a question for the Christian consciences of the couples themselves. However, all sides of the question must be seriously examined, and the counsel of a doctor and, in every case, of a priest must be obtained. The present crisis of the Pope's teaching authority cannot become an opportunity for confessional self-justification but must, if possible together with the Roman Catholic brethren, lead to reflection on the Pope's problem and on the entire question of teaching authority which is being seriously attacked today not just in the Roman Catholic Church but in all the Churches.

It is interesting to note both the statement of principle that each person should responsibly follow his own conscience and the admonition to consult the "experts"—the doctor and the priest. This illustrates the idea of formation of conscience, a process which synthesizes the contributions given both by human reason and the wisdom of the gospel. The recognition, as well, of the fact that a crisis of authority and of the magisterium is developing in all the Churches suggests that their desire is for a common search, and this is an essentially constructive ecumenical position.

Perhaps the most interesting opinion, however, on account of its complexity and subject matter, is that of a group of lay people and pastors of the *Folkekirkens evangelisk-lutherske grund* (Evangelical Lutheran Foundation of the People's Church) in Denmark. The statement by this group of thirteen persons is fairly complex since it supports the encyclical's view and especially the motivations behind it—motivations which (they say) are above all, drawn from the gospel and are also in defense of human freedom and dignity. The interesting point they make is the fact that the encyclical is being judged, above all, as a defense of conscience and personal responsibility, against outside interference, especially by authority, and even papal authority. Therefore, on the one hand it gives a completely positive interpretation of the encyclical and on the other it takes issue on several points in the encyclical itself. On the whole it is a very mature and complex judgment which could be used profitably as the basis for constructive, ecumenical dialogue. The statement is as follows:

In the face of the numerous strong attacks against the papal encyclical and the Pope's No to artificial birth control, we, the undersigned, wish to declare:

1. We note with displeasure that the protest against the Pope on the part of the *Folkekirken* has been prompted more by humanist attitudes than by an Evangelical Lutheran position.

2. From the point of view of Lutherans, the Pope would be compromising himself if he preached against sacred scripture and the confession of faith, but he is not compromising himself by taking up a stand against public opinion when he feels obliged in conscience to do this after having prayed and studied the Bible.

3. We are happy that the Pope in opposing a commission majority has stressed that neither ecclesiastical authority nor secular competence can substitute for the conscience of the individual bound by the Word of God, and we would like to add that not even the Pope's permission could replace this.

4. We stress that the fact that our Church has not made a declaration against contraceptive methods cannot be interpreted as an authorization for the use of these methods, but as a sign of its conviction that everyone must render an account of his own life and that on the day of judgment he will not be able to shield himself behind papal or governmental declarations for or against any particular course of action.

5. Hence we protest against the affirmation that a papal permission need be any more or less ecumenical than a papal condemnation of contraceptives.

6. We maintain that the Pope is following biblical thought when he states that no human being may have unlimited disposition over his own body and that a child not yet born may not be killed.

7. We maintain, from the Evangelical Lutheran point of view, that the individual is responsible and must decide to what point the use of contraceptives is in conformity with fidelity to God and the sacred scriptures. But we are glad to see that many women see the encyclical as a protection against the opposing trends found in materialistic declarations and stated by materialistic men.

8. As citizens of a country in which a vast sector of the public does not protest against the introduction of obligatory instruction on

190

the use of contraceptives in schools, we express our thanks to the Bishop of Rome who is defending the freedom of the human race against the tyranny of sin, experts, and public opinion in an age in which men are more and more being reduced to becoming cogs in a machine. We are glad that the sanctity of marriage is being defended and that experts are being encouraged to find solutions to the problems of population growth—solutions, however, which can be accepted by both Christians and non-Christians—and we are glad that the encyclical indicates a natural method of family planning providing it is used responsibly.

The statements made public by the *Kristeligt Dagblad* of October 21, 1968 naturally aroused no small interest in the rest of the Danish Lutheran Church. What, in fact, interests the signatories is more the general intention of the encyclical as a defense of man, and not so much the actual arguments it uses. Moreover, all the statements are deeply Protestant. It seems, in fact, that some sections of Nos. 3 and 4 are a Protestant interpretation of the encyclical.

Because the overall judgment of the encyclical is positive and because the encyclical reaffirms the importance of responsibility before the Word of God, the thanks "to the Bishop of Rome" acquires a special significance. It expresses one of the most positive, present-day aspects of ecumenical dialogue: all the Churches are finding themselves facing the same serious problems which exist in the world today. The same controversies and confessional theological discussions pass through the reality of the world and man's urgent, concrete problems. All this serves to produce a more immediate, sincere dialogue which was in danger of becoming abstract and academic. Seen in this light, the encyclical could become, instead of a serious ecumenical problem, an opportunity for a healthy crisis and a test for all Christians on their capacity for living and interpreting the message of the gospel in the context of today's world.

Chapter 5 Pincus, the Encyclical and Demographic Statistics

I have defended oral contraceptives. I have taken part in the campaign for the diffusion of contraceptives organized by the inhabitants of Maciel Island, and at the moment I have just been studying the possibilities of injectable contraceptives. It is only forty-eight hours since I first heard of the papal encyclical and I shall have much thinking to do in the next few days. Who knows, maybe the Pope's decision will tomorrow be acclaimed as a prophetic gesture! Certainly, contraceptives were a convenient solution. Just as certainly, as a doctor and as a Catholic I don't know what I shall do in the future.

This is how Dr. Emilio Ottuli, a gynecologist from Buenos Aires, expressed himself in an interview reported by *Perspectivas de Dialogo* of July 1968. The same issue gives a short, colorful statement from another gynecologist, Prof. Robert Nicholson: "We must now descend into the cellar again and await the return of fine weather. It would be a good idea to go into exile for five years; goodness knows if it will be long enough!"

Why should scientists show so much concern? Is it because the Pope's decision does not seem justified when it is contrasted with real scientific solutions, or is it because as Catholics they are aware on the one hand of the problems and solutions proposed by scientific research, and on the other, that the Pope speaks not in the name of science but of moral and religious principles? Moreover, there is a far more serious question to be answered. The possibilities of directing man have greatly increased today—biologists even speak of planning a particular type of man. This so-called manipulation has no immediately negative meaning in itself. At this point, however, we must ask what criteria are to be established which will limit this manipulation, and who is to determine such criteria. Above all, however, is it conceivable that what man has succeeded in achieving by means of his intellectual powers should now be limited by introducing criteria of a different kind?

The more progress the medical and biological sciences make, the more serious these problems become and the more they distress those scientists concerned with man's general welfare. These men are well aware that it is not merely a matter of improving the human situation biologically and economically, but of not bringing an imbalance into the factors which together compose an essential, integral part of man's personality. Above all, the problem is that of competences—not in the sense of the exclusion of one by the other, but in the sense of a reciprocal integration. Each sector which affects man cannot ignore the other sectors—this would constitute a real danger for man himself.

The Question of Competence

To what extent is it necessary and allowable for religious authorities to intervene in a question which concerns not only a religious fact—since marriage is a sacrament for a Catholic—but also a psychological and biological problem? If we admit even to a minimal degree the possibility of a relationship existing between the religious magisterium and this order of reality and its problems, we need to find the underlying reasons for it.

On August 6, 1968, a week after the encyclical was published, the ex-Archbishop of Bombay, the Jesuit Thomas Roberts, who is already well-known for his open statements in favor of a revision of the classical teaching, said: "In the final analysis, the law is as strong as the power that authority has of enforcing it. The Church, however, has not the power to ensure that its laws be observed in the bedroom."

The archbishop's words do not pay much attention to prelatic modesty. Without any sidestepping they attack a magisterial intervention which, according to Roberts, is unjustifiable. Clearly such a position, which is representative of many others including those of Catholics, presupposes the double conviction that a decision by religious authorities on this matter should not be based on the concept of the law of nature, considering the difficulties and discussions now revolutionizing the concept of "nature," and that the individual's conscience in his private life should, at the most, be advised but not commanded by an external authority even if it be a religious one.

When addressing "men of science," No. 24 of the encyclical, for its part, seems to suggest some motives for the religious magisterium's claiming competence for its reasoning in this field. No. 24 states: "We wish now to express our encouragement to men of science, who can considerably advance the welfare of marriage and the family, along with peace of conscience, if by pooling their efforts they labor to explain more thoroughly the various conditions favoring a proper regulation of births." It is particularly desirable that, according to the wish already expressed by Pope Pius XII, medical science succeed in providing a sufficiently secure basis for a regulation of births, founded on the observance of natural rhythms. In this way scientists, and especially Catholic scientists, will contribute to demonstrating in actual fact that, as the Church teaches, "a true contradiction cannot exist between the divine laws pertaining to the transmission of life and those pertaining to the fostering of authentic conjugal love."

In this short text there are three quotations, two from *Gaudium et Spes* and one from the 1957 discourse of Pius XII. The three quotations refer to the grounds which justify, on the one hand, the religious magisterium's interest in the problem of procreation and, on the other, the reasons for the men of science dealing with the problem—obviously in addition to those of a scientific nature. First, it should be on account of their interest in "making a great contribution to the good of marriage and the family." Certainly this does not mean directly contributing to marriage ethics but rather to marriage "hygiene," in the widest sense of the word. The scope of this, however, is to contribute to "peace of conscience" by clarifying more and more the different conditions "which favor an honest regulation of births."

It is admitted, then, that ethical honesty in married and family life is based on presuppositions involving biological behavior which is understood by the encyclical as the order in which the law of nature is revealed. It must also be noted that the quotation from *Gaudium et Spes*, No. 52: "They can give a great contribution . . ." simply says, "They will seek to explain more thoroughly the various conditions favoring a proper regulation of births." Immediately afterward, this invitation is defined and given its objective according to the basic thought pattern already given in the encyclical: ". . . that . . . medical science succeed in providing a sufficiently secure basis for a regulation of birth, founded on the observance of natural rhythms." This is the line which *Humanae Vitae* has chosen, which is however a continuation of the line already chosen by Pius XII. In fact, this quote, too, is simply taken from the famous discourse of Pius XII in 1951.

The last reason does not directly concern the help that the doctor can offer "to the welfare of marriage and the family," but is of an obviously apologetical nature, for it concerns the contribution that the doctor can make to proving factually that ". . . a true contradiction cannot exist between the divine laws pertaining to the transmission of life and those pertaining to fostering authentic married love." This last phrase is taken from *Gaudium et Spes*, No. 51, and is applied to marriage in particular.

On the other hand, in relation to the topic of contraception and usable methods, Dr. Paul Chauchard, a vigorous opponent of the use of contraceptives, acknowledged that the moralist must have a say in the problem because it concerns not just the welfare of the individual but a much wider welfare encompassing the whole of society. In a book written in 1967, *La pilule et le planning familial,* in a discussion with Dr. Lagroua Weill-Hallé, Chauchard says:

It is not only the Pill that should worry the confessor and that concerns the examination of conscience. How can it be denied that all the psychotropic medicines affect the moralist just as much? After all the massacres caused by the automobile, more and more is being said about a motorist's morality. Here, too, the moralist must be concerned over the abuse of drugs which attenuate responsibility and self-control. The religious problem involving the Pill is not a question of prohibitions and permissions. It is the problem that men and women must face when confronting their sexuality in a responsible way.

Chauchard, a specialist in sexology and the author of many works on this subject, gives a good statement of the position of many doctors when he concludes his treatment of the topic by giving reasons for his opposition to the use of progestatives:

I am against the Pill, not on account of moral or religious prejudice, but only after serious, exhaustive thinking on the way in which it acts. First, the Pill is a hormonal treatment and it is dangerous to administer it habitually to a normal person. The Pill is bad biologically, not because of the immediate or long-range side effects it may have, but because it encroaches on the very nature of the woman by disrupting her hormonal cycle. Therefore, it is much more insidious than local contraceptives which are limited to interrupting the sexual act. This disruption of female sexuality runs the risk of being unwittingly unbalancing from the psychological point of view.

196

On the other hand, like every contraceptive device, as a defensive measure which denaturalizes sexuality, the Pill is against the harmony of the couple. It is also harmful in that it brings with it a certain servitude and anxiety over the fear of forgetting, which increases the risk of pregnancy. Besides the fact that it is unsatisfactory, the Pill has the added unsuitability of often leading to abortion—especially the modern forms of abortion which are neither more nor less than pre-natal murder: use of antimetabolic and antinidatric pills, the danger-ous intrauterine ring, not to mention surgical sterilization. This does not mean that the female cycle may not be regularized in pathological cases. In these cases it is a legitimate therapeutical measure. This is what a "good pill" or a "good use" of the Pill would consist of. It could also be used as a means of *dépannage* for emergencies in diffi-cult cases but on the condition that this occur as an educative measure which will enable it later to be done manually.

To say No to the pill and all contraceptive devices is not the same as rejecting birth limitation or preferring the other "natural" technique which is the temperature method. It is to want to promote sex education based on self-knowledge and self-control, for it is these that make a man and a woman free before their sexuality which then becomes more valuable to them. This allows them to procreate volun-tarily in an ever-deeper interpersonal communion, not just in the sex-ual act but in their whole life.

Up to this point his rejection of contraceptive methods ap-pears to be a typically medical and psychological problem, even if Chauchard asserts that it "concerns the moralist" by reason of the implications it has for the education of the married couple and the family. However, Chauchard then emphasizes this aspect even farther:

The serious problems of family and world stability which people want to resolve in a simplistic way by means of the Pill, affect politicians, moralists, and religious counselors who are the people responsible and who must take an interest in these problems. Enlightened by biological arguments, they must then use them to put technology at the service of man and not to open the door to a dehumanizing technocracy be-cause of poorly understood sentimental reasons.

The moralist's and religious counselor's competence is hence to be based on the information given by biology, and in this way they can prevent the use of contraceptives giving rise to an excessive manipulation of man and interfering with the well-being of married life.

The religious magisterium's competence, therefore, finds its justification in its service to man's well-being. Consequently, since man's well-being is dependent on his biological conditioning, the religious magisterium should, in a way, sanction the biological order. This is what Chauchard seems to be stating (and we repeat, he is the representative of this position) when he says: "It is because the Pill is psychobiologically harmful that it should not be legalized in the civil, moral, and religious spheres."

It can be queried however, whether, simply because this may be true in the civil and moral spheres (and in the sense of a purely anthropological ethics), it is equally true in the religious sphere. In the first two cases it could happen that a deepening and widening of our psychobiological and pharmacological knowledge could suggest other solutions in civil legislation and different conduct in the moral sphere. In the third case, the religious magisterium may change when the above alteration occurs, or it may not change because there are other principles on which it bases its judgment on any given mode of behavior or intervention in the biological order. In fact, once it is admitted that the religious counselor must be "enlightened by biological arguments," it must then be admitted that such "light" is not necessarily *infallible* and *irreformable,* and that the religious magisterium also depends on an order of things which by its intrinsic nature allows of a range of development of which we do not yet know the extent.

Hence the competence of biological and medical science should be limited to suggesting what is here and now revealed by the *present state* of its knowledge and without thereby dictating the choice of the religious magisterium. The religious magisterium, in turn, should not put forward an already known truth in the religious field as a cogent starting point for psychobiological research, or as an end point which their research must attempt to attain. In the quoted text of No. 24 of the encyclical, however, it is stated that the task of men of science consists "in providing a sufficiently secure basis for a regulation of birth, founded on the observance of natural rhythms." Hence it is assigned a precise field of competence which certainly does not mean that it is attempting to force those in research to pursue their general investigations in only this one direction. It is simply an invitation for them to provide the details and discoveries which will facilitate a surer, less mechanical use of "natural" means.

In this way the field of competence, as well as being made more specific, is also given definite boundaries and made smaller. It would also seem to suggest that the area of the religious magisterium's competence is restricted to a very precise area—that of ethical principles as seen from the standpoint of a religious teaching. The fact that this teaching is "enlightened" by psychobiological data does not mean that it is conditioned by this data unless it is admitted that there can be an evolution on the basis of this same psychobiological data. In that case the problem then passes from the realm of competence to a specific issue; namely, to the far wider and more delicate one of the relationship between the data provided by nature and the religious judgment and consequently to the problem of the historical nature of religious teaching and finally to that of its value and its justifiability.

On the other hand, Paul VI himself, when the vast discussion on the encyclical was getting under way, made certain clarifications at Castel Gandolfo on August 5, 1968: "The norm we pronounced is not ours but belongs to the structure of life, love, and human dignity, which is derived from the law of God." The intervention, then, is within the scope of a religious magisterium which reads in the laws of life the law inscribed there by God, and which has no intention in so doing of interfering in the wider, strictly scientific field. Therefore the Pope, as well as anticipating the objection that this procedure excludes all possibility of taking into consideration the concrete information revealed by science, also states that we are here dealing with a moral norm. Paul VI says:

It is not a norm which may ignore the sociological and demographic conditions of our time. Nor is it of itself opposed, as some seem to think, to a reasonable birth limitation, nor to scientific research and therapeutic treatment, even less to responsible parenthood and to family peace and harmony. It is simply a severe and demanding moral norm still valid today, which forbids the use of methods which intentionally prevent procreation thereby degrading the purity of love and the mission of married life. Through the power of our office we have spoken in the interests of duty and pastoral charity. We therefore send a paternal wish to all the couples and families who are trying to find their moral courage and true happiness in the order willed by God.

The competence of the religious magisterium, therefore, lies only in this "order willed by God." It is clear, then, that the consequent reading of this order willed by God from the data given by biology of the process of procreation has repercussions on the concrete choices made by the couple when choosing their course of action, and on medicine, which prescribes what intervention may be employed. Just as the religious magisterium cannot determine the laws proper to the fields of biology and medicine, likewise medicine and biology can, at the most, help the religious magisterium to "read" in the biological law what the religious magisterium calls the "law of nature" and the "divine law." The problem, in any case, now turns on whether the religious magisterium can really interpret the biological law (as it is known today) as the divine law, and if the law of nature must be understood in the way that the magisterium today understands it.

It is precisely these two aspects which are being questioned today, while the magisterium and another line of theological thinking reaffirm their validity. It is in this way that Prof. A. Günthör in his volume *Kommentar zur Enzyklika "Humanae Vitae,"* Freiburg, 1969, affirms the ecclesiastical magisterium's competency in matters touching natural law, and examines the theological basis of this competency. He sees it as an act of loyalty to divine revelation and creation, as well as a sharing in the office of service for the good of man. At the same time, however, Günthör is anxious to free the encyclical from any accusation of "biologism," as if it had placed the human person and love below the level of biological laws, and he reinstates the encyclical's concrete and spiritual vision of married love. The encyclical's thought is thereby once again placed in a field of competence, which as Günthör states, is that proper to it: the personal relationship of the couple in each expression of this relationship escapes division and fragmentation and assumes its true qualities when seen in an overall view which can be defined as the structure and the law of man and love in their totality. Hence every infringement

—such as that of contraceptive methods, and above all the interruption of maternity—is an infringement on love, and consequently on man.

It can safely be said that it is not the encyclical which has surpassed its proper field of competence—all the more because Paul VI himself, as we have seen, clarified his thoughts on the matter. It should be said, rather, that the commentaries on the encyclical are to blame and, unfortunately, especially those commentaries of an apologetical nature. They have attempted to justify it in every possible way, and to avoid and foresee every possible objection, and have thus tended to take it into fields which it did not directly intend entering.

Prof. Bruno Gherardini, in *L'Osservatore Romano* of February 15, 1969, in presenting Günthör's work, observes that one of the merits of this "serene interpreter," as he calls Günthör, is exactly that of "getting back to the essential content of the encyclical. The encyclical's subject is not more or less one of giving a broad teaching with respect to the problems of birth and overpopulation in the world. Its topic is absolutely different and deals only with 'the correct ordering of the transmission of human life within the field of marriage understood as a community of love.' " For this reason, says Gherardini, all this has been brought to the attention of "too brash commentators and critics who took the encyclical into different regions from those outlined by the Holy Father."

If it is not the magisterium as such which has gone out of its territory but rather its commentators, then the problem of competencies must be faced, first and foremost, when the problem of the function of men of science, especially biologists and physicians, is posed. Both the negative and positive reactions to this question can betray a measure of ambiguity. If negative, there can almost be detected a satisfaction that the religious magisterium agrees with the unfavorable opinion of the physician and the gynecologist on contraception. The risk here, however, is of drawing the religious magisterium into a compromise in which logical conclusions are easy to foresee. No matter how illustrious the physician and biologist are, they have a poor knowledge of the categories of theological science and how demanding these are. The positive reactions reveal an aggressive reaction toward the magisterium, almost as if the latter's intention were to put a stop to research, even if not directed just toward the deepening of knowledge of natural rhythms as indicated in No. 24 of *Humanae Vitae.*

Yet it must be said that too much importance was attached to the presence of noted experts, as for example in the Papal Commission, who were then almost all found to be in favor of allowing the use of contraceptive methods, from a scientific point of view. This consequently led to too much insistence on the fact that the Pope had to make his decisions from another point of view, independently—of course!—of the scientific judgment. All this created a violent reaction on one hand, because the opinion of the "greats" of science, whose presence had made everyone so proud, were not followed and, on the other hand, it had to be said that a religious magisterium cannot have scientific opinions as its basis since it operates in an entirely different sphere. In this way the ambiguous nature of the "agreement between faith and science" became all the more apparent and, moreover, the impression which was given, quite unintentionally, was that of a superficial *embrassons-nous* which turned out to be of little use for science and completely useless for the religious magisterium.

Once the respective areas of competence have been clarified and once it has been said that it is at least dangerous, if not useless, to appeal to medicine and biology for either an opinion "for" or "against" the magisterium, what remains to be done? There still remains the individual problem for the physician and the biologist who, wanting to be believers faithful to the religious magisterium pertaining to their faith, can find themselves faced with being forced to choose between a correct course of action toward their scientific convictions and a correct course of action toward the religious magisterium.

There also remains the problem of the person who opposes in the name of medical, psychological, biological, or demographic science a teaching which, although intending to remain in the strictly religious sphere, also necessarily involves an interpretation of the biological law as a law of nature and divine law which are included in the religious sphere. The real debate cannot be obscured by a skirmish of this type, but must arrive at a more dialectical and realistic confrontation of the issues. The question thereby becomes a brutal one but must nevertheless be asked. Is a religious faith bound up with a sacralized vision of the world still possible in a world which is tending more and more toward rejecting both the halo and the interpreter's key to the sacred?

If a faith which preserves a "mythico-sacral" vision of reality wants to survive, will it still find any common ground with, and a place for, a science whose future we gaze at anxiously but whose progress we cannot stop? Jean Rostand has said, from the purely scientific point of view, both spine-chilling and exalting things about the future of man.

Professing Faith but not Repudiating Science

That, then, is the question. It is a personal question for the scientist who does not, just on account of this, intend denying his faith. It is a question for the man whose knowledge forces him to face a dilemma when dealing with people involved in this problem. Should he follow what science recommends as useful, safe, and not immoral in that particular case, or should he decline to help in that particular, human case because a religious magisterium is opposed to it in the name of general principles? The man of science cannot deny his religious faith for that single case just as he cannot deny his scientific convictions.

This is the problem voiced by Dr. Michel Chartier, a leading hospital gynecologist, legal expert in gynecological problems, and member of the International Center for Sexological and Family Research and Study of the University of Louvain. He wrote in *Le Monde* of August 14, 1968 on the subject of professing one's faith and not repudiating science.

Dr. Chartier realizes that "by force of circumstances the Catholic gynecologist finds himself caught between the decisions of the magisterium and the day-to-day life of both Catholic and non-Catholic couples. It is difficult for him not to express what the couples feel and what his experience has taught him even if doing this can become a little disconcerting."

First, Dr. Chartier states that a Catholic gynecologist "is aware of the value of human life and the respect due to it, so much so that he is anxious to inculcate it in the many childless couples who consult him." He then says he knows the difference as given by the "traditional" morality between the observance of the female cycle and so-called contraceptive methods, and he laments the fact that the latter are too often reduced to the Pill, which is only one of the numerous methods available. The gynecologist observes that couples are scarcely aware of this difference in practice. Their first, immediate request is for a temporary or definitive halt to their biological fertility. He also maintains that couples understand very well that it is more important to reflect on the motives for regulation than on the licity of the methods. It must also be recognized that everyday experience proves that periodic abstinence may be employed without respect for the fundamental values of married life and that these values may be pursued and lived by couples who do practice contraception.

For this reason this same Catholic gynecologist

questions the value of a law which seems to consider women as if they were all perfectly normal with ovulations which are always regular, whereas it is known that approximately 20 percent of them are exceptions to these general norms. On account of this, he is sorry for the difficult lot of those women whose higher nervous centers are sensitive to climacteric, emotional, and affective stimulations which make all the rules irregular for them and which make ovulation inconstant and variable.

There is a further difficulty to complicate matters; namely, that "the rhythm method is inapplicable in the premenopause period even though fertility is not necessarily to be excluded—who does not know instances of women being pregnant after the age of forty-five?"

It can be objected, however, that the encyclical itself urges the men of science to deepen the knowledge of natural rhythms and to clarify "more thoroughly the various conditions favoring a proper regulation of births." Dr. Chartier replies to this with a certain amount of skepticism:

The discovery of a treatment which will allow the female rhythm to be efficiently regulated is not unthinkable, but this hope for the moment is still very much in the realm of hypotheses for anyone who knows the fragility and variability of hypothalamico-hypophyseal interactions which control the exclusion of the ovulation process. The Catholic gynecologist is therefore surprised concerning how this regulative treatment could possibly be contrasted with ovulation inhibitors. Probably the mechanics would be different but the purpose is the same: to guarantee that any given cycle remains infertile. On the other hand, let us not delude ourselves. Such a medicament, if it does one day exist, will like every other therapeutical intervention, have its limits and its drawbacks. It is a scientific fact which can be observed every day—the humble aspirin is no exception to this rule.

Over and beyond these scientific objections, however, there are others of an eminently human nature which a doctor conscious as a Catholic of his service for men cannot pass over. In fact, he feels it with special intensity. One instance, for example, no longer as hypothetical as imagined in the casuistry of book morality is the following:

How is it possible to impose one and the same attitude on those couples who normally live together and on those whose profession or socioeconomic conditions separate them occasionally or for long periods of time? These couples can only have intercourse on the weekend or during short periods on leave, and often find themselves faced with the insoluble dilemma of either abstaining or risking a pregnancy.

There is, on the other hand, the argument of pleasure-seeking, of a hedonist attitude combined with the intention of avoiding fatherhood or motherhood and hence finding it useful to have recourse to preparations which remove the fear of unpleasant and unforeseen repercussions. Some have even gone so far as to satirize on these subjects and appeal to a "dolorous" and even "masochistic" view of Christianity, which once again shows just how dangerous it is to speak on matters as if one really understood them in depth. For example, Maurice Clavel in the *Nouvel Observateur*, among his various arguments in favor of the encyclical, has included the following:

(1) We are no longer in the time of Innocent III and no one is forced to be a Catholic. (2) Nobody, either Christian or non-Christian, has ever said that being a Christian is easy. (3) The most insidious and ignoble temptation of our age is that of cheating and of playing on both tables, spiritual honor together with full, temporal enjoyment, traveling to eternal beatitude by bus.

Clavel, consequently, mentions the pontifical offense of "non-assistance to a person in heat" and is at odds with those Christians who would like to see the Pope proclaim the dogma of original innocence in the place of that of original sin. He concludes by inviting the reader to smile with him at the "moving disappointment of those who, when they are ready to begin the thing, would like the Holy Father to come in person and tuck them into bed." We quote this "lay" defense precisely because it is typically lay and feels a certain amount of superiority over the poor Christians floundering in their ideas of original sin, struggle against the devil, evil of the flesh, etc. Unfortunately it reveals to excess another characteristic of this type of laicism: it thinks of Christianity precisely in terms of the time of Innocent III when *De bello contra carnem et diabolum* was written, and when the devil and the flesh were seen just about everywhere, especially in the marriage bed, as long as it was not that of the feudal lord taking advantage of the *jus primae noctis* by divine grace and with papal and episcopal blessing.

To not want to admit that on this level we are certainly not in the field of Christianity (the "Christian" Middle Ages have other characteristics which entitle them to be called Christian!), means that either one does not understand anything about Christianity, or does not want to understand it because it is comforting to make an amusing puppet for oneself and thus remain in one's own enlightened and overdeveloped laicism. The simple fact of the matter is that while Christianity, on the one hand, has never rejected the dogma of original sin, at the same time, it has never conjured up the dogma of the vocation to universal suffering and, in any case, it has the dogmas of a redemption and a resurrection which—at least according to Christianity—do not wait till the end of time to begin being effective but are already operative in history.

If God has given man the intelligence to find something to calm his worries and his sorrows—and ours, in an age of enlightened laicism, are no less than those of the obscure monastic and Christian Middle Ages; they are simply more scientific!—he does it because he has put nature in the hands of his sons so that they may work as collaborators in his good and paternal creative action.

As for the intelligent man who becomes a physician, there has existed such a personage well before the time of Innocent III; that is, even from Paleo-Christian times, the image of *Christus Medicus* who cured man's sicknesses—including the flow of blood from the poor woman suffering from hemorrhage—as a manifestation of the divine, renewing life that he carried with him. Physicians, too, were seen by Christians not as Satan's aides who convinced men "to go to paradise by bus," but as helpers of Christ the physician and good Samaritan. All this is certainly more Christian than satirizing on "Christians in heat" and on a Holy Father as one who is anxious to tuck in the blankets of love-making Christians.

Unfortunately these lucid, "lay" examinations of Christianity's intentions are understood by a number of those who defend the encyclical to the bitter end, as unexpected assistance from *extra moenia*. They do not realize what a Trojan horse it will turn out to be to draw it in just for this small, limited, political action, when seen in the time and context of what the whole of Christianity is. In such cases it is much more Christian to answer these objections with the observations of Dr. Chartier who, although criticizing the encyclical, still wants to remain a Christian and a Catholic, and evidently has no intention of going to paradise by bus. He says:

The Catholic gynecologist refuses in the name of his experience to think that the couple practicing contraception has no other purpose in mind than their own convenience and pleasure. He knows the anxiety of women who are afraid of a pregnancy and for this reason alone refuse their husbands. This anguish is the wellspring of marriage conflicts, incomprehension, and affective separation from each other, and cannot but reflect on the manner of bringing up the children already born and those to be born. He has seen a good number of couples, including Catholic couples who, on account of lack of foresight or unfortunate results with the so-called natural method and because they cannot accept any further pregnancies either psychologically or physiologically, search for a solution in abortion. The promise of an efficient contraceptive technique in the future which will make their married life livable is frequently the only thing which gives them the courage to accept this new, undesired pregnancy.

This is certainly more Christian than smiling at the "moving disappointment of those who, when they are already to begin the thing, would like the Holy Father to come in person and tuck them into bed." This is just seeing the "thing," and not the great reality where love for the Christian does not consist, platonically, of great, learned debates on love and expensive, "moral" flirtations which only well-to-do people—that is, those with the money and the many other necessities—can afford, but where it consists also in derided, ironized "sex," willed in any case by God in the same way as he willed grace, redemption, and paradise.

What matters is the basic genuine meaning of the realities which the Christian sees, so that instead of concentrating on the "thing," as do ignorant Christians who do not know history and who grumble because they believe they are still in the time of Innocent III, there is the observation which the doctor can make, for example, as Dr. Chartier has done. He observes that

experience shows how when a couple decide to begin employing contraception it is an opportunity for them to make an examination of conscience of their responsibilities, and it gradually leads them to real moral progress in which the recognition of the other as a person and of the child as a human value to be advanced, reveal the presence of real charity. The Catholic gynecologist notices that their idea of sexual pleasure is often false, as if this were not indispensable to the structuring of a deeply human, fruitful love. Moreover it is surprising to notice how this pleasure is too often absent from sexual encounter and dialogue.

If the question of competence is an ambiguous one in the relationship between medicine and the religious magisterium, it is no less so in the relationship between the doctor and the couple who consult him. The problem has been repeatedly put by Catholic doctors after the encyclical in this way: "What constructive meaning can our help have if these couples know that by coming to us they expect no more than a precise, straight-out rejection by us of the use of all contraceptive methods? If we do it by appealing to our scientific convictions they will be able to take our advice, but if they know that it is only on account of complete loyalty to a religious teaching they may make up their own minds with possibly dangerous consequences or else go to doctors who do not have these scruples."

This, too, is a real problem with which the physician is faced.

Is he allowed to use his scientific authority to impose a particular solution? If this solution were purely and simply one of accepting the encyclical's teaching, when applied would it lead to a disturbance of normal growth and the couple's peaceful development, or would it gradually help them to overcome their difficulties? The principle, says Dr. Chartier, must be that of a respect for freedom and a realism which takes the couple's present situation into consideration:

The Catholic gynecologist respects both the freedom and the story of the couple who come to him. He guesses that by means of what can appear to be aberrant behavior it is really unity which the couple are looking for. He also knows that their doubts and uncertainties can lead them to a greater human and spiritual maturity. On the whole, he is more ready to put his confidence in the couple than not to do so. What seems essential to him, if he is to guarantee a healthy regulation of childbirth, is to consider the couple in their historical reality, keeping in mind their sociocultural conditions and their psychoaffective and spiritual maturity in order to promote what is essential; namely, unity, fidelity, and fertility, in a word: the love lived by the couple. The gynecologist does not want to replace the couple in making their final decision or definitively enslave them to any particular technique. For this reason he experiences no difficulty in helping the couple to choose a method—cyclic or otherwise—which will best allow them to fulfill the overall fertility of their married life.

It is clear that at this point a moralist can advance some reservations, if not direct objections. Msgr. Lambruschini has already observed that the encyclical rejects the possibility of the formation of a contrary opinion. The encyclical itself, in No. 27, urges doctors and hospital personnel to "promote on every occasion the discovery of solutions inspired by faith and right reason, striving to arouse this conviction and this respect in their associates." Dr. Chartier takes his standpoint not from the principle but from the concrete situation which can arise in his relationship to the couple. He makes allowance for the fact that his attitude after the encyclical is possibly a surprising one, and yet he then goes on to examine the possibilities for tomorrow when married couples will come to him with their problems which he must be able to solve, not with the moralist's impregnable logical principles, but with the means that his science offers him. He draws a historical parallel which possibly to a trained moralist will not have much value, but for us men in the street cannot but be significant since we cannot see what possible hidden difference can exist between the two instances. Dr. Chartier says that

today the surgeon can cure certain diseases of the kidneys by mutilating one of them as long as the patient agrees to it. Everyone permits this. Yet there was a time when the authorities condemned this practice as being "against nature." What the Catholic gynecologist wants, today as yesterday, is to be able with technical methods to help the couple better promote their unity and their fertility in a progressive spiritual and moral maturity and with full responsibility.

But Dr. Chartier says that there is a preoccupation which affects the surgeon on a deeper level: "In a word, this is what he wants: to affirm his faith without repudiating science."

This certainly does not mean that the encyclical's teaching is completely being rejected. It appears, rather, as a norm which the physician utilizes but which he must put in the real context of his help to the harmonious growth of the couple. This outlook is considerably different from that proposed, just to quote an example, by the Protestant Church in Austria in a letter of the bishop Dr. Gerhard May, of August 12, 1968: "It is not the Church, but the conscientious physician who must decide if the use of the Pill, of another contraceptive method, or abstinence in each individual case, is the most suitable for the couple." In this case a precise area of competence has evidently been outlined while in Dr. Chartier's case there is more nuance since the normative and formative value of the Church for the physician's conscience is not being rejected.

Evolution of Marriage Morality and the Contribution of Medicine

The position of the physician concerned with the moral implications of his assistance to the couples who turn to him with their problems was not an easy one even before the encyclical *Humanae Vitae*. This is not to say, either, because of the situation where a concrete choice has to be made in each individual case, that every problem has now been solved by the publication of the encyclical. Moreover, the encyclical itself, while reaffirming a principle, admits—in the section devoted to pastoral exhortations—that it is an overall ideal to be aimed at in a global view of married and family love. If this ideal is to be realized, it requires the contribution of all those who are directly or indirectly responsible in this field. Those directly concerned are physicians and biologists, and above all, gynecologists. Why, then, have they found themselves in difficult situations, and why do they claim that they are still in these situations to a certain extent?

From this point of view the problem is not scientific in the proper sense of the word. It is concerned with another problem and an objective, factual datum—the evolution brought about in the understanding of marriage morality, and its consequences on the practical course of action the couple adopts, and the consequent contribution given by the physician. This side of the problem has already been disclosed in Dr. Chartier's attitude. It returns in the double perspective of Prof. C. P. Sporken, gynecologist and pediatrician of Nijmegen, and president of the Commission for Family Problems of the Dutch Pastoral Council. It appeared in *De Tijd* of August 3, 1968. The double perspective is given by the outlook on sexual and marriage morality and by the consequences which have arisen from these new problems. After observing the problems which were slowly being created for married life within, and on account of, the sociocultural evolution of our time, Prof. Sporken states that problems such as these

have had, of necessity, an influence on ethical thinking. Among Catholic couples an opposition was becoming evident to the fact that only a "pastoral" solution was being offered for their problems. This stimulated a reorientation in thinking on morality, which was made all the more pressing by the development of anthropology and the sciences related to it.

First, there has occurred a separation of sexuality from procreation. For centuries only one purpose had been assigned to sexuality —that of procreating. This interpretation determined every moral judgment, even of the motives underlying it. The marriage act had to be carried out according to the "natural laws," and it was not to be sought in order to satisfy the desires for pleasure. Only a few decades ago it was noticed that in the case of a human being, even from the biological point of view, there is no necessary relationship between the marriage act and procreation—this is how Dr. Ruygers treated the question in 1952. Anthropology and psychology on their part have demonstrated that sexuality is much more than a simple activity with a view to procreation. It is the expression of married love in all its aspects. The ethical question thus underwent a change. No longer was it formulated: What is the scope of the procreative act? It was now formulated: What is the authentic meaning of human sexual life?

This change in the awareness of the problem itself which was favored by the development of scientific knowledge is of the greatest importance for the moral questions which are connected with it. There is evidence, for example, that the moral judgment of the marriage act can no longer depend solely on its biological finality and that there can be no dissociation between the different "ends" of marriage (if the term ends may be used in this case). It is married love in itself which is directed toward its own specific realization and its own fertility. "Fertility" must be understood first as truly human fertility, which means a rational, responsible fertility.

The second side from which conventional morality was to suffer severe attack was from the criticism of "natural law" and the possibilities of manipulating nature. Even though it is not a term directly belonging to St. Thomas' teaching (as the theologian Prof. Arntz proved in 1965), it seems that the term natural law had undergone a continual development in traditional Catholic moral thought to the place where it had become a starting point which equated the physical nature of the human being (his biological laws) with the ethical norms themselves. Clearly this idea leads to an infrahuman morality. Only anthropological thinking based on a view of human nature endowed with reason can serve as a starting point for moral reflection. Moreover, if reason is seen as the distinctive sign of human nature, it means that the natural law is as dynamic and historically conditioned as the human being itself.

The real evolution of traditional moral thought was of a far more fundamental nature. It gradually came to be seen more clearly that the starting point of Christian morality could not be found in a natural law with its Greek origins, which has been badly interpreted and sanctioned by the official magisterium of the Church. The demand gradually became stronger for a reorientation of Christian morality by research into the fundamental principle of the gospel message as understood today in the living faith and moral sense of the majority of the faithful (Sporken dealt with this in 1967). This is the reason that marriage morality cannot have its starting point in the biological structure of the sexual act, but must find it in the message of salvation presented to mankind.

Even though this idea had already been in existence in the Church for ten years, it seemed impossible to be able to develop it systematically until recently. The moral problem always remained centered on the sexual act, and the question remained that of knowing if it was licit or not to intentionally prevent biological fertility by means of a deliberate intervention. This old question was always being asked in the old way and the answer was always given according to the old categories and ideas. Logically enough, the answer was always negative because it was simply moving in a continuous, vicious circle.

It is interesting to note that a physician gives the same clarification which we felt necessary when dealing with the question of competence. The physician is always led either to completely separate the two fields—the biological and the moral—or to reason as if the two were identical. In this way several physicians praised *Humanae Vitae* as if it were a scientific discovery or a divine ratification of a scientific discovery. Prof. Sporken indicates how it is one thing to hinge the moral judgment concerning the meaning of the marriage act on biological laws and another thing to hinge it on the message of salvation, to the extent that revelation has given married relations and procreation a meaning. Does this different view, which has been called "new" and which had made considerable progress before the encyclical, now risk being checked and forced to undergo an involution? It may appear to be so in certain cases, but Prof. Sporken is not the only one after the publication of *Humanae Vitae* to restate that it is a factor which can no longer simply be rejected.

The fact that the meaning of the sexual act should be based on the religious message of salvation and not on biological structures does not mean depriving every intervention of man of its moral value, nor does it exempt him, therefore, from making a moral judgment on this intervention. In fact, a different notion of the reality of sexuality and of married relations taken in their entirety, logically entails a different attitude toward man's conscious, willed intervention into it. Prof. Sporken observes, moreover, that it was at this stage of moral thinking that oral contraceptives appeared. They made the regulation of births possible in a totally different way than former methods in use up to that time. In a discourse in 1958 on the inhibitive means of ovulation, Pius XII had stated that to make a moral judgment on these means, it was necessary to take the principle of "double effect" as the starting point. Traditional Catholic morality taught that sterilization is only permitted as a secondary effect of a therapeutical operation—indirect sterilization.

The first publications by moralists after this speech by Pius XII consequently took the direction indicated by the Pope: the use of contraceptives is licit on the condition that it be desired first as a remedy for a pathological state (thus, for example, van Kohl in 1958). This gave rise to a tendency to search for the cause of married problems in pathological causes; for example, by considering cycles with an irregular duration as "abnormal" to the point of considering an ovulation produced in the lactation period as "unnatural" (Férin in 1961).

All this reasoning, however, gives the impression of being no more than a way of avoiding the ban in force on all contraceptives and any willed form of infertility. It is all very understandable, however, if it is remembered that, according to the opinions current at the time, the judgments of the Church were seen as having an absolute value. Rock in 1962 and Janssens in 1964 confronted the problem from a completely different viewpoint. According to them, the use of the Pill for the sake of avoiding ovulation is a licit method and, as such, is to be put on a par with the method of periodic continence. In both cases procreation is positively excluded but in such a way that the physical structure of the marriage act remains integral. As a second argument they maintain that the suppression, or the holding back, of ovulation is not strictly sterilization because sterilization in its strict sense is the destruction of the generative power which does not happen in this case.

Beemer, in 1963, brought attention to the fact that in the judgment of the Church the phrase "to render infecund" is understood in too biological a sense. The sole form of sterilization which is morally inacceptable is "integral" sterilization; that is, the form bearing on the person himself. Van der Marck arrived at the same conclusion by another path. According to him, the problem of knowing whether sterilization is permitted cannot be solved unless one sees it in the light of the totality of the human act. One and the same material action may have, according to the context of the situation, a very different significance on the human level. Msgr. Ruess in 1963 strongly underlined the idea that a specifically human and marital sexuality be seen in its totality and judged as such. It is by this standard that he judges a sterilization of the biological and physiological processes morally licit, even though this intervention takes place for the sake of the marriage act. In 1964 Prof. Bernard Häring referred to the fact that in Rome there was a certain tendency to refer to the use of oral contraceptives by the name and under the heading of "indirect" sterilization (and therefore licit). The reason given was that contraceptive methods have as their objective the creation of an infertile period and therefore only an indirect sterilization of the marriage act.

It is not surprising that Catholic married couples saw these debates as offensive and non-Catholic saw them as ridiculous. The English-speaking countries seemed to be following a more traditional understanding; for example, McDough in 1965. The discussion suddenly came alive when Bishop Thomas Roberts (ex-Archbishop of Bombay) stated in 1964 that he had never understood the arguments against contraceptives and that now he had serious doubts about the arguments from authority. In 1964 the German theologian Bernard Häring clearly gave the warning not to stop at the letter of the Church's declarations. He said that a distinction must be made between the fundamental meaning of a thing and its historically conditioned formula, that the fundamental sense contains nothing but a condemnation of every willed interference in the consummation of married love and of fertility on the personalist level.

This was the stage that the various attitudes and hypotheses had reached by 1964. As can be seen, there has been a whole evolution of ideas on married love, personal love, the meaning of the marriage act and the basing of it on either biological and physiological structures or the more general structures of man's personality. Consequently it can be seen how scientific discoveries have revolutionized the whole meaning of human love and sexuality.

In 1965, however, convinced that the special nature of oral

contraceptives (the Pill) had not been sufficiently taken into account, Prof. Sporken himself reformulated the problem in a different way. He wrote:

We are dealing with a completely new form of intervention into the physiological processes of the female organism. The moral problem to which it gives rise cannot simply be solved with the traditional categories of thought such as "acts having a double effect" or "direct or indirect sterilization." The moral question is not, "Can I see here an act having a double effect?" or "Can I prove by means of (astute) reasoning that we are dealing with indirect sterilization?" The issues revolve, rather, around the profoundly human and personal meaning of an intervention on the physiological plane. The basic question of oral contraception is of a *strictly medical and moral* order.

It must be asked, in other words, if the influence that contraception exercises on the hormonal structure of the female organism is of such a kind as to harm the personality of the woman as such, and hence the sexual relationship itself. It is certainly a question of intervening in the woman's physiological integrity, but is it of such a nature that her personality itself is not affected? If in all honesty it can be answered that the use of oral contraceptives is basically favorable to the personality of the woman as a woman, and therefore to the human dignity of the couple's sexual relationship, then this method may be approved from the medico-moral point of view, and the insurmountable objection from the point of view of Catholic marriage teaching can be lifted.

All this leads to still more basic conclusions which touch on the fundamental reorientation of marriage morality and its medico-moral aspects. Prof. Sporken says:

The anthropological starting point and the emphasis placed on the personalist aspects reveal a deep change in the direction that moral thinking has taken. Marriage is now considered as basically a community of love which implies, morally speaking, the obligation for this love, of its very nature, to develop into responsible parenthood. The moral judgment of how births are to be regulated will not, therefore, be determined by biological laws but only by considering marriage and sexual love in their entirety.

As can be noticed, we are once again looking at the same lines of thought that have been constantly reappearing from the first chapter (the "prehistory" of *Humanae Vitae*). What interests us here is the fact that they are seen more in the medical and moral context. While on one hand we notice the carefulness of the physician to separate the biological and physiological order from the moral and religious order, on the other hand it can be seen that this separation does not entail the separation of married love and the sexual behavior connatural with it from the moral judgment. Rather, it means that they must be subject to a moral judgment which is not simply conditioned and determined by debatable foundations themselves subject to evolution. The broadest basis which has been suggested, evidently also the most secure, is an anthropological one which takes account of every aspect of the human situation. It can be noted that the "principle of totality" is thereby being introduced. Moralists have increasingly been suggesting that it is the guiding principle even in those cases where the medical treatment proposed is contraception.

Humanae Vitae makes two references to the principle of totality, one implicit and the other explicit. For the first, No. 14 states: "To justify conjugal acts made intentionally infecund, one cannot invoke as valid reasons the lesser evil, or the fact that such acts would constitute a whole together with the fecund acts already performed or to follow later, and hence would share in one and the same moral goodness." Msgr. Lambruschini notes in a statement following the appearance of the encyclical that

these words refer, more than simply to the principle of totality, to the so-called comprehensive morality and to the morality of the totality of all human acts in any given field. The Pope wanted to state the moral and personal responsibility involved in each individual aspect of human behavior by closely following the traditional position of the moralists. It can be said that the global and comprehensive viewpoint is a variation of the principle of totality.

This principle is explicitly faced in No. 17 of the encyclical:

If the mission of generating life is not to be exposed to the arbitrary will of men, one must necessarily recognize insurmountable limits to the possibility of man's domination over his own body and its functions . . . and such limits cannot be determined other than by the respect due to the integrity of the human organism and its functions, according to the principles recalled earlier, and also according to the correct understanding of the "principle of totality" illustrated by our predecessor Pope Pius XII.

The principle of totality had already been enunciated by St. Thomas. According to him the parts of an organism are subordinate to the good of the whole; that is, the organism itself, which includes the being and reality of the parts, seen under both their organic and functional aspects.

In the convention on medicine and morality held in Rome in the first half of October 1968, the moralist Fr. Anselm Günthör spoke of the "principle of totality." His lengthy report was summarized by *L'Osservatore Romano* of October 28–29, 1968. Günthör explains:

The principle of totality can be understood in various ways. Vatican Council II in the constitution *Gaudium et Spes,* for example, insists on the unity and totality of man in both body and soul. This has enormous repercussions on medical practice which cannot focus its attention solely on the diseased organ but must be concerned with the whole person. The principle of totality in the specific sense states that part of the totality of the human being exists for the whole, that it is consequently subordinated to the whole, that the whole determines the part and that it can utilize it in its own interests (this is how Pius XII explained the principle).

Even though this is a fairly evident principle, its application is not always an easy matter. The principle itself, in fact, has undeniably undergone development. While Pius XI spoke rather of the body to which the parts are directed, Pius XII increasingly considers the whole person which the parts serve. In this way, for example, such things as psychosurgery and just aesthetic medical care find their justification. The problem of organ transplants from one human body to another also finds a solution in this perspective because the transplant is not only beneficial to the person receiving the organ but also benefits the donor who thereby actuates the ontological social structure of the human person.

In *Humanae Vitae* the Pope does not permit certain applications of the principle of totality to marriage questions. For example, the single act cannot be considered to be part of the totality of married life because each single act would then no longer be a total surrender. Moreover, neither can the principle of totality be applied to marriage when looking at it from another point of view; namely, that man may manipulate his nature for the sake of his own personal good and that of the partner. Anyone following this line of reasoning forgets that the concept of nature is analogous. It can signify certain physical data, more or less contingent, which can be and in some cases must be manipulated within the limits of the principle of totality. But nature can also mean those human attitudes and acts abounding in profound meaning and sublime significance. It is in this sense that nature cannot be manipulated but can only be either realized or destroyed.

The reason that the "principle of totality" may not be used to justify interference with the reproductive powers is clarified by Msgr. Lambruschini when, concluding the article just quoted, he notes:

The encyclical *Humanae Vitae* while not going into details, simply intends reaffirming that the appeal to the principle of totality is not enough to justify contraceptive practices. Important as recent scientific developments have been, man should always be seen as a beneficiary; that is, endowed with a useful, reasonable domination which is not despotic or absolute over his body and its functions. In a sphere as delicate as this, precise formulations are indispensable because a slight change in one of the principles, no matter how insignificant it may appear, entails quite serious consequences which must be given the fullest consideration.

Msgr. Lambruschini recognizes the fact, however, that in spite of the encyclical's implicit and explicit rejection of the principle of totality, "there is a tendency today, which can be observed here and there, of substituting for the principle of double effect, the principle of totality, and thus arriving at conclusions which give considerably wider liberties." Rather than the question of considerably wider liberties, possibly the issue is really one dealing with the problems which Prof. Sporken had explained; namely, that while following the reasoning of the principle of double effect one is led to a series of problems and solutions which give the appearance of being rather mechanical—a kind of abstruse and unrealistic game, an escape route which smells strongly of the scholastic hankering to find abstract solutions to problems. This is at least how it appears to many at the moment.

Difficulties in Understanding the Distinctions

Besides this problem there is also a certain difficulty in understanding the distinctions proposed by the encyclical. Certainly these distinctions are obvious and clear to specialists in theology or morality, but not always so for the physician or scholar. Possibly the first two move in a world of concepts and language which is no longer that of the scientific man of today or, more simply, the man in the street. This naturally does not mean that the encyclical's language and distinctions are useless. In any case, on several occasions a certain incoherence has been observed in the use of these distinctions precisely on account of the fact that by proceeding along the lines of rational interpretation of the data of the natural law, the encyclical's thinking has remained on this same level. For example, Mario Tedeschi, dealing with "Catholic Morality and Ogino-Knaus" in *Gazzetta del Sud* of August 14, 1968, notes:

The other question on which we must dwell is that referring to the licity of recourse to the infertile periods as sanctioned by the encyclical. Contrary to what the encyclical observes it does not seem that the Church is coherent with herself when she maintains that there is "an essential difference: in the former, the married couple make legitimate use of a natural disposition; in the latter, they impede the development of natural processes." This means nothing because the limiting of intercourse to only infertile days by means of a precise, premeditated choice, in order to avoid relations during fertile days, is perfectly analogous as regards both its effects and its morality to the use of contraceptives. It is quite superfluous, moreover, to dwell on the fact that "only in the former case are they able to renounce the use of marriage in the fecund periods." It is as if in exchange for eight days of continence a month the couple were given the prize of being allowed to be incontinent for the remaining period!

Pius XII himself, whose teaching the present Pontiff has employed on more than one occasion, and not least of all, as he himself is well aware, in this encyclical had this to say when referring to the Ogino-Knaus method: "If carrying out this theory means only that the couple can exercise their matrimonial right also on the days of natural sterility, there is nothing against it. If, however, it means more than this—that is, permitting the conjugal act on those days exclusively—the moral rightness of such conduct would have to be affirmed or denied according to whether the intention of constantly observing those days is based on sufficient moral motives. To embrace the married state, to continually use the faculty proper to it and licit within it, and on the other hand, to continually and deliberately avoid one's primary duty without a serious motive, would be to sin against the meaning of conjugal life."

Hence it would have been better for the sake of coherence either to have condemned the Ogino-Knaus method along with all the other methods inasmuch as it aims to exclude procreation and is therefore just as harmful to Catholic morality, or by leaving it to the individual to decide whether he wants to use the infertile days or not, to have also given him the chance of deciding whether to use contraceptives or not.

This reasoning could hardly be accepted by a moralist, but it must also be recognized that it has a value for those who question whether morality is based on the biological structure of the cycles.

De Volkskrant had an interview on August 20, 1968 with Prof. J. T. Snijders, rector of the University of Groningen, professor of psychology, president of the Dutch Catholic postgraduates, and president of the first and second sessions of the Dutch Pastoral Council. Dr. A. Snijders-Oomen, a specialist in child psychology, was also present at the interview. The considerations treated above were examined in a wider perspective which takes into account at the same time the validity of the religious magisterium and the validity of the interpretation of the natural law as a norm.

"Looking at it from a religious point of view," said Prof. Snijders, "I cannot succeed in seeing the encyclical as a religious document, as a message of Christ. Scripture is not mentioned. Only once is a text quoted and this has nothing to do with the argument. The name of Christ is found mentioned only in relation to the authority of the Church. Not only the text but also the whole spirit of the document is distant from the gospel message. In fact, the central idea is that of natural law. This word is never found in scripture. It is an extra-Christian concept which the apostles would have considered to be totally worldly. Love, sin, grace—these are Christian concepts, but not that of 'natural law.'"

"Are the encyclical's arguments valid?" Prof. Snijders was asked.

"They are antiquated philosophical arguments," said the professor. "A concept like that of natural law comes from the phi-

losophy of Aristotle which has been given a biological orientation, and this teaching penetrated into Christianity during the
Middle Ages. It is curious how this concept has been preserved
in Rome while in the scientific world and in the Christian world
outside Rome it has been abandoned a long time ago. I can say
without a doubt that you will no longer find any teachers in this
field in Holland who have anything to do with the present way
of reasoning and who use the concept of natural law in the way
the encyclical does."

Hence this better explains why it is difficult for a scientist
to permit the distinctions, as given by the encyclical, to direct
the course of action he adopts on contraceptives. He finds the
notion of natural law, as it has been presented, difficult to accept.

Since the encyclical, even though seeking to remain in the
realm of strictly religious moral teaching, in fact rests on a concept of the law of nature which in turn rests on a biological fact,
Prof. Snijders sees that this entails in a certain sense either going
outside the territory belonging to it or reopening it to debate,
since the concept of natural law is now back in the opinion realm
of scientific discussion.

"From the scientific point of view," he said, "the encyclical
speaks of things which in the last analysis have scientific implications. These are questions which cultural anthropology, sociology, biology, etc., treat. They refer, for example, to matters
like the diversity and development of humanity and the relationship between nature and culture. Now it seems that all this has
simply been denied by the blanket statement that it is not so.
Modern science will then say, however, 'That human nature of
yours, biological, uniform, and immutable—take a good look and
you shall see it does not exist.' Don't get me wrong; I am not
denying the deep, general, moral impulse which is at work within
man. But in such a case we are dealing with broad outlines of
love, mutual respect, and honesty, and not with a code of prohibitions and orders. The time has come to start an open discussion on this point and to really listen to the opinion of Catholic
lay people and experts."

At this point Mrs. Snijders-Oomen made a sharp interjection:
"And not to say, as you hear at times, 'if you don't accept it, get
out!'"

Is the possibility still open, then, for true research, which does not exclude once and for all research not directed to finding a more secure basis for the use of marriage according to the cycle and temperature methods? If the experts were to restrict themselves to this, is there not a risk that the outcome would be what one person has called a thermometer and curve morality?

El Pueblo of Lima of August 9, 1968 wrote on the "Path Not Closed Off by the Encyclical," where it said among other things:

Since the use of marriage which is limited only to the days when conception is not possible can create in the couple, and especially in the woman, a strong psychosis which would cause difficulties in married life, it is desirable that men of science "succeed in providing a sufficiently secure basis for a regulation of birth, founded on the observance of natural rhythms" which would also solve the more serious difficulties involved in this procedure. Scientific experiments in this direction are already under way, and we have news that in Australia some Catholic doctors are experimenting with a "pill" which "isolates the fertile periods suitable for impregnation to two days in the month." The doctors inform us that it is not a contraceptive formula but simply a pill designed to control periods. Prof. H. Carey, head of the Obstetrics and Gynecology Clinic of the University of Sydney is carrying on his studies and experiments in this direction in strict collaboration with Dr. W. Murray who is a renowned Australian theologian.

Nobody therefore should think that the encyclical has closed all the doors to further investigation in the search for ways of obtaining an adequate means of regulating births in harmony with the moral principles defended by the Church.

El Pueblo has admitted that besides the fact that there are difficulties from the moral point of view regarding the moral difference of the two methods, there is also a negative factor of a psychological nature—especially for the woman.

In the meantime, research continues along the lines of finding a way of ascertaining exactly the days on which conception is impossible so that the couple are not being continually exposed to anxiety. Naturally it can always be asked if this, too, is nothing more than playing with "nature" just to salvage a morality based on it.

This does not seem to be the opinion of Prof. Luigi Gedda,

a specialist in the study of pregnancy and twin births and director of the Mendel Institute in Rome. He was one of the Pope's medical consultants for the encyclical. In *Orizzonte Medico* of August 1968 he states that "the physician is the priest of human life understood in its physical sense, and since this papal document's judgments and commands are in the realm of human life, it is up to us to go deeper into the encyclical." But in which direction? Prof. Gedda says that this does not include research on the Pill (how would he judge Dr. H. Carey's research in Sydney? It is still a "pill" even if only a "regulative" pill), and he gives his reasons against those who hold that the Pill reconstructs the "natural state." Therefore he first condemns

the ambiguity of those who maintain that the Pill reproduces a natural state. It must be remembered that progestines produce a state which would be natural during pregnancy because, as the name progesterone clearly indicates, the effects produced by it help gestation. The condition resulting from the Pill is, on the other hand, extremely unnatural. It is not produced by nature and is unbalanced and dangerous outside of pregnancy, and all the more so if the woman has taken the Pill to avoid conception.

The only way left open, then, would be that of research into the cycles where conception is not possible in order to calculate the infertile periods with greater accuracy and thus remain within the realm of the "natural law."

This, however, is precisely the problem which other doctors find to be an insoluble one at present, while at the same time there is the crying need for a solution to be found to those problems involving the personal needs of couples and, on a far wider level, demographic trends.

A Problem for Present-day Biological Science

The reactions to the encyclical range from extremely negative criticisms on the one hand to a search for positive motives underlying the encyclical on the other. They also range from giving reasons why the use of only those methods permitted by the encyclical is difficult to why these same methods justify the solution as set forth by the papal document.

The Association of German Catholic Physicians, for example,

in the Berlin medical journal *Berliner Aerzteblatt* of October 1, 1968 states in an editorial that

Paul VI is completely out of touch with reality and is going against scientific discovery. . . . For many physicians, the Pope's encyclical is an insoluble conflict between faith and medical knowledge. Catholic doctors live in the world as it is and not in an ideal world longed for by the Pope.

Also the Dutch psychiatrist Dr. P. Trimbos in *De Tijd* of August 1, 1968 states that

the encyclical is almost totally unacceptable on account of a scarcely understandable language and a way of reasoning on marriage and sexuality which is foreign in our time. The most serious objection, however, can be brought against its pseudoscientific procedure, and for this reason the gap between teaching and practice will become even wider than it already is.

In the same issue of *De Tijd* the Nijmegen gynecologist Prof. Mastboom attempts to uncover

some illuminating points. . . . The method of periodic abstinence can be made to give noticeably better results. The general percentage of failures now between 10 percent and 25 percent could be reduced to 5 percent. There is still no clear, scientific information available on a way of verifying ovulation. Many factors still remain which make periodic abstinence impracticable.

Prof. Mastboom maintains, however, that the encyclical allows for "the possibility of finding, where periodic abstinence is impracticable, a better therapeutic method adapted to the psyche and the economic, social, and medical circumstances of the patient."

However, it is precisely from this standpoint—namely, one of studying the papal document "from the point of view of the evolution of the human group"—that Prof. Jacques Ruffié in *Le Monde* of November 7, 1968 brings to light not a few problems.

Prof. Ruffié notices that "a careful reading of the encyclical gives rise to a certain confusion over the term natural law, willed by God and from which man cannot prescind." The professor observes:

What are natural laws if not biological laws, the sum total of the

225

physicochemical processes on which the beginning, balance, and continuation of the species is founded? These processes have guaranteed during the course of billions of years the successive appearance of living groups. They are at the basis of evolution and condition animal behavior. They are "laws of iron." Animals do not have freedom. They can only act within the strict limits which are imposed on them by biological imperatives. The physicochemical structures of a being endowed with life form remarkably stable units, endowed on the other hand with self-regulative mechanisms. They can only be transformed extremely slowly, excluding accidental cases which are always rare and isolated—mutations. For this reason the evolution of the species takes periods of time which are scarcely imaginable and are to be measured in geological eras.

At this point Prof. Ruffié gives an outline of the plan of evolutionary phenomena on their different levels, from the biological and cultural to the psychosocial. Especially on this last level

mutation is replete with consequences. Coming from animality man arrives at reflex consciousness, the source of responsibility. This difference between animal societies and human societies is easily observable. In the first, each individual is directed by natural laws in a series of biological processes—which are translated into tropisms—that guide the behavior written into its hereditary patrimony. No room is left for choice. The bee "knows" what it must do in the beehive when it is born. It has nothing, or almost nothing, to learn. The queen of the swarm is never threatened by a coup d'etat. She rules over an unchangeable society, the evolution of which can be understood only in terms of "geological time."

On the other hand, the organization of human societies is the fruit of reflective decision. It be modified at will, and rapidly, in order to adapt to new historical circumstances. On the human level, the dominant characteristic of evolution is the acquisition of a greater consciousness which allows man to be freed from servitude to biological constraints and to come to a freedom which is indispensable for his full self-realization. Turning his back on animality, man becomes responsible for his destiny. For this reason, every reference to natural laws for the sake of regulating human behavior runs the risk of turning into a dangerous regression.

Let us take an example. One of the most fundamental natural laws is that of selective pressure which eliminates, by means of a process of preference, those subjects which are weak or carry genetic faults. This is the price which a living group pays to maintain its "biological quality." However, all human societies which have reached a certain stage of civilization have attempted to decrease this process of natural selection. Who would dream today of not curing physical infirmities or subjects with defects? Yet by doing this we are going against a natural law which is among the most fundamental in the development of the human group. Thanks, however, to the progress of medical science, man has the possibility today of voluntarily protecting the group without following this law of natural selection which, on account of the level of development which man has now reached, appears simply monstrous to us. All this is nothing new and it is widely developed in Teilhardian thought, which the encyclical seems to have ignored.

The ovarian cycle also goes to make up part of the biological constraints to which the human group is subject. We cannot put the blame on human inventiveness for having controlled it and as a result of this, having made possible conscious, voluntary "parenthood," which in the present state of the evolution of the world, is the only type that can be allowed. Every other attitude is tantamount to putting in doubt the privileged position which man occupies in the world of living things.

Prof. Ruffié's observations are particularly impressive because they place the whole question in a far wider context; namely, in the grand plan of the evolution of the human group. On the medical level this intervention is seen then, as part of man's effort to escape from the "biological constraints" belonging to the human group by the use of his power for "growing in consciousness" which belongs equally to the whole human group once it has evolved from the preconscious stage of development. All attempts at medical, biological, and genetic modifications appear, basically, as an effort toward promoting this process. Its sole intention is that of favoring man's development and of not inflicting traumas on him. On the moral level this entails a necessary revision of the meaning given to the concept of the "law of nature." The question must be asked, then, if the present notion and interpretation of natural law, at least in the way proposed by the encyclical, is theologically correct. In fact, we already know that in connection with biological and anthropological science, the most delicate and fundamental question which theological thinking after *Humanae Vitae* has posed is this one of natural law.

In one case (the purely scientific) as in the other (the theological), the question is precisely that of applying to the human species in its present state of evolution this capacity for reflective understanding which it has acquired after a long evolution measured in "geological time."

Along the same lines, Dr. Roger Géraud, specialist in the psychological aspects of maternity, in his work *La limitation médicale des naissances* (Paris, 1968), after studying the evolution of the ideas and facts on the matter of birth regulation and giving extensive documentary evidence, insists on the idea that when scientifically studied and sufficiently certain so as not to have adverse effects on a person, human intervention must be understood as an "application of intelligence to the perpetuation of the human species." It is man himself then, who once he has arrived at the stage of self-consciousness of the group in which he lives, intelligently and respectfully takes his place within his species to promote its further development and not allow it to be abandoned to biological constrictions.

To this outlook on the general biological development of the human group, could be raised the objection that it has the inherent danger of "manipulating" the person and is consequently a danger for the human species itself. This objection, however, can be leveled today against every sector of human research. Seeing that the possibilities for manipulation are so great and are, practically speaking, unimpedable, what principles are there to guide or slow down this manipulation? Clearly it cannot be rejected *sic et simpliciter,* for this would be equivalent to denying any possibility of an intelligent development of the human species.

If in the specific case of fertility manipulation there is introduced a principle like that introduced by the encyclical, it must then be asked if this principle could not also be logically extended to every other sphere. To admit this would be to completely dissociate oneself from the undefined possibilities which are now in the hands of man himself. Is this not also a falling back into a purely mythical understanding of God's intervention and providence? It is a question which spontaneously comes to our lips when our subject is examined from the viewpoint of the possibilities and the difficulties proposed by the biologist and the anthropologist.

In any case, the problem of the dangers involved is still a very real one, as has been underlined in No. 17 of *Humanae Vitae,* and hence cannot be ignored. The experts themselves are aware of it and are attempting to overcome in a positive way this real difficulty which exists first of all on the level of scientific conscience and honesty. The basic problem, in fact, is that we cannot speak of a useful and positive service to man unless every intervention is based on scientific knowledge which is continually being deepened. On the other hand, neither is the problem solved simply by laying down prohibitions. In fact, the encyclical's arguments in No. 17 are only arguments "of convenience," as the theologians say.

There are difficulties then, but they follow two different lines. There are difficulties on the part of medical and biological science regarding the encyclical because, as Prof. Ruffié has observed, it does not take into consideration the wider issue of the overall development of the human group, and difficulties regarding the so-called artificial methods, once again in the name of medical and biological scientific information. In the second case, however, the difficulties tend to focus on the problems for the individual person which arise from chemical and biological intervention.

There are several instances where a study of the "pros" and "cons" has been undertaken with the intention of arriving at some possible solid basis involving the least possible number of disadvantages in the use of contraceptives. This Dr. C. Thibault and Dr. M.-C. Levasseur in their volume *Bases et limites psychologiques du controle des naissances* (Paris, 1968), state that there is still too much empiricism involved in determining the social repercussions, human significance, and moral value of contraception. It is necessary above all, they say, to have a well-grounded knowledge of the physiological mechanisms of reproduction and of the way in which contraceptives operate.

For this reason they have completed a study from which they have deduced a general panorama of the biology of the reproduction of mammals and particularly of man in the light of the most modern scientific findings. On the basis of these findings they show in a very balanced way the advantages and the serious or less serious risks of the contraceptive methods in use today. They state that nevertheless these must be seen as only provisional.

Once again we hear this same note of "provisionality." It seems to be the one most frequently heard in scientific circles.

On the other hand they insist more directly on the disadvantage which, from the biological point of view, contraception has in every case. Once again it may be noted here that there will be revealed a certain ambiguity in the attitude adopted toward the encyclical if it is granted that the Pope's answer could not have been different from what it was, given the biological difficulties involved.

It is along these lines that Pierre Grassé, professor at the University of Sciences of Paris and director of the Laboratory of the Evolution of Living Organisms, in an article in *Le Figaro* of October 8, 1968 voiced his difficulties. Prof. Grassé says:

Almost all the commentators on the encyclical are in favor of a temporary sterilization of the woman by chemical means. . . . The use of the Pill would seem to be the only way of confronting the problem of overpopulation in any positive way, of bringing clandestine abortions to a halt, and of giving each couple the possibility of procreating according to its choice and bringing only those children desired into the world. In other words, the use of the contraceptive Pill could only bring advantages from the physiological as well as social point of view.

If we study the issue in depth, however, its unsuitable qualities and its dangers, be they bodily, moral, or social, become apparent. Thus when criticisms of the encyclical come from Catholics, priests, and lay people, we cannot but remain surprised. These criticisms witness to a serious lack of reflection and knowledge of human physiology and Christian morality. Paul VI could not have made any other decision. This can easily be proved by using biological arguments.

When a biologist castrates a mammal he notices a whole series of anatomical and functional modifications which vary in extent according to the species being experimented upon. There are alterations in the basic metabolism, in the secretions and bacterial flora of the genital tracts, in the cellular composition of the hypophysis and of its hormonal secretions, and in almost all the internal secretory glands. In the woman, the Pill produces the effect of a temporary castration. In adult women it does not have any noticeable influence on the secondary sexual characteristics. However, the fact is known that it acts on the internal secretory glands—hypophysis, thyroid, suprarenal cortex—and on the liver. Up to now these influences have been generally considered as mild. On the whole, by some strange privilege, the woman is less affected than animals by chemical sterilization.

It has been said that, thanks to the obligatory medical examination required, only those women capable of tolerating the effects of the Pill without detriment to themselves take it. This may be so in legal cases, but it does not happen on every occasion because the Pill is mainly taken secretly, outside of all medical control. What, therefore, is the role of medicine in the problem? We believed up to now that the function and ideal of medicine was that of curing and preventing the sicknesses which attack man, but what about when this changes course and devotes itself to either developing or suppressing man's most noble functions? For that is what the question is about and nothing else. This is why I would like to highlight what is the most important point about the action of the Pill. Will an ovary which for years has been rested and not been irrigated by blood containing hormones that normally animate and regulate its function still keep its faculties intact? Will absolutely nothing happen?

It is to preliminary and vital questions like these that the supporters of the Pill, particularly its legitimate father, Dr. Pincus, answer that this general inhibition is beneficial for the ovary and that in any case no harm can come from it. But the truth of the matter is that they do not know if this is true or not. There are no accurate statistics which can give us information on the frequency with which abortions result from a long treatment with the Pill, nor do the anomalies of aborted embryos tell us anything.

Several points which are well-known to biologists but not known by the general public must be kept in mind; namely, the division of the ovum which reduces the number of chromosomes to half, partly depends on the nature of the cytoplasm of the oocyte. The deficient distribution of chromosomes, as Turpin and Lejeune have proved, is the origin of mongolism and several other sexual, bodily, and intellectual anomalies of man.

At this point Prof. Grassé quotes several examples of side effects such as the fact that the average duration of pregnancies decreases considerably if pregnancy is followed by a long treatment with contraceptives, as well as other side effects observed from the characteristics of aborted fetuses in similar cases. From all this he concludes:

What biologist conscious of his responsibilities will chance stating that even though the ovary is subject to a long period of rest and there is in the blood which irrigates it an artificial hormone which should not be there, this will leave the germinal cells completely unaffected and will not disrupt the emission of polar globules which are liberated under the control of the hypophysis and the follicle?

Together with many other endocrinologists and genetics specialists, I maintain that the use of the Pill to avoid a pregnancy is as excessive as using a club to push a cork into a bottle. This fact must be recognized by all. I apologize for these few technical observations, but they were indispensable for putting the debate in its right perspective.

The artificial inhibition of the female sexual function, however it is viewed, constitutes a clear aggression against the physical person. First, the individual is accorded the right of modifying the normal regularity of his natural functions. What lack of logic legislators show! Doping in sport, a practice which is far less fearful in its consequences, is repressed and the regular working of the reproductive functions is allowed to be destroyed! The serious side of this question is that governments by either authorizing or directly recommending the use of the sterilizing Pill, have opened up an era of legal aggression on the human organism, both in its physical and its moral aspects.

Prof. Grassé, therefore, is totally opposed for biological reasons, to the use of any form of contraception. Although he is clearly thinking of the present state of knowledge in this field, a certain difficulty arises when he says that "Paul VI could not have made any other decision. This can easily be proved by using biological arguments." What is to be said, then, of the numerous biologists and gynecologists in the Papal Commission who apparently did not find conditions as catastrophic as those suggested by Dr. Grassé? Or do they all by chance fall under Grassé's verdict, "But the truth of the matter is that they do not know if this is true or not"? It may well be asked where all those specialists came from who were willing to admit the possibility of the use of contraceptives. Or did those on the commission just want to examine the matter from an "ethical" point of view, and thus not find that an interruption in the regulation of the female cycle was a real attack on the person? If they had been as convinced as Grassé, would they have admitted as much as they did in the so-called Majority Report? And after the encyclical had taken up the opposite position, is it right to call them, even indirectly, incompetent?

Once again the whole ambiguity of the favorable and unfavorable medical justifications has been revealed. The specialists on the Papal Commission were asked to give only a medical opinion; and on this basis they put forward the opinion that, within limits, the traditional moral teaching could be revised. The "post-encyclical" specialists now give their medical opinion and whenever it turns out to be opposed to the use of the contraceptives, they claim that the encyclical could only have given a negative decision. Possibly the latter's pretenses are more developed than those of the former. An opinion like that of Prof. Grassé cannot but astound a theologian accustomed to using other categories in his interpretation of papal documents.

What would Prof. Grassé say if a celebrated theologian were to use theological categories to reject or accept a scientific discovery of his? In fact, this biologist says:

The Pope has spoken as the defender of the individual and of all humanity. The encyclical *Humanae Vitae* in its noble terms guarantees not only the preservation of Christian morality and teaching but also the development of true scientific humanism. The encyclical concords with the data of biology, recalls the physician to his duties, and puts man on a path where both his physical and moral dignity will not suffer attack. For us the controversy is closed!

It is a peremptory statement but one may well ask whether the controversy is closed because Christian doctrine does not allow contraception or because the data of biology militate against it. It may be observed in the former case that there was no need then for biology's contributions, and in the latter, that it is enough to add the word today to the phrase "the data of biology" to conclude that at least from the scientific point of view the controversy is not yet necessarily closed. At least that is how Prof. Ruffié thinks.

If we compare the two positions of these two equally famous and competent biologists, at least one thing becomes clear: while Grassé, in saying that the controversy is closed, seems to be supposing that the present state of biological science is definitive to say the least, Prof. Ruffié, in saying that the evolution of the human species allows a continual overcoming of the "natural laws," seems to suggest that there still exists the possibility of major clarifications of the behavior of the hormonal mechanism as well as the possibility of finding a chemical method which will gradually eliminate the dangers still inherent in the present method.

Have Scientific Developments Come to an End?

The position held by many physicians, as represented by Prof. Ruffié, seems to suggest that paths open to research on birth planning by chemical methods have finally petered out, not so much on account of any moral drawbacks which they may involve but, rather, because of reasons of a biological nature that would in turn support the moral objections.

It is, in fact, for these same reasons that on several occasions the invitation offered in No. 24 of the encyclical has been warmly welcomed; that is, "to succeed in providing a sufficiently secure basis for a regulation of birth, founded on the observance of natural rhythms." For this reason, a group of doctors and biologists under the direction of Prof. Huant have decided to found in Paris a *"Humanae Vitae"* center for "the study," as the statute of the foundation says, "of problems for the protection and the amelioration of human life, and particularly for the study and application of the natural methods of birth regulation. This center intends, as well, to fight against the unlawful propaganda which vested interests use in favor of contraception in general, particularly of the pharmaceutical type." As can be seen, its intention is that of studying the question scientifically but also to act as an opposing force against any kind of solution which is not in line with the "natural" means of contraception.

The *Tablet* of December 14, 1968 reported the founding of another institution in America pursuing scientific study along these same lines. The *Tablet* says:

America's Catholic bishops are preparing to invest a million dollars in research designed to improve the reliability of the rhythm method of birth control. The notorious unreliability of the so-called safe period derives from the difficulty of pinpointing the period before and after ovulation when a woman is unable to conceive. Attempting to perfect simpler and more reliable methods of determining this period will be one of the principal aims of the proposed research foundation, according to Dr. Germaine Grisez, associate professor of ethics at Georgetown University. . . .

Another possible research goal, Dr. Grisez explained in an interview, is to find ways in which ovulation may be triggered by hormones or other medicines. This would have the advantage of fixing the time of ovulation beyond question. The contraceptive pills now in wide use act by suppressing ovulation. This was condemned by the Pope as an unlawful intervention in a natural process. Dr. Grisez suggested that hormonal triggering of ovulation would not meet the same theological objections as suppression. A third objective would be to attempt to determine with greater precision the effective life of spermatozoa. Because medical science is doubtful on this point, practitioners of the rhythm method either have to add a substantial safety margin to the time of presumed fertility, or take chances.

While remaining on the level of research into rhythmic cycles, it has been recognized how extremely necessary research is for a certain matter which has not yet even been clearly defined and whose solutions are therefore not definitive. One of the primary reasons for research, apart from that of hormonal imbalance as outlined by Prof. Ruffié, is the fact that on account of the lack of a certain margin of security in the use of the rhythm method, a psychological state of tension comes to be set up within married life which is caused by this fear and insecurity that act as a psychic stress at the very moment when the couple have the greatest need for their actions to be done with complete calm.

The theme of mental stress has already been treated, in fact, by the World Federation of Mental Health in a convention held in the first half of August 1968, and was fully reported by *The Times* of August 13. The convention gave particular attention to the subject treated by Prof. Morris Carstairs. He observed that

illness and premature death has seen to it that the rate of numerical increase of the population was kept at a low level in previous generations—but at what price of suffering! But today we are in a position to order things differently if we are authorized to improve on what nature undertook to do in the past. . . . Now the Pope has said to his faithful that it is legitimate to practice birth control by making use of our medical knowledge for recognizing the so-called infecund period, but not by making use of other medical knowledge which permits a more certain control of fertility. I personally share the opinion of many people within and outside the Catholic Church regarding the negative effects that this teaching could have not only on the universal campaign for the limitation of births, but also on personal relations within the families. . . . It would in any case be premature to establish a precise relationship between any particular method of birth control and mental health.

The subject of mental health with reference to the possible stress that can arise in the couple's interpersonal relationships, has been developed on several occasions by physicians, and above all by psychologists. With the limited guarantees which medicine can give at present, this topic is always seen in the perspective of further research since there is still always a certain uneasiness in the use of the rhythm method. Hence the reaction of Dr. Guido Caprio, secretary of the Association of Italian Catholic Physicians, is significant in this regard. He stated on August 1, 1968:

If he does not want to betray the trust of his patients and his professional ethical code, the physician must himself feel free before the Pope's definition on birth regulation. . . . The encyclical, in fact, contains incomprehensible and insoluble contradictions from the strictly medical point of view. . . . The Catholic physician who decides to follow the encyclical's teaching would be adopting a course of action that entails advising the use of a method which he knows to be inefficient and at least aleatory, thus knowingly giving false advice against his professional conscience. One is left deeply shocked and seriously disoriented by reading the encyclical because it cannot be understood how two such contradictory statements can be reconciled—responsible parenthood on the one hand, and on the other, the authorization of one single method based solely on risk and aleatory data, as has been proved besides by the extremely high failure rate.

This excerpt, too, is a testimony of what an expert has observed. Apart from the fact of the uncertainty of the scientific data, it reveals a professional ethic itself. This is particularly understandable in a physician who is continually in contact with his patients while it is not as noticeable in a physician engaged in research.

The fact that the "controversy is not yet closed" is also indicated by Prof. C. Thibault, professor of the physiology of reproduction at the Faculty of Sciences in Paris, who in an article in *Le Monde* of November 13, 1968 after attempting to clarify the terms of the problems involved in the two different contraceptive methods, observes:

We hope that this information will allow everyone to understand better the freedom of spirit which they must acquire in the face of all those —philosophers, moralists, and also experts—who are concerned with giving absolute replies and who attempt, contrary to their calling, to imprison people in false dilemmas.

While Prof. Ruffié outlines without ambiguity or confusion the sad but necessary consequences of the use of "temporary chemical sterilization," Prof. Thibault attempts to give the possible reasons for the genetic accidents which have been observed, showing that even the use of so-called natural methods can produce them just as frequently as, if not more frequently than, chemical substances—"pills"—which suspend ovulation. Prof. Thibault notes, in any case, that these can be easily avoided as soon as their mechanism is better understood not only on the scientific level but also on the level of public opinion, by having objective information widely disseminated on the subject.

Hence Prof. Thibault practically challenges the arguments of Prof. Grassé but also warns of absolutizing tendencies which are "contrary to the calling" of the scientist, all the more so when the scientist would like to use them to suggest or justify ethical or religious behavior. This brings us back to what Prof. Ruffié had underlined; namely, the awareness that within the realm of the living group, the human group is to be considered in the light of its evolution and its surpassing of "biological constraints."

Prof. Thibault observes, however, that

with regard to such an important problem it is normal to have a personal opinion and to have others share it, but it is blasphemous that it should be based on very inexact scientific arguments . . . above all, if it is done with public opinion in mind. Public opinion trusts an author's credentials and vigorous style, and will surrender to the fear reflex when faced with progress—a reflex which the author can instill either consciously or unconsciously. It is vital that specialists objectively synthesize for the general public the ideas and the essential conclusions of the thousands of essays and communications published every year on the problem of fertility.

For this reason Prof. Thibault makes a synthesis of the more recent information available "on the problems raised from the scientific point of view by the two contraceptive methods: the use of contraceptive steroids (the Pill) and the use of thermatic curves." Prof. Thibault says:

Contraceptive steroids—or progestines—are no longer used in strong doses (from 5 to 10 mg. per day), but in medium doses (from 0.5 to 2.5 mg. per day) or even weak doses (at the most, 0.5 mg. per day). Under these conditions the ovary continues to secrete steroids— estrogen and progesterone—and its structure remains normal. With medium doses ovulation is not produced. With weaker doses the menstrual cycle and ovulation are unaffected in more than 60 percent of cases. However, the contraceptive action is total and everything points to the fact that the primary effect occurs on the level of the secretions at the neck of the uterus which remains impervious to spermatozoa. These substances would then act primarily as a *chemical diaphragm.* It is clear, therefore, that the main accusations brought against contraceptive steroids lose all force and that to compare the effects of steroids (the Pill) to those of castration which definitely deprives the organism of its genital glands (ovaries and testicles) with all their physiological or psychological consequences, is a grave error.

After the termination of contraceptive treatment, even if it has lasted for several years, the natural menstrual cycle very soon returns. Ovulation reappears for more than 90 percent of women during the first three months, and even in the rare cases—less than 3 percent— in which the cycle remains erratic for a year or more, fertility reappears either spontaneously or by the use of ovulate substances.

Prof. Thibault reminds us as well that the difficulties for pregnancy, lactation, and birth after a period of treatment with steroids are no greater. He concludes:

It is not possible to deduce any reasonable case against contraceptive steroids from the period intervening between the halting of contraceptive treatment and the voluntary beginning of pregnancy. If this happens on the biological level, the problem remains on the biological level. . . . Even here, too, no serious danger for the mother or child has been found. First, no data exists on a relationship between the rise of contraceptive steroids and the frequency of the formation of

238

tumors. As well, no vascular difficulties are produced unless there exists a natural predisposition which can be determined by a prior medical examination, and in these cases it is evident that the use of contraceptive steroids must be forbidden. Nor can we conclude anything regarding an increase in the frequency of children affected by classical congenital deformations. However, it must be emphasized that the statistical data we possess at the moment is *insufficient* to reveal any slight frequency variations. . . .

Finally, the elevated frequency of modifications of the number of chromosomes—cellular elements bearing heredity characteristics—observed by Carr in embryos resulting from spontaneous premature abortions (6 embryos in 8), has led some to formulate the hypothesis of a long-term action of contraceptive steroids on the germinal cells of the ovaries so that in such a case the woman finds herself malfunctioning either definitively or temporarily.

The sum total of the observations we possess at present leads to a completely different interpretation. In fact, we know on the one hand that the first and second menstrual cycles after the suspension of treatment are slightly abnormal. Their duration is longer and ovulation takes longer to commence. On the other hand we know from a recent study done on rats, that when ovulation is 24 to 48 hours slower in occurring, the proportion of embryos manifesting these chromosomal anomalies is tripled.

In the present state of our knowledge it must be concluded that the increase in the frequency of abortions with chromosomal anomalies after the cessation of long-term treatment with contraceptives is not due to the direct action of the contraceptive on the ovaries but to a disturbed development of the first, or first two, cycles following the suppression of the Pill, which may lead to abnormal fertility. It is correct, therefore, that the couple should not begin procreating until the third menstrual cycle to guard against these risks.

Dr. Thibault, therefore, does not deny that there may be disturbances, but he tries to clarify the fact that they are not so catastrophic in every case and that they can be avoided by means of more accurate medical control and scientific research. Seemingly this research is still quite far from having said the last word on the matter. The objection could be raised that the danger of these possible disturbances is great enough to discourage all chemical contraceptive methods. But to reason in this way would mean admitting that there are an infinite number of similar situations which come under this same, general rule, beginning with nuclear research and extending through to the conditions to which the greater part of the workers in the chemical industry are subject today. Likewise it would not be acceptable—and Prof. Thibault himself rejects it—to reason that the risks are therefore not great and, in any case, can easily be overcome.

In the field of genetics there is the serious question of the risk of forming embryos bearing chromosomal anomalies. On this point Prof. Thibault observes:

These risks exist just as much for the couples who practice the rhythm method of intercourse with the help of the thermic curve and the duration of preceding cycles. In actual fact, there are large variations from cycle to cycle in the same woman. In a recent study, Bartzen shows that out of a group of 24 women only 1 had seven successive, regular cycles. This variability leads to errors in detecting the moment of ovulation, or else leads the couple to accepting a "calculated risk." They may stop having intercourse too close to ovulation or resume it too soon after ovulation. If fertilization does take place, first, the spermatozoa may have remained for 1 or 2 days in the genital tracts before penetrating the ovum, and second, the ovum may be fertilized 1 or 2 days after being freed from the ovaries. During this prolonged period of waiting the germinal cells age and degenerate rapidly.

Experiments done on rabbits show that fertilization with "old" germinal cells is often abnormal and provokes the formation of embryos carrying chromosomal anomalies. . . . The error or "risk" attached to this method can, therefore, have dangerous consequences; and there exists almost no means of avoiding it unless, as a last resort, by the almost permanent abstention from intercourse.

A solution which would give a certain amount of tranquility, even from the biological point of view, does not seem possible even with the rhythm or temperature methods. It is true that the encyclical has urged further research so that this method may be given greater certainty, also that the biological dangers involved will become avoidable and that the same may be done with the chemical method. Hence, any value that the encyclical's teaching may have does not lie in the fact that it defends, for all practical purposes, a solution which for the moment is the least dangerous from the biological and genetic point of view, but only because it is based on an ethical and religious understanding of intercourse and the beginning of life. Consequently, it is dangerous to try to justify the papal document by basing oneself on any scientific, medical, and biological data. When this danger is realized, it will not be difficult to recognize the fact that the encyclical, because it makes a decision for ethical and religious reasons, has not closed the doors to science in one way or the other.

Henry Perroy in *Project-Civilisation, Travail, Economie* of October 1968 states, for example:

Medical science is still searching for words, and our knowledge of natural rhythms and psychophysiological behavior during fertility is an almost totally unexplored region. Will not the encyclical help stimulate the fervor for scientific research in this field?

This seems to be the most logical and understandable possibility from at least the scientific point of view. In the meantime the problem facing the doctor is one of either following his conscience as assisted by the encyclical's teaching, or following his conscience from the scientific and clinical standpoint according to the complex situations which couples find themselves in. Excessive enthusiasm, apart from acceptance of the teaching for reasons of faith, could in the long run lead the doctor and biologist to irreparable conflicts arising from a confusion over the different levels of reasoning and moral behavior involved.

The synthesis presented by Prof. Thibault is not an isolated one, and it is shared by many other scientists and research workers. Even though it is an opinion which favors the use of chemical contraceptives (from the medical and biological point of view), it also appears to be urging prudence rather than the formation of absolute judgments, as Thibault himself has observed.

The weekly *Tempo* of August 13, 1968 published a full, scientific inquiry directed by Prof. Ernesto Servida with the collaboration of the specialists Dennis Cahal of the English Ministry for Health, Hilary Hill of the English Association for Family Planning, who based his work on the experience of 770 clinics, and Prof. Corrado Scarpitti, director of the Maternity Institute of the University of Milan. This extensive study was put in the form of questions which a couple would be most likely to ask. It has no intention of advancing preferential solutions, and the

241

specialists wished to remain within the field of a synthesis of the knowledge available at present. What are the primary effects of the Pill? What are its secondary and long-term effects? Can it cause cancer of the breast or womb? Can it cause uterine fibroma or thrombosis? Can it damage the liver and can prolonged use result in female sterility? Other similar questions were also answered.

In every case, as Prof. Thibault has already admitted, there are drawbacks on account of real dangers in the use of estrogen and there are cases in which its use is absolutely advised against. The overall view is not encouraging even though, as Thibault notes, the dangers are not in every case serious, imminent, or certain, and much is the result of the lack of an exact knowledge concerning many factors in the biological and genetic process. The specialists in the inquiry conclude with a glance at the future:

What developments will take place in the Pill in the future? Enormous sums of money must still be spent to perfect research into contraceptive drugs. Recent discoveries show that to obtain contraceptive effects it is no longer necessary to stop ovulation. At the level of the neck of the uterus—that is, in the part where the uterus begins and is closest to the exterior—there are special glands which excrete mucus. It has been estimated that by modifying the physical and possibly even the chemical characteristics of the mucus which is positioned like a stopper at the entrance to the uterus, it is possible to prevent the male semen from passing into the organ of pregnancy and, in the last analysis, the ovum from meeting the fertilizing male cell. All this can be achieved by administering daily in very small, continual doses (0.5 mg.) a derivative of the acetate of progesterone, clormadinone. In this way the menstrual cycles will not be interrupted and there will be no alteration of the rhythm. Up to now the results obtained from this method have been rather encouraging.

If what these experts say is true, and it does open up possibilities for the future, we may make the following observation: Since it is so evident that the paths opened up by science are still far from their end, is it prudent to base the validity of a doctrine like that of *Humanae Vitae* on the undeniable dangers present today in the use of chemical contraceptives? The experts quoted above note that on account of the complexity of the female endocrine apparatus, the prudent attitude of medicine in not pronouncing the last word on the matter until after further experimentation, is more than justified. Fortunately, many of the pessimistic predictions suggested by some have not materialized up to now. On the other hand, it must be remembered that even though the first experiments with oral contraceptives were conducted more than eleven years ago, the use of the Pill has only become widespread in the last six or seven years.

If these latest studies on the use of clormadinone prove to give positive, effective solutions, the strong objections summed up by Prof. Grassé will become groundless and hence the motives that couples and doctors had for either supporting the encyclical or holding another opinion will need to be found elsewhere. The experts quoted above, after examining this chemical preparation now being studied following observations on the glands at the neck of the uterus, in fact note:

Another positive feature is that with these pills not containing estrogen many objections will disappear together with the scientifically unproved suspicions about the cancerous action of estrogen hormones. Besides, in contrast to what happens with the Pill in use at present, there is no observable interference with the rhythmic activity of the hypophysis and the ovarian hormones, which is at present looked on by some with great misgivings.

From this point of view the fear of genetic and biological side effects from estrogen is thereby reduced. The same experts, however, recognize that there is another problem remaining which although created by chemical methods, has an immediate moral significance. They say:

Another problem envisaged in the future is that of a pill taken the morning after, which will prevent fertilization just as effectively. To prevent conception after intercourse which probably occurred during the female ovulation period there must immediately be administered high doses of estrogen for from 4 to 6 days. This stops the implantation of the fertilized cell ovum in the wall of the uterus. However, this contraceptive procedure goes against our morality, for when does the product resulting from conception have the right to be considered a human being? This disquieting question is at present occupying biologists and theologians. It is of immense practical importance; for if this contraceptive system should fail, the fertilized ovum may suffer alterations which will not stop its growth but result in congenital abnormalities in the child that is to be born. This is why all these procedures together compose the future.

This attitude is possibly the most prudent one if we think back on what Prof. Ruffié has so stimulatingly said on the evolutionary idea which belongs to the present state of self-consciousness of the human group.

The future will also see another development which could quite possibly be connected with the problem of contraceptives —that of "the pill for men." It is a topic which has been reported so far on the sensationalist level. It has, however, a precise scientific ancestry and is not pure fantasy. The experts consulted by Dr. Servida admit this. They say:

A pill for men is also being studied. A certain number of chemical compositions interfere very actively with the process of the maturation of the male seminal cells. Tests made on American prisoners have given positive results. When the tests were repeated on volunteers who, unlike the prisoners, had the liberty of drinking alcohol, violent general reactions occurred, quite similar to those caused by antabuse (a drug in use for discouraging the drinking of alcohol) when a small quantity of alcohol is taken. Many other types of male contraceptive drugs experimented with have proved up to now to be too toxic for men.

So even on the purely scientific level we are once again confronted with "disquieting questions." It does not appear prudent, therefore, to justify a teaching such as that of *Humanae Vitae* by using scientific arguments of which the author of the encyclical himself is aware and which he certainly wanted neither to canonize nor to condemn—all the more so because he realized that his could have been a "crucifying word."

Disquieting Questions

Aside from the purely scientific level, the disquieting questions will circulate into the everyday life of couples and of specialists who deal with couples' problems in the psychological and social spheres. It is not just medical science, in fact, which is brought to trial by the problem that *Humanae Vitae* has put before couples. It is the whole, wide sector of those sciences engaged, rather than in the medical side of procreation, in all the other extremely complex aspects which go to make up a balanced married and family life and which have become more evident in present-day society.

Particularly engaged at present are the numerous centers of sexology, marriage counseling, and gynecology, instituted by movements based on either religious or social principles. To all these groups and to the individual specialist, *Humanae Vitae* has brought particular difficulties which they had previously thought could be faced along lines differing from those traced out by the encyclical, or else has given a shot in the arm to research aimed at finding new ways of giving constructive help to married couples. Quite frequently, therefore, the questions have "disquieting" features on account of the difficulties which the encyclical is believed to have created. Thus, for example, a statement on August 15, 1968 by the French Association of the Centers of Marriage Counseling, at a meeting presided over by Dr. Lemaire, states that marriage counselors

have felt in the Pope's words, and share with him, his anxiety over the use which men can make of their liberty of intervening into the very source of human life itself. The more this liberty grows, the more new possibilities it offers man to humanize his nature, but it also allows him to feel all the more the risk of denaturalizing it. Therefore, we marriage counselors interpret the encyclical as a pressing demand made on all men of goodwill to reflect together on the essential values which must be promoted.

Farther on, however, the statement continues:

A progressive and almost universal consciousness today is leading couples to question the value traditionally given to not intervening into the process of procreation. The respect due to the other insofar as he is a free and autonomous human person, rather than an abstract physiology, seems to them to be a higher value, more difficult to live out, and more demanding but also more liberating and fruitful. This respect for the other cannot exist without a deliberate intervention into the natural processes of fertility. This intervention always involves an artificial element, no matter what method is chosen, be it a

245

mechanical, chemical, or thermic test. Is it not perhaps necessary for nature to be made artificial before it can be made human? The question which, according to the Association of the Centers of Marriage Counseling, now remains all the more disquieting is that of a "deepening of the values of sexuality knowing that truly human love cannot exist without a full acceptance of sexuality."

The themes which the statement found to be motives for disquieting questions become a "crucifying word" in the statement that Drs. Gaudefroy, Grimbelle, and Liefooghe, together with the priests Drs. Guilluy and Mathon, members of the Group for Sexological and Family Studies of the Catholic Faculty of Lille, asked to be published in *La Croix* of August 8, 1968. This crucifying word, however, is seen by them as a springboard for research which they maintain has not been suffocated but rather stimulated by the encyclical. They say:

The Pope has therefore spoken solemnly and his word is sorrowful and crucifying. This is our first reaction on reading the encyclical *Humanae Vitae*. It is crucifying for thousands of Christian families who, during the years of hesitation and silence, had often sought and had often found harmony in their marriage and family, thanks to the methods which are now "excluded." It is crucifying for a good number of counselors, priests, and doctors immersed in the heart of couples' sexual dramas and for whom the new paths which in all loyalty they had considered "honest" have now been closed off. It is crucifying for the numerous research workers like us—biologists, psychologists, theologians—who have the direct impression that their work has been useless and not understood, and that the encyclical misunderstands the new values which seem essential to the men of today and which were reconcilable with traditional morality.

Yet we feel we can detect, ever and beyond these decisions which grieve us, a certain number of signs telling us to go forward. They will be experienced as we experience them by all those who are ready to read humbly and fully a text which can only be cut short at the risk of betraying its thought.

The invitation to pursue an ideal, and no doubt a very high one, is at present, therefore, an invitation which the majority of Christian couples cannot accept. The Pope recognizes this serious difficulty and, without ever condemning persons themselves, urges couples to make greater use of the spiritual support of the sacraments and family groups.

246

It is an invitation to an integral vision of the human person, thereby giving the bodily and spiritual dimensions of the human person their full value. We are only at the dawn of a civilization which is being shaped by technology, and already we may catch a glimpse of some of the menaces it brings for this integral vision of man. The contestation now being expressed against our consumer civilization is surprisingly similar in nature to the Pope's anxieties for the future of man.

The encyclical is an explicitly expressed invitation for research to continue among biologists and doctors, philosophers and theologians, psychologists and economists, to determine even more exactly the characteristics of man's true nature. The encyclical refers to this on numerous occasions but with an outlook which to many gives the appearance of being too traditional, if not fixist. We warmly hope that for their assistance those doing research will be able to have access to the results of the work produced several years ago by the Papal Commissions which has up to now been held in secret. In these results there can be seen an encouraging sign of hope for the future.

The encyclical is finally an invitation toward an enormous effort for the education of all—children and adults, believers and non-believers—in order that they understand and create the conditions for a true, balanced growth in married, family, and social life so as to define the most human expression of love in the civilization of tomorrow.

The difficulties which have emerged on the level of scientific opinion also made themselves felt in the General Assembly of the National Center of French Catholic Physicians held in Lille on October 13, 1968. After the discussions, it was noted that there had emerged express reservations on *Humanae Vitae* which Henry Fesquet reported in the October 15 issue of *Le Monde*:

With 146 votes against 65, 19 blank cards, and 1 invalid, the assembly has adopted a declaration which affirms in a special way that the choice of birth-regulation methods depends in the final analysis on the couple themselves, that periodic abstinence remains "inapplicable" for a certain number of couples on account of the fact that it can lead to "serious disruptions." The declaration notes besides that the arguments regarding "the norms publicly proclaimed in such a precise, rigorous, and exclusive manner by *Humanae Vitae* seem for many very difficult to follow. . . . It is the first time in the history of the National Center of Catholic Physicians, founded in 1962, that a large majority of Catholic physicians has dared to openly express itself against a position adopted by the Pope.

Seeing, however, that this criticism on the part of the National Center of Catholic Physicians had been used as an instrument to criticize the value of the encyclical as a document of the religious magisterium, Dr. Rudalesco, gynecologist and president of the family and marriage commission, made it clear to the October 18 issue of *Le Monde* that

in the research that the Center pursues, contestation is a simple epiphenomenon and not, as at Nanterre, the object of our concern. Moreover, when this spirit of contestation is presented in this way, it really veils our almost unanimous concern which is that of helping physicians to fulfill capably and validly the multiple and complex requirements of family pastoral care. . . . The Center has insisted on underlying the positive values which we have found in the Pope's document. . . . In fact, we do not have any reservations to formulate of *Humanae Vitae*, which would be going outside the task we have set ourselves. We place ourselves in the field of medical research and reflection, and in the long run, the marriage relationship and the couples' illnesses. If we highlight the debatable character of certain statements of a scientific nature, or if we often deplore the moralizing style of the text, it does not imply any reservations concerning the teaching on our part, but solely a desire to free the document from every scientific proposition which has yet to be proved.

We do not allow ourselves to oppose the Pope's position, but we do state our perplexity over certain facts regarding married intimacy. If in spite of this, some want to attribute to us a spirit of contestation, this does not refer to the teaching which we accept, but at the most, to certain affirmations of a biological, physiological, and medical nature.

This statement could give the impression of having second thoughts about the original criticism of the encyclical, but at the same time it seems the most obvious and most honest position to adopt. After all the insights we have obtained from the ambiguous medical reactions, this seems to be the most logical and honest path to follow. On the one hand, there is the teaching itself, with its ethical and religious basis and formulation, and on the other hand, the medical questions and difficulties. Dr. Rudalesco's statement does not treat the encyclical as a scientific document, but as a document of the religious magisterium. If the physician finds difficulties of a scientific nature in it, that does not mean he must reject it, but allows him the possibility of continuing his free research unhampered by prejudice from a field which is outside that of his research.

Nevertheless, this fact does not hinder Dr. Rendu, president of the Center for the Coordination of Research Groups from affirming:

We think that periodic abstinence based on a scientific knowledge of the female cycle, thanks to the technical "test," interests only those Catholics who feel unable in conscience to employ contraceptive methods. We have estimated that this type of attitude to the problem was found to be very positive for furthering love and, at the same time, it gave couples the chance to foster voluntary procreation and, on the other hand, to avoid it with almost total certitude. We have observed this fact also among numerous couples who, deluded by contraception, came to us afterward to seek help. To these, we clarified the incumbent dangers which the habitual use of contraceptives holds for the quality of their love.

Up to this point we are in the perspective of the medical profession and no objections can be brought against it if we keep in mind the difficulties involved in both methods. What is debatable, however, is what follows: "We are thus led almost experimentally to discern the value of the Church's teaching. We are therefore profoundly happy that this teaching has been solemnly reaffirmed by the encyclical *Humanae Vitae*." However, a confession follows:

We know very well that a certain number of couples feel they cannot regulate their fertility by observing the "thermic" test. However, we have also noticed the great willingness to learn which all couples show. It is also true that a certain number of couples are not immediately capable of learning the method of regulating their fertility with periodic abstinence without serious risk, at times, of creating disunion. But we think that the Church, as both mother and educator, will not prefer to see a couple become divided rather than employ a contraceptive device. She is hence led to tolerate this evil to avoid another more serious one.

This certainly poses the question of which of the two—the principle laid down by the encyclical, or the good of the couple

—we want to serve. Which of the two is to have preference? If the ethical and religious principle is supreme and untouchable (even if not infallibly expressed), can its opposite be allowed in order to save the good of the couple which is being seriously compromised? We know that cases like this are not few and far between. Is not the point at issue, however, really one of totally accepting a principle (as many groups and persons especially intent on embracing the encyclical without hesitation, at the same time trusting in Divine Providence with the same act of faith, state they are doing) rather than one of seeking half measures which finish up putting the principle itself in crisis?

The validity of the principle remains, but as the Church's present conviction—susceptible to further development. The unique fact that *Humanae Vitae* was commented upon by the episcopates of almost all the countries of the world, would seem to suggest this. In fact the bishops' commentaries, while obviously accepting the encyclical, read it in the light of the real-life situation of couples and families, and thus seem to be interpreting it in a certain direction. Since we are persons who realize the importance of the formation of theological opinion in the Church (and especially on the episcopal level), this hardly makes it difficult for us to become convinced of the truth of what we have said about the need for redimensioning the "absoluteness" of the principle. The difficulties and disquieting questions which science has raised possibly serve as a direct, concrete introduction to this line of thinking.

We have noticed at the base of all the reactions from the medical world a certain amount of ambiguity which becomes dangerous on the strictly religious level, and certainly negative on the level of theological methodology. Perhaps, however, there is another factor involved, that which Marc Oraison—doctor, priest, and specialist in problems of married life in relation to moral issues—mentioned to Henry Fesquet during the Assembly of the French Catholic Physicians at Lille: "The medical world is evolving even more slowly than the clerical world." Has not the same thing been said quite a number of times of magistrates, or at least of men in the law profession in general?

With all respect to these groups which contain first-class men and to which humanity owes so much, is there not perhaps a historical and sociological factor which renders them particularly inclined to conservatism with the result that they find the evolution of principles outside their direct competence difficult to accept, and even tend toward supporting the status quo by justifying it with scientific data? Possibly the "contesters" of our society could tell us more on this matter. In fact, they have already given us the explanation, and with respect for the truth, their diagnosis is not to be despised. It certainly makes one think. Molière bitterly satirized more than just the doctoral wigs of the eighteenth century.

Is Demography Just an Opinion?

The demographic experts do not seem to have as many of these slightly cunning explanations to suggest, even if here and there they have been maligned by being accused of being prophets of doom who work for rather bad and interested motives. Demography, the daughter of mathematics, seems to have abandoned the unambiguous, fastidious precision of its mother to arrive at the more restful shores of opinion. On the other hand, it is connected with medical problems of birth and it became one of the serious questions which led to the problem being so widely discussed before the encyclical.

In reality it is almost impossible to establish the intrinsic importance of the encyclical's decision on the basis of world-scale demographic surveys, seeing that it poses a variety of different problems for different areas of population and these themselves have differing problems in which that of demographic increase or decrease is not always the most pressing.

Dr. Roger Geraud, for example, observes in *Le Monde* of November 13, 1968 that "if it is true that politics is a 'dimension of the person,' then no human problem is foreign to this political dimension and the Pill enters quite literally into this category"— and this will in fact be verified in the next chapter. While on the one hand the use of oral contraceptives is accused of causing "empty wastes" (as a Japanese said with reference to France, and note the conversation with Don Jure in the next chapter), and while on the other hand it is generally admitted that at least for Europe and the United States there is no real demographic problem, the idea is held that it is not the use of contraceptives which has caused the lowering in the rate of population growth. Although it is rather ingenuous to suggest that the only solution to the demographic problem where it exists is to use contraceptives, it is just as ingenuous to blame contraceptives for depopulating countries, or to use this line of reasoning to justify the truth and wisdom of a teaching which outlaws them.

In the article quoted above, Dr. Geraud observes:

The decrease in births is not a phenomenon belonging solely to France. . . . It affects the majority of the European countries. . . . The demographers, however, agree in attributing this to decrease in expansion more than to contraception, which, in any case, has had a very high failure rate. In France there are calculated to be approximately 380,000 women who use the Pill as opposed to 11 million who use it in the United States. Only the Pill could be called the absolute weapon —with a theoretical failure rate of zero and a practical failure rate of 0.8 percent. The intrauterine spiral is not widely used because it has an average failure rate of 4 percent, and all the other methods are found to give variable results. Thus it is the Pill which causes the demographic anxieties.

We admit, with Alfred Sauvy, that European countries are estimated to have a growth rate of a little over 1 percent per year which is equivalent to 2½ children per family, which also represents the aspirations of today's French couple. The birthrate decreases especially rapidly in those families with three children. On the other hand, the decrease in marriages has an influence on this demographic deflation, and the principal reasons that people put off marriage would seem to be of an economic and social nature rather than hedonism. The Pill only stops those from marrying who do not want to marry. The Pill is not what is forcing municipalities and churches to close down. It is rather the lack of social sense and the uncertainty of what tomorrow will bring. This is a pill which those who hold the responsibilities for our future find hard to swallow.

Referring to the French scene which is in an especially precarious position on the question of births and which is consequently saddled at present with a complex problem regarding legislation on contraception, Roger Geraud states ironically:

During the period when the legislator is preparing to undertake those reforms which affect the citizens in an interior as well as exterior way, he may find it profitable to first get an objective, and not a dramatized, view of the problem instead of looking at the Pill as if it were the monster of the seven seas. This would only land us with more prohibitions and hence further transgressions. It would be better if he directed his efforts to the university education of those who will later be prescribing the Pill. This would evidently be far more expensive but much less complicated.

May our little Pill—which set so many poor people aghast when four women happened to lose their hair by accident—not be accused of society's predicaments. There remains much to be done in order to give back to citizens a taste for fertility. Mercy on the Pill—it is not the only one in this prison not to mention that possibly it should not even be there! A humorist once said, "There is nothing harder than grabbing a black cat in a black room . . . especially if there is no cat."

It will not be the Pill which will solve the demographic explosion where it exists, but neither is it the Pill which is producing the decrease in the birthrate with all its consequences. This, too, could well be an example of the ambiguous reasoning like that already noticed in medicine, and it has not been slow in coming to the surface.

There are those who criticize the encyclical for not using a realistic position based on demographic data as its starting point. This criticism has as its departure point the presupposition that "like all institutionalized religions, Christianity has become to an extent a religion whose adherents are born into it" as *Le Journal de l'Université et des facultés françaises* states on November 1, 1968. It then goes on to draw a picture of the influence which historical factors and the pertinent demographic trends had in gradually shaping this "natalist" outlook:

For 2,000 years it has been evil to not have children and good to have as many as possible. It could not have been different. The human species is very poorly physically equipped to fight against a stifling and unwelcome nature. The woman is, relatively speaking, very fecund. In primitive conditions, two thirds of the children brought into the world perished before descendants were assured. They died as victims of numerous contagious diseases, malnutrition, etc. Since many women died or became sterile well before their menopause, the burden laid upon fertile women became overwhelming. The more perceptive among them were certainly aware of the slavery of this chain maternity. In certain groups this point of view prevailed and led to their limiting the number of births.

These collectives, however, purely and simply disappeared without leaving a trace. Only those which brought the greatest possible number of children into the world survived. For this reason populationist teachings had almost unconditional hegemony in historical societies. It is for this reason, too, that all religions and moral traditions appear as populationist. We know only that history which has survived. Birth limitation was practiced only exceptionally in periods of decadence, and only among the privileged classes. This is what happened in high Roman society at the beginning of our era. This social group, however, had disintegrated well before the disappearance of the empire itself. Within this populationist context, however, human demography underwent enormous fluctuations and grew very slowly during the course of centuries.

At the birth of Christ there were approximately 200 million people on the earth, and it was only in the middle of the seventeenth century that the number reached 500 million. More than 16 centuries were needed for a growth rate of two and one half. The technological and economic revolution which began in the eighteenth century produced a massive movement of growth of productivity, and this movement has never stopped. It was followed, as well, by a great development in Western medicine. During the nineteenth century anti-smallpox vaccination, quinine, and above all, hygienic practices diminished infections and contagious diseases. . . . In the entire Western world the general mortality rate was characterized by a continuous decrease. It was the beginning of vast demographic development.

Europe and its American extension then underwent a population explosion. Europe—including Russia—and North America had 185 million inhabitants in 1800. In 1910 the total had jumped to 490 million while China, for example, in the same period had only advanced from 300 to 450 million. The economic and medical revolution was restricted to the Western world. The European demographic expansion has shown that in these new conditions the woman's natural fertility produced excessive multiplication even if this was moderated by the late age at which unions took place. In other words, contraception became a necessity for civilization.

The newspaper of the French University does not think that the encyclical's influence will cause any particular, unexpected phenomena of demographic increase. In fact it thinks that "in all developed countries, the majority of Catholic couples act differently from what the encyclical demands and it is not likely that this will change."

If an effort is made to have the Pope's intentions taught and understood, will it really produce any effect on the demographic level? In *La Stampa* of December 4, 1968, Diego di Castro asks himself this question. He observes:

One of the reasons that the encyclical has put many people against it can be summed up in their concern for its effects on the future, world-population trends. It can be noted that in the face of the predictions of a catastrophic population increase (6 billion people in the year 2000), the encyclical avoids this problem in order to favor an increase in births, while everyone else thinks it should be discouraged by every means possible. This is not the place to discuss whether or not there exists a real danger of overcrowding on our planet. . . . The catastrophic predictions are not just exaggerated, but they repeat the same error that Malthus made at the end of the eighteenth century. They do not take into account the enormous increase possible in the subsistence level, and the certain spread of birth control. The problem we now want to face is that of the influence which the encyclical may have on the increase of births in the world.

The Catholic religion is more widespread in the world than any other, as can be seen from the information published by the well-known scholar D'Agata. Yet it is practiced by only 18 percent of the world's population; that is, by a little less than 600 million of the 3,400 million inhabitants of our globe. If all Catholics were to stop birth control without warning, this would certainly result in a slight increase in births on a world scale, even though the number is just a small fraction of the human race. However, certain aspects of the question must be given further attention.

Almost two thirds of Catholics live in Europe; namely, in that part of the world where culture and economic welfare are higher, and therefore where birth control is more widespread. Of the 170 million or more who live in America, that part living in the United States and Canada has an even higher standard of living. It is not likely that the mass of Catholics will change their attitudes on restricting the number of their offspring. The encyclical, moreover, is about understanding as is possible, leaving priests the task of resolving concrete cases of conscience. It may also be added that birth-control material was already being disseminated everywhere and to everyone in France during the last century and at the beginning of this century, even if the present Republic may be and is the bastion of Catholicism which has never approved of or allowed this control.

The same observation, except for the period when the spread of birth regulation began, goes for Italy, Austria, and now also for Spain and Portugal—all states with almost exclusively Catholic populations. Many other adherents in the world of the Roman Church, in India, Africa, Central and South America, do not yet control births on account of their extremely modest cultural and economic level. They would not understand the statements coming from the Church of Rome or the propaganda of those seeking to spread contraceptive methods even if it reached them.

It can be said, moreover, that the planning of offspring is spreading throughout the masses because the hostility which was shown it in the past by all Christian religions has not succeeded in affecting the new family trends, either by raising the birthrate or by halting the decline. The demographic campaigns of Fascism and Nazism had no better success, and likewise those being conducted at present in several countries. Therefore, from the demographic point of view, the repercussions the encyclical will have cannot cause concern. They only affect a very limited elite of persons who are culturally developed and deeply religious, but can have no perceptible numerical effect on the behavior of the masses, even of those 18 percent of the world population whose faith has its roots in the teaching of Rome.

Yet it seems that it is precisely this "teaching of Rome" which has violently shaken the "demographic sensibilities" of various different milieus, almost as if the encyclical were a serious danger for the future of humanity.

Naturally these reactions vary in intensity and significance. That of Addeke H. Boerman, general director of F.A.O. is, for example, very moderate, and he makes it clear that he wants to limit himself to the concerns proper to the UN organization:

The uncontrolled demographic expansion of the population can contribute toward nullifying the benefits which modern technology brings to the developing countries . . . I am not in a position to discuss the religious aspects of contraception but, just like the other organizations of the United Nations that are concerned with increasing the standard of life of the disinherited populations, I think that the regulation of births must become an intrinsic element of the infrastructures needed to improve man's conditions of life.

Likewise at the World Pharmacy Days held in the first few

days of September 1968 at the University of Hamburg, Prof. Gerhardt Martius, head of the gynecology department of the Martin Luther clinic in Berlin, said that "the existence of humanity seems to be in danger in the near future. . . . The world population is growing at a rate which will bring it up to 4 billion within 50 years and to 30 billion around 2060." For this reason Prof. Martius said that he felt

it would be useful to find a solution which would guarantee the couple physical and psychic balance in the matter of limiting births, family size, and eventually humanity itself. The essential reason for birth control is to prevent the multiplication of abortions and all the dangers they entail.

Leaving aside the violent reaction, already quoted, of *The Economist* of August 7, 1968, the document sent to Paul VI and signed by 2,600 American scientists and scholars of the United States in which they protest against *Humanae Vitae,* has made a big impression. The document, which was circulated in the last few months of 1968, expresses very clearly that reaction which intends attributing to the encyclical a negative influence on the present demographic and economic situation in the world:

The undersigned scientists strongly protest against the encyclical *Humanae Vitae* of Pope Paul VI on birth control. More than half the world is undernourished, and its social conditions are deteriorating rapidly and perhaps irreversibly. The menace of a pestilence on a world scale increases as malnutrition and overcrowding become greater, and the means of transport between the various continents could permit an epidemic to spread rapidly from one corner of the globe to another. Furthermore, demographic pressures contribute to political tensions and increase the probability of a bacteriological and thermonuclear war. Any action that blocks the efforts for halting the numerical development of the world population perpetuates the misery in which millions of human beings are living at present, countenances the death by starvation of millions of men in the course of the present year, and will render inevitable the death of an even greater number during future decades. The discovery of the killing of six million Jews during World War II led civilized people to attribute a share in the guilt to those who were not directly implicated in the executions. But what shall we say of the maimed lives and the slow and prolonged deaths of an equal number of people who do not have enough to eat? Does the fact that the Pope believes himself to be compelled by his religious convictions to take up such a position make these deaths less horrible than those caused by political motives? We do not think so.

It has been claimed by certain Roman Catholics that the Pope is not moved by bad intentions—we quite agree. Nevertheless, whatever may be the motives that have inspired his encyclical, its negative consequences are quite obvious. For a long time the world has used prudence and circumspection in its dealings with Rome, hoping that the Church would abandon its antiquated and inhuman attitude toward sexual problems. Humanity was encouraged when the Commission on Birth Control nominated by the Pope recommended a change of policy. Today the hope for a change has been destroyed. The moment has therefore come when we must make clear our position in the face of the encyclical. We declare that the appeals for world peace and pity for the poor made by a man whose actions help to promote war and render poverty inevitable do not impress us anymore. The world must rapidly realize that Paul VI has sanctioned the death of innumerable human beings with his badly inspired and immoral encyclical. The fact that this incredible document has been emanated in the name of a religion whose teachings are inspired by the highest respect for the values of human dignity and life should serve to render it even more repugnant to the eyes of humanity.

The accusations are strong and cogent. Possibly they are all the more impressive because they are signed by almost 3,000 scientists, while many others, as *The Tablet* of January 1969 reported, did not sign because they did not agree with the way the document was formulated. It could be objected that they did not keep in mind the fact that the encyclical is not opposed to family planning and birth control, as the Pope stated on a number of occasions afterward.

No less energetic is the reaction of the Italian scientist Adriano Buzzati Traverso in *L'Espresso* of August 11, 1968. He uses the Italian scene as his starting point and gives a rather bleak judgment:

Even though our birthrate is relatively low, the Italian population is growing at the rate of approximately 500,000 babies a year; and these, within a decade, will bring further problems of emigration and unemployment to our economy. Once again the observance of the new pronouncements of the Church magisterium has a class orientation insofar as the priest will succeed in his work of persuasion of the poorer and more underprivileged classes. This could make the social and economic dissimilarity between North and South even greater. Too often, reference is made to the population problem as if it affected only the Third World. It is forgotten that it is also being posed in urgent terms for us, citizens of the Western world, even though on a less tragic scale. Prof. Paul Erlich of Stanford University, for example, recently wrote that the United States should immediately begin taking measures to lower its birthrate: "If things continue in this way, not only will there be a progressive lowering of the standard of living for all (following the deterioration of the environment due to the excessively high number of citizens), but the democratic institutions themselves will inevitably be destined to perish." . . .

The appeal made to "men of science" to make an effort to give "a sufficiently secure basis for birth regulation based on the observance of natural rhythms" cannot be reasonably accepted. Scientists who professionally study the demographic progress of the world or the physiology of the reproduction of our species know that by now the game has been lost.

They know that humanity must now face the inevitability of enormous famines and that each child born "by mistake" will be the innocent victim of the ignorance of a society which forces him to die by deprivation. They know that already today 350 million children of six years or under, which means 70 percent of the world population of children of that age, have an abnormal development lower than that of the average among well-fed populations and that they are listless, irritable, and resist education. They know that the terrible scourge of kwashiorkor in Africa and culebrilla in South America due to protein deficiency in the diet of the child and the mother during pregnancy, means the psychic retardation of entire nations for several generations. They know that for science it is just as "natural" to employ antibiotics to control infant mortality as to prevent the conception of children forced to suffer the consequences of ancient taboos.

They are aware of that sacred tradition which three centuries ago thought it "natural" that the sun should orbit the earth even if the data presented by scientists up to then had shown without a possibility of doubt that the earth was not the center of the world, nor was the Chair of Peter the center of the human race.

Buzzati Traverso quotes what the editor of the English magazine *New Scientist* observed:

Bigotry, pedantry, and fanaticism can kill, mutilate, and torture those who become the victims just as much as bombs, pogroms, and gas chambers—even if they are dictated by noble intentions, even if they obey healthy dogmas. The harm they cause can easily exceed in scale and duration the damage produced by hundreds of famines.

Here, too, the accusations are serious and the judgments not always tranquil, even though a scientist faced with the situation just described can hardly be asked to preserve "tranquillity" in his judgment.

Nevertheless it may not be said that the Pope was not aware, as the American scientists state, of the gravity of the problem. He himself said several days after the encyclical's publication:

We heard the outraged voices of public opinion and the press. We heard . . . those of so many people, especially of very respectable women distressed by the difficult problem and by their still more difficult experience. . . . We read the scientific reports on the alarming demographic issues in the world, often supported by studies by experts and government programs. Publications came to us from various parts, some inspired by particular scientific aspects of the problem and others by realistic considerations of the many grave sociological conditions or by considerations, so predominant today, of the changes breaking out in every sector of modern life.

A moral theologian, Dalmazio Mongillo, in *Rocca* of September 1, 1968 stated on this issue:

Since the primary problem for which *Humanae Vitae* has been most directly attacked is the demographic problem, the Pope has clearly said that the demographic problem is an extremely complex one which cannot be solved by any simple methods such as those which interfere in a harmful way with the transmission of life. The demographic problem is solved neither by killing men nor by interfering in a destructive way in any of the dimensions of the human person. It is a complex problem which requires the coordinated intervention of all peoples who should search for a way of solving it not by harming man but by putting the resources of nature at every man's disposal. The demographic problem has its own structure, complexity, and dynamism, and it is not solved by harming human life. . . . *Humanae Vitae* is not in favor of overpopulation and irresponsible, unlimited, and arbitrary procreation.

The problem certainly involves more than simply the use of the Pill, just as can be said that it involves much more than simply banning the Pill. May it not have been necessary to defend this papal document which, for purely ethical motives, prohibits the use of contraceptives, and then both to insist all the more vigorously on the overall, world-scale responsibility of all countries to all men—above all, of those nations which enjoy the benefits of an affluent, consumer society—and to recall them to their duty in conscience? Already Paul VI had said at the Sixth Assembly of the United Nations: "Your task is to ensure that bread is plentiful enough at the table of humanity and not to favor an arbitrary control of births which would be irrational if done for the purpose of decreasing the number of those partaking at the banquet of life."

The long article by Henry Perroy in *Project-Civilisation, Travail, Economie* of October 1968 also takes up this complex topic and speaks of the "deplorable indolence" of those nations and governments that should and could be intervening, but stand with arms folded and then begin waving them about when the completely free prospect of a less costly and more remunerative possibility like that of birth planning is taken from them. How true is the accusation? This will be the opening topic of the next chapter—a topic which is moral, demographic, and "political." The Pope may not have had it directly in mind, but when the problem is one of feeding hungry mouths, then every problem runs from one end of the world to the other, from the Third World to the Iron Curtain.

Chapter 6 "Third World" and "Iron Curtain": Two Judges for the Encyclical

A disaster for the poor and underdeveloped countries
They will not stuff us with pills: *"Humanae Vitae"* and "pentagonism"
A new quarrel between Altar and Throne?
The encyclical "enters" politics
An accusation against Christians of affluent societies
"Europeo-centrism," "North Atlanticism," and "Third Worldism": three fields for *Humanae Vitae*
A "one-dimensional" encyclical?
Pills for the underdeveloped
The paths of the Pill also pass through Africa and India
Behind the Iron Curtain: between light and shade

With a violence and irony hardly ever before used in the British journalistic style, *The Economist* of September 3, 1968 attacked the encyclical *Humanae Vitae* without sparing even the person of the Pope, so much so that it provoked bitter reaction on the part of *L'Osservatore Romano*. The columnist of *The Economist* declared:

In Latin America, which the Pope ironically enough is due to visit later this month, where Roman Catholics are in the overwhelming majority, the average rate of population increase is 3 percent a year. Most of these countries now have too many potential schoolchildren per adult, let alone too many schoolchildren per potential teacher. The leaders of opinion there, both clerical and lay, had begun to accept the need for national policies to reduce population growth. They will find themselves gravely impeded. Even in the majority of developing countries which are not Catholic, the poor will have to pay for this papal failure. The concerted efforts of the richer countries to promote family planning through the medium of the United Nations and other agencies will now have further serious obstacles to overcome because some rich Catholic countries will feel that they cannot support them.

This is an extremely dramatic and realistic aspect of a doctrine which seeks to be only religious, and Paul VI himself affirmed on August 5, 1968: "The norm we have reaffirmed . . . is derived from the law of God." Why then such a strong reaction from the economic and demographic standpoint? And what was the reaction from the countries in question? The answer is clear, even though, from the many voices raised in protest against the encyclical, it will be particularly interesting to note the way in which the countries of the Third World reacted in general. The reaction of various quarters behind the Iron Curtain, be they typically Marxist or openly religious and Catholic, will appear equally strange and original. The motives underlying agreement to the encyclical in these two zones of opinion are strangely similar. Likewise, the motives for criticism and dissension, even if clearly differing among themselves, can be reduced to an underlying series of local and regional problems.

A Disaster for the Poor and Underdeveloped Countries

From April 21 to April 27, 1968 there took place at Beirut a *Conference on World Cooperation for Development* sponsored by the World Council of Churches and the Pontifical Commission *Justitia et Pax*. This conference marked a decisive step forward in the collaboration of Christians toward the development of the Third World, and the cooperation on a worldwide scale of various different movements and tendencies. Dr. Richard Fagley, a well-known expert on development problems and for many years an organizer at F.A.O., and Fr. Arthur McCormack, one of the founders of the commission *Justitia et Pax*, presented the conference with a report in which they widely discussed the present situation and provisions for the future. (The report, "The Demographic Increase, the Family and Development," was published by IDO-C in its bulletin of September 29, 1968.) In this report the two authors, after a long discussion of this theme, say: "We are led to think that unless there are drastic changes the great part of the human family will continue to be undernourished and tens of millions of children will grow up impaired in mind and body."

With these "drastic changes" the authors also foresee a "demographic policy," and they speak of the plans completed in different countries; for example, India. However, they do not hold that scientifically these plans are the only solution, nor do they advise them; but they maintain that these plans must be considered.

Now that *Humanae Vitae* has clearly stated its position, we must consider what effect this teaching—which is opposed neither to demographic planning nor to "responsible parenthood," but which in fact tends to take away one of the most concrete means of realizing them—could have.

The judgments and reactions on this point after the appearance of *Humanae Vitae* have been numerous even if not all of the same quality. Moreover, the fact that the encyclical does not oppose family planning itself, but is opposed to a certain method for realizing this planning, means that the problem must be studied in a different way. The favorable reactions to the encyclical on this particular issue of development normally recognize and actually insist upon the fact that the freedom to employ contraception is not only dangerous, but is irrelevant for solving the real problems of the Third World. On the other hand, the unfavorable reactions, under the same aspect, hold that the encyclical is "a disaster for poor countries." This is the line of thought which emerges in the criticism of the Jesuit L. M. Janssens, professor of the economics of development with the faculty of economics at Tilburg.

In *De Tijd* of August 17, 1968 Prof. Janssens writes:

I think that the decision of the Pope will seriously retard the solution to the demographic problem of developing countries. This means a prolongation of the period necessary for the development of the Third World, and this may be considered disastrous. Pope John wrote in *Mater et Magistra* that the problem could be solved only through socioeconomic means. In *Populorum Progressio* Paul VI recognized at least the task of authority. He revealed his understanding of the problem and recognized its seriousness. Now this encyclical suddenly appears and turns the whole process backward. There are countries where the influence of the Catholic Church is so small that the encyclical will have little influence. However, the situation is different for Catholic countries like those of Latin America. One could point out that the inhabitants of these countries do not really give much attention to the Church's teaching. Why, then, should this strict moral teaching have any real influence?

This reasoning would be valid if the people sought nothing else in their lives but birth control. This, however, is the whole issue. In these countries an enormous effort is required on the part of the authorities and private institutions like the Church. Up to now there has not been this effort—above all, on account of the Church's resistance. This is most understandable, for how can one recommend birth control if all the efficient methods—and periodic continence is inefficient —are morally prohibited? . . . The encyclical reaffirms the existing situation, and is hence retarding the solution of the demographic problem. I am not saying that the situation has become impossible. Development will continue notwithstanding, and experience teaches that the number of births decreases if material well-being increases. This is one of the reasons why the encyclical demands of us Catholics of the developed countries a greater obligation to contribute to the economic solution of the problems of the developing countries, and this in turn demands an increase in aid toward the development of these countries.

Even if greater help is given, however, the fact remains that the lack of a good population policy retards development. This is a tragic fact, since the standard of living of people in underdeveloped countries is so low. In other words, no matter how great the effort toward an economic solution, research for a demographic solution always remains indispensable.

This is more or less the judgment of specialized circles concerned with development. It must be noted, however, that we are speaking here of European or United States circles; and we shall immediately see how this attitude is reversed in the circles in underdeveloped countries, equally concerned and engaged in the development of their countries. Their judgment is not very flattering for those Europeans and Americans preoccupied with resolving problems of underdevelopment by means of contraception.

Nevertheless, in some European circles also very much involved in campaigns for helping the Third World, positive judgments have been expressed along the lines taken by the encyclical to the extent that those lines coincide with the attitudes of the movements involved in the Third World. Dr. Ulrich Koch, general director of both the campaign and the association *Misereor* in Germany, which gives considerable help to underdeveloped countries, expresses his reaction to the encyclical in a completely different way from that of Prof. Janssens. In the Dutch medical magazine *Katholik Artsenblad* of September 9, 1968 he writes:

The opinion of the Pope coincides completely with the experiences of this movement in the underdeveloped countries. The significance of the encyclical is very different for industrial countries. In the industrial countries the discussion on birth regulation revolves entirely around the Pill. This, however, is not the only aspect of birth regulation. The Pope has clearly underlined the fact that to resolve the demographic problem in the underdeveloped countries, we must abolish the unjust structures of society and substitute them with more just structures. It is thought, and not completely erroneously, that the West, through a refined form of biological neo-colonialism, is seeking to suppress the just social demands in many underdeveloped countries. To achieve an efficient system of birth regulation we must start by making the people conscious of it. Only later will birth regulation be accepted not as a coercion but as a social need. The developing countries, however, now find themselves in the stage of a growing consciousness.

Dr. Koch has suddenly changed the outlook by introducing a strong doubt that maybe the insistence on demographic planning by those countries enjoying an affluent, consumer society, and consequently their criticism of the encyclical which they fear could halt the use of contraceptives, is really a very subtle justification of a new type of colonialism—"biological colonialism." The doubt is serious, and one can easily see how the countries affected could immediately react.

They Will Not Stuff Us with Pills: "Humanae Vitae" and "Pentagonism"

And they do not react as was foreseen; on one hand they are worried because of what is happening in their own countries, and on the other, by what the "others" would like to see happening.

Typical and extremely significant is the reaction of Helder Cámara, the well-known Archbishop of Olinda and Recife, in Brazil. We know what Dom Helder means for Latin America— he is sometimes accused of being a Communist on account of his decisive action toward development. On September 27, 1968 while at a conference in San Paulo, Dom Helder was asked for his opinion as regards *Humanae Vitae* in relation to development in Latin America.

The Latin-American, Asiatic, and African masses would very soon have been stuffed and drowned with birth-control pills if Paul VI had not issued the encyclical *Humanae Vitae*. I will never forget the words of the American President Lyndon Johnson when he stated: "Five dollars spent on birth control is far more profitable than a hundred dollars spent on development." I am hence grateful to Paul VI for his encyclical, even if I realize that it may create problems for developing countries.

As we can see, Dom Helder did not speak as most other bishops did, including those of the Third World, by referring, that is, to the specific value of the encyclical as a document of religious teaching, and not as a document for the solution of demographic and developmental problems. He entered directly into a problem to which the Third World is particularly sensitive. Because this sensitivity is particularly acute in Latin America, we shall examine above all the reactions from that sector. In his statement Dom Helder did not mention names; but as to the allusion, for one who knows the strong anti-United States feeling of those Latin-American circles deeply concerned for and involved in a radical policy of development, there can be no doubts: Old "Uncle Sam" is ready to spend five dollars today for supplying the Pill, and he knows very well why: there will be less risk of his having to spend a hundred dollars tomorrow to obtain what he can obtain immediately by means of his so-called aid for development. The fewer the "peons" and the "campesinos" the fewer the dangerous surprises!

The reasoning is cruel; but if it is true, the policy which is behind it—including that of "aid for development"—is even more cruel. And the drama is that an increasing number of Latin Americans are convinced that this is more or less the true situation—in regard to the United States first of all, and then also the other European nations.

Humanae Vitae did not descend, in this case, on a (relatively) quiet world where people can permit themselves the luxury of dissertations on nature, the collegiality of bishops, the infallibility of papal documents. It descended on a world where the conversation centers around whether one's work should be done calmly and hopefully, with confidence that a day will come when this work will bring about the end of neo-colonialism, or whether one should take a machine gun and join the guerrillas in order to solve matters more quickly. In both cases there are those who discuss whether the work is in accordance with the gospel, or even if it is the gospel which demands it. Behind the reactions to the encyclical lies this world (and one hears it in the words of Helder Cámara), and this world is the key for understanding the motives underlying the Latin-American reactions.

Is this opinion, however, which may hardly be called tempting, really even credible? Is it true that millions of "desperadoes" have set themselves against old Uncle Sam even to the extent of being the key to the interpretation of an encyclical? What also of the suggestion of using it as a moral weapon against the "gringos" and "gorillas" who came from the affluent North of the huge continent?

It is clear how complex the problem is. It has already been amply treated, for example, by Jean Claude in *L'Empire Améri-cain*, Paris, 1968. We will limit ourselves here to sketching the outline of the more immediate feelings of the Latin Americans to the encyclical, or better, to Uncle Sam.

The *United States News and World Report* of October 20, 1968 poses the question bluntly: "Is there still any hope for Latin America?" and it answers, "The reply given by the most competent observers is a very weak Yes; the hope reduces itself to a very tiny light on the horizon. But the immediate outlook is that of a Latin America dominated by poverty, instability, and tyranny." It then proposes solutions to poverty, inflation, and political instability, and the order of priority is as follows: "control of demographic growth, struggle against inflation, limitation of a nationalism that slows down the necessary inflow of foreign capital and paralyzes the efforts for the unification of the hemisphere." The three things are closely connected with each other, and one can understand how "reduction of nationalism" is very much united to *control of demographic increase*.

A week before, Robert McNamara, president of the World Bank, had made a strong defense on the subject of birth control in underdeveloped areas. In a speech given at the closing of the twenty-fourth assembly of the I.P.S. (Inter-American Press Society) at Buenos Aires, McNamara spoke at length on the "urgent need for population control." In fact, the project of the "Pill for the poor" has been presented at Washington on several occasions in World Bank circles.

In Latin America it has ironically been called the "basic panacea," and the project has been denounced almost everywhere as a form of "planned genocide." One example suffices: the "birth surveys" conducted by experts from North America in Amazona, caused a public uproar in the fall of 1968 in Brazil, which accused the United States of "promoting a limitation of births and hence of the repopulation of Amazona in order to get a better control of its wealth." In addition, great publicity was recently given to an enormous project undertaken by some North-American companies for an intensive exploitation which included all Amazona. In the meantime, M. Hübner Gallo, professor at the University of Santiago in Chile, denounced the "population explosion myth" in a book showing great technical expertise. He expressly stated that "the campaign in favor of 'family planning' in the Third World, is animated by powerful political, economic, and marketing forces" (cf. M. Hübner Gallo, *El mito de la explosion demografica*, Buenos Aires, 1968).

The Latin Americans are obsessed by the new form that the old colonial capitalism, or as they call it, *pentagonism*, has assumed in the Third World. It is interesting to note that an old liberal like Juan Bosch, formerly president of the Dominican Republic, conducts an exhaustive analysis on the matter and in no half terms: "What is happening today in Latin America, Asia, and Africa no longer fits under the old imperialism defined by Lenin as the highest stage of capitalism. It is 'pentagonism,' which is the direct result of overdeveloped capitalism" (cf. Juan Bosch, *El Pentagonismo, sustituto del imperialismo*, Madrid, 1968). Marcel Niedergang, commenting in *Le Monde* of October 24, 1968 on Juan Bosch's book states: "Some will surely find Juan Bosch's conclusion a little schematic. His cry of anger, however, expresses the fear of the last of the liberals who find themselves abandoned to the discretion of the bayonets supplied by Washington."

In figures, the presentation of Latin America's present wrath and of that which may soon arise (as Juan Bosch observes) in Asia and in Africa, is provided by sources which are unexceptionable for their technical precision. The American magazine of the Department of Commerce, *Survey of Current Business* of September 1968, states that the earnings of the principal American companies have increased in the last 10 years by 90 percent in Chile, 30 percent in Argentina, and nearly 90 percent in Venezuela. In turn, the German magazine *Deutsche Aussenpolitik* states that General Motors makes profits of 25 percent in the United States, of which nearly 80 percent comes from its Latin-American branches. After this, one can well understand the aggressive reaction of Ivan Illich, director of the Latin-American Center at Cuernavaca in Mexico. In 1967 he attacked in the American magazine *America* not only the mass intervention of American interests in underdeveloped countries, but also those interventions involving aid not directly profit-making in themselves. Everything seems summed up in the proposal of the World Bank to offer substantial aid for the purpose of birth control. It is the famous "five dollars today." . . .

The above reaction finds valuable support of both a moral and a religious nature in the Pope's encyclical. On the one hand the encyclical not only condemns the methods of birth control proposed by the World Bank, but it also puts forward as the real solution, reforms which the world interests behind the bank certainly do not intend to undertake voluntarily. On the other hand, in countries which are predominantly Catholic, the moral weight of the Pope's words is also an important political force.

The Peruvian agency *Noticias Aliadas* of October 5, 1968 gave a rapid synthesis of this reaction in which the opposition to family planning financed by the World Bank is seen as strongly tied up with the moral influence of *Humanae Vitae*. "Various personalities," the Peruvian agency says, "as well as many Catholic organs, have pronounced themselves against the proposal of the president of the World Bank, Robert McNamara, who has offered the aid of this credit organization for birth control. The president of Bolivia, René Barrientos, states that in his country birth control may not be implemented "because," he says, "my country is contrary to the thesis of McNamara." An investigation by the daily *El Diario* of La Paz arrived at the more or less unanimous conclusion that McNamara's proposal "is intolerable."

A group of Catholic doctors and biologists stated that McNamara was committing "an insult by offering the sale of the Catholic Bolivian conscience in exchange for generous credit." *Radio Fides*, in turn, calls this process a "disgraceful trade," while the daily *Presencia* of La Paz declares: "Although the problem of demographic explosion is serious, it must not be solved by the use of those methods which have led, as a result, to the Negro ghettos in the United States. These methods presuppose that we men and women of the underdeveloped countries can be 'planned' like cattle."

At Bogotá the chancellor of the archbishopric's Curia, Msgr. Luis Carlos Ferreira, stated that the Catholic Church opposes completely any economic aid by the World Bank to underdeveloped countries if given on the condition that it be used for birth control. The magazine *Oiga* of Lima, in an article entitled "McNamara Attempts a Take-over of Latin America," highlights the fact that Paul VI foresaw the World Bank's plan, and this gave him incentive to issue his encyclical *Humanae Vitae* condemning the methods of birth control proposed by the "controllers." The same article quotes Harold Griffiths as indicating how "McNamara has started a distressing plan against the underdeveloped countries," and that the president of the World Bank "without the least scruple insults human dignity and man's free self-determination."

Besides this insult to the underdeveloped countries, there is another reason for refusing the plan, which is that the "demographic explosion" is a false problem blown up by the capitalist forces so as to be able to intervene more easily in direct control of those countries. Therefore the Argentine magazine *7 Días Ilustrados* of October 2, 1968, in an investigation on the Pill, holds that

the population explosion is a false problem. *Humanae Vitae* indicates that there is a double conflict. There are acute problems pressing on the already dramatic demographic situation, highlighted by underdevelopment and infra-consumption; and it is also difficult to obtain a workable solution. . . . When Paul VI in his recent encyclical reaffirms that the primary end of marriage is procreation, not only does he jump into the abyss, separating doctrine and the practical behavior of Catholics, but he also challenges a whole army of sociologists and statisticians who maintain that the weaknesses and economic crises of the Third World can only find a solution in the reduction of the high birthrate.

The same magazine then treats of the social problem and states that

the real question is this: Is human society in a position to supply food to all its members? Dr. Julio Notta, author of the book *Crisis y solución del comercio exterior argentino,* says in this book, "If we take into consideration what nature gives us, and the technical knowledge at our disposal, at the present time conditions are favorable for feeding a population 5 or 6 times that of the 3 billion people on our planet. One just has to think of the 135 million square kilometers of land surface, not water, of which 54 million are uncultivated. What is more important, only a small portion of the cultivated area—Europe, United

States—produces the maximum possible. . . . While some scientists state that the future depends on the Pill, others have been able to extract proteins from gasoline. Synthetic foodstuffs are the solution of the future, but for now it would suffice to better exploit the available land. Obviously it is an economic problem. If the foodstuffs are insufficient, it is due to bad and unjust economic organization. What must be changed is economic organization and not the birthrate."

The Argentine experience seems to agree with Dr. Notta. Argentina is suffering from chronic economic fatigue. Its demographic index is very low, and it also suffers in many cases from overproduction. Even if there are many who do not eat enough, there is still a surplus production of Tucumán sugar; tons of fruit from the Paraná Delta are destroyed for price reasons, and the same is done with grapes from Mendoza, while no outside market can be found for the meat produced in Argentina, not to mention that in the last few decades land fertility has been jeopardized, plantations have not been renewed, and production per hectare has been reduced. Hence all the international plans for birth control defined by those promoting them as "a medicine which will check the falling economy of the underdeveloped countries" are worthless.

What is unquestionably true, however, is that statistically speaking, all the developed countries became industrialized simultaneously with the dizzy rise in population. At the end of the last century the United States annually accepted thousands of immigrants, and Argentina accepted tens of thousands. The efficiency of the birth-control plans elaborated by international organizations must be strongly criticized. They are supposing as a prerequisite something which is illusory to want to reach in a brief period of space and time; namely, a rapid improvement of the education of underdeveloped peoples. If, in underdeveloped countries, it is found to be difficult to promote birth control with rigorous efficiency among women of the upper and middle classes, then its diffusion among the poor and illiterate masses is well nigh impossible.

This problem of the education and betterment of the people is also felt in the Dominican Republic, where the rector of the Catholic University of Santo Domingo, after having stated that he is very familiar with the problems of his people, adds:

The solution does not lie in corrupting the people's moral outlook, but lies rather in educating them so that they may better use their available resources. We must fight the moral laxity which is filling this

273

country with illegitimate children. We must fight for the desired reforms which will bring about an equal distribution of goods to all. . . . It would be impossible, with an agriculture at an almost primitive stage, with such unequal land distribution, with only a restricted nucleus reaching a certain development, to tolerate a large increase in population without seriously endangering the present order of things. To do this, however, we must not start thinking of closing the wombs of Dominican mothers to keep matters as they stand. Rather, we must think of better exploiting the possibilities which this land offers, even if to achieve this we must destroy the present egoism.

Here then, is a realization of the real demographic difficulties, which is also an occasion for saying that a birth-control campaign would end up by leaving matters as they stand, to the benefit of those who should be facing the real reforms of education, land exploitation, increasing the peasants' standards of living, subdivision of the vast estates, etc., instead of thinking of pills. The statement of the rector of the University of Santo Domingo, Roque Adames, was understood by a newspaper of the Dominican capital as a condemnation of the government, which according to unspecified voices, favors a hidden but effective campaign of birth control. The university immediately made it clear that the rector had no intention of attacking the government.

In Latin America, however, there are governments with clear demographic policies which include education for birth control; for example, Colombia. The recommendation of the encyclical to the ruling powers, in No. 23, is clear:

Do not allow the morality of your peoples to be degraded; do not permit through legal means, practices contrary to the natural and divine law to be introduced into the fundamental cell—the family. Quite different is the way in which public authorities can and must contribute to the solution of the demographic problem; namely, the way of a provident policy for the family, of a wise education of peoples in respect of the moral law and the liberty of citizens. . . . The true solution is to be found only in economic development and in social progress.

This statement naturally aroused apprehension among some Latin-American governments, and also produced clashes and debates.

274

A New Quarrel Between Altar and Throne?

On August 10, 1968, the Colombian foreign minister, German Zea Hernandez, announced his resignation after a meeting with the president of the Republic, Dr. Carlos Lleras Restrepo. The political observers at Bogotá stated that this resignation was related to the criticisms which he had leveled against *Humanae Vitae* and to the fact that in a Catholic country such as Colombia, it would have interfered with the government's birth-control policy. Because the Pope was coming to Bogotá on August 22, the minister's criticism was judged "imprudent and inopportune" in the capital's political circles. The Catholic weekly of Bogotá, *El Catolicismo*, making itself spokesman for these criticisms which appeared on various levels, stated in its editorial of August 11, 1968:

It is a hurried and unusual declaration made by the responsible officials of the anti-birth campaign of Colombia which states that the encyclical *Humanae Vitae* will in no way interfere with their program. In the light of the peremptory declarations of the encyclical, a demographic policy like the Colombian one, which uses any available method of birth control, is objectively immoral. Consequently, all the people who directly or indirectly participate in the application of this policy and who call themselves Catholics, should henceforth not continue to support it, under pain of falling into an evident contradiction with the principles they claim to profess. . . .

In future the officials in charge of the birth-control campaign in the country, will no longer be able to keep up the pretense in the public eye that the Catholic Church is in agreement and is collaborating with the development of such an ill-fated policy. As Catholics we cannot but be surprised that the supreme magistracy of the nation during this exceptional present period should continue placing under divine protection government plans which include a policy that —as Paul VI states in his encyclical appealing to public authorities— leads to the degradation of the people's morality by permitting practices contrary to natural and divine law to be introduced into the fundamental cell of society.

This accusation directed at the government's policy was clear and precise. At present, on the basis of the agreement between the two parties which alternate in governing Colombia, the

Liberals, to whose party the president and the dismissed minister German Zea Hernandez belong, are in power. Even the outlawed anti-government movements, which do not in any way share the official attitude of Catholics and the hierarchy whom they accuse of collaboration with the oligarchy, are nevertheless in this case in agreement with the "conservative" Catholics and the hierarchy. In fact, the Catholic hierarchy did not avoid facing the matter on the occasion of the encyclical, but did so in a very subdued and diplomatic way, thereby convincing the movements of the so-called Camillist Catholics that there is dangerous collaboration and mutual support between the Catholic hierarchy and the government. It is sufficient to note the speech of the apostolic administrator of the Archdiocese of Bogotá, Msgr. Aníbal Muñoz Duque, president of the Colombian Bishops' Conference. He stated on Colombian radio on August 4, 1968:

The Church teaches that we must undertake a careful family policy and a wise education of the people which respects the moral laws and the liberty of the Colombians. In saying this, the Church indicates the path which rulers must follow in the revision of their programs. The hierarchy as such will put no questions to the government as regards its official family planning programs. The church informs the rulers that it is they who are primarily responsible for the common good and that they can do much in safeguarding public morality.

The bishops' statement is considerably restrained, conscious of what a more direct intervention on a political plane could produce. *El Catolicismo* interprets the archbishop's words in a more direct sense as an invitation to review the government's demographic policy. *El Catolicismo* says:

The Catholic hierarchy, by its nature and mission, does not intervene coercively against the public powers in order to make them follow any one particular line, but it states with firmness, as in this case, the moral criterion based on a correct interpretation of the natural law; and this must be the guiding influence behind those concrete policies which, like the demographic ones, are related to public morality, which is the indispensable safeguard of the authentic common good. The practical task of carrying out such a revision of policy is the Catholics' duty, and the fields of action are many: government, legislative chambers, exercise of the electoral vote, communications media, and all the intermediary groups which constitute society.

276

As we can see, it is a real strategy to ensure that the government concretely revises its demographic policy. The Catholic weekly is categorical:

We cannot permit it to happen that, in a nation which is almost homogeneously Catholic, a certain government, using the excuse of common good, insists on propagating equivocal criteria contrary to the principles of religion, when that same state has constitutionally undertaken to recognize and safeguard these principles as being those of the majority of the citizens.

In any other country where there is a similar agreement between Church and state, but where there is also a consistent parliamentary opposition, a similar stand might well unleash political battles and a crisis in the government. (One thinks of Italy where No. 23 of the encyclical caused strong reactions in political circles and also in Parliament, where already a proposal on birth control was being examined. The same applies to France.)

Other situations arise in countries where the Catholic movements more committed to development as well as the government, find themselves in agreement against a demographic policy initiated or sustained by public interests. Even where there exists the advantageous situation of a separation between Church and state, the encyclical has produced an agreement which evidently lies more on the political level than on a moral or religious level—or better, the moral-religious sphere undertakes to support a policy of independence in the face of outside pressure. This situation is typified, for example, in Peru. In *La Prensa* of Lima, of August 2, 1968, Federico Prieto Celi wrote an article already indicative from its title, "From the Vatican to Washington," in which he says:

Humanae Vitae bears the date of July 25, but was made public on July 29. On that same day President Lyndon Johnson signed a law for aid to underdeveloped countries, in which provisions were made for birth control. The disgraceful decision of the Washington government is nothing new. It takes the form of a systematic campaign presented under the halo of super-affection and dollars but deprives thousands of men of their right of procreation. It is true that increasing demographic development is posing many governments with acute

277

problems. But to go so far as to propose a systematic control of a nation's births as an ideal solution is, to put it bluntly, like suggesting the elimination of invalids, the abnormal, and the aged because they do not directly contribute to the state. Materialism, egoism, and error unite forces to form a single, aggressive evil which could not remain hidden for long.

Number 7 of the statement by the Peruvian episcopate released on January 27, 1968 alerts the country against Washington's attitude. The clear, pastoral words which do honor to our episcopate for their strength in defending, six months before the papal pronouncement, the rights of marriage and the family, spoke of the foreign intervention: "This strong restriction on births does not take into consideration the fact of personal liberty, nor does it take into account the country's legitimate hopes and possibilities. If it is accomplished also by moral and economic pressure, using the help of foreign aid for the campaign of family planning in the way we have indicated, the dignity of the human person and the sovereignty of the nation is harmed. It must therefore be rejected, and we strongly reject any intention to limit the population increase at all costs. . . . In other words, Washington has decided, notwithstanding the Catholic doctrine ratified by Paul VI, to diffuse the Pill and egoism among the developing nations as the first and indispensable condition for the loan of dollars and aid.

The reply of the Catholic hierarchy of Peru was clear, and is now supported by *Humanae Vitae*. The government and people of Peru have before them the Christian teaching of the Pope and the nation's bishops, and the plans of the powerful brother country in the North. It lies with the government to interpret not only the feeling of the Christian conscience of our people but also its best interests.

This last phrase offers a rapid and effective synthesis of the reactions that *Humanae Vitae* has caused in Latin America: "The feeling of the Christian conscience of the people and its interests."

Nevertheless, the unequivocal reaction of Peru, which finds an echo in other Latin-American countries, reveals the real and grave local difficulties that exist, besides the problem of relations with the "powerful brother country in the North." The encyclical produced uncertainties and maybe ambiguities, if one is to believe the article which the same newspaper, *La Prensa*, dedicated on the same day to the announcement of the Peruvian minister for health, Dr. Javier Arias Stella, that "the Peruvian Catholic Church, as in many other parts of the world, has accepted the use of the Pill during certain periods, especially immediately after childbirth."

The minister specified in his statement, that the acceptance of the Pill on the part of the Peruvian Catholic Church, did not constitute a definite policy but that the papal encyclical coincides in part with the policy carried out by his Ministry of Health. Dr. Stella said that the only fundamental objection on the part of the Church, was against the use of the intrauterine device, even when used as a means of avoiding an excessive population growth rate and only with the couple's conscious agreement. Dr. Stella also revealed that in the talks held with the Peruvian Catholic Church an agreement had been reached on the method to be followed. Before the appearance of the encyclical, the minister added, the ecclesiastical hierarchy accepted not only the biological methods but also within certain limits, the hormonal treatment. From what we read now, the hierarchy's new attitude reveals a change of opinion [the minister is referring to the new statement by the bishops issued after the appearance of the encyclical—EDITOR].

The minister then said that the encyclical coincides fundamentally with the policy that the Ministry of Health had suggested regarding this problem, laying particular stress on education as a fundamental element in the stability and equilibrium of the family. "It also coincides with the line of policy that we had traced out in agreement with the meaning of responsible parenthood." The "revelations" of Dr. Stella are rather interesting, and they arouse the same curiosity as did the news a few years earlier concerning the admission on the part of the hierarchies concerned that nuns who had been raped in the Congolese war and in Poland by the troops could use contraceptives. Nevertheless this indicates how in reality governments together with Churches are ready to follow demographic policy in certain spheres, especially in conjunction with the efforts being made at mass education. If what the minister, Dr. Stella, says is true, the harsh rejection of the Peruvian bishops to the policy of Washington takes on a rather new light.

One fact, however, is clear: the Church, through a particular hierarchy, is attempting to find a compromise with a given demographic policy. In each case—whether the Church opposes it, or whether the Church adopts a position different from that of the encyclical—a new problem has now been proposed which Alberto Methol Ferre, in the magazine *Vispera* of Montevideo, of October 1968, calls "The new quarrel between Altar and Throne."

The point made by Methol Ferre is extremely interesting and is on two levels: the "domestic" one, as he says, and the "political"; namely, the significance of the encyclical for the individual family and individual person, and its significance for society as a whole. Methol Ferre holds that he expresses a situation which is typical of the underdeveloped countries when he says that the first level affects rather those countries with a high standard of living while the second is prominent where the political element —that is, commitments on a social scale—are felt more, since they are problems which involve large masses of people as such. Maybe it is for this reason that the hierarchy's interventions in these countries, even when the hierarchy attacks a government clearly pursuing demographic plans programmed and financed from outside, give rise to fewer reactions than No. 23 of the encyclical does in European countries.

Methol Ferre affirms:

The encyclical forces us to leave the *domestic ego* of our family, to pass to the problems of our neighbor, to give total consideration to the other. For this reason, it is my conviction that when we pass calmly from the *I* to the *We*, and this the encyclical obliges us to do, with a little reflection we shall understand the Church's and Paul VI's reasons. . . . The encyclical's statements lead us to visualize them not in an abstract way but in relation to the contemporary political scene. We must therefore dwell on certain aspects of the tension existing between we Christians and the states, which is that complex, historical world in which *Humanae Vitae* is born and is inserted, and not close ourselves within ecclesiastical walls. . . . *Humanae Vitae*, in its discourse and its language, has two dimensions: what it says and what it signifies. And so its significance ceases being that of an abstract, formal absolute, and is seen instead to be significant in a real, practical, and social context. . . .

Thus to be better able to understand the encyclical one must ask in which historical context and when and why *Humanae Vitae* was promulgated. To what concrete and historical situation does it rely and refer? We find the answers in the encyclical's text, and they are the guides for going even farther than the text itself. In fact, this encyclical is a message which is directed not only to Christians but also to states. It calls Christians to task but also formally interrogates the states, so that they are "the other subject," which every exegete of the encyclical must keep in mind. Not to answer this fundamental demand is to complicate matters and to be lacking in clarity. It is with reference to the states that the encyclical poses the issue *which comes before all others:* the question of certain demographic policies connected with developing countries. This is not a new question for the magisterium since John XXIII brought it to the forefront and Paul VI does nothing but restate it.

A whole "pseudo-progressive" exegesis has tended to separate the acts of Paul VI from their continuity with the directives opened by John XXIII, and tries to introduce a foreign "individualistic" and "subjectivist" interpretation of the motivations of Paul VI. This is a thesis which does not stand up to even the most rudimentary analysis. First, an individualistic interpretation of history is naïve and shallow, all the more when one is treating of the acts of the supreme "pastor" of a whole community. We can only understand Paul VI by having as a point of departure the global reality of the Church, and the specific tensions it is subject to. Second, because *Humanae Vitae* fits naturally, without a break, into the series inaugurated by *Mater et Magistra* (1961), *Pacem in Terris* (1963), *Gaudium et Spes* (1965) and *Populorum Progressio* (1967) . . .

How does Rome see the situation of the states in the present day? From the time of *Mater et Magistra* onward, the popes have been repeating the following fact, which in itself is certain and obvious: "Probably the most difficult problem of the modern world concerns the relationship between political communities which are economically advanced and those in the process of development. The standard of living is high in the former, while in the latter countries, poverty—and in some cases, extreme poverty—exists" (*Mater et Magistra*, 41). The text goes on to say: "But the bigger temptation with which the economically developed political communities have to struggle is the temptation to profit from their technical and financial cooperation so as to influence the political situation of the less developed countries with a view to bringing about plans for world domination. If this takes place, the fact must be explicitly declared that it would be a new form of colonialism" (*Mater et Magistra*, 46).

All the important texts from Rome, from *Mater et Magistra* to *Populorum Progressio,* do nothing other than insist on this viewpoint, so full of criticism against affluent, consumer societies and the sight of rich countries becoming even richer and the poor ones remaining poor. Obviously these tensions are an essential part of the Christian *We,* since the Church is found both in the rich, affluent dominating countries and in those proletarian countries dependent on them. This innermost, violent contradiction within the Church immediately becomes apparent when viewed both before and after the appearance of *Humanae Vitae,* which is the encyclical which most deeply penetrates this contradiction. It is for this reason that the encyclical has shaken the entire Church with a violence it has never before experienced. In fact, the encyclical has been placed directly and forcefully in between married couples and states.

There are various versions of the circumstances which led up to *Humanae Vitae*. One of them deserves particular attention on account of its relation to the general historical context: "In certain Roman circles the reasoning goes as follows: The Pope was not excessively interested in officially pronouncing himself on the Pill and he did not dismiss—even if he did not approve of it—the possibility of leaving the problem to the decision of the married couple, as some orthodox Catholic groups desired. Undoubtedly, some plans of lay and religious foundations, intent on imposing rigorous norms favoring birth control in Latin America, are said to have led Paul VI to express himself as he did on the question" (in *Análisis*, Buenos Aires, No. 387). All speculations on the intimate intentions of Paul VI are superfluous if one does not keep in mind the whole of his policy, its link with the series of objective actions in which he has shown his conduct, and his government of the Church. If the objective context of these preceding factors makes this version the most probable one, its *objective effects* on all the various fields makes it certain.

Is it pure coincidence that on July 29, the day the encyclical was issued, President Johnson also signed the law which determined "Food for Peace" aid in favor of the underdeveloped zones, for the birth control of the states being "aided"? Is this not the flagrant neocolonialism that John XXIII spoke of in his encyclical? Is it not "the temptation" which Paul VI refers to? Is it not the objective, fundamental reason for his appeal to states? Or is it pure chance? To invoke chance is ridiculous, because the North American plan for the control of the "population explosion" has been in existence since 1953 and has been slowly increasing in the last five years. Who has not seen in the past few years alarmist, coercive, and organized propaganda which has been unleashed in Latin America to regulate its birthrate? And who is the principal agent of this campaign in the Third World if not the United States, and for exclusively national reasons? Why spend a hundred dollars when one can save by spending five on birth control? Paul VI now reverses Johnson's reasoning and threatens the affluent society. Is this a new "quarrel" between Altar and Throne?

As can be seen, the problem of birth control is not only that of the single couples with their questions. It is the problem of the couple and the family before the state, and before both foreign and national powers, when the latter allow themselves to be tied down by the former.

Thus the encyclical is before all else a sign of the times—of the times when one type of society is repeating what man has always been doing. When it is well off, its egoism leads it to ensure that there will not be others who may take away or diminish its well-being tomorrow. Undoubtedly this is just one key for understanding *Humanae Vitae*. Why then is it so evident and acute in Latin America and not in other countries of the Third World? Possibly the reason is that the Latin-American countries are those which have best understood their own situation and the extent of foreign intervention with all its relative advantages and dangers. That is why it is the Latin Americans who can most clearly ask: While in the Middle Ages the quarrel between Altar and Throne raged over the meaning, and the purity and liberty of the Church, and over how Altar and Throne were to divide the government of the world among themselves, is there today another such quarrel, set in a modern context of a new domination, more dangerous and cruel than the previous one, which may get the upper hand? May the encyclical, then, be read "politically"?

The Encyclical "Enters" Politics

Methol Ferre himself says:

In this way do we not risk giving a political interpretation to the encyclical? Yes and no. We prefer to call it a crude and Christian interpretation, seeing that politics is included in Christianity and not rejected by it. We are inseparably citizens of the Church and of the world. There is a judgment which men and nations make of the Church, and it is one and the same—can we remember it? Of course. If not the Christian, at least the ecclesiastical hierarchy has specific functions: it has no direct powers in politics even though it must always consider politics and view it from the point of view of the preaching of the Word and sacrament, yet without sacralizing any one particular political body. For this reason the Pope must necessarily confront the various demographic policies from the standpoint of the dignity of the person and of the couple—where sacrament and politics meet. To adopt these policies as such would be tantamount to formulating pure opinions in precarious, changing, and much disputed ground. For this reason John XXIII cautiously approached the demographic problem in *Mater et Magistra* (cf. *Mater et Magistra,* 50).

Today, however, what the Church must face are the Malthusian policies now in full swing. What is it like to face them? What is it like to refute them with authority? From the point of view of the couple and the traditional teaching of the Church (not in relation to revelation but to the natural law, even if this is directly connected with the former), the Church must do it by reaffirming and not changing this teaching. It is for the good of humanity.

Thus the problem of the couple, of human dignity, of the continuity of the Church's doctrine, "enters" directly into politics, or better still, is faced with the various political forces which today in Latin America may be best summed up as neo-Malthusian.

Once it has entered into politics, what is to be the fate of the encyclical? Clearly it will have an effect on all the possible channels, as *El Catolicismo* of Bogotá observed—first, on the governments, and then on the legislative chambers, etc. Though from one point of view this is desirable, it is generally feared and criticized. This was the situation for the minister of health in Colombia. The reactions were directly given by one of the interested parties; namely, the Population Reference Bureau, which in its PRB service of August was already reporting from Washington and co-jointly from Bogotá, on the session, held on July 31, of the Organization of American States (OAS), and the *Comité Asesor en Población y Desarrollo* (CAP), a member of the general secretariat of the OAS. It stated that in a declaration issued by the *Unión Panamericana*, CAP expressed its grave concern over the possible hindrances created by the papal encyclical *Humanae Vitae* to the economic and social development of Latin America.

This committee of the OAS, composed of eminent personalities of the hemisphere, expressly stated its concern in a special and extraordinary declaration, drafted at the end of the business of the first reunion, declaring unanimously, that

in view of the cultural, religious, and economic characteristics of the great majority of the Latin-American population, one cannot ignore the fact that the message of the encyclical will translate itself into greater anguish, misery, despair, and infirmity for millions of individuals if it succeeds in obstructing in a large number of families of that population the decisions they had made before the encyclical. . . . The encyclical makes an unusual appeal to heads of governments, asking them not to sanction practices contrary to the laws of the Church. In this connection the committee points out that in contemporary pluralist society the decisions relating to any element of population policy fall within the competence of the public authorities of each country.

The committee then treats of the theme of the government's actions in their population problems, remembering that

the reunion of Caracas [September 1967, in which the committee was created under the auspices of the OAS and of the Pan American Organization of Health: PAHO—EDITOR] recommended paying attention to the conditions of each country and every existing demand, thus supporting the familiar planned economy of government programs, providing adequate information about the public's planned economy, based on unbiased dialogue.

The PRB then explains at length why the Assessor Committee of the OAS intervened and commented on the possible influences and interferences of the encyclical, and again quotes paragraph 5 of the declaration:

In strict terms the discussion of this matter does not fall within the competence of the committee: first, because the Population Program of the OAS has the task of offering technical assistance to the countries for the purpose of increasing the effectiveness of their national policies in the matters of population and development, and because within these policies the purely instrumental problem of choosing different methods of contraception is of secondary importance; second, because the committee has neither authority nor competence to influence the decisions that each couple must make in complete liberty; third, because the decision made by the encyclical is fundamentally based on principles of a theological and moral nature and not on technical considerations.

The PRB goes on to say that after having explained why, strictly speaking, the committee should not initiate a discussion of the encyclical, CAP then outlines the grave consequences which the papal document may have when it states in paragraph 6 of its declaration:

It would undoubtedly be impossible not to admit that the low educational levels and the religious tendencies prevailing in Latin America can transform the encyclical into an instrument which will exercise an unfavorable influence on the attitude of governments, institutions, groups, and individuals when faced with demographic problems.

The first reunion of the committee, continues the PRB, was closed by the new secretary-general of the OAS, Signor Galo Plaza Lasso. In a speech in which he reaffirmed the positive attitude of the OAS regarding the population problem in Latin America, the secretary-general stated:

Here we touch the aspect that most concerns us as an institution dedicated essentially to the development, and therefore to the quality, of human life. In the humanistic tradition of our Western Christian civilization, we are always mindful of the ethical and moral values which indicate to us that man is the center and measure of all things.

After affirming that "in considering the population factor as a quantitative variable which we view in its relation to the unity of the family, this unity must be formed on the basis of responsible decisions of fathers preoccupied with the dignity and well-being of their children," the secretary-general recalled what the Inter-American Economic and Social Council (CIES) had stated in its fourth annual reunion when it underlined:

It is the specific responsibility of the governments to adopt necessary measures for guaranteeing to each family the freedom to decide the number of children they want, in accordance with their particular situation; and to ensure this possibility, it is necessary that families have opportune, objective, and sufficient information.

A very cautious use of language as well as a circumspect attitude may be noted in both the statement of the committee and the statement of the secretary-general. However, the care taken to establish the fact that a demographic policy can only be determined by the governments responsible, is evident. The fact that a papal encyclical based primarily on religious and ethical reasons can have a determining influence on countries with strong Catholic majorities is seen as an intrusion in a sphere which is strictly "political." Paragraph 5 of the statement indicates this very discreetly—that both CAP and OAS have been set back in this area, and this is shown by a subsequent statement of the PRB in August, where it reports at length a statement of the Jesuit Dexter L. Hanley, director of the Center of Human Rights of the University of Georgetown in Washington, and the first Catholic priest and delegate member from the United States to the United Nations. Hanley's statement is interesting for the way in which he poses the question of the relation between Church and state authorities on the matter, referring to Vatican Council II. The PRB states:

Father Dexter L. Hanley declares that according to the tradition of the Church it is not the function of the state to impose private morality upon the citizens because this could be a violation of the religious liberty reaffirmed by Vatican Council II . . . The Pope has not claimed infallibility, indicating in this manner that he does not want to change the teachings of the Council. The Pope says to the leaders: "Do not accept that the morals of the peoples become degraded. Do not accept that practices contrary to natural and divine law are introduced into the fundamental cell represented by the family by legal means.". . .

Did the Pope want to enter into the very complex field of the relations between the Church and the state by means of a simple passage in an encyclical which is dedicated to the teaching of private morality? It is not possible to consider the encyclical on its own. In order to interpret the precise sense of this extraordinary appeal made by the Pope one must also look at the other sources of the teaching of the Church. . . . The Church and the Christian tradition teach that the state—or civil society—is a natural and independent society, founded on natural law, with its specific rights and functions. The state has neither authority nor competence to make decisions in matters of faith or private morality. This is the mission of the Church and not of the state. If the state were to act in a different manner it would risk the abuse of temporal power. In a society the individual must be free to determine his choice in the exercise of his rights and in making his convictions operative, always provided that the exercise of this freedom does not harm or interfere with the rights of others or the common good. . . .

In practice, the declarations of Vatican Council II are of a much higher order than any papal encyclical without the character of infallibility. The declarations made by a Council of bishops with the approval of the Pope are one of the most solemn forms of the teaching of the Catholic Church, and have a far more compelling force than

287

any declaration made by the Pope. The encyclical *Humanae Vitae* does not have this character, and it did not therefore intend to change the lines laid down by the Council which, in their true significance, can justify official action in programs of family planning. [Hanley then goes on to explain how the conciliar declaration on religious liberty recognizes that man has the right of free choice in matters of faith and morality, and particularly stresses the passage which says that "if in view of special circumstances prevailing among certain peoples it becomes necessary for the constitutional law of society to give special recognition to a particular religious organism, it is nevertheless necessary that the right of all religious organisms to religious liberty be recognized and effectively put into practice."]

It is clear that the Pope did not want to suggest that the state has the right to impose private Catholic morality on its citizens, not even when these citizens are Catholics. The only thing with which the state is concerned is the promotion of the common good and the defense of public order, respecting the exercise of religious liberty. The formation of the Catholic conscience is in the last analysis a question of faith and not one of public policy; this is evident for two reasons: in the first place because the Pope himself appeals to revelation as the inspiration of his teaching, and then because other religious organisms have adopted contrasting positions. The Catholic position cannot therefore be the one preferred in government policy.

From Hanley's remarks it is evident that he intends to establish the fact that the Pope's recommendation to governments cannot be understood as an intervention into political choices. But demographic planning is precisely part of the "political," and rulers as such may not go so far as to establish a moral norm of conduct for citizens to observe. In both cases it means remaining faithful to the principles of religious liberty; that is, to freedom of conscience. The Pope may not therefore expect a government to renounce or impose a given policy in the name of ethical and religious principles—and these are the principles within which the encyclical operates. On the other hand, and for the same reasons, a government may not impose a policy, be it only a demographic one, when by doing so it makes demands on the citizens' consciences. It could be said that this is the problem, though in another sphere, of countries predominantly Catholic (for example, Italy) where a government intends legalizing divorce, and where the Catholics (at least part of them) do not intend imposing an anti-divorce policy arising from a religious law opposing divorce, on the government.

If, theoretically speaking, Hanley's statement could calm the governments and international institutions concerned about an unlawful political interference, the practical question remains as to how a government or an institution is allowed to undertake a demographic policy which also includes the use of contraceptives. Would it be solved by means of a popular referendum or a tacit consensus with the local religious hierarchies? It is difficult to say with any precision on account of the delicate problems posed by local situations.

In any case, Hanley draws the logical conclusions of his treatment of the problem by indirectly answering the question posed by Alberto Methol Ferre: "A new quarrel between Altar and Throne?" In the way Hanley poses the question there is really no room for a medieval quarrel updated to a contemporary theme. In fact, the PRB reports:

Dealing with the legitimacy of the intervention of the public authorities in questions of family planning and population, Hanley quotes the declarations of Vatican Council II and the previous pronouncements of Paul VI. Paragraph 87 of the constitution *Gaudium et Spes* says: "Within the limits of their competence the governments have rights and duties in connection with the problem of the population of their respective countries." And Paul VI himself, in paragraph 37 of his encyclical on the development of peoples, said the following with regard to family-planning services organized by the state: "The public authorities can certainly intervene within the limits of their competence, carrying out appropriate informatory services and adopting suitable means, always provided that these be in conformity with the requirements of moral law and that they respect the just liberty of the married couples."

At this point Hanley descends more directly to the concrete, grassroots level and thus draws theological conclusions to his arguments:

Governments therefore have the right to concern themselves with the demographic problem. In practice the leaders have the duty to face up to these problems, basing themselves on social norms and the common good. . . . It is undoubtedly in accordance with natural law that state competence be recognized so that the state may attain its legitimate objective such as the promotion of peace, prosperity, public order, and the common good. On the other hand, it is quite clear that the state is not competent to aim at different objectives. In the same way it is in accordance with moral law that the state should grant the civil right of free choice to all citizens, even when the choice of the citizen is contrary to private Catholic morality. If the state has decided that there is a need for the elaboration of family-planning programs, it must permit all its citizens to freely exercise their liberty in the choice between the various methods which are scientifically acceptable. The only limitation derives from the interests of the common welfare, not from the morality of the methods.

However, since the state is not some kind of abstract idea, but is made up of single men and these may be Christians, Hanley now touches a very real problem. What attitude must Catholics take toward the family-planning programs of their government? Hanley believes that

a Catholic can perfectly well give his political support to programs that offer contraceptive information and services, even when the use of contraceptives is recognized as being contrary to moral law. In that case his position implies only this: supporting his government in the legitimate effort of promoting the common good and public order by means of a program which is intended to balance the population and the resources.

At this point Hanley touches on the problem of criminal or intentionally induced abortion, which in Latin America today has reached "frightening" proportions:

In view of the fact that abortion offends not only against private morality but also against the common welfare, governments are entitled to administer *effective* contraceptive procedures within the framework of a necessary effort aimed at reducing its incidence. Contraceptive programs can be justified, at least on the basis of the principle of accepting the lesser evil, because abortion is both socially and morally a far more serious evil.

At this point it is obvious that a conflict can arise: Does accepting a political argument of this kind not really amount to giving the Pope's decision little real weight? Hanley cannot see this danger and attempts to answer the objection. He says:

I believe that one must promote among Catholics a filial respect for the teachings of the Pope, but that these teachings must be read and understood in the light of all the pontifical teachings, and particularly in the light of the declarations made by the Vatican II Council. . . . The paragraph in which the Pope appeals to the governments cannot be interpreted separately from the rest as a contradiction of the principles laid down by Vatican II. The Pope did not seek to decide questions of public policy in this manner.

Hanley's line of interpretation regarding the encyclical which has "entered" politics, is itself an interesting political interpretation. Whereas in Europe, in order to lessen in a certain sense the excessively strong weight of the papal document, some have made an attempt to prove that it is not in continuity with the teaching of *Mater et Magistra*, etc., in America an attempt has been made to establish some kind of continuity for precisely the same motive but on a different issue: the minimizing of any possible political repercussions which the papal document could have.

Consequently, while some—as does Methol Ferre—perceive and in fact uphold the encyclical's "political" plan and function, others make an effort to save the demographic policy by playing down the encyclical's political significance.

Is there really any different treatment of the problem over and beyond—or rather, at the root—of this political discussion? Are not the different "keys" for understanding *Humanae Vitae* really nothing other than one's basic opinions? If Ferre maintains that the encyclical cannot be read in an abstract or "meta-historical" context, but must be inserted into the historical and political context in order to be understood over and beyond the text as such, it is obvious that one must search for these possible ideological components, or historical and geographical concerns, which lead to different interpretations of the encyclical.

An Accusation Against Christians of Affluent Societies

It has already become obvious that there are different ways of interpreting the encyclical, from the purely religious, ethical, and theological—including the problems of authority, magisterium, natural law, etc.—to the medical and biological. The fact is that the encyclical, whose most controversial decision is that of paragraph 14, necessarily includes these themes. In fact, like few other papal documents, it touches on an extremely delicate and intimate part of human behavior and consequently has an immediate repercussion on the broadest possible spheres of society and human community. It is for this reason that Methol Ferre's suggestion of the two levels on which the encyclical may be read—the level of the domestic *I* and that of the Christian and social *We*—allows us to develop a more dynamic criticism of *Humanae Vitae*.

If on one hand negative criticism is based on the fear that the encyclical will make successful demographic policies more difficult and thus cause new traumas and difficulties among the underdeveloped nations, on the other hand the fear exists that direct or subtle imposition of large contraceptive projects amounts to nothing less than genocide, which would suit those societies which are well developed and characterized by affluent, consumer civilization.

The first criticism, attacked almost unanimously by the underdeveloped countries as redolent of "North-Atlantic terrorism," bases itself, in any case, on a particular analysis of the world situation. Even though this criticism can easily serve the more disreputable and questionable interests, in all honesty the admission must be made that it has objective reasons in its favor. There is at least less risk of reading the encyclical in terms of the political scene whether in an "Atlantic" or "world" context, and it gives greater possibility of directing the problem to the essential content of the encyclical, which is of an ethical and religious order.

The second interpretation certainly has the advantage of revealing the more dynamic, concrete, historical, and existential dimensions of a doctrine which could become the subject of parlor talk centered on rather egoistic and private problems. At the basis of this second interpretation is certainly an unfavorable judgment on the part of the underdeveloped nations toward the nations of the consumer civilization, and more specifically toward the Christians who live in this society and who criticize the encyclical for not taking into account the sad situation of Christians who are forced to live in a civilization with enormous development problems, who are now further tormented by a moral law which forbids them to employ a given solution to solve some of their problems.

This is an interesting aspect of the discussion on the encyclical and may be viewed as a "challenge" to the affluent society, which instead of offering sincere and open help to the underdeveloped world, complains because the Pope has not permitted a morally valid solution, the one most comfortable to them. One can understand, therefore, how a certain type of reaction and judgment is characterized by a sense of offended dignity on the part of some significant representatives of the underdeveloped countries. A complete outline of this interpretation characterized by its challenge to and "accusation" of the Christian in affluent consumer societies is given by Methol Ferre. He asserts this interpretation in the much wider context of a judgment on the general attitudes of this type of society, including its political aspects which include the North-Atlantic policy on one hand, and the religious and theological policy which logically corresponds to it on the other.

Hence the rather cruel attacks begin against those theologians who in Europe and in America had voiced criticisms of a theological nature against the encyclical. However, it is possible to perceive in this the questionable nature and weakness of the political interpretation when its criticisms are directed at theological criticisms, which thereby come to be evaluated on the political level. If, in fact, one is to admit that the sociopolitical reasons for which one accepts the encyclical have their own validity, one must also admit that the strictly theological motivations for which a theologian criticizes it also have their own validity. Moreover, just as one may not reject the Third World interpretation simply because it tends to enhance the theological value of the encyclical, in the same way one may not reject the theological criticism because it holds that one must not overemphasize the encyclical's teaching, even if this criticism happens to come from developed countries. In both cases the real issues involved would simply be used as instruments to justify one's own interpretation.

What exactly then is this Third World interpretation which

sees the encyclical as an accusation against the Christians of the consumer society? Methol Ferre has formulated it with particular insight and has achieved a complex synthesis of the position in *Vispera* of October 1968. He writes:

This accusation of Paul VI against the affluent society is first an accusation against the Christians in this affluent society. The day following the publication of the encyclical, a non-Catholic friend said to me, "If the Church were to change her traditional teaching on birth regulation just now—when it is in the empire's interests to 'regiment' countries so as to keep them in the status of colonies—it would be the most irresponsible act imaginable." It is of little help to know that an eminent theologian like the German Hans Küng has declared that the papal encyclical is a "second Galileo affair," because the traditional doctrine has not been changed.

What is this new Galileo affair? Surely it is the fact that Christians of the affluent part of the world have concentrated on the problem of the couple and have forgotten the political problem. What a strange confusion of conscience! This division of the Christian We makes itself most apparent in the declaration formulated by the North American theologians in Washington and also signed by authorities in moral theology like Bernard Häring. Here their complicity with the affluent, domineering society is most obvious. The whole document limits itself to competent reflections on the Church and natural law but completely ignores the political dimensions of the encyclical, even though a few feet away the government of these men had simultaneously promulgated this neo-colonialist law as part of its demographic policy.

None so deaf as they who will not hear! This silence radically undermines the position of Häring and the other signatories, and makes us lose faith in their seriousness. Moreover, in their reflections they do not even take into consideration the declaration of the North American bishops, issued from Washington in 1966, which saves the honor of the Church in the United States by adopting a firm stand against this neo-colonialist politics.

We could add examples to prove our point, and when taken in all their breadth and depth what do they reveal? They show that "progressiveness" in the affluent world does not necessarily coincide with progressiveness in Latin America and that we must exercise incessant criticism. The opinions of Hans Küng and Bernard Häring are a symbol. Do they not lead us to initiate a "critical sociology of knowledge in affluent societies" and to its incidence in our societies? Will it not be our duty, in dialogue, to "demythologize" certain so-called progressives, reveal to these progressives in the *northern hemisphere* that really they are not what their name implies, and demonstrate their objective complicity with the dominating powers?

The criticism of Methol Ferre, as can be seen, goes farther than the matter of the encyclical, calling into question the "progressives" who are accomplices of the dominating powers. Naturally these progressives could ask whether they must introduce politics into their critical theological methodology simply to not risk unknowingly offering a hand to the demographic-planning campaigns mentioned by the OAS. They could also ask if they may use such criteria in other theological disciplines (seeing that they are approaching the encyclical from this point of view), and if they may not, what other criteria could be used to determine this point. In fact, Methol Ferre suggests a theological methodological category which it would be interesting to apply to all theology, but on account of its dialectical character, not to mention its reasoning, would become rather discouraging. His response to the "ecumenical" problem is an example of this. While we have understood it in a theological sense, he applies the category of "politics" with the following results:

And if this is so, do not certain forms of "ecumenism" also come in here? When *Humanae Vitae* is taken by our separated Protestant brethren as an obstacle to ecumenism, can we not see how, strangely enough, Pastor Malthus is also quietly included along with the fathers of the Reformation, Luther and Calvin? Is it by chance that the recent assembly at Uppsala, in some of its workshop discussions on the development and underdevelopment of nations which ignored all the neo-colonial questions (they limited themselves to "racism"), affirmed that "many Churches are of the opinion that we must promote family planning and birth control as a priority problem"? Does not silence on neo-colonialism and giving priorities to demographic issues reveal a coincidence with imperialist interests? Nor is this rectified by their feeble final observation: "We recognize, nevertheless, that there are Churches which have moral objections against certain methods of birth control."

Does not this aspect of the ecumenical movement lead us to observe that the Protestant areas coincide almost completely with the affluent world of the northern hemisphere, while the Catholic Church is in the position of having to bear the tensions which come from having a third of her flock in Latin America? And if we see that the integration of the North Atlantic world is continually progressing, are not, then, certain forms of ecumenism one of the more recent ideological phases of imperialism? Our Protestant brothers of Latin America must face this both obvious and acute problem together with us. Look at the force of *Humanae Vitae* in reacting against it!

Put in these terms, the issue immediately passes from the political level to that of relationships between nations. We may say rather that it takes on a "class" aspect because, as Methol Ferre notes, it deals with nations which, according to their position on the ladder of power, each adopt a definite viewpoint on the encyclical, which is determined by their vested interests. These interests include greater wealth, security, and development on one hand, and survival and safety on the other. Certainly we have the right to ask whether he is adopting an outlook which is present in the encyclical itself or whether this outlook is extraneous to it. This second hypothesis certainly does not derive from the premises laid down by Ferre, for although this hypothesis is formed within a "political" context it then enters into a *context of political forces* and thus even the other interpretations of the encyclical come to be seen as different facets of the one power game or as an ideological metamorphosis of imperialism. Ecumenism is an example of this.

It must be noted, moreover, that this judgment naturally suggests another judgment which, over and beyond the problem of the encyclical, involves all of Christianity, for it now finds itself before the supreme judgment of its responsibilities; namely, whether Christians in the economically developed sector of the world can still call themselves Christians. Our author arrives at consequences like these when he transposes the "political" or the "Christian We" aspect of the encyclical into the unstable equilibrium of concrete political forces as they reveal themselves in relationships between the human masses. Methol Ferre says that

Latin America is not simply a conglomeration of proletariat nations in comparison to the affluent, North American world. In its more advanced and forward-looking regions it also contains the powerful forces typical of the affluent society, the attractiveness of the way of life of its landowners, and the blinding fascination of its tastes and fashions. This leads to noticeable but inevitable contrasts. In the outlying areas of southern Latin America it is customary to divide the human groups into rich, poor, and *remediados,* who are the middle class. It is among the last that the discrepancy between health and sickness is most acutely felt. Especially in the capital cities and in coastal regions the middle class and the new proletariat are emerging from the immense world of marginal groups.

It is from these emerging groups that there arises the initiative to protest, the impetus to develop, and the criticism of oppression and archaic structures. On the other hand, these groups also collaborate with the established order and they feel to a very high degree the impact of the old, colonial culture and the alienation arising from the customs and ideas introduced by the consumer society. It is at the same time a fruitful but a dramatic combination of opposites. All the most useful energies for a transformation are put in a state of tension. This makes it difficult to implement practical political projects. A popular movement has appeared but without a people. Literate revolutionaries have appeared but together with a violent rejection of critical reflection which eventually dissolves into self-destroying action. The *remediados* are not the most numerous sector of Latin America, but they are certainly the most important sector for revealing the present state of affairs.

The more dynamic segments of the Church in Latin America are in no way removed from this situation. It is primarily these sectors that *Humanae Vitae* hits most directly and most personally. Indeed, as in the affluent societies, it is among the vast sector of *remediados* that *Humanae Vitae* arouses opposing reactions, and it affects them on their deepest level. It is here where one finds the most conscientious couples and the most united families, but they have innumerable difficulties on the ethical level—because in Latin America one does not speak of families and married couples with the same facility as one speaks of them in Europe or the United States—and it is in this sector where the better-known clergy work. Given this state of affairs, it is logical that the reactions of a great number of priests to *Humanae Vitae* are related to the couples' difficulties, and one understands how a wide range of reactions has arisen.

At one extreme, for example, there is the position taken up by the Centro Pedro Fabro of Montevideo, one of the best theological centers in Latin America. It holds that "neither directly nor indirectly does *Humanae Vitae* allude to the birth-control policies which are being used by rich countries on poor countries" (*Perspectivas de dialogo*, N. 25). Hence it then feels free to expound on the role of the laity in the Church—not in the world—and on the married couple. It puts forward no suggestions to eliminate the problem of countries' demographic policies. In so doing it evades the real problem. Possibly it is a reaction springing from the conviction that other Christians take into account only the political aspect of the issue and forget the problem of married couples, which would also be an oversimplification of the problem. A third position, and the most widespread one, is that expounded, for example, by the Argentine priest, Alejandro Mayol: "The encyclical has a positive side only on the social level: it curbs the mass sterilization projects by the United States in Brazil, Puerto Rico, and Colombia—planned to avoid social conflicts which would endanger the capitalist system" (*Primaera Plana*, No. 293).

Let us leave aside the optimism of the curb and reflect on the "only," which would have us believe that the encyclical fares well in "no other" than the political sphere and that it would fare badly in the sphere of marriage. This "via media" between the married couple on the one hand and politics on the other is the most common reaction, possibly because it is also the most comfortable one. But it is no answer to the concrete questions posed by the encyclical. It is a tactic of dividing and separating to make the obstacles easier to overcome.

This contrast, which seems to be suggesting a completely different "political" interpretation of the encyclical, hence does not come to light simply in the relationship between "North Atlantic" attitudes and "Third World" attitudes, but can also be seen to be present within the underdeveloped societies themselves, with the difference that here it is easier to find a middle course. Indeed, on one hand, we have the universal problem for the couple—one of "domestic policy"—and on the other, the demographic problem—the risk of falling into the hands of foreign powers and vested interests. Which is the more realistic interpretation, the purely domestic or at the other extreme, the purely political one, or that of finding a middle course? Possibly we cannot afford to dwell too long on dissertation of this kind when there exists the pressure of misery on one side and the offer of dollars and technicians in exchange for agreeing to use the Pill on the other.

"Europeo-centrism," "North Atlanticism," and "Third Worldism": Three Fields for Humanae Vitae

The pressing nature of the problems results in the issue of the encyclical being thrust even deeper into the historical and sociological context, and this in turn opens up three different fields of study in which the same seed produces fruits—a strange, unnatural phenomenon which in this case gives the appearance of being quite natural. A "European-centered" theologian would perhaps find the encyclical an excellent chance to prove that one and the same truth takes on a new voice and a new face when transplanted into different times and places, and he would arrive at some valuable conclusions on "demythologizing." Methol Ferre says:

Let us look at the historical context. Paul VI issues the encyclical a month before his first visit to Latin America, which holds one third of the world's Catholics. Since in fact the official statement of the Church must be directed primarily to those areas where they really can have an influence and where the Church is in some way called into a particular field, one can objectively uphold that *Humanae Vitae* is above all, and on account of its effects, an encyclical for Latin America and for the powers which hold sway there. One cannot imagine it having any real effect, for example, in China or India. And where did Paul VI go? To Colombia, the paradise of imperialist birth-control programs.

And what does the gesture signify? First, it intended revealing in the clearest possible way to Colombia, to Latin America, and to the world, the complete separation between the Church and politics of this kind. At the same time, however, it placed the fact and the consequences of politics such as these before the conscience of the entire world. It led to a very wide discussion and public diffusion, and hence in a dramatic way it warned the Catholics of Latin America and of the whole world of the affluent society. It transferred the question on to its most concrete level, into everyone's domestic issue; nobody could elude it, ignore it, or feel that he was innocent. . . . Nobody could wash his hands of the matter, whether living in the northern hemisphere or in the privileged farmlands of Latin America, since the encyclical has brought politics into his very house. Has not Paul VI raised up the cross of other people's misery before a society of consumers and waste-makers? Has he not made the unity of this suffering Church felt? The ecumenical unity of the Christian people has never been revealed in such a sad and stagnant state in our very midst.

After being inserted into "history" and "politics" the encyclical is thus now taken into the "geography" of the conscience of peoples. Even though Latin America was the point where the "geographical" application of the encyclical was made, insofar as it is a paradigmatic representation of the problems and contradictions of the Third World, this will not necessarily convince everyone that *Humanae Vitae* is "above all an encyclical for Latin America." If it is, determining what, in fact, it really is, becomes all the more difficult unless it represents that "catharsis" of the cross raised up before a "society of consumers and waste-makers."

Is the encyclical what Paul calls the "scandal of the cross," updated and presented in terms of history, politics, and geography? Is it not placed rather at the crossroads of three roads along which travel three different worlds of culture, interests, concerns, sufferings, doubts, reciprocal tensions, hidden fears, balance-of-power politics, and wars cloaked over by smiles and dollars— the Third World, the European-centered regions, and the North Atlantic?

Methol Ferre seems to affirm this when he states that the "reaction of the *metropolitanos* powers was exceptionally and unanimously furious, just as much as that of the Christians closed within the circle of the problems of married couples. The reactions ranged from that of *The Economist*, which left aside its elegant English calm and called the Pope an 'Italian bachelor,' to that of the Herodian Lleras Camargo who spat out infamous remarks against the Church in his editorial in *Vision*, while the Colombian minister for external affairs was dismissed and the OAS called the appeal of the Pope to public powers 'obsolete.' Need we say more?"

What are some examples of this provocation which goes beyond (the insistence is symptomatic) the problem of contraceptives to include even the very equilibrium of the world?

Methol Ferre quotes some facts and statements:

The very day of the publication of the encyclical, Fr. Curran, vice-president of the North American Theological Society, said in all certitude, "It is incredible that the Pope on his own could think of making a declaration which reaffirms the past teaching." We have shown that Paul VI has not defrauded the expectations of Fr. Curran. The incredible thing is that many do not understand this. Certainly this lack of perception has profound historical and social roots in this divided world of ours. But the irrefutable fact is that Paul VI—overcoming the "domesticated" treatment of the reports from the majority and minority of the Papal Commission on Birth, as well as evading the ideological terrorism of North Atlantic hypocrisy on the population explosion—has brought about a Copernican revolution with *Humanae Vitae:* in the problem of birth he recognizes the intimate bond between family and population, between married couples and politics, in the light of the contemporary situation. It is this which is unbearable.

Let us take a look at some symptoms. In *Informations Catholiques Internationales,* a magazine open and full of authentic ecumenical pursuits, we can ascertain the tenor of North Atlantic reactions, which occupy the greater part of its contents and which are almost unanimous in restricting the problem to the couple. Its most pathetic expression comes from the eminent philosopher and theologian, the Jesuit Hayen, to whom we owe so much intellectually and who is so entangled in the painful difficulties of married couples and of himself, as a priest, before Christ and the Mystery of the Church. The same magazine informs us of the "motives" which appear to be special to Latin America—the stress on their rejection of imperialist population-control policies. Likewise, the motive for the support of *Humanae Vitae* in Africa is included among the difficulties that the Union of South Africa, the country of *apartheid,* has put forward.

What more does this do than flash before our eyes the *European-centered* nature of this interpretation, since the "general" element is implicitly the Latin-American? And is Black Africa almost nonexistent? We can, from our point of view, reverse the procedure, taking ourselves as the general element and saying that the "special" element is the North Atlantic and the couple. Neither one nor the other are valid, however, because we are thereby adopting a partial *urbi* perspective whereas the Pope speaks *urbi et orbi.* He takes the two terms —family and population—as the two extremes of one and the same problem: birth and the procreation of human life. Thus there are no "special" motives from this or that sector, but it is the one problem and the one motive which absorbs the energies of the whole people of God, unites all the members of the Church, and transforms the special into "universal."

The encyclical ensures that the body of the Church does not put aside her crucifixions; it makes the cross of the poorest be borne on the shoulders of all, and not only in a literary, abstract way, but with an ecumenical, flesh-wounding "carnality" that transforms *Humanae Vitae* into the deepest sign of Christ's mystical body, of Catholicity, in such a concrete and personal way as to make it a "sign of contradiction" and a "sign of the times."

I know of no pontifical document which is so deep in meaning, so incarnate, so historically great, or so much a sign of the times as *Humanae Vitae*. For this reason it has raised a storm. What married couple (or what North Atlantic theologian) found themselves in a crisis because of the failure of the recent conference at New Delhi where the Third World found itself cheated once again? Will not someone now convert this failure into "pills"? This is no fiction! The fact is that population programs touch the very sources of life, of the couple; and the problem of the couple reverts back to the problem of population programs. Any type of exception allowed for the married couple, rebounds like a boomerang into population programs and vice versa. At the same time, population programs are intimately connected with economic policies. The pastor in his wisdom must know this, even if his people become hostile to him. Even if it hurts the pastor, he must be aware of this.

Is not the progress of "colored peoples" perhaps at stake? Today more than yesterday? Today, Spengler's successors have decreased in brilliance and have taken on a simple, more bureaucratic elegance— sophisticated experts, technocrats of organs like the UN or the OAS or of countless other abbreviations, new types of international toys offered to the highest bidder not batting an eyelid as they cover over the so-called population explosion. We prefer the remark of a good historian such as Fernand Braudel: "Latin America is an immense space. Its population is sparse and spread over an immeasurably large area. The area is superabundant and this abundance dazzles men" (*Las civilizations actuales*, Madrid, 1966). One can say the same for Black Africa. Even though the encyclical is for the whole world, practically speaking its important repercussions are on Latin America and Black Africa, where the Church feels its worldwide future being compromised.

This "geography" of the encyclical's intentions, however,

could easily give the impression that it is being used for its own ends despite all its premises and explanations of its "domestic" and "political" value. Methol Ferre senses this difficulty and he asks himself "whether it does not also involve the whole world. Is now the time to change a traditional teaching of the Church on the conditions of sexual relations and on procreation? Is it opportune and prudent to do it at this moment? Is it not essential that Christians reflect on all its consequences and implications? How also does *Humanae Vitae* contribute to this?"

Humanae Vitae certainly involves the whole world. It is one thing to say this at the beginning, however, and another to say it when it has already been inserted into a political and geographical context explaining how the world should be involved by the encyclical. If the "North Atlantic" theologian is challenged for interpreting the encyclical as a domestic fact, the Third World could be challenged just as much for interpreting it as a political or geographical fact. This, too (from a Christian point of view), is an instance of the encyclical's being interpreted in a theological tone. To speak of "opportunity and prudence" and of "a suitable time to change a doctrine" is already to place the issue on the level of criticism and evaluation, and consequently even here the theologian is given full scope to interpret the encyclical over and beyond its political and historical aspects. The theologian must ask himself other questions—in addition to the political ones.

Why attack the theologian, then, as if he were an imperialist agent or a crypto-Malthusian? The danger in this quite acceptable political interpretation of the encyclical, is that this principle will lead to a chain reaction so that the revolution could also be theologized with the consequent danger that it be "absolutized," and thus very soon become atrophied. In this chain of dangers it is certainly the theologian, interpreting an encyclical only with the categories proper to it, who is exposed to the least risk. It is also admissible to use other categories, but it is difficult to see the exact reasons for those categories being used and no others. This applies all the more when one sees how historical (and this the theologian accepts) and hence open to opinion (and he accepts this also) they are.

Hence, when the historical and political contexts change, an

303

encyclical which today is so much in the forefront can tomorrow be cast into oblivion. Theologians prefer a more logical path, even if a less pleasant one—that of saying in this present moment that a text is valid for certain reasons and not valid for other reasons, but always for intrinsic reasons. Anything else would be an extrapolation and that is the most dangerous procedure to follow for any type of reasoning, even the most straightforward. Hence the key in which the encyclical is interpreted by the Third World seems to be a highly emotional one, in spite of the disagreements with it and in spite of the search for a "via media." Admittedly, it can give a new outlook on a problem which no doubt could become enclosed within a circle it would never break out of. The true, dramatic picture that a document like *Humanae Vitae* puts before the conscience of the world, especially of Christians, is even more emotional.

All this, however, does not increase the intrinsic theological value of the document by one inch, just as—imagining the opposite case—it does not take an inch away from it. This is so because the Third World's interpretation is a political issue. It is as saintly a "politics" as one could desire: pure in its intentions, realistic toward facts and possible, present-day solutions, and as wise as the wisdom of a pastor. However, it cannot be the one, definitive key in which the encyclical is to be interpreted. Nevertheless, it is a key which must be used.

A "One-dimensional" Encyclical?

We have made allowance for a "key" in which to interpret the encyclical only because it offers a fine, clear summary of one aspect of the widespread Third World interpretation. The reason we have chosen this key and have given the greatest reference to it in Latin America is precisely because of that phenomenon of the *remediados* which Methol Ferre spoke of. Unfortunately, there are as yet no *remediados* in Africa, India, or Asia who are able to speak like a Latin-American *remediado*. This means that Latin America can almost be termed the voice of the Third World, keeping the appropriate differences in mind. The same phenomenon that is in Latin America is in the Third World. Just as in Latin America the really "poor" have not reacted because they are not even in a position to do so; likewise in the Third World the real "peons" have not reacted. It is only the *remediados* who have reached an awareness of the problems.

Providing, however, that this voice does have a deep, authentic, and paradigmatic value (and it does), does it not risk creating the appearance of a "one-dimensional" encyclical?

Methol Ferre himself senses this difficulty and asks: "Are we relativizing the encyclical in this way?" And he answers:

Yes and no. Our viewpoint does not exactly coincide with that of Paul VI in his encyclical. If it were only a question of married couples and not one of demographic policies, I confess that I would share the viewpoint of the majority on the Papal Commission. This, however, as I have already said, is partial and limited, and we must give an answer to a more general question. As an overall answer, no better one can be found than that formulated by Paul VI in *Humanae Vitae.* Our partial disagreement then changes into total agreement, since I feel that partial disagreement today is negative from a global point of view, being destructive of the common good of the Church and humanity. Admittedly, from time to time, as the Church's consciousness grows, the data of the solution can vary. Is this relativism? Not at all. It is an act of prudence which for us now is necessary, Christian, and obligatory for the entire Church.

Is not this, however, going against the very interpretation of the encyclical, which formulates a special, "ahistorical" interpretation of the natural law? No doubt Paul VI is restating the traditional interpretation of the natural law in essential and not prudential terms. For this reason he gives the impression that the couple's problem will solve itself while the demographic question will be solved by an "addition" —of vital importance, no doubt, but all the same, an addition. But in fact, Paul VI gives an absolute No to certain types of demographic policy by using as his starting point a series of absolute statements on the couple. It is his strongest, most invulnerable position before those countries which today have started on the road of Malthusianism.

Hence Paul VI has already made a certain number of qualifications which, although retaining all their "political" and "prudential"—in the noblest sense of the word—value for the interpretation of the encyclical, serve to lessen the one-dimensional impression which could be given to the encyclical. In fact, he has been forced to rescale the political dimension and it is important that this is being done precisely by one who upholds a political key for the encyclical's interpretation. "Paul VI's confrontation with the empire," says Methol Ferre; "no matter how frontal it is, is still obscure since it begins from the specific sphere of Catholic religious tradition and thereby remains on more solid ground, and never descends into the field of 'pure politics.'"

To be excluded, then, is the field of pure politics since the encyclical moves on the "more solid" ground of traditional doctrine. Also to be excluded is the single dimension, since it cannot be denied that there is another, in fact, the primary dimension, which is clearly ethical and religious, even though "ethical and religious" does not simply mean personal, private, and interior. The "political" interpretation, however, does reveal other dimensions of the encyclical—dimension which in different areas from that of the Third World are possibly the prevailing ones. Nevertheless, they are not altogether absent from the discussion in the Third World. The following are examples: the value of the encyclical, its comparison with topics of morality, family life, couples, the Church, nature, the responsibility of man and of the believer, etc.

Remaining to a certain extent in the political dimension, to which the Third World is particularly sensitive, and at the same time broadening our outlook to include another area of our responsibilities, it is interesting to note the connection which has been seen between the Pill and the "bomb." This is not a quip, considering that *Venezuela urgente-Semanario del la izquierda cristiana* of August 15, 1968 calls one of its editorials just that, "Of Pills and Bombs," which says among other things:

This time it is papal authority itself which has been brought into question. . . . With respect for truth, we must recognize the loyalty and courage of the position taken by the Pope in this delicate problem of fertility and marriage. Paul VI is more concerned with the meaning of the married couple and the authenticity of the marriage act than with the population explosion. He is even more concerned over the possible uses that governments could make of an "opening" by the Church to artificial methods for birth control than of its consequences for responsible parenthood. He cannot be accused of defining the conditions for correct marriage morality to the finest detail. However

—and this, too, with respect and honor for the truth—it must be admitted that the Church did not show the same concern in the field of international and social morality, principally as regards war.

What are we Christians to do with the problem of the atomic bomb? Shall we accept the fact that the United States and the Soviet Union hypocritically control the experimentation and the production of nuclear arms? Are we to let France and China perfect their thermonuclear bombs with impunity? What are we to do about the "napalm" which the "Western and Christian civilization" lets fall on Vietnam every day? What shall we do as regards the "flying incendiary bombs" with their destructive shrapnel? What are we to do about the 250,000 corpses of Vietnamese children who died as a result of this type of bomb between 1961 and 1964 (figures from UNESCO)? Who is to help us *see more clearly* the kind of pressure we can employ to put an end to the organized and rationalized massacre which is called the Vietnam war, a symbol of all wars?

It is still a timid gesture on the part of FUMEC (Universal Federation of Christian Students) and the Methodist Missions to withdraw their money from the First National City Bank of New York in order to protest its conversion of money in racist countries as, for example, South Africa. Just as timid is the gesture of nineteen North American bishops who demand the suspension of the use of napalm until the shareholders of Dow Chemicals make a decision on this issue. These gestures, no matter how symbolic, are not sufficiently effective against machines designed to kill. Defining the conditions for the birth of human life is a sublime and absolutely necessary task. Analyzing and affirming the demands of respect for and preservations of human life is just as necessary and possibly even more urgent.

Even in this passage, the encyclical is seen to some extent on the "political" level, although its true content and intention is understood as a "domestic" issue of the problems of the couple and human life. The political context is widened even further so that the writer seems to be saying in opposition to the previous view: even though it is true that the future of the Church in the world lies in Latin America, and that *Humanae Vitae* has a particularly strong bearing on it, this does not necessarily mean that the encyclical is a doctrinal intervention in favor of the "campesinos" and that it disregards some other, equally impoverished people who do not entail as much uncertainty for the future of the Church but who are now just as loudly proclaiming their accusations against the conscience of humanity. Even in this case, however, the encyclical's dimension is an acceptable one, all the more if this dimension reveals the difference between a *promulgated* encyclical and a *deficient* encyclical; namely, the difference between the times when the Church, or better, Christians, had the chance of intervening into serious problems and when they did not intervene.

At the same time this reveals the weakness of the political interpretation which is that of possibly establishing the principle of the sociopolitical "functionality" concerning the religious magisterium's official proclamations—which, however, is not to be excluded on principle. This could lead to the return to more modern and updated forms of Cesaro-papalism, and to a religious magisterium's being influenced to the point of once again being forced into political commitments at the very time when the necessity for it being liberated from this form of commitment has been seen. For cannot an encyclical risk becoming a program for a Catholic political party, especially in a country where the majority of the population is Catholic?

This same difficulty is felt, ultimately, even by those who accept the encyclical as a message for the Third World. Ricardo Bernardi, in *Vispera* of October 1968, after observing that "the last few public pronouncements by Paul VI—namely, *Humanae Vitae* and the declarations made at Bogotá—were a swift blow and a considerable source of difficulty for all those who held that the incarnation of Christianity in the categories and aspirations of the man of the twentieth century is one of the essential tasks of the post-conciliar Church," states:

Humanae Vitae, apart from the initial consternation over its condemnation of an opinion which had enjoyed a wide consent even within the Church, has come to be seen in another dimension which has been justified by the presumably political implications of the text itself. It is quite reasonable, in fact, to think that if the Pope ordered the free growth of population and thereby went against the interests of capitalist countries which would like to see births subordinated to their development plans, the logical consequence should be that the populations of underdeveloped countries should not limit themselves to the right of bringing children into the world but should also demand the chance of a decent life for them. Viewed from the sociological standpoint, it could have been hoped that the population explosion would have given life to a human and political explosion; that is, a revolutionary explosion.

However, a short time after, and on Latin-American soil, Paul VI rejected violence as a means of transformation, and in order to obtain social justice, resorted to the usual appeals to the Christian conscience of the wealthy, repeated now for four centuries, during which this "Catholic continent" has slowly developed into its present outlandish situation. But now, the very sociological reasoning which led to a manifesto in the revolutionary, historical change of the masses, whose right to procreation was now recognized, showed at the same time, paradoxically, that this change was impossible, because it transferred the initiative for it into the hands of the classes who hold power and whose impermeability to moral and religious exhortations has been recorded by history. After the dilemma has been posed in these terms there only remains to ask whether any common base exists to both the declarations of *Humanae Vitae* and the religious and sociological speeches at Bogotá, apart from that of defending the more or less traditional norms in the Church. If such a base exists, what can it tell us of the Pope's present line of thinking?

This, then, is the dilemma of a "one-dimensional" encyclical: if its "political dimension" is allowed, then the dialectic of the political game must also be accepted. The comparison between the two papal texts, however, leaves us perplexed precisely for this reason, since the recognition of the right of underdeveloped peoples on the one hand—the right to defend themselves against birth-control campaigns—is not accompanied by a recognition of the right to develop a policy of human and social emancipation even in a revolutionary direction. On the other hand, while the choice of *Humanae Vitae* is very much a political one (even though basically religious), the invitation and the appeal directed to public powers and the rich to "allow" and "favor" the development of their peoples is purely an ethical and religious one.

Is there not then a more basic issue not only in the encyclical but also in the last few official declarations of the Pontiff? To search for this issue would be the same as undertaking an internal criticism of the encyclical, be it positive or negative. The political interpretation could give the impression of being a complete, overall acceptance of the encyclical even if this leaves a certain margin for criticism. To search, however, for the underlying motives which explain this political dilemma means to enter into the topics which on a preliminary reading are almost absent from the vast amount of Latin-American material (apart from a general acceptance), and which are precisely the topics most in evidence in the European and American reactions—the so-called North Atlantic and European-centered reactions. This indicates that the political interpretation of the encyclical is not the only one possible, even in the Third World countries. It is not absent, for example, in Africa and Asia.

At this point, however, we are justified in asking a question: Which of the two readings is the more positive with regard to the encyclical, the "political," which seems to accept, or at least include, the document's entire reasoning process, or the "thematic," which seems to raise certain difficulties regarding some of its underlying reasoning? Maybe the first makes it possible for the document to open onto the broader, worldwide level, while the second, although appearing to be less respectful, does it—in fact, a more penetrating and constructive service insofar as it does not intend destroying the encyclical and even less the authority from which it proceeds, but intends rather to clarify—within the sphere of the present difficulties (which are one-dimensional and political), certain problems that the encyclical could do nothing but present.

Ricardo Bernardi begins from this basic problem by adding a "limited anthropology" to the reasons which create the dilemma already indicated. He says:

I think the confusion which has been created is basically the result of a mistaken interpretation of the two pronouncements, but particularly that of *Humanae Vitae*. In the great social encyclicals of John XXIII, of Paul VI, and in many documents of Vatican II, the analysis centered on the historical process and on the deep, underlying dynamism which animates the present-day world. The accent was put not so much on problems of conscience but rather on historical problems. The Christian's ethics were not seen so much from the personal point of view, but rather as part of the historical process which was being examined and of which a global appreciation revealed the norms for the Christian's ethical behavior. In our case this does not occur. Paul VI does not ignore the historical and social dimension of the problems regarding sexual life or violence. However, he prefers to adopt an individual and moral perspective when he deals with them, which transforms them primarily into a personal question of conscience. *Humanae Vitae* centers around the appeals addressed to different groups of persons (governments, scientists, families, etc.) that they respect (or prevent anything which degrades, etc.) an ideal of marriage presented in an abstract and ahistorical form.

At Bogotá, the conflict of classes and of nations from which Latin America suffers is solved, in principle, by an appeal to charity, by means of the different duties of status: the generosity of the powerful and the rich, the effort of workers, etc. One can certainly object: Is it not legitimate for Paul VI to speak directly to the conscience of the faithful to remind them of the demands of Christian morality? There is no doubt that Paul VI has clearly and wisely seen the necessity of remembering the ascetic demands of the Christian life. Even from a purely psychological point of view, a psychoanalyst would affirm the domination of one's basic drives, like those of aggressiveness and sexuality. This control is necessary if these energies are to be freed for social and religious goals. The real difficulties do not have their roots here, but in the limited anthropology which serves as a basis for the ideal of the Christian life as proposed by Paul VI.

Family life at present is faced with various kinds of difficulties, according to whether one is dealing with a less-developed society, a socialist society, or a capitalist society. Ideas regarding the development of fundamental values of life arise in each of these, but they are seen within a comprehensive view of man in society. The encyclical does not take up the task of reading these aspirations in the light of the gospel. It limits itself to indicating some very general characteristics (married love must be human, total, faithful, and fruitful) and to pronouncing on methods of birth control from a perspective which, even if it is postulated as comprehensive (natural and earthly, and at the same time supernatural and eternal), sinks into an essentially aesthetic and oversimplified concept of human nature, based exclusively on a biological fact and removed from the movement of man in history.

This nature ends up by becoming the expression of the "order established by God" (No. 16 of the encyclical). We are dealing with a sacralized nature. . . . When, however, these transformations of which man is capable (as both their subject and object) are considered as artificial, then this mutilated and sacralized nature becomes inadequate as a criticism for moral norms.

This anthropological deficiency, as Ricardo Bernardi observes, goes to the root of the difficulties raised by the encyclical. He says:

The encyclical begins with the existence, willed by God and proper to married life, of a relationship between married love, its sexual expression, and procreation. The unity of these three terms is based on its expression in two distinct spheres: (1) This unity can be rooted in the anthropological significance of married love. In its very structure, this love is at the same time unifying and procreative. Having noted this twofold dimension of married love, vertical and horizontal—that is, for the married couple and for the species—the encyclical then ascribes to this love all its depth and gravity, and preserves it from the growing triviality with which modern man views it (cf. *Humanae Vitae*, No. 12). (2) Yet this basis seems to have received an inadequate development in the encyclical. It is a basis which presupposes that one can accept the "principle of totality" and a dominion over the laws of procreation, both of which Paul VI rejects from the very beginning of the text (cf. No. 2, sec. 2). The encyclical, in fact, moves along quite different lines and adds that biological laws are an expression of God's will.

This identification of the divine laws with physiological laws occurs throughout the encyclical. . . . It is true that it is said they are "laws inscribed by God in its nature" (of the transmission of life) (No. 24), and hence that they are "biological laws that make up part of the human person" (No. 10), but they are considered as existing outside of or above the human person who is the natural normative totality. It must also be noted that in the encyclical the plan of God is not related to the processes of the organism by way of conscience, but by the opposite process: of the two spheres that we have mentioned, it is the biological sphere which determines the overall meaning. From this flow some consequences, then, which destroy that very inner dynamism which exists between the three terms—"love, sexual expression, procreation"—which the encyclical is so concerned to safeguard and to ensure that they do not lose their true significance, since the approved method (temperature or Ogino-Knaus) certainly does not result in this dynamic union being created automatically.

Bernardi, farther on, sees a "lameness," as he calls it, in the reasoning of *Humanae Vitae* when it

considers as disordered the possibility that man has of modifying the functions of his organism for legitimate purposes; as, for example, spacing births when there exist "serious motives" for doing so. Indeed, what is the essential difference between *knowing* that an act will be infertile, and making it infertile, when the end is lawful and the means used do not have in themselves negative consequences for health or married life? The difference between *foreseeing* an infertile act, and *rendering* an act infertile supposes a divorce between the intelligence of a man and his organism—a divorce that alienates, estranges, and dehumanizes him, by assigning to nature what belongs to man. God has given man dominion over the earth; yet man cannot project his potentialities onto nature. It is very difficult for man today to feel that by regulating his functions for just motives he is offending God. To oblige him to consider it as a rebellion can lead to strengthening the idea, central to the problem of atheism in the twentieth century, of a Promethean man and of a God jealous for the fire of the earth.

"Prometheus and God"—an image which seems to have come from ancient Europe, full of these types of problems; and yet it comes from the Third World. Are not these problems perhaps already there, and not just problems of development? Or better, is not this latter problem one which is included in the former? If we descend to this innermost level of criticism of the encyclical, do not the judgments of a political nature also assume a different aspect? The latter problem does not become any less important, and it retains all its values. Perhaps it can even receive solid support just by taking into account the criticisms of the weaker points of the encyclical. At the same time we are no longer dealing with a *single dimension* but with a *plurality of dimensions*, which allows a functional utilization of an ethical and religious document, and also keeps at its correct distance the presumably convincing weight that the document's underlying intentions, which are certainly valued ones, could bring to bear on the political dialectic. It may be noted, therefore, that the political interpretation of the encyclical, while not simply leading to a domestic interpretation, as in the case of Ricardo Bernardi, does attempt to bring about this synthesis. Bernardi says:

I wish now to refer to the political aspects of this encyclical. It has been said, and said with great emphasis, that *Humanae Vitae* puts the Church against not only the concrete programs of family planning under the auspices of the United States and its satellite governments, but also against the interests of this power to maintain in Latin America, by means of these programs, the status quo, which favors their plans of imperialist expansion. I think that it is necessary to recognize the courage and independence of the Pope in preaching the moral law over and above any sort of human respect. The Church did not change her position even when the largest economic and political interests of the world urged her to do so. In fact the Church has hit these interests hard, and it is sufficient to glance through the reactions of many representatives of the "Western, Christian world" to discover an unusual hostility toward a religious force which they believed they could depend on as allied to their plans. We cannot see political Machiavellianism in this, as we cannot see it in the condemnation of violence.

I insist on saying that to pretend to carry the reasoning of *Humanae Vitae* over and beyond the moral sphere into the political sphere, is to fall into opportunism and oversimplification. Above all, a simple reading of the encyclical is enough to show that it has no political interests for this is denied by the document itself; and the encyclical goes on to "appeal to the legitimate concerns" of public powers and to the help of international organizations in resolving the socio-economic problems, for they themselves may have been involved in causing them. . . . Second, it is necessary to evaluate the significance of the family-planning programs.

What is the relationship between family planning and population planning? And how is one to decide on the effectiveness of a demographic policy? The tendency is to see family-planning policies as the instrument that the United States prefers using to limit population growth in areas under its influence. Family planning is thereby identified with population planning. Hence one is led to believe that by fighting against the former, one is defending a nation's population potentialities. I think that this notion is politically simplistic, and that it is only jumping from the frying pan into the fire. I say this without wanting to deny that in some places it could be a human and political work of the highest kind to fight against family-planning programs.

After having thus redimensionalized a possibly too "one-dimensional" aspect of the interpretation of the encyclical, Ricardo Bernardi observes that the essential problem is quite different, and he quotes Kingsley Davis, professor of sociology and director of the Department of Demographic Studies at Berkeley University in California to indicate how in the United States this aspect of the problem is already seen in a different light. The whole position of Davis, and of a good part of the best American experts and centers, can be synthesized in the words of Davis himself:

"The ministers of economy and education, and not the minister of health, should be the ones who direct population policy." Bernardi then comments:

What are truly uppermost are the economic and cultural conditions which are exertive pressures in this direction—from the misery that prevents the establishment of family nuclei to the spreading of the *American way of life* that is driving us toward a spurious culture, in the sense given by Darcy Ribeiro. Do not be mistaken. It is not contraceptives which are the all-important factor, but rather, the "catalog of horrors" which our socio-economic situation goes to make up and which will be an efficient deterrent against any desire to have numerous offspring. Contraceptives just close the circle and reveal the problem: birth is subordinate to the economy because initially man was at the service of the economy and not the economy at the service of man.

Thus the theme is at the same time broadened and balanced. To fight against "pentagonism" and "North Atlanticism" by using demographic weapons, including the encyclical, can make us forget that the more pressing problem, to be faced by another encyclical just as peremptory, and not by exhortations, is the problem of the world's economic and social condition. Does this mean that there is really no population problem? Or else, would there be no sense in making the use of contraceptives easier? And if there is a sense and a usefulness, then how does a decision which can affect those actually concerned so closely, the *favelados* and the "campesinos," really influence them?

Pills for the Underdeveloped

It is the Brazilian magazine *Ponto Homem* of December 1968 which speaks in this bitter way on the contraception issue among underdeveloped people. We shall not quote here the numerous testimonials of those who live in the most desolate and abandoned areas of the *true* "Third World," among those voiceless masses who have not even understood what has happened among them and because of them. From these testimonials we can deduce a fact which emerges continually: the overwhelming majority of true *probres*, the *desemparados*, and the *favelados* do not even know what the Pill is; and if they do happen to know, it is because some doctor, or in some countries, social welfare, has pro-

315

vided them with it. When matters are at such a stage, it is easy to understand the fear and aversion for any type of program involving planning. With no education and no awareness, these masses are the perfect target for being "flooded" with pills, as Dom Helder Cámara says. The first problem, that of education, is coming to be seen more and more as the primary and most urgent problem.

Yet, besides the encyclical's having received an enthusiastic reception in most cases from those "committed" to the work of defending and promoting the Third World, it has also received another reception which is bitter, filled with sadness, and over-burdened with the pains of reality. "Pills for the underdeveloped" then becomes not a heading for the defense of the use of con-traceptives and of criticism of the encyclical, but a heading for the sad "witness" to the many situations of misery and ignorance. At times the Pill is only a "lesser evil," seen as such by those who live in the midst of this "catalog of horrors," as Ricardo Bernardi calls them. There is never a defense of the Pill as if it were *the* solution to a serious problem; but at most there is perplexity over the fact that it is not even *a* solution, and certainly it can neither be imposed nor proposed as a *sine qua non* condition for solving the problem.

The heading Pills for the Underdeveloped is hence crudely and realistically written at the head of a story which is so concrete that it makes the rather abstract reasoning of the encyclical diffi-cult to understand. Hence Ricardo Bernardi asks: "To whom is the encyclical directed?" and the answer turns precisely to that concrete and immediate world of the "underdeveloped" which in the reasoning of ethics and natural law, has been so little under-stood. Bernardi says:

Paul VI addresses himself to an ahistorical and abstract man, without specifying his problems by referring back to his particular social and cultural conditions. Such a man, however, does not exist; and the encyclical seems directed, judging from the universalistic tone with which it reasons, to the middle classes or upper classes. What meaning, though, has such a way of speaking for the family life of the two thirds of the world who must go hungry? We are thinking of the inhabitants of the Peruvian *barriadas*, the Uruguayan *pueblos de ratas* ("village of rats"), the Brazilian "Northeast."

Can we speak of responsible parenthood where the family has no stability, or of birth control where diseases carry out this function? We are also thinking of the simple working women who do extremely tiring work. How can they regulate their married life by calculating natural rhythms? It is clear that the encyclical should have taken another standpoint if it really wanted to have an influence on the great Latin-American masses and on the masses of the Third World. The basic conflict which the family is suffering from is not the "introduction of practices against the natural and divine law," but the alienating conditions which prevent the very fulfillment of the natural law. This situation is not solved, nor are the possibilities exhausted, by a simple appeal to public authorities (encyclical, No. 23) who are often the ones directly responsible for this situation.

Bernardi's phenomenological observation is very simple. It could be taken on to a more technical level where huge, more basic, and more distant problems would once again appear. But what of the here and now? What of this concrete reality? Andres Cox Balmaceda, in an interview conducted for *Vispera*, a Uruguayan magazine, has a vivacious and strong dialogue with his interlocutor, who states, picturesquely, that the solution is not to reduce the size of the family but to make the house larger, just as when his son's shoe is too small he solves the problem by lengthening the shoe and not by shortening the foot. To this the interviewer says: "Maybe you are right, but in fact, in our day-to-day procedure, today, here and now, what are we to do? Fill ourselves up with children and get farther and farther behind in the opportunities which life offers us?"

The interlocutor replies: "Today, here and now, Pope Paul has committed himself to human nature to save it once and for all from manipulation and from the mutilation of its powers. Today, here and now, one may do what nature itself indicates. But neither today, nor here, nor now, nor tomorrow will human nature be permitted to go against nature, much less to give unfounded arguments for it. There are already many forms of slavery in the world: the slavery of money, of underdevelopment, of the exploitation of one man by another, of servility in order to climb up the ladder of ambition; the slavery of propaganda which directs tastes and creates needs; the slavery of political and scientific dogmas. Should the Pope be allowed to become one more ally of the slave drivers of human nature and give them a free rein to carry out a new mutilation which in this case would touch man's innermost structure in which nothing less than life itself is rooted?"

Hence today, here and now, the problem is one of not allowing another form of slavery to develop because the other problems can be solved by acting "according to what nature itself indicates."

Yet this "today, here and now" takes on an entirely different coloration in both the attitudes and the statements of someone who lives continually immersed in the today, here and now of the suburb of a big city; as, for example, a priest whose testimony (anonymous for reasons of prudence) has been included in the magazine *Perspectivas de dialogo*, No. 25. He is a worker-priest who also exercises his ministry among the *baraccati* and who himself lives in *bidonville*:

The attitude of the encyclical, in fact, presupposes a lack of esteem for the woman. The encyclical, in fact, rejects all forms of infidelity. In society, however, man's infidelity is an accepted fact, whereas the woman is considered as an object to be used for reproduction. St. Augustine's doctrine, according to which the sexual act is licit when it has reproduction as its objective, seems to have been revived once again. It is a doctrine based on a negative, pessimistic outlook on sex which today is outdated. The Church has the duty of keeping up with the rhythm of historical and social change. In underdeveloped countries the person finds himself placed between two, usually authoritarian orders: the United States, on one hand, pretends that it can impose contraceptive practices as the condition for economic help. The Vatican, on the other hand, has ordered that these pills not be used. In neither of the two cases is freedom of choice respected, and the problem of responsible parenthood thus ends up outside the realm of personal responsibility.

The worker-priest is aware of the danger of "gulping down pills," but he does not hold that it can be avoided by an order to the opposite effect. On both sides it is always authority which is being used, and in the middle there are always the underdeveloped. In both cases these, rather than being helped, are once again being ordered, which is not exactly the starting point

318

for treating them according to their personal human dignity. This is undoubtedly one more aspect of the problem of "pills for the underdeveloped." It makes us think. On one side you have the authority of the dollar applying pressure to the empty stomach of the *subdesarrollado,* and on the other the authority of religion applying pressure to his conscience. Which of the two is more honest and which of the two is more unjust and dangerous?

Indeed, the problem of authority when seen from this point of view is new to our reflection on the encyclical. It is one aspect of the more general problem of authority which has emerged in the North Atlantic and European-centered discussion. While in these two spheres the discussion has been more along the lines of conscience and authority, here it once again takes on a lightly political tone. Once again the immediate problem becomes a key with which to interpret the encyclical.

The Lima newspaper *Accion* of August 7, 1968 has, for example, an editorial which carries the title "Back to Authority," in which it brings out the contrast between the direction and the way in which John XXIII faced the human problems of our time and the way in which his successor faced them. There is in it a certain amount of criticism of the consequences which the gestures and unexpected words of a Pope like John XXIII had at times, but also a sympathy for this man who looked at the world as it is, without becoming pessimistic, with love for the men in the world, and with clear-sightedness. This is followed by the passage: "Back to authority: what it means and what it has achieved":

John XXIII, who was undoubtedly one of the most attractive men of this century, wanted to teach that the Catholic religion is a state of mind which is capable of existing in any human spirit. This way of thinking, unique in Christianity from the time of Paul of Tarsus, produced the revolutions and upheavals which we have all seen and heard. He opened up the unexpected by going to scandalous extremes and by most scandalous commitments in social life. . . . The truth of the matter, however, is that the humanism of John XXIII brought the world face-to-face with serious and noble problems, since, I repeat, never from the time of St. Paul until today has there been in the history of the Church an epoch in which the Church has been so

319

close to life, so bold, and relishing so much to be in the midst of the disorder of problems in all their dramatic vitality. It will be for others to see how much good there was in this.

When the country Pope died, the Church elected Paul, so different from his namesake of Tarsus. He, like John, wrote two or three encyclicals because it was necessary to keep up the state of war which John had stirred up. But the guerrillas applied pressure; the Third World was awakening and burning; a despairing Christendom was also burning. In opposition to what some economists have said, what was created by the Johannine revolution was a lucid understanding of necessity and of nature, of the supreme preeminence of necessity as the moving force behind history. Of the great lines which direct human history, John XXIII opted, between authority and necessity, for the latter. Instead of hesitating for a long time and calling in the authorities of science and women with marriage problems, his successor opted for the solutions of authority—of authority which would like to be a spirit and which instead is an order, of authority which puts the supernatural below the natural, as if the supernatural were a law for the society of human beings and not a sublimination. Therefore he proclaimed that the marriage union must lead only to having children.

What does this encyclical on the transmission of life achieve? It achieves a return to the sad, Christian families, both numerous and enchained. Those who are rethinking his philosophy, by seeing the encyclical as the result of the sad fact of the publicity given to contraceptive pills, those who think that the Pope wants to populate Latin America in opposition to capitalist Malthusianism, are mistaken on the means and the ends. Paul wants a society made up of poor families, fearing another, heartbreaking conception, in a world of misery and underconsumption—and if he does not want this, then let us admit it. The encyclical is at its best on young women made slaves to pregnancy, who end up hating their husbands, sex, the very nature which dragged them to love, and on men who free themselves from the burden of fertility in brothels. Because this is the story of an uncontrolled marriage, its consequences are that the couple eventually turn from hating nature to loving authority. . . . And we can see the picture of the poor, working-class families, depressed and hungry, who end up taking God's command more as a punishment than as a blessing: "Increase and multiply."

The comparison between Pope John and his successor, the heavy *barrios*-style irony, and a certain amount of not very understanding animosity at the most understandable reasons which led the Pope to write the encyclical—these are all rather questionable. There does remain, however, a kind of harsh, immediate reaction which the worker-priest could not permit himself but which is basically the same.

Is what Ricardo Bernardi calls "ahistorical" and "abstract" possibly a kind of lack of realism which can only be acquired by direct contact with the hungry and the ragged?

Antonio and Margarida Acauan, a married couple who are presidents of the Christian Family Movement of Rio Grande do Sul, in an interview with *Ponto Homem* of December 1968, observed among other things:

It makes us sad to think that the encyclical is lacking in "openness" —an open attitude of love which is the basic point of the gospel— precisely when it comes to considering in all its reality the state of so many families, especially those of the poor and the ignorant who are unable to observe the method of natural periods of infertility. How can the illiterate of Brazil, for example, who are 50 percent of the population, plot graphs, mark dates, read and write calculations, and check thermometers? And at what time are you to note the temperature if the woman has not been able to sleep at night on account of fatigue and pain from caring for creatures who are a bundle of needs? Thousands of these poor women knock at the doors of family planning clinics and ask for any kind of method to free them from desperation. After all, it is to Christ that they come and to whom they state their demand, to him who says, "Come to me all you who are tired and afflicted and I will give you rest." Some points in the encyclical show how it could have gone much farther ahead, for example, No. 8: "Marriage is not, then, the effect of chance or the product of evolution of unconscious natural forces; it is the wise institution of the Creator to realize in mankind his design of love."

This couple engaged in the work of helping the families of the *favelas* seems to be saying that opening up farther and drawing out more logically this admission would already have been an answer to this tragic "today, here and now" which worries wide areas of poor and unprepared nations.

This is the same concern as that of Nely Capuzzo, who lives in the *morro da Maria degolada*. The *morro* is a human agglomerate where one can find all the horrors of the *favelados*, where the people live in their primitive goodness and simplicity but which can unexpectedly become aggressive and a hive of delinquency. When asked by *Ponto Homem* about the effectiveness of the Ogino-Knaus method, which in the concrete conditions of the *morro* is permitted because it is natural, Nely Capuzzo wastes no time in giving an answer:

In the *morro*, experience has shown that this method has very few concrete possibilities for various reasons. First, ignorance: it is very difficult for the women of the *morro* to have any idea of their menstrual cycle. They make mistakes; they lose count; they think that all this mathematical calculation is nonsense and a waste of time. We have followed them as they have gone through the various courses brought into operation even in the primary school, in the period of puberty itself, and this is what we are trying to do now. Then there are the poor health conditions. For this reason many women do not have regular cycles. During the past few years I tried giving instructions to a woman who already had eight children. I gave her the book, the table, and long, private explanations. Result? Today she has twelve children and she insists that she scrupulously stuck to directions. There is also the lack of acceptance of this method by the husband. In the majority of cases I have treated, the problem was one of the partners not accepting periodic continence. Even by organizing guidance courses we did not succeed in overcoming the difficulties.

I remember well the case of a woman who was allowed to leave the sanitorium and to whom the doctor had advised a period of abstinence so as not to make her health worse. The husband's reaction was: "Well then, why have I a woman in the house?" In the man's case it is always more difficult to get anything done because you must overcome his egoism and a good dose of willpower is needed for him to control himself, which requires education on every level. Even someone who is rich and enjoys all the things that life can offer has the same difficulty. How much harder it is then for those whom life has denied everything. They do nothing else but suffer from hunger and cold, and they can only enjoy the pleasure which their bodies offer them. Someone told me that hunger increases the sexual appetite: Would this be a compensation?

It is a sad and squalid atmosphere, but how can we accuse or even lightly scorn these creatures? In the words of the social-worker Nely Capuzzo, we have the reality, with no rhetoric or sentiment. Then we pass on to the most tragic problem of all:

abortion. When asked what her attitude was to this before the encyclical, Nely Capuzzo said:

A considerable number of women of the *morro* used the Pill—some instructed by the doctor, others on their own initiative. In this way they were able to avoid being among the numerous cases of abortion, which is the serious problem of the *morro*. There are midwives who are specialized in the district. At the moment we are attempting to bring them together to face the problem, but it is very difficult because the majority of them work clandestinely. At times some women who are very knocked about and in great pain come into the surgery room and they say, . . . "I have had a loss," but they do not reveal the name of the midwife who attempted this unfortunate operation. The encyclical has not had many repercussions in the *morro*. The majority have not even heard of it. And the people's usual question is: "What is better: a pill or abortion?" For many there is no other way out. . . . At times I think: "Is it worthwhile bringing children into the world who will then pass their lives under these conditions of hunger, cold, ignorance, and pain—children who in many cases do not really succeed in becoming men?

I remember the case of a woman who came to speak to me fifteen years ago. She was expecting a child and was afraid of having it. I spoke with her of the crime she was about to commit. We talked for a long time but eventually the creature was born: a *guri* [untranslatable, it means a "small, malformed person," used in an affectionate sense—Editor]. To support her *guri,* the mother had to work outside the house, leaving him behind; then her husband left her. At five years of age the *guri* had already been left to himself and he used to go out into the alleys of the *morro* and beg for food. The mother always worked on the outskirts. At eight years of age he was already a shoeshine boy in the center of the city where he tried to "get something going" together with some friends of his. Last year he robbed a bank and stole twenty cruzeiros and started becoming a regular customer of the Tribunal for Minors. A group of specialists of Fr. Casa are trying to help him recover. Today, however, I often find myself asking: "Was it worth the effort to let him be born just to lead this life?"

The question is tragic and certainly the Pill cannot be the answer to it. And yet, while admitting that there are many more solutions, one asks if it is worth the effort to go to so much expense just to see the Pill condemned, and if it would not have been better to issue a direct condemnation of the societies which keep on producing *guris* who continue to *catar bagana* ("get something going"), like the small *guri* of the *morro*.

The motive for such a procedure is that "to lead this life" also means knowing, learning, and loving; and while the ban on contraceptives is intended to safeguard love, in these *morros* it does nothing but produce more people who are incapable, in the misery and degradation in which they live, of really loving. They can do it, but how difficult it is. Nely Capuzzo puts it in a cruel, factual way:

What is love like in the conditions of the *morro* where the lowest and most widespread level of underdevelopment exists? I won't answer this question; I'll tell you some facts. You may draw your own conclusions from them. In a meeting with some people already addicted to a life of violence we were talking about the young person who falls in love, and one of them said that he had "hooked" a *guris muito bacana* ("a fine girl"). Another one commented: "You are not even happy yourself. How can you give happiness to your girl? I will fall in love when I can make a girl happy. I will not fall in love now because I am sure that if I fall in love she would soon run into maternity because people don't hold out for very long; so for the present, then, it is better not to fall in love."

The social worker then follows with an even sadder story— a story which is like a symbol and which can be summed up in the popular saying of the *morro: Fulano casou prá nois* ("Fulana is married among us"). Beneath this innocent phrase lies an allusion to a state of misery which has led the young woman—as long as she is young—to become *prá nois* ("a wife to everybody"). Nely Capuzzo notes that this is not always the case. Fortunately, there are "good families who love one another and who fight together to survive, but they are few and far between. Is it, possibly, that *misery* kills *love?*"

It is in this bitter, unanswered question that the two terrible words *misery* and *love* are left suspended before us.

In a contribution marked by a bitter and biting irony which the Lima daily, *Expresso*, published on August 2, 1968 in its social pages, written under the pseudonym of Sophocles, the two terms return in all their crudity: Sophocles says:

324

I understand that the Holy Father (so-called because he has never had children) should be alarmed at the arbitrary use of the Pill on the part of irresponsible people—like my sister who is heading for her fourth consecutive dreaded pregnancy. One thing which is a thousand times more concrete that the famous Pill, however, is that in the world there exists hunger, misery, wealth poorly distributed, the growing impoverishment of those already poor, rickets, filth, horrifying infant-mortality rates, and it is absurd to pretend that man must face the alternatives of renouncing the natural imperative of his sex or filling the world with babies with no hope—or very little—of surviving. It would be just as absurd as pretending that one should ban all electric lights because some will die from electric shock, or condemning automobiles because some happen to lose their life under their wheels. . . . It is one thing to increase and multiply life, but it is another thing to increase and multiply the number of cemeteries.

Before condemning the Pill, the Vatican should clearly condemn, without playing on words, the systems of exploitation which have given hunger and misery to humanity. I think that the Vatican has lost sight of both man and hunger. Who knows if the pope in Colombia will not be able to free himself for a moment from the drapings and the multicolored bishops, and cast his eyes on those *barriadas* of Bogotá, anonymous ambassadors for tuberculosis, and revise his ideas a little, because—who knows?—from time to time one can even be mistaken before one's God.

The bitter irony aside, there still remains the question: Ban a "pill" or ban a type of society? In other words, should one legislate on the morality of marriage and birth, or rather on all those things which go to make up the *barriadas*, the *favelas*, the *morros?* In this case the reasoning would stretch farther afield and the trial would no longer be one of *Humanae Vitae*, nor of the Pope's discourse in Latin America, but would be a trial of Christianity: Is Christianity really capable of helping man? Is it always capable of helping man, even when the "quarrel" between Altar and Throne is no longer one with the emperor and his feudatories but a more dangerous one because it occurs between a Church so old and yet so alive, and new Thrones that are no longer backed up by fierce feudatories and vassals but by World Banks and missile ramps?

The Paths of the Pill Also Pass
Through Africa and India

The enormous Latin-American "dossier" on *Humanae Vitae* risks giving the impression that the Third World is only Latin America. The Third World is also Africa, Asia, and India. However, the Latin-American dossier extends farther than Latin-American problems. The whole series of issues are no other than the general themes of underdevelopment, development, misery, education, colonialism, and imperialism. They are themes which remain alive, even if obviously under different forms, in the other great areas of the Third World.

What is characteristic of Latin America in this confrontation which *Humanae Vitae* has given rise to, is that there the thought, the reactions, the religious and political forces, have all been able to find a voice. European colonialism influenced native ambients at a time when any kind of political awareness was impossible, and moreover, when conditions were almost totally primitive. It then left the colonies behind, at a level which was not generally too evolved. The Latin-American type of neo-colonialism, however, affected countries which already in some way possessed a cultural and political tradition, and in the process of making its profits it involuntarily contributed to a way of life and activity which became useful in helping the self-awareness of continually broader groups.

The differences between Latin-American neo-colonialism and the *post-colonialism* in Africa, Asia, and India have also created differences in problems regarding education, population, etc. Even though the rest of the Third World feels acutely the dangers marked out in Latin America, nevertheless these dangers take on apparently far less dramatic proportions. Moreover, they take on a varying importance in different countries of the same continent. "The paths of the Pill" are not seen everywhere against the stark, "anti-pentagon" outline of Latin America, even though these paths of the Pill pass through all continents, especially India.

Africa's biggest problem, for example, is that of finding means of exploiting its resources and of fighting against disease, rather than that of overpopulation. This does not mean that the problem is unknown, although the real population problem includes instead, that of bettering the living conditions, national hygiene, and giving planned help to those tribes which are more backward and easily liable to become extinct.

A superficial observation, however, could lead one to think that the problems which exist in Latin America are in fact nonexistent in Africa. But it suffices just to mention the similarities of population density, the possibilities for exploiting large but barely profitable or unprofitable areas to get an idea of the facts of the situation. In some places, for example, after examining the economic problems incurred by a poor nation (lack of sufficient markets, lack of funds and incentives to develop infrastructural services, etc.), Richard Fagley and Arthur McCormack in their wide study *Population Growth and the Family in Relation to Development* (IDO-C, September 29, 1968, No. 68, 39–40), indicate how necessary it is to look at the population density to get a realistic picture. But then they observe:

Population densities as given above and in demographic yearbooks are an inadequate guide, though they may give rough indications. For example, the population density of Kenya at 17 inhabitants per sq. km. does not take into account the fact that two fifths of Kenya is either desert or largely marginal land. A truer picture is given by the figures adjusted to take into account cultivable, habitable land. In that case, the figure would be nearer 120 per sq. km. Around the Kadamega area at present, the population is about 800 per sq. km. The United Arab Republic density is 30 per sq. km., but adjusted density is 847 per sq. km.

It is a fact that some countries such as Kenya could usefully have more people. However, here we come to the crucial point; many countries which are in that position do not need the rapid increase they are getting, and in fact such an increase is detrimental. The example of Kenya may be taken to illustrate this point. Kenya's rate of population increase is 3 percent; its population in 1965 was 9 million. This means that without population regulation policies, the population would be 30 million by the end of the year 2000; that is, more than three times the population in 1965. It may well be that Kenya could feed such a number of people; the food potential is there. But it would have to step up its food productivity very considerably to do so, by a figure which many would indeed regard as theoretically possible but practically unrealizable.

It is not only food that is involved, however. It is the provision of more schools, more jobs for those who are educated, more public services, more hospitals. For example, it is reckoned that if present rates of fertility are unchanged, the number of illiterate children of primary school age will likely double in the next 25 years, in spite of present plans to improve and expand education. With a country such as Kenya with a per capita income of less than one hundred dollars, such an increase of population would put an intolerable strain on resources of money and manpower. With the population policy suggested by the *Population Report*—namely, a reduction to 1.5 percent from 3 percent in fertility in 15 years, the situation would surely be much more manageable.

This is only an example, but it could be repeated in different areas of Africa. Since the problem of population planning really seems to exist and the problem of development clearly does exist, what effect has the papal decision of *Humanae Vitae* on the African scene?

In *La Croix* of August 30, 1968 the correspondent for Africa, Simon Kiba, observes:

Africa has not as yet become a continent of hunger and misery as has happened elsewhere. There is more often bad nutrition rather than a shortage of essentials, and witch doctors and taboos play an important role in this bad nutrition. The birth question, however, does not leave Africans indifferent. Traditional Africa, that of the farmers and many others, welcomes every birth as a blessing from God. The more children a woman has, the more she is respected in the village. The more living children she has, the more she is considered as the natural counselor for the other women, especially the young ones. In fact, she must know what the best herbs and roots are for healing children's diseases. She becomes at one and the same time obstetrician, nurse, and social worker. The clan and the tribe are always happy over birth, and abortion is considered a very serious evil. Moreover, to tell an African woman from the bush to contravene the natural law of bringing children into the world, would be considered just as bad as to tell a youth not to respect his elders. In traditional Africa, then, the encyclical finds a people already well-disposed, not so much to responsible parenthood, but to parenthood whatever the circumstances. The missionaries, then, who live in the bush will not have many problems to face.

The same does not apply, however, to the large African cities.

Leaving aside the problem of girl mothers which is becoming a scourge in these cities, all the more since this gives rise to the fear of abortion, there are other social problems which force city dwellers to rethink the birth question in a different way than is done by those in the villages.

Living in an African city presupposes that one has work, that one can feed his own family and many other relatives. Unemployment, however, is a reality which is making inroads into all African countries, and many city dwellers seem to stay alive only by a miracle. To have babies in African cities raises not just the problem of feeding them but also the problems of further care, housing, and education. Medicines come from Europe and are very expensive. The free dispensaries are often short of the essentials. The hospitals, too, are always overcrowded. The countries' modest balances do not allow them to deal with all the sick and all the sicknesses, especially those which take on an endemic form. As for the dwellings in the cities, it is enough to see the thousands of African shacks to realize that certainly the house is chiefly responsible for the infant mortality which all the doctors deplore so much. To build a house requires funds, and money is the thing that is in shortest supply.

The education of children in the cities is either free in principle or based on fees, but education is a considerable expense to all the relatives because a child who is malnourished never applies himself well. There is also the problem of transport. When children get out of school many of them must walk many kilometers to return home.

In the face of all these problems there are many different attitudes toward births. The greater part of the aged or comparatively wealthy Africans make no attempt to hinder nature, and it is not rare to see 10 or 15 children in families in these categories where polygamy is also often customary. An African who is gradually becoming rich first thinks of finding a wife, and if his religion allows him, he then acquires several of them. We may notice in passing that money has made polygamists of not a few baptized persons.

On the other hand, the young tend to think more and more of responsible parenthood. Many of these young city functionaries, who were students and then entered skilled professions, employ artificial methods of contraception. It is true that in French-speaking Africa the former French legislation still exists, and therefore contraceptive products are sold only under the counter. But these products do exist and quite a few make fortunes from them, not to mention the fact that the greater part of African cities are ports where smuggling is a flourishing trade.

Some governments have put forward a population policy. Others have never even spoken of it. In French-speaking Africa only a few states have a legal code for the family, and it is generally thought that this is the best solution to the problem. The encyclical *Humanae Vitae* may accelerate the formation of these legal codes for the family. In fact, the most serious question in Africa, even before that of birth control, is that one can raise a family only after having overcome the obstacles of dowry, clan tradition, forced engagements, etc., and these are questions which are a long way from being solved. It must be noticed, however, that among Catholic couples the opinions for and against the encyclical *Humanae Vitae* have been expressed for the most part privately.

This last observation in the picture drawn by Simon Kiba gives us some explanation for the lack of individual reactions in Africa which can also be explained by the African situation itself as he outlines it. The fact must also be remembered that African Catholics are still very much under the influence of European missionaries and there are very few lay people with the necessary degree of emancipation to be able to express themselves publicly. This is certainly not a result of fear or inability but because of their very live awareness of indebtedness to the missionaries and the Church for the African sensibilities regarding the birth of children, and the family subsumed and hence deepened by Christian preaching.

The impression that the Africans do not speak a great deal on the subject is highlighted by the African Archbishop of Cotonou, Msgr. Bernadin Gantin, who therefore makes himself a voice for the Africans "who also themselves," he says "have the right to speak." Msgr. Gantin observes that

Europeans and Americans have a remarkably quick reaction to events, but they have the advantage of rapid, perfect communications media. As a result they make their voice felt far and wide: this risks impressing and even influencing opinion. The Africans, however, also have the right to say what they think and feel. After the Pope's encyclical on birth control they have spoken and have written, but what they have said does not appear to be very well-known. . . . Underdeveloped Africa is a long way from being overpopulated. Dahomey, which has one of the densest populations of any African country below the Sahara, has only 21 inhabitants per sq. km. Yet some rich countries think that the best help they can give Africans is to push them into putting a brake on their "galloping demography." They prefer investing capital to help underdeveloped countries introduce contraceptive methods rather than allowing them to attempt industrialization.

A little more than a year ago, the director of the World Health Organization for Africa warned us against this danger. He wrote: "If one considers Africa's resources and the numerous fertile areas which have not yet been developed, then the problem is not one of overpopulating but one of underemployment of resources, including human resources. For this reason, Africa must be on guard against certain forms of international action and oversimplified and often unfounded propaganda.

Certainly we also think that in Africa as elsewhere in the world, the time has come for conscious and voluntary paternity and maternity. We know what heartbreaks numerous families experience, especially a certain elite, who examine their future and who do not want to give birth to life unless they are sure that they possess the necessary prerequisites for its development in all spheres. To these we want to say that Paul VI did not want to close the road to responsible parenthood but that he did want to put a stop to that dangerous permissiveness which does not want to accept any objective norm in the married couple's sexual life . . .

The problem of birth regulation for us is not an isolated problem which can be solved with one, simple move, but is one facet of the problem concerning the development of the whole man and of every man. Together with the Pope we say No to sexual liberalism as to economic liberalism, in the conviction that the road to development passes through the rejection of egoism on every level where it is to be found. These Africans who put the problem of birth control to themselves are precisely those who have reached a certain level in the consumer civilization which has been imposed on Africa. It is proof that our real problem lies in finding paths to ensure a community development based on solidarity. . . .

Far be it from me to want to throw the stone at those who are contesting, or at those who have been slow in believing and adhering on account of their whole education, their whole past, or their long, painful searching. Respecting others' sufferings and sharing them are duties in charity. Today, however, there is a greater tendency to be more attentive to the individual and to personal cases than to the good of the whole, and to be more aware of the immediate and of the superficial than of the future and of the heart of matters.

If we read carefully, we see that Msgr. Gantin's words reecho several themes which we have already noticed in Latin America. Possibly the population problem is less stressed, and inside accounts of the type of life lived in underdeveloped nations less often heard. These nations are at a more primitive state and not in a state of regression. Hence these accounts are more the expression of a world which is still to be faced and to be developed than the expression of a developed society which has been left on the outskirts of humanity.

It must also be realized that in Africa special attention is given to the person and function of the Pope in the Church as well as to the human and spiritual values he affirms. The relatively young age of the Catholic communities and the very live religious sentiments of the people, who still preserve the primitive values carried over from their previous religious traditions, are factors which favor this awareness of more directly moral and spiritual values.

The problem of underdevelopment is thereby easily related to moral and spiritual problems. In *Effort Camerounais* of October 1968, two African lay people confront and strongly criticize those who affirm that the Pope did not keep in mind the misery of the Third World. They state:

The problem of underdevelopment is a moral and human problem, and not just an economic and material one. The Pope is possibly the only person who has really understood this. He has taught the integral development of every man, and in Bombay threw out an appeal to the rich to give the Third World one tenth of the sum they spend on stock-piling nuclear weapons. Instead of wanting to sterilize us with the Pill, the rich would do better to satisfy our just economic claims which they are always deferring, *sine die*.

The two African authors then introduce a theme which recurs frequently and also, it must be said, rather monotonously among the African reactions—the theme of the values proper to African society which give it its originality and its specific mission and which are essential to its balanced existence and growth. They say:

In a society where the supreme values are veneration of life, esteem for fertility, passionate love for children, and respect for the woman as the sacred depositary of life, a policy favoring the Pill could not be put into practice without contradicting these fundamental values and introducing disequilibrium in the life of this society. For us Negro-Africans, life is sacred in two ways. It is consecrated by its source who is God, the first cause of all life. It is also sacred because it is ordained to guarantee the continuity of life in line with our dead ancestors, whom we believe to be united with God. . . . Africa wishes to announce to all the people of the earth a message which has an original freshness—respect for life that merits being faithfully transmitted because it is sacred and beautiful. It is only by remaining faithful to our profoundly human values which are necessary to fulfill this supremely divine mission that we will be able to achieve this task.

Few articles have been able to produce such an emotional and typically African synthesis as this one. It synthesizes a view in which life becomes the fertile and benign mother nature deriving from God, which is at the basis of *Humanae Vitae* and which is an essential part of the values of "negritude"—values of which many Negro-Africans who have come in contact with the present white cultures geared to development feel they must be the messengers.

The same theme has been taken up in Malawi by the bishop of Blantyre, Msgr. Ciona, who on September 7, 1968 while speaking on the encyclical also dwelt on the "mission which God gave the first family, to 'populate the earth,' and before which we are in no way justified in giving in to our egoism." He then continues: "Traditionally, in Malawi we have a great respect for human life. In our society a family without children is considered to be a failure because we hold that the fundamental aim of marriage is procreation."

There are no problems then, seeing that his last point, that marriage has procreation as its fundamental aim, is replete with difficulties for others. The view on marriage which the people of Malawi have, has been canonized by *Humanae Vitae*. Possibly the encyclical is more perceptive, however, since it states that marriage must "remain open to procreation."

"Africa has special reasons for accepting the encyclical on birth regulation." This is a statement made by Msgr. Thiandoum,

Archbishop of Dakar, on September 28, 1968. His contribution appeared in a publication edited by the bishops of Senegal where he states:

In Africa artificial birth regulation is not a thing to be feared, because a large family is always considered a blessing by God. There does exist, however, the danger of "irresponsible parenthood," which consists in imposing on the woman innumerable pregnancies because one has no desire to take on the restrictions involved in self-mastery, which is required for spacing and limiting the births and thereby being better able to take on one's responsibilities.

After all the praises of the African love for the family and for children, the panorama has now become less idyllic. In between these two contrasting views there is the woman, all her pregnancies, even a little egoism on the part of the man and also a little irresponsibility, because children are a blessing from God, but God entrusts them to the goodwill and sacrifices of men. Does each and every birth, then, reveal the pure ancestral values of African civilization? The black bishop, who knows his people well, insinuates that this, understandably, may be a little doubtful. He also introduces an entirely new concept, that of irresponsible parenthood, after so much talk of responsible parenthood.

Archbishop Thiandoum continues his diagnosis with a wisdom truly characteristic of "African values" and also with a certain amount of courage, when he says, for example, "A simple line of behavior—imposing numerous pregnancies on the woman because one is not capable of controlling oneself—is not a better one than that of using artificial means to avoid pregnancy in marriage relationships." He also sees the "special reasons for Africa's support of the Pope" from the very concrete viewpoint of auto-education, and the respect for the woman and for the family. The archbishop says:

Africa cannot remain indifferent before the high vision and clear-sightedness of Paul VI and the trust which he shows for man's generosity and capability. . . . In territories situated at the South of the Sahara the fundamental necessities like the advancement of woman, comprehensive education, the rule of austerity, all find solid support in *Humanae Vitae*. The encyclical's reminders fall on a ground fertile with traditional African values; namely, the idea of God as the first cause and ultimate aim of all things.

This is an "African" value which is essentially religious and Christian. Is it equivalent, however, to a total and fatalistic abandonment to Providence, a closing of one's eyes and rejecting the good intention of working to better man's condition? No—in Africa, too, the problem of development is felt as a fundamental problem. Fr. Souillac, general secretary of INADES (*Institut National pour le Développment Economique et sociale*) of Abidjan on the Ivory Coast, in an extremely long and documented article in *Présence Chrétienne du Togo* of September 1968, faces the problem of African development in relation to the demographic campaigns and the proposals of *Humanae Vitae*. In the author's opinion the encyclical gives rise to two problems which are not to be confused: on the one hand, that of the growth of humanity as a whole, and on the other, that of the number of children which each family desires. This yardstick for interpreting the encyclical already varies considerably from the normal one proposed in Europe, and reechoes, even if at a long distance, the issues in Africa as they have already emerged.

Souillac observes, however, that this is a problem which particularly affects the feelings of individuals and cannot be solved absolutely or juridically. In fact, "man's spiritual liberty within faith itself is guided by the interior light of love and charity." The author then dwells at length on the general, humanitarian aspect of birth regulation:

It is on this level that the prophetic character of the papal teaching obliges those responsible for the future of humanity to find, over and beyond short-term, Malthusian solutions of expediency, the difficult, long-term, and ennobling solutions for the whole of humanity. . . . In the face of the difficulties experienced by some countries in making their economic progress proportionate to the growth of their population, their governments have proclaimed that births must be controlled and that it is the duty of everybody to bring into the world only those children whom the parents and governments can guarantee a good standard of living, education, and work. Unfortunately, the solutions put forward—the use of artificial means—will facilitate the appeasement of sexual instincts rather than give encouragement to couples to dominate their procreative functions.

It is not very helpful to reduce the number of men in such an artificial way, which is so unworthy of man. It is an easy solution which dispenses those responsible from putting the processes of education and development into action. In certain parts of Africa, for example, it is not because the people are less numerous that countries progress more rapidly. . . . Only development can answer the questions posed by population growth. Specialists must continue their research: financiers must continue investing their goods; governments must keep working for the common good . . . the population must be made active. It is by following these paths that men will be fed and educated. . . . From this point of view Africa represents an immense hope. Her agricultural potentialities have been quite poorly exploited up to now. Correct techniques, a just repartitioning of goods, communitarian organizations inspired by the traditional structures, active and efficient functionaries, disinterested governments: these are the solutions to the population problem. It is also along these lines that the solutions to the problem raised by *Humanae Vitae* have been suggested by *Populorum Progressio*. . . .

If Christians have read *Populorum Progressio* and have understood that development is a strict requirement of faith, and that one cannot be a Christian and not be a promoter of development at the same time, then the future of the world can be said to be safe. Christians can become those who transform the earth and make of the desert an oasis of peace.

A personal choice by the couple in the planning of their family, which Souillac calls "spiritual liberty," is hence permissible but must be based on self-control and not on the use of artificial methods. The real solution to African problems, however, will always be one of putting all the resources with which Africa is endowed to their fullest use.

As well as examinations of the encyclical from the developmental aspect, there has also been no shortage of study meetings on the themes proposed by the encyclical. A symposium was organized at Kensington (Johannesburg) in the first half of September 1968, in which several hundred nuns and married women took part. The topics of the three speakers, which were reported and synthesized on several occasions by South African newspapers like *The Southern Cross* of September 4, developed in general the problems presupposed and left open by the encyclical. These speeches, however, manifested some of the very few reservations to the encyclical which appeared in Africa. Dr. W. Whelan spoke of the natural rhythm and of modern conditions which have led to a noticeable increase in the fertile period, and hence to greater difficulties for couples both practically and morally in following the course of action they have chosen. Moreover, he raised some doubts about the encyclical's logic. It encourages men of science to "find a secure basis for birth regulation," when the Pill, all things considered, is already a secure basis and yet has been entirely disapproved.

The theologian M. O'Brien in turn praised the encyclical in general, and indicated the values which it has as its departure point and which it intends safeguarding. Following this, he raised doubts as to whether it is entirely credible. First, what is called "traditional teaching" can only be called traditional from the time when artificial preventive methods were introduced; namely, from approximately a century ago. Moreover, the use of artificial means was not officially condemned until 1930, by *Casti Connubii* of Pius XI. Second, the natural law is too variable and too uncertain to be used as a criterion for human behavior.

The Jesuit G. Garry presented a long treatment of the ecclesiastical hierarchy before Vatican II. He observed that at that time the chief authority was invested in the Pope, who normally acted without consulting the opinion of the bishops and the "ordinary magisterium." Today, a greater awareness of "episcopal collegiality" has come about. If a particular teaching like that of birth regulation had the consensus of this ordinary magisterium and the total assent of episcopal collegiality, then this teaching would become infallible, which is not the case at present. In any case, a general opinion emerged from the symposium that it is necessary both to give much more thought to the meaning of the Pope's authority and its exercise in the Church and to go deeper into the exact meaning of "natural law."

As can be seen, the basic problems which the encyclical has given rise to have also been treated in Africa.

The Society of St. Augustine of Khartoum also organized in October a very interesting "forum" on the encyclical. The panel was composed of the more well-known scientific personalities of Sudan: theologians, doctors, gynecologists, and married couples.

A deep analysis of the encyclical was made, attempting to bring positive aspects into light. From an examination of the African reactions it appeared that Africans generally received the encyclical well, that its teaching was very relevant and has contributed greatly, during this particularly tense time, toward promoting the spiritual and material welfare of the African family.

There was also a staff consultation on *Humanae Vitae* at St. Peter's Seminary of Hammanskraal in September 1968 and a priests' discussion group also met at Johannesburg on August 27, 1968 when almost all the same topics of discussion and criticism as had been included in the European discussions were mentioned, and there was no shortage of dissent on the now familiar issues.

From the point of view of the universal episcopal consensus, the two documents of Dr. D. Hurley, the Archbishop of Durban, are very interesting. He had already made a strong impression by his first immediate statements after the appearance of the encyclical. The first document was a letter to the clergy, and the second a pastoral letter. Although much more balanced than the archbishop's first immediate reactions, they show more nuances than the other African episcopal documents and although indicating the path of reflection and obedience to the Pope, leave room for rethinking and deepening those questions which the encyclical has not solved even for a considerable number of Africans.

Possibly the most critical position, however, came from 78 Algerian Catholics in a letter addressed to the Archbishop of Algiers, Cardinal Duval, in which they did not recognize the cardinal's adhesion to the dictates of the encyclical as their own. It must be noted, however, that Algiers contains a typically "metropolitan" Catholicism which has resulted from a very long French presence in the country. Hence the reaction reveals one side of the "urbanized" African civilization of which Simon Kiba spoke. The Catholics addressed themselves to their archbishop thus:

Father, the diocesan magazine of September 5 published a letter which you addressed to Pope Paul VI after the publication of the encyclical *Humanae Vitae*. "Every time that Rome speaks," reads the very first line, "Christian Africa welcomes the Vicar of Christ with joy and fidelity, and thereby puts an end to the discussion among the sons of the Church." The public and official character of the document, as also the guarantee of being a faithful interpretation of the feelings of our community, which it purports to give, seem to demand a public stand from us. First, we want to express our astonishment at the circumstances in which this letter was drawn up—far from the diocese, outside the country, and without the summoning of the Christian community in whose name you intend speaking. We believe that this way of proceeding is very abnormal; namely, that your personal initiative should substitute the exercise of our responsibility as adult Christians, an exercise which we incessantly and justly recall to mind.

We—unmarried lay people, Christian couples, the first to be interested in a lived fidelity to the sacrament which has been given us—ask that the right we have of expressing our feelings by ourselves, whatever they be, be respected with facts and not just with words. We are sad to see that on such a serious question, which is at the very center of our existence, the ecclesial community has been reduced, as all too often happens, solely to its hierarchical dimension. We are also forced to express our disagreement, which is also that of numerous other Christians whom we have met in the last few weeks, on certain too hurried affirmations in your letter. In fact, far from bringing to an end the discussions among the sons of the Church by the simple imposition of authority, the encyclical *Humanae Vitae* is causing numerous and deep dissension with the universal Church. There is no shortage of information on this. It is no less true, however, that it has also given rise to dissensions within our community.

The words which we are addressing to you are intended to be both information and witness. We believe, in fact, that it is useless and dangerous not to look this situation in the face. Useless, because public opinion today is a more important element in human society and hence in the local Churches than before, and it cannot be disregarded without harm. Dangerous, because under the tower of deep silence, the numbers of those for whom faith in Jesus Christ cannot be reduced simply to questions of discipline and who hence quietly leave, become greater and greater. Many Christians in fact think, like the bishops of England and of Wales, that "neither this encyclical nor any other document of the Church can limit our right and our duty to follow our conscience," once it has been truly informed. Where this right has been denied in practice, what other attitude is possible if not that indifference which we see all around us and which is so widespread?

We also feel obliged to state in conscience that it is inexact to say that the encyclical answers the difficulties of married people. Too many of the publicly expressed reactions in the international press and on the radio, the experience of numerous married friends, and also that of many of us, are sufficient evidence for this. Even though the encyclical's ban does not bring any change in the attitude of many Christian families, others today find themselves anxious and staggering from its blow. It causes an anxiety with often tragic consequences for the equilibrium of couples and of families, and often reveals itself to be destructive of married love. How can we ignore all this? Should not we also say that, instead of solving the problems of our priests, the encyclical's teaching seems to have notably aggravated them in certain cases. How can we fail to notice that the relationship of trust which we had with this or that priest has become more difficult after the encyclical. Areas of silence have been created; barriers have been raised—the attitudes range from a pure and simple refusal of any type of dialogue to admissions of a profound embarrassment. We feel too much in sympathy with this uneasiness and too much hit by it to behave as if it did not exist.

At the same time we are not too sure that non-Christians have found in the encyclical the solution to their problems, whether on a collective or an individual level. Many of those whom we have met, in fact, think that the papal position risks putting a halt to the evolution they had looked forward to. This then, Father, is what we wanted to say. Although it is a taking up of a stand, information and an expression of our feelings and our uneasiness, this letter is dictated primarily by a twofold rejection: the rejection of silence and the refusal to remain apart, comfortable as these may be during this period of weariness. It is once again this rejection which leads us to ask a question that we hope will not remain unanswered. Is it perhaps not urgent that the fossilized structures which are the vestiges of a psychologically and sociologically dead past, be laid bare and that there be erected within our community new institutions which are elastic and open to all—priests and lay people—where it would be possible to discuss both frankly and freely all the different questions that present themselves? A great publicity would be given to this work within our community, and this would allow the effective participation of all. It is in this way that we become more responsible within the Church.

Although the problems which seem to be more urgent in the Third World are only briefly mentioned here, one extremely interesting fact appears: as soon as one comes upon an environ-

340

ment where there are lay people who are relatively conscientious and culturally prepared, then immediately the universal problems which do not involve the content of the encyclical so much, but which get to the very roots of issues, reveal themselves. The problems then become ones of the Church—community and responsibility. Which is better, the good Christian community which accepts the encyclical because it recognizes *en bloc,* once and for all, the authority that emanates from it and because the encyclical defends "typical values," or the Christian community which reacts, challenges, criticizes, writes, and speaks like these Algerian Christians? The answer does not concern just the Catholic communities of Africa or India. It could be extended to include the whole world where almost everywhere the Church, the hierarchy, and the institutions are contested, are objects of criticism, and are in crisis.

Will the Church which is born of the radical "crisis" introduced by the creative Word of God, be afraid to accept this criticism—criticism which does not remain on the level of theological diatribes but which feeds on the concrete, human contexts in which the Church is inserted? India, for example, is a country whose tragic state we all know well—a state caused by famine, flood, disease, enormous population growth, and infant mortality. The government has concrete plans and the Churches, whether Catholic or Protestant, are in charge not only of social welfare activities but also of institutions specializing in family and marriage problems. The encyclical has put these institutions in a particularly delicate position on account of the policies they had adopted before it appeared and also because of their connection with government plans. Moreover, at present there is a growing feeling of distrust in nationalistic Hindu circles toward missionaries and the Churches for their interference in national affairs.

At the moment a strong, openly declared course of action on the part of medical and welfare institutions of confessional origins could provoke a real crisis. This is felt very much by the Jesuits, who are engaged in many of these activities, and it explains the scarcity of clear declarations and official positions. On one hand it is impossible to dissent from the papal encyclical for local reasons, and on the other it is impossible to condemn a government policy clearly geared to birth control by appealing to the papal decision. Moreover, daily contact with the Indian masses suffering from hunger at its worst, does not give cause for excessive enthusiasm for the more logical, long-term programs.

This explains why, outside of the statements of adherence to the encyclical by the bishops (Cardinal Valerian Gracias of Bombay wrote a letter of adherence to the Pope, inviting the other bishops to do the same since initially they had refrained), there are no comments of any real importance. Significant, however, is the comment by the Jesuit Anthony D'Souza, director of the Indian Social Institute, who said that "it will now be necessary to diffuse birth control in India." He added, however, that

in doing so, one will have to respect the ideals of marriage and responsible parenthood, and in any case no method of birth control can be accepted by Catholics if it menaces the sacred character and the honor of conjugal relations, if it tends to cause the degradation of women in the sense of sexual exploitation, and if it would eventually become the cause of a decadence of morality in social life.

In other words, according to Fr. D'Souza, Paul VI's encyclical should at least give rise to a new awareness on the part of Christian couples in India, but this does not mean that they will accept artificial methods of birth regulation.

Massimo Olmi, special correspondent of *Témoignage Chrétien* to India, observes:

Many priests, however, are not ready to share Anthony D'Souza's words. One of them told me, "I don't think that I'll have the courage any longer to hear my parishioner's confessions," and another elderly person said, "It is the first time in my life that my faith has been deeply injured." From his point of view an Indian Catholic doctor said, "It is a problem in which there are so many scientific aspects which are not for the Church to solve." A Jesuit was asked by a Catholic woman, "Father, from now on will you find us all guilty of mortal sin?" The Jesuit said that these words were full of both bitterness and irony. And when a woman in India begins ironizing on the faith, it is a serious thing, a very serious thing.

Massimo Olmi then attempts to give an outline of the situation as it has been created in India:

The fact is that in the last two years the growth of a more liberal outlook among a considerable number of couples had led priests and Indian Catholic doctors to soften their attitudes. Priests became more tolerant in confession. Now they find themselves in the position of having to give an explanation to their people of an encyclical which could have been written in the time of Pius XII—an encyclical which takes into consideration neither the conclusions of the majority of Catholic experts on this matter nor those of the "sensus fidelium" which was slowly but surely being formed on responsible parenthood, independent of the methods, artificial or natural, chosen to achieve it.

It is too often forgotten that the first plan conceived by the New Delhi government to induce couples to limit the number of their children was based purely on the Ogino-Knaus method—147 family-planning clinics were founded for this. The results were negligible, a complete failure. Why? Because a birth-regulation program based exclusively on natural methods requires, to succeed, a minimum of education and instruction on the part of the people. It must be remembered that in India there are 250 million illiterate people in a population of 520 million. It is difficult to follow nature if one cannot read or write. For this reason, in the second plan which was adopted, the government adopted artificial methods. Even though some of these methods (sterilization, for example) have always received, and rightly so, the reprobation of all the Indian Catholics, who see it as a mutilation of the human being, other methods (especially the oral Pill) did not seem to them to justify such a clear opposition on the part of the Church.

A young Catholic woman, far from what one would call "progressive," told me: "Facts speak for themselves. And what are the facts? One seventh of the world's population lives in India. Every day 55,000 children are born here—one every second and a half. This represents a total of 21 million newly born each year. The net population increase is 13 million. In 1966 we had 500 million; in 1967, 510 million. Now we have already passed the 520 million mark, and in 1994 we shall reach the 10 billion mark. In our country it took five thousand years to reach a population of 500 million. At the present rate, it will take only 28 years to reach 1,000 million. It is true that in 1929 our birthrate was 49 per 1,000 and today it is 41 per 1,000. In 1921, however, our death rate was 48 per 1,000, and today it has fallen to 16 per 1,000. From 1 per 1,000 in 1921, the difference between birth and death today is 25 per 1,000—all as a result of the progress of science. Our food production increased by 17 million tons between 1951 and

1966, but the distribution per head decreased, precisely on account of the population excesses.

"The problem, then, is not one of convincing 100 million to regulate their births. Numerous obstacles will have to be overcome: the vastness of the nation's area, the difference of language and customs, the resistance which has always existed toward anything new— and above all, illiteracy. And yet it is a question of life or death: India risks being strangled. In a case like this, what we need are exceptional measures." There was no doubt in this young woman's mind that among these exceptional measures artificial birth regulation would also have to be included.

Fr. James Tong, director of the Association of Catholic Hospitals of India told me: "What do we know about human nature? They have always told us that birth control is strictly connected with the natural law. But as regards marriage we know far more today on the natural law than we did in the past. Just in the last thirty years we have been able to discover what human nature could do in the field of reproduction if all the obstacles of sickness and hunger were to be removed. An uncontrolled population is like a cancer: cancer is an uncontrolled multiplication of cells which in the end kills the victim. In the same way an uncontrolled population can be a social cancer which kills human society. We are told in reply: Utilize natural means of birth control. Here in India there is practically no literature on this subject. The little that there is, is in English. But even if this literature existed, who would be able to read it? There are 250 million illiterates. To imagine being able to teach the Ogino-Knaus method to 250 million illiterates seems morally impossible to me."

A play on figures, more figures, and still more figures, a whirl of hundreds of millions, but also of men, and children who suffer for a few days and then die after having made a woman suffer for months and causing her anxiety when the children are finally born. The Pill is not the solution. India, absurd as it is, does not even have the same expectations as Latin America, although even the people there are still far off. It is easier to speak of development there. One can attack capitalism, imperialism, Atlanticism, and pentagonism. In India one cannot even do that. In India it is also possible to talk of development and it would be fearful not to do so, but the first logical thing which must be said, and the first thing one always hears from anyone committed to solving the problems of India's development, is: "In 1966 there

344

were 500 million of us, today there are 520 million. In 1994 there will be 10 billion. Leaving aside the not-far-off 1994, there are still the 55,000 thin, little Indians who come to 'enrich' India every day!

"We can understand how Massimo Olmi, returning from India, could tell us: 'In a word, we are in anguish—the anguish of the faithful, the anguish of the priests, and the anguish of some bishops. Maybe within fifty years, when the fight against illiteracy will have borne its fruits, the natural methods of birth control can be taken into consideration by the great mass of Indian Catholics. But today? Today I leave India with a feeling of great uneasiness.' "

A short while ago an Indian Catholic priest, formerly a professor at the University of Banares and today teaching in various American universities, a great expert in Indian philosophy but one who lives poorly among the Indians in Banares told me: "If the person who translated *Humanae Vitae* into Latin had come here to Banares, I would have taken him for a walk along a street in my city. I would not have said anything to him, but I fear that had he gone for that walk before he had started his work he would no longer have been able to find Latin words in his head with which to clothe the encyclical's concepts."

Can we call it pragmatism, hypersensitivity, situation ethics? I think that deep down we are still discussing the encyclical simply because we have not gone for a walk in a street of Banares. Had we done this, would a papal document still be of any interest to us? Why should we be surprised, then, if an Indian views it as an object which has in some strange way rained down from heaven onto this earth, which is so rich with mud from floods and with babies who remain silent because they have no strength left with which to cry?

At the same time other countries, classical for their over-population problems but in themselves not belonging to the Third World, have no intention of arriving at the same state as India. Japan, for example, has, together with an enormous population growth rate, strongly organized government campaigns for family planning. The silence of the Japanese Catholic bishops on *Humanae Vitae* does not suggest that it is an expression of their

345

acceptance of these government campaigns or even a political maneuver (considering that Catholics are such a small minority), but rather that it is reserve on their part before the fact of an undeniable population problem. It is a very real problem even though Japan is not in the position of having to avoid overpopulation in order to increase development, since Japan has a very high level of industry and commercial development and its food resources and diet standards attain very high figures.

The problem can be expressed in what may appear to be trivial terms, but it indicates the last consideration necessary in our thinking on the present and future relationship between development and population: Where shall we put all these people? Once again a political problem rears its ugly head but this time it is "pure" politics, which means that Japan will not hesitate to use arms to solve it if necessary. Everyone knows the kind of arms the small, refined Japanese may prepare on that day if they find it necessary to "emigrate."

Another more illuminating situation is that of the Philippines. Richard Fagley and Arthur McCormack, in their study quoted previously, observe:

The Philippines is a country of high population density and high rate of increase. It provides a good illustration of the urgent need for a population-regulation policy. It has a very good climate, great areas of fertile soil, great potential for food production if a policy of land reform is implemented; the need for this can be judged by the fact that 1/10 of 1 percent of the people own 40 percent of the land. When one of the authors was there in February 1968, it had just signed an agreement to import 350,000 tons of rice. Its population of 33 million is increasing at a rate of 3.4 percent—just over a million per year. The population will double in 20 years. The population density is at present 112 per sq. km., rather high for a developing country.

Here again there is surely a case for regulating population policies together with social, economic, and especially agricultural reforms, and with great efforts to step up production. This could be done using the famous "miracle rice" which—admittedly under the ideal conditions of the International Rice Institute at Los Banos—can produce 450 bags per ha. per year instead of the 38 bags that are the normal harvest. Without a restriction of human fertility there would also be a continuing and compounded upward spiral after the first doubling in 20 years time.

This then is a typical situation; a country is in full economic development but also in full demographic development. Even though the present situation does not give reason for excessive concern (at least, not as in India), even a superficial glance at the near future is disturbing. Population growth will become a far more serious problem than that of economic growth, serious as the latter may be.

The reactions to the encyclical, then, are rather complex. On one hand, those responsible for government and developmental action hesitate in stating what position they will adopt realizing that the Philippine government has already been studying various demographic policies for a considerable time. On the other hand, however, the absolute majority of the population is Catholic. The episcopal letter and certain articles by professors at the Catholic University are decidedly in favor of the encyclical, while others are more aware of the real situation and their interpretations contain various nuances as well as posing various difficulties, but these are expressed in a very cautious manner. Fernando López, the vice-president of the Philippines, expressed his opinion on the occasion of a voyage to Latin America. It was reported by *La Prensa* of Lima on August 25, 1968. The vice-president, who is also the secretary for agriculture and natural resources, states that

the encyclical *Humanae Vitae* is at least disputable. This is all the more true for us since we are at present studying a plan on demographic policy. The Philippines has 35 million inhabitants. It is one of the most populated Asian countries and has the greatest number of Catholics, who make up 90 percent of the population. The Philippines has an annual population increase of approximately 1 million per year. There is also the difficulty that its 35 million inhabitants are distributed over 7,200 islands and islets.

At Manila, Dr. Rivera, who is himself the director of the birth-regulation campaign which is supplying approximately 1 million Philippine women with contraceptives, stated in the first days of August that the whole system of government campaigns will be revised, and that in any case progress will now be more cautious. The encyclical's positive side is that it has led to reflection on certain problems which could become serious if all the factors are not kept in mind.

How can we formulate our overall impression of the effect of the encyclical on the Third World? As we have seen, the elements which have come to light are complex and very different from those which have emerged in other human and cultural regions. In some cases they are even confusing and ambiguous. There is a tendency to overvalue or at least justify the theological worth of the encyclical because it has, or can have, a concrete "political" value. There is no shortage, however, of balanced deep analysis which reveals a real ability at getting a lucid grasp of the two factors involved: the socio-demographic factor of the Third World and the "religious" and "ethico-moral" factor.

Since it is impossible to give an exhaustive analytical and critical treatment here, we shall condense our global impression into the judgment given by the famous Brazilian sociologist Alceu de Aporoso Lima: "The Pope's theological outlook is conservative and his social proposals are innovative." The problem is one of not attributing the characteristics of the second to the first, because it would be of no service to the ethical and religious doctrine of Christianity or to the Pope's spiritual authority. In fact, it would be Machiavellianism which—although understandable from the dramatic nature of the situations, which require the collaboration of all the possible forces if a solution is to be found —would not be justifiable on the level of serene, objective logic.

Behind the Iron Curtain: Between Light and Shade

Why read the reactions to *Humanae Vitae* from the Socialist countries behind the Iron Curtain, as they are commonly known, in the same vein as those of the Third World? We certainly do not want to give the impression that the situation is so similar that an identical interpretation is possible, and even less that we wish to include the Eastern Socialist countries within the area of the Third World. The only reason comes from some of the general outlines which have emerged from a reading of the reactions be they of Catholics or of strict Communist adherents in these countries.

The outlines of a political interpretation of the encyclical—and we have already dealt at length with the meaning of political—also seem to emerge from some of the Eastern countries, especially in the satellite countries. On the other hand, this political interpretation is openly evident in the expressly Communist reactions. Although there is no clear and precise line of reaction, we can perceive a certain ambiguity arising from the local problems as here, also, demographic policies make their weight felt. On one hand we have criticism of the Pope because he has imposed something from on high which has fettered man's liberty and which has interfered with state politics, and on the other, a kind of poorly concealed agreement with its opposition to birth-planning policies to which less and less attention is being given by the popular democracies.

It is interesting, besides, to note that this same concern is shared by Catholics in satellite countries and by the Communists of Soviet Russia, and for exactly the same reasons, even though they are naturally in opposition to each other. The full acceptance of the encyclical on the part of Catholics in the satellite countries also has a highly spiritual and political significance. The Pope's authority is a constantly recurring, underlying theme, as well as the fact that the Pope's concerns coincide with those of Catholics in the satellite countries. It is clear that it is not possible to weaken the Pope's moral authority on one controversial point without weakening it on other points, when he intervenes to proclaim the sacred rights of a people, or of an ethnic or religious minority, and to condemn various forms of cultural, religious, or demographic genocide. A parallel can be found in the force with which the small Catholic minorities scattered throughout Protestant areas have always fiercely defended the moral and spiritual authority, the wise judgment, and the equanimity of the Roman Pontiff. All this obviously does not diminish the value of the acceptance, but should be kept in mind if we are to ensure that the reactions be understood objectively.

In fact, the magazine *CSEO-Documentazione* of August 1968 rightly notes that it is different to judge the encyclical in Holland than in Czechoslovakia, or in Bonn than in Zagrabria, and not just because it is a question of objectively different situations, but even more because the price that the Church must pay to say what it wants, to express its own message, is immensely higher in the East than in the West. When the price is high, then one is forced to say only what is essential. Consent or dissent, be it unconditional or with reservations, has a different weight when expressed in the East. We Westerners must come to recognize the fact that we have a modest role to play in the debate which is in progress. The Christians we have frequently betrayed, those of the Socialist world and those of the underdeveloped world, have a right to speak first.

But the obstinate severity of the official Church and the indignant tenderness of the dissenters toward couples who apparently no longer have the right to use the Pill, have disclosed an unprecedented liveliness. The traditional way in which the Churches of the West reacted against the loss of liberty on the part of their brothers in the faith, in one world or the other, cannot compare with it. One can sympathize with the woman "condemned" to the Ogino-Knaus, but one should sympathize just as much with the victims of violence and colonialism both in the East and in the West. When the hour of judgment comes, many of our "crusades" will be found to have been "luxury crusades."

One thing, however, is evident in the reactions which have come from the East: they are all from clerics, and lay people have not spoken a word unless privately or through anonymous inquiries organized by various agencies. On this silence of the lay people the same *CSEO-Documentazione* comments:

We know that there exist, particularly in the East, serious difficulties which explain this state of affairs. We must realize, however, that it would be harmful for the Church and for its dialogue with society if the problem remained an "ecclesiastical affair" in the strict sense of the word, giving the clergy a kind of professional immunity or at least professional priority. The problem is one for the entire Church. This is especially true in the East where certain clerical superstructures so rigidly fossilized here among us, have either been eliminated through lived experience or may eventually be eliminated so that the Church can show the world its true face.

When the situation is viewed in this light, one cannot speak of an "ecclesiastical policy," but must instead speak of an "ecclesial life." Possibly the very fact that it is still the clergy and the hierarchy who express themselves, in preference to the laity, indicates their inheritance of a "professional priority" and a certain age-old recognition of the laity's incompetence. It could also be the expression, however, of a unity of hearts and minds, now that the rigidly fossilized form of ecclesiastical structures has been dismantled. The concrete drawbacks involved in lay people expressing themselves clearly on religious problems must also be kept in mind. In many cases these lay people do not want to give any opportunity for interference and interpretations on the part of the regime, which is concerned not so much—at least in some countries—with personal religious sentiments, but rather with the fact that these sentiments may be the vehicle for political and nationalistic "reactions." It is enough to think back on what the celebration of Poland's millennium, with all the tensions and misunderstandings on both sides, represented.

It was in Poland that the reaction to *Humanae Vitae* reached a high point. The Polish government has imposed a very liberal legislation in order to reduce the rate of increase in the population. Abortion is practiced legally in hospitals, and there has been wide propaganda in favor of contraceptives. A few days after the publication of the encyclical, the newspaper *Trybuna Ludu* of August 10, 1968 announced that the first Polish-made pills would be on sale by the end of the year. At present, pharmacists stock pills which are produced in East Germany and which are provided for clients on request.

The Primate of Poland, Cardinal Stefan Wyszynski, in often-violent terms, openly criticized the government's policy on several occasions and denounced the law that legalizes abortion. The cardinal, speaking on the first Sunday in August 1968 before 60,000 pilgrims who had come from all parts of Poland to the monastery of Swieta Lipka in the northeastern part of the country, said: "The Polish nation has received the encyclical with great reassurance, since it is convinced that only this can be the Church's teaching, and that only this can be the Pope's word." Later he stated: "The preeminent values in human life and culture must be saved to avoid the danger that the triumph of egoism and love of comfort will lead humanity into becoming a crowd of half-wits, imbeciles, and degenerates."

351

The primate's speech is in a general vein, but does he not hint at the fear that the Polish nation could be badly affected by a population campaign which is certainly inspired by concern for the nation's well-being, but also by political motives encompassing more than this?

This judgment is developed in greater detail in an article by Oto Mádr in *Katolické Noviny* of August 18, 1968 where he admits that "the papal documents are always reactions to present needs and problems. *Humanae Vitae* is directly related to the life of the individual person, to the intimacy of the family circle, to a problem which every conscious Christian realizes as extremely important." He immediately goes on to note, however, that it is not just these "interior" motives which caused the reaction to it, and he continues:

The discussion on the subject of birth regulation has been continuously going on throughout the whole world for many years and may be traced back to two factors. The first is the population explosion; that is, the rapid growth of population in many parts of the world which has been putting men on their guard since the eighteenth century, and which has given birth to the theory of Malthusianism. The second factor, especially important for the Catholic world, is a new means of contraception that was developed, the so-called anti-baby pill, which was rebaptized for a short time by journalists as the Catholic pill. It was a method that appeared to be morally acceptable. It interrupts only the biological process of fertilization and does not destroy the true and proper encounter. Thus it is not so very different from the method of periodic continence which Pius XII declared as morally licit. . . . The encyclical resolves the issue by reaffirming the traditional line. . . .

Those whose hopes were dashed by the encyclical will possibly ask if this is an immutable judgment. It is not immutable; it is not an infallible dogma; it is a problem which enters into the field of moral theology. Practically speaking, what counts for the conscience of individual Catholics is the fact that the Church's state of awareness at this moment is the one which has been expressed by the head of the Church, whose faith is not dependent on public opinion or on the possibility of his giving reasons for the norm.

Our delusion, however, does not destroy all hope. The Pope has invited scientists to investigate the best methods for the forms of family planning that are morally allowed. Possibly it was the high moral authority of the Pope himself which retarded the process of research into these methods—who knows? Christian marriage, however, has received important recognition and a strong impetus on the moral level. . . . We must also remember that Paul VI had no small number of difficulties to face when treating this problem, and that he feels the tragedies which occur in this sphere of life no less than we do. His concern was not to make the life of many Christian couples unhappy, but to defend the highest values in marriage, which are being menaced by technology and the baser orientations by contemporary civilization. In individual cases the moral norm can even be painful, but it is essential that the matter be viewed from beyond a limited standpoint. The life of the Christian, like that of any honest man, cannot be continuously without sorrow if it is to be a worthy life. . . .

The Church cannot and does not want to impose more duties on her sons than those which God imposes, but neither does she want to remove any of them. This is for the benefit not only of the relationship with God the legislator, but also of the only true progress of humanity, outside of which all progress is progress toward nothingness. It is in the interests of the greatest authenticity and dignity of man, as the Pope continually restates. This also means the greatest happiness for the greatest number, the only kind which counts, that which is given to those who live according to the norms of charity, even if this entails sacrifice.

Oto Mádr notes some of the perplexities and delusions arising from the encyclical's decision, but he attempts to see the Pope's statements and intentions from a wider viewpoint. He says that in the face of the difficulty felt by individual couples and the evil which could arise from contraception for all humanity at this moment, each must accept a personal sacrifice which in the long run will turn out to be for the good of all.

"Against the devaluation" of love is how *Glas Koncila* of August 18, 1968 views the theme of the encyclical. Among other things it says that

the first alarming reports which came from the press were simply not true . . . it was stated that the Pope had banned, had condemned, had wanted to bar the way. What was not seen was that by means of this encyclical the Pope wanted to prevent only one thing: *the degradation of love.* In this our age, when it is so difficult for anyone to succeed in thinking with his own head and feeling with his own heart, and when films, newspapers, television, and books make us accustomed to sex at an early age, it is easy to forget that love is something more than simply mating. We see that the world is extending the liberty of sexual relationships more and more, that it is appreciating chastity and virginity less and less, that a devaluation of love is under way. In a world of sexual liberty, divorce, abortion, and the Pill, there is no love. Since there is no love, those capable of sacrifices are few. Since those capable of sacrificing themselves for others are few, then there is less and less love. It is in this vicious circle that all civilization, it seems, is slowly heading to its destruction.

In Europe and America, parts of the world which could feed children but which do not want to have them in order to live more comfortably, the Pill is put forward as the golden opportunity for one to love on a certain "cultural" level. In South America, Africa, and Asia, countries where parents are eager to have children but where there are insufficient resources to feed them, the Pill, sterilization, and abortion are offered in the attempt to deny the people their lawful, social rights. In these "liberated" countries, children now must not be born because it is up to the colonialists of yesterday to feed them, and they do not even want to feed their own children because they never seem to have enough material goods.

Moreover, scientists, like those who were "glorified" in the Third Reich, are already presenting their governments with very efficient methods of mass contraception—methods with which one could ensure the death of entire nations without violence, or their growth in exact accordance with the plans which their economists arrive at. Mass production and the introduction of the legal use of contraceptives thus become the vulgar substitute for love and justice. The Church had to tell the truth and it would not be rash to say that future history will be grateful to the Church, just as it will be grateful to U Thant, who stated that the problem of birth regulation is a question for the conscience of the individual couple. The Pope's encyclical here agrees perfectly with the statement of the Secretary of the United Nations. No public power has the right to tell people when to procreate and when not to procreate. The Church is acting here not as a public power but as *the conscience of humanity*.

The first theme, then, is the Church as the conscience of humanity, operating within a society which is dangerously inclined to assign too great an importance to its technical prowess, with the result that essential values like that of love risk being destroyed. The second theme brings us closer to the Third World theme which we have already fully investigated when referring to the situation in Latin America.

Glas Koncila, also recognizing the fact that the encyclical did not want to put a halt to research or close all possibilities to science, observes:

It must be remembered that none of the chemical, technical, and mechanical means of contraception which are being disseminated today are perfect, and that none of them, even from the purely medical point of view, can be accepted without reservations. The Pope has affirmed that the Church is ready to accept and promote that method which is in full harmony with the biological, psychological, and spiritual aspects of human nature.

These two themes of respect for love and life and respect for nations, which may not be forced into decreasing their populations, recur in numerous occasions in the Eastern countries. One notices their concern for the values which they have always held in high esteem as well as a kind of noble pride toward their own nations. Also in *Glas Koncila* of August 18, a Croatian priest with the pseudonym of Don Jure published a conversation with a young doctor from his parish. There is obviously no sense in asking whether the dialogue really took place. It is the themes which interest us. They are vividly brought into the limelight one after the other, and reveal an awareness and an attitude which are typical of the Catholics from these regions, as also in great part, of all those persons animated by patriotic sentiments.

Don Jure says:

Now I am dealing with Davor. Davor is a doctor, and he says he is Catholic and pig-headed like all good Croats. He has studied medicine but is not yet practicing because in the city, where he would like to go, he still cannot find a post to his liking. Nor is the province to his liking, and on account of this he is now thinking of emigrating to Canada or Australia. At the moment he is sitting in my study, nibbling at a piece of ham and criticizing the Pope's new encyclical. He criticizes it as a doctor, or as he puts it, in the name of medicine, but I know that it is all a facade. He has a single son and he has decided not to have any more. I shall let him have his say, for I have already said enough about him.

"Don Jure, the Pope has made a bad move this time. Nowadays a man cannot afford to have his house full of children!"

355

"It depends on what kind of house he has," I reply, with a seraphic air.

"And if he has no house?" Davor wisely asks.

"If he hasn't one, then he'll have to build one, and if there are no children he no longer has a reason for building it. He will let the house go to ruin and he will loaf his way around the world, just like you, Davor."

Davor looks at me and does not understand this; then he starts speaking with fury, waving his hands about: "Stop giving me your theories, Don Jure. By what criterion could I bring children into the world? By what criterion could our people bring children into the world? Here am I, a doctor without work. I even have to go overseas to earn something."

"And let Croatia go to rack and ruin!" I prod, knowing his weak point.

"I would give my soul for Croatia!" he exclaims. "But what can I do? There's nothing to eat here. Very poor conditions, overpopulation, low standards of living, almost no prospects . . ."

"And thus the Pope should have allowed you to use the Pill and all those other things so as not to have children, to live how and where you want, so as in the end to have a fine, empty land—right? But I tell you, my dear Davor, the Pope does more good for Croatia with this encyclical against contraceptives than all you young, intellectual charlatans put together—you who cry for the fate of your people but have in fact never shown any concrete concern for them. How can you, a Catholic and a Croat, rebuke the Pope for this encyclical when you know that our people are dying out, because there are fewer Croats being born than there are dying, and besides, a huge mass emigrate to go looking for fortune! How can this people survive if there are not enough children born?"

"You are jumping from one thing to another," and he tries to laugh.

"And you laugh, but not here; go into the big, wide world, there in some part of Australia. You will build a beautiful house; you will adorn each room with a Croatian flag; you will bring up your only, beautiful son, and you will tell him about the past in a language which your grandson will no longer even understand."

"But what can I do?" he asks, making an attempt to justify himself. "You have to stay alive!"

"Don't try to pull my leg, Davor. You're not interested in living!"

"Hey, what's got into your head? For what reason, if not to survive, would I go tramping all over the world?"

"No, you don't love life. You've had enough of life. You don't believe it's worthwhile living. You want to run away from life," I attack, as if I were in the pulpit.

He looks at me and says, "Is that the sermon?"

"Yes, dear Davor, that's the sermon; that is exactly what the sermon is about. And if there hadn't been these sermons, and if your father and mother hadn't listened to them, you would not be here today. There was no Pill then to cancel you out when you were just a seed. I'm back on the point of saying that all you young people who want no more than one or two children don't love life. This is the reason that you don't bring children into the world. And the country people of Posavina, of Moslavina, and of our other areas, who don't bring children into the world, they, too, don't love life. Our unhappy people don't want to live; that's why there are no children born. And you cry for Croatia. But it's you who are leading it to ruin!"

"You are just like the Pope, Don Jure. You don't know how to look at the concrete economic and social conditions. If there's nothing to love with, why bring children into the world?"

"Just what I wanted to hear you say. All that talk about over-population is just so much hot air. In the city there will be no more room—but who is obliging you to be squeezed into the city? There is so much empty countryside around, dear Davor; if you really love your people, you must learn how to sacrifice yourself for them!"

"Huh, priests' utopias! What use would my sacrifice be? What could I do?" Davor asks.

"You, my dear young man, if you could only do it! Go into the Croatian province; there's work for doctors there. Walk in the mud and among the thorns. Live with the country people in their misery. Teach them to work and to bring children into the world. In this way our land will no longer be deserted. You will also have a big house and a courtyard where the children can play, and you will have bread, clothes, meat, and other things to go with it. You will also have a car. Our people are good. You won't have asphalt. But you will live longer. And you will teach others how to live and to love life—when the country people get to like you, Doctor, when the country people get to like you!"

"You're dreaming, Don Jure," he says, shaking his head.

"Certainly, I'm dreaming. I know how to dream, and I'll dream until you wake up. You, thousands of young intellectuals, who leave your country because there is no means of survival! Because the country is overpopulated, you say. But you know that it is not true. Other-wise, why should our people die out when others, like the Chinese and Indians, keep growing? We clean our houses for strangers, don't we? This is our wisdom! The old die, the young emigrate, no children are born. Perfect! Then you attack the Pope when his wisdom doesn't coincide with yours."

The dialogue goes on, gradually becoming more anxious. Emotions over a dying people slowly overtake the two speakers. "Both of us are sad," concludes Don Jure. "Around about us no noise can be heard. In the nearby houses the old women are preparing supper for the tourists who are still on the beach: the foreigners and the local people, the barefooted children in shorts, the daughters-in-law in bikinis with their varnished fingernails, grandsons and granddaughters, only sons and only daughters. Thus we wait for autumn and winter, when the old men and old women left at home by themselves will clean the rooms to get them ready for the next tourist season. It seems that this silent twilight is falling all over our fine country. Everywhere I see old men and old women cleaning rooms which nobody else will ever use while they wait for a letter from overseas that keeps taking longer and longer to come.

Maybe Don Jure and Davor never existed. Maybe the two speakers in the presbytery in the Croatian countryside are the two voices of a single soul: the soul of a people murmuring its swan song, not with strength but yet with pride. This sad chant is heard not only in Croatia but also in Slovenia. And yet hope has been offered by a spiritual authority who, in his very prohibition, means to have uttered a life-giving order. The Slovene newspaper *Druzina* of September 1, 1968 asks why the encyclical was written:

Why? . . . There is so little respect today for human life, as can be witnessed in Vietnam and Biafra. . . . Multitudes are killed on account of vested interests and egoism. The Pope said in the encyclical that human life is sacred and that hence it must be given the highest respect. . . . We can add that the Pope's words were necessary even for us and for our situation here in Slovenia. . . . If we look at our country's birthrate and that of our compatriots overseas, we shall gradually become convinced that the Pope's encyclical on the transmission of life and on the grandeur of the marriage bond will have beneficial effects for our people. Even among us there are men belonging to other ideological systems who want to purify whatever is unhealthy in the life of our society. We think that this work could become a truly fertile ground for dialogue.

358

The significance of this hand held out toward "men belonging to other ideological systems" in a Socialist republic is quite clear. It is a discreet reminder of a question in which the authorities themselves are interested, even though they do not want to insist on the matter so much as to provoke problems of a political nature —after the Pope's encyclical, the Catholic position has become an unhoped-for help. The problem is fully treated in *Tedenske Tribune* of Ljubljana of August 7, in which there appears an interview with Msgr. Jozef Pogacnik, Archbishop of Ljubljana and interim president of the Yugoslav Episcopal Conference. The questions put to Msgr. Pogacnik often refer to world population problems, and then come down to the problem of Slovenia:

In Slovenia, every year approximately 9,000 women have an abortion which is allowed by law; and not all of them are atheists. How will the Church act toward those faithful who will not respect the encyclical's principles? The average income in Slovenia is approximately 100,000 old dinars, and the amount in child-endowment checks is going down. Forty percent of the women are employed. Many parents cannot afford a larger number of children. Is not banning contraceptives equivalent to increasing poverty?

In his reply, after stating that the sum total of abortions in Slovenia comes to about 18,000 per year, that the Church holds abortions to be a crime, and that from the medical point of view, Prof. Bogdan Tekavcic had also revealed what is happening, he [Msgr. Pogacnik] makes it clear that

whoever attributes the Church with the doctrine that every family must have a crowd of children shows that he has completely misunderstood the doctrine. Could parents who brought children into the world and then abandoned them to a wretched existence be called loving, responsible parents? . . . The number of children cannot be controlled, however, by unjust means. There are other lawful, clean systems which even the encyclical itself calls to mind. The task of science should be that of studying the licit methods of birth regulation in greater detail, in order to safeguard them against possible psychic drawbacks and thereby help the many people who find themselves in difficulty. . . . There is no easy way out for contraception.

The same clarification is made by the Polish *Tygodnik Powszechniy* of August 25, which states:

From some of the critical comments by the press, one could get the false impression that the Church is generally opposed to all forms of family planning. Nobody, however, can conscientiously state that birth regulation, whether in relation to individual families or to those societies faced with overpopulation, is unjustifiable. The encyclical itself at no stage affirms this.

Even though all these attitudes in the Eastern countries reveal adhesions and judgments which are quite straightforward, they also reveal certain clarifications which do not diminish the value and moral force of the encyclical in any way, but which are designed to make the point clear that the Church is not closing her eyes to real problems which, although not present in a very acute form in Eastern Europe, nevertheless, do exist in other areas of the world.

The reactions from the Soviet Union are by no means as clear, and the reasons are not hard to find.

The Russian reactions come only from cultural, scientific, and government circles, and not from ecclesiastical circles. Some idea of the reactions from ecclesiastical circles can be obtained from the direct attitude of the Metropolitan Nikodim, already recorded in the chapter entitled "A Grave Question for Ecumenism," where we attempted to understand the motivations behind the reactions of the Russian Orthodox Church.

The first Russian reaction appeared in *Literaturnaya Gazeta* of August 7, 1968, in a very modest form, and referred rather to the Western criticisms. It stated:

The Western press says that the papal message does not take into consideration the serious demographic problems which numerous countries must reckon with and that, in the encyclical, theology is given the upper hand over life. . . . One observer also feels that the encyclical will lead to a victory for hypocrisy among those Catholics who, as the surveys show, practice birth control.

The article in *Literaturnaya Gazeta* bears the title "Must One Now Hide Sin?" This contribution by the Soviet periodical seems to be part of a complex, rather hidden controversy. In the previous issue and in that of August 7, the periodical rebukes the Soviet authorities for the very same thing for which it rebukes the Pope: banning the Pill. It bewails the fact that in the U.S.S.R., birth control is practiced with methods which are "not modern," among which is included the interruption of pregnancy. "If the woman has been recognized to have the right of a consciously desired maternity," says the latter issue of *Literaturnaya Gazeta,* "this right must not be guaranteed by means of a brutal surgical operation but by effective contraceptive methods."

The most interesting fact is that the authoritative Soviet organ took as its target in this controversy first the Soviet authorities and then the Pope, although obviously on different issues. In the above mentioned article it is disclosed that three quarters of the couples who practice birth control still resort to abortion, which is permitted by law on the condition that it is done in a hospital and that the pregnancy has not passed its third month. Then the article makes an appeal for the production of contraceptives. It is not that they do not exist in the U.S.S.R., because they are in fact on sale for low prices in drugstores. The people, however, do not put their trust in them because they maintain that the contraceptives are of such a poor quality that they are practically worthless.

Later, the wish is expressed that a "matrimonial institute" be founded to examine the problem, because statements by various persons have underscored the urgency for methods which are not surgical. Dr. Truietseva, director of the Gynecological Institute of Moscow had in fact said earlier: "The mass production of efficient and harmless contraceptives is one of the most important problems in Russia at the present moment." A debate is also in progress among physicians because experiments with the Pill have already been carried out, but the Pill did not meet their full favor insomuch as excessive or mistaken use of it may produce frigidity or aphrodisiacal effects. Therefore, up to now the great majority of Russian doctors seem to prefer other types of female contraceptives. Soviet legislation has undergone a rather complex and mixed fate on these issues. At present a campaign is under way for the defense of the rights of the woman, who is too often sacrificed to male egoism. The most recent provisions in family law, which were approved in the July 1968 meeting of the Supreme Soviet, have been prompted by these needs.

Soviet legislation, however, has passed from the extreme

tolerance of the first years after the revolution when the "free love" theories of Alexandra Kollontai were very much in vogue, to the puritanical severity of Stalin. After the war, Khrushchev and his successors attempted to establish some kind of balance by permitting divorce and abortion but under certain conditions. In practice, the official attitude is more prudent and conformist than that of many Western countries, and tends to favor family stability and the procreation of children. This explains the ambiguity which may be found in the Soviet reactions. It also explains why some of the problems in the U.S.S.R. have finally been faced by using statistics.

On one hand, after the intervention of *Literaturnaya Gazeta* in August the reactions to the encyclical have become more severe. On the other hand, various scientific publications admit that situations do exist which would justify the Pope making the decision he did.

Thus *Literaturnaya Gazeta* on October 3, 1968 attacks the encyclical saying that it "proposes an 'archaic' system of birth regulation and that it tramples on the honor and dignity of all men on earth." The article is signed by the eminent physicist and pediatrician George Speransky. He says:

The Vatican's position is still inspired by the teachings of St. Augustine, which go back to an era when the world was not populous and the populations were periodically decimated by wars, diseases, and famine. . . . The Vatican is interfering with the couple's private life by giving them directives which are completely out of date. The Pope is condemning millions of women to abortion. Only an evil and cruel man would want to stop the use of effective and harmless contraceptive methods.

Obviously we know where we stand, especially when the renowned scholar passes over from his field of study, where he uses a moderate language, to the field of invectives, where one feels that he has not had much experience.

However, Dr. Edmund Stevens, in *The Times* of August 14, 1968, writing from Moscow, observes that "when compared to the worldwide controversy caused by the encyclical, the Soviet attitude is a model of reticence. Quite apart from the Russian tendency during recent years to show a certain tact toward the Catholic Church, a look at Soviet statistics can suggest some reasons for this reticence."

Dr. Stevens affirms that the U.S.S.R. is faced with a serious population decrease. From 1960 to 1965 the annual birthrate fell from 25 percent to 18.4 percent. In Central Russia the percentage fell in the same period from 20 percent to 14.6 percent. This overall picture is altered by the fact that high percentages in the birthrate are registered among ethnic minorities of Muslim culture in the areas of Russian expansion toward the Caucasus Mountains and right into Central Asia. The most productive seem to be Turkomans who reached a figure of 37 percent in 1965. The percentage curve seems to be falling even farther, in spite of a series of efforts which have been made to both stop and raise it. While the urban population keeps growing, the rural population fell from 108,500,000 in 1960 to 106,400,000 in 1967. The decrease in rural population is certainly due in large part to the emigration of the younger age-groups to the cities. Transposing these figures into human terms, this means that all rural built-up areas, in the East and in northern European Russia in particular, have slowly been depopulated. Dr. Stevens says: "I have seen villages where a third of the huts had been abandoned and the huts were closed and boarded up; they included the kindergarten. There are villages where neither marriages nor births have taken place for several years."

Thus there is a continuous flow toward the city. This has been in progress for about 4 years; namely, from when Stalin launched the first five-year plan of industrialization. In the last 5 years the flow has been increasing, from the time when the institution of the rural policy attempted to keep the population within privately owned areas, with privately owned fields and herds. It is at present hoped that the new agricultural policy begun 2 years ago by Brezhnev, by slowing down some of these restrictions and by increasing the agricultural shares in the national income, will put a halt to urban immigration and possibly even attract people to the country. There is a shortage of work power in industry as well as in the country, especially in the huge, new projects in Siberia and in the farthermost regions in the East. Here, besides the immediate, economic necessities, there is also the problem of building up a front against the strong pressure of millions of Chinese.

The Central Soviet Office of Statistics admitted that its research into the causes for the decline in births had been inadequate, that it had even made gross blunders, and that in the face of these dangerous errors, it was necessary to take immediate measures to rectify them. This explains the more recent Soviet legislation on divorce and abortion, which has become more severe and detailed. How do Russians react, however, to an encyclical which supports the need for family and birth planning but does not permit the use of methods which are not used much in Russia anyway? This is where the ambiguity in the Russian position may be observed. Dr. Stevens notices, in the article we have quoted, that

the Russian leaders evidently do not sympathize with the Pope's theological premises for opposing artificial birth control, and they have also said so. But going against the Pope in this case would also mean going against their own efforts for stopping the decline in births. The government has no objection at all if the Pope's word will induce Russian Catholics, concentrated above all in Lithuania, in the West, and in the Ukraine, to put more children into the world. But there is a great ambiguity and even an open controversy in Soviet attitudes to this vital problem. A. Verbenko, a famous Russian doctor, recently wrote that "Marxism has for a long time condemned the Malthusian theory of overpopulation as a subterfuge aimed at confusing the workers and distracting them from the class struggle against capitalist exploitation." Starting from the criticism of Malthus, Dr. Verbenko describes Soviet legislation, putting into relief the advantages of motherhood and underlining the value of the measures intended to encourage mothers to have large families. . . . The author adds that, as part of the effort for improving the birth rate, doctors are now untiringly instructing their patients about the harmful effects of artificially interrupting a pregnancy.

Dr. Verbenko gives a long discourse on abortion, chemical methods, the difficulties which exist in Russia, and what should be done, and also addresses himself rather vigorously to the minister of heath, urging him to find and produce safer contraceptive methods. This is not for the sake of decreasing the number of births, since the birth curve is falling, but to better the condition of the population and to free woman from painful situations. With problems of this kind on his hands and when faced with a statement by the Pope which is basically positive for the U.S.S.R., it is clear that Dr. Stevens' reactions become rather ambiguous, or as he puts it, "a model of reticence." Dr. Stevens himself observes that there is an underlying tension among the ethnic groups themselves in the U.S.S.R. In his observation he quotes the newspaper *Kommunist* published in Yerevan in Armenia, which criticizes the background as presented by Verbenko, not to mention that of Mrs. Lidie Skorniakova, president of the Mother and Infant Education Department.

Dr. Stevens says:

Perhaps the Armenians feel themselves free to comment because they have the highest birth rate in the Soviet Union and can therefore hardly be suspected of wanting birth control. Somewhat ironically the newspaper pointed out that the greater part of the parents throughout the world undoubtedly agreed with the Pope that birth control should be left to the will of God. The mass of humanity lives in Asia, in Africa, and in Latin America where the cultural and economic level is still low. Nevertheless, in view of the growing population and the low standard of life, these countries regarded the new effects of contraception as an unexpected gift. But *Kommunist* criticizes the Pope because he wants to make a dogma about the facts of life, just as happened long ago in the case of Galileo. . . . In her efforts to attain a regulation of births that will give a balanced order to her population model, Russia will also have to consider the problems caused by a great preponderance of women over men, which is due to a higher death rate among men. The entire dilemma is perhaps best summed up by a phrase attributed to the Armenian Radio; when asked whether in a Socialist regime the birthrate could be determined by the state just like other things, the mythical oracle replied: "No, as long as reproduction remains a private matter."

Possibly it is the key, too, to the Soviet reticence and ambiguities. On one hand, in fact, we have the concern of the people over the decrease in population in relation to other ethnic groups, which have generally been added to the Socialist bloc groups, which have generally been added to the Socialist block by force, are more productive precisely because of what they hold in conscience to be a religious and ethical duty. In this sphere it is precisely the private and personal decision which matters most, and this is facilitated by adherence to a faith. (This applies both to the Catholics of Lithuania and the Muslims of the Caucasus!) The Socialist state could hence appeal to the Socialist ethics of class struggle and to the old theme of the mystique of the working classes. Apart from the fact, however, that this would sound anachronistic in the present situation created by the phenomenon of urbanization and higher living standards, it would end up sounding like a Socialist encyclical against birth control!

Once again the "political" element has entered into an eminently religious and ethical problem. Is it a political interpretation which has been added on to the encyclical or is it that the encyclical, by facing such a concrete issue, must necessarily give rise to repercussions in all the dimensions in which this human problem is found?

The long observations we have made on the issue in the Third World and in what has already begun to be called the Fourth World—that is, the Socialist World—tend to make us opt for the second hypothesis.

In any case, one thing has clearly become evident: there are problems which strangely coincide in continents as far apart as Russia and Latin America. Also, the motives underlying the various interpretations can help us to be more attentive and less hurried in our reading of the encyclical.

Finally, when reflecting on the story of *Humanae Vitae* in the Third World and behind the so-called Iron Curtain, we cannot but in all honesty ask a question which others have already seen as an affirmation: Will not the encyclical in a few years' time be found to have been really correct after all? Shall we discover that, even though not an infallible religious teaching, it had very wisely managed to see through the cracks of the present, confused reality?

Chapter 7 *Roma Locuta, causa finita*—or: Is the Encyclical the Last Word?

Roma locuta, causa finita: these famous words of Augustine always reappear whenever the central authority of the Church is invoked to decide and define a controversial question. Augustine's phrase, however, has never met with as many difficulties as in the question of *Humanae Vitae.* In the present context the translation could be: "Is the encyclical really the last word?" or "Must everyone else be forced to keep quiet because Rome has spoken?" The more delicate presuppositions of this question evidently entail far more than the concrete, particular instance of an encyclical which after all is only an encyclical; the great uproar which has surrounded it increases the risk that it will receive more attention than is in fact due. On one hand, it has been made into a question of schism, on the other, into a "handbook" of the faith. Individuals' intelligence and openness are judged by whether or not they accept the encyclical humbly or whether they criticize it. For some it is a guarantee of fidelity and orthodoxy, and as far as they are concerned the affair is over. These, however, are only the picturesque, banal side issues of a far more important problem.

The Debate on Infallibility and Irreformability

To ask whether a document of the Church's magisterium is the last word on a particular question is to presuppose another question: Is this document *infallible?* This question is immediately followed by another which logically follows from it: Is the document *irreformable?* By *infallibility* we mean that prerogative which, according to Catholic teaching, pertains to the Supreme Pontiff when he defines a point of doctrine with the intention of using his supreme teaching authority. In this case we have what is technically called an "ex cathedra" definition. Infallibility can be clearly declared, or it can be implied in the forms of expression used when the magisterium wishes to express its intention of giving an ex cathedra definition. Examples of this latter usage are the formulas used in the definition of the dogmas of the faith; namely, when the Supreme Pontiff establishes that a truth already believed in by the Church and the faithful is to be held as a dogma; that is, as an essential point of the faith.

Apart from these cases, it is impossible to speak of infallibility in any real or proper sense. This does not mean that other decisions are without value, and we will immediately observe how their interpretation is much more complex. Once it is admitted that a document is not infallible, is it then possible to say that it can change, and that the doctrine it affirms can evolve? It is clear that if the document fulfills all the requirements for infallibility, it is also irreformable in the doctrine it proposes. In any other instance it can admit of a subsequent evolution in one direction or another, and hence that doctrine is reformable.

Never, perhaps, has this whole question been as sharply highlighted as in the present document. Might it be because such a reaffirmation of teaching was not expected? Might it be because the question has already been so deeply investigated and subjected to theological evolution that it is hard to believe the encyclical could really be the definitive statement on the subject? Is it perhaps rather because of modern man's extreme sensitivity to decisions in which he can take an active part? The motives are certainly numerous. However, we must reject some which are often suggested; for example, that the insistence on the noninfallibility and reformability of the encyclical is due both to bad will in not conforming to the correct norms of the divine law and to capitulation to the spirit of hedonism and immorality current nowadays. This accusation may not be leveled at theologians who have spent years of study on these problems, and who are now seeking to clarify the sense in which the encyclical is an "authentic" teaching even if it is neither "infallible" nor hence "reformable."

The Vatican theologian Ferdinando Lambruschini opened the discussion when he presented the encyclical to the press. He foresaw that one of the first questions to be asked would be in connection with infallibility. After presenting various considerations on the Church's magisterium expressed in the encyclical, he posed the question:

We may ask ourselves at this point: What is the value of the pontifical pronouncement on the regulation of births? While admitting that the magisterium can define infallibly some of the aspects of natural law, explicitly or implicitly contained in revelation, most theologians consider that this has not yet come to pass in the field of morals. Attentive reading of the encyclical *Humanae Vitae* does not suggest the theological note of infallibility; this is also shown by a simple comparison with the Profession of Faith proclaimed on June 30 during the solemn rite in St. Peter's Square. It is always a matter, however, of an authentic pronouncement, all the more so since it is included thus in the continuing line of the ecclesiastical magisterium.

At the time of the appearance of *Casti Connubii,* a certain theologian thought it constituted an infallible and hence irreformable definition which condemned contraception. The great majority of theologians, however, do not hold the pronouncement of the said encyclical to be infallible or irreformable, while they recognize the force of its formulations. Although artificial, evil intervention by a married couple in the marriage act, which interferes with the natural possibility of a new life arising, was peremptorily condemned, with the consequent stern measures imposed by confessors, not many theologians today look upon this as an ex cathedra definition. It would have been easy for Paul VI to declare *Casti Connubii* infallible, as was actually suggested to him by some. It would be difficult, however, to discern the extremes of a definition in the quiet, serene exposition of the encyclical *Humanae Vitae,* the pronouncement of which may be called Catholic doctrine, but not of defined Catholic faith, nor even proximate to Catholic faith.

Lambruschini's phrase "nor even proximate to Catholic faith" may appear surprising to those not familiar with the technical language of theologians. The phrase is a translation of the Latin term *proxima fidei,* and it refers to the essential elements of the faith defined in the form of dogmas. When applied to any one particular truth, the phrase *proxima fidei* means that there are sufficient elements in the truth to warrant its being made the object of a dogmatic definition. That situation, observes the Vatican theologian, does not exist here. This is not to say, however, that *Humanae Vitae* is worthless. The problem, rather, is one of trying to establish its true value. Lambruschini continues:

Nevertheless, just as no one refused assent to the conclusions of *Casti Connubii,* likewise no one may refuse not only external, but also interior and spiritual, assent to the decisions of Paul VI. His pronouncement is an act of the authentic magisterium, which is binding on the consciences of all the members of the people of God, including pastors. The Pope is called to confirm this people in the faith in the same way that Peter was called for the other apostles.

A little later the theologian adds for clarification:

Even if not infallible, it is a decision of the magisterium of the head of the Church, whose directives should be followed. In No. 25 of the Constitution on the Church, *Lumen Gentium,* we are told that the authority of the magisterium instituted by Jesus Christ is endowed with a special charisma even in the interpretation of the natural moral law. If the authority of the Church's magisterium were binding only in infallible pronouncements, it would be very limited in extent and we would not be far from the deteriorated forms of Protestantism which are lay aligned and which declare the complete arbitrariness of the individual Christian's conscience in his behavior.

Lambruschini thus made the clarification that even though the encyclical is not infallible, it is nonetheless binding; we shall later examine the question of individual conscience and also the question of the right of inquiry. We shall then deal with further criticism of the consent due to this act of the magisterium.

Lambruschini himself later returned to this topic and made some points which did not appear to have been clearly expressed in the few excerpts from his press conference that were included on television. He clarified his ideas first of all in the *L'Osservatore della domenica,* and again in his book (F. Lambruschini, *Problemi della "Humanae Vitae,"* Brescia, 1969). In the latter he says:

It was pointed out to me that viewers of the second transmission could have deduced that the decision with regard to birth regulation, not being a definition "ex cathedra," and hence not an irreformable judgment, was therefore not binding on the consciences of the faithful. Such a deduction is completely false, and it is one which has been heard frequently in subsequent polemics, especially in the press, which has reported the opinions of those theologians who disagree with the pontifical document. Without wishing to blame those responsible for the television program, who may have found themselves faced with deadlines and time limits, I must say that in connection with such a delicate point, a greater theological sensibility would have done no harm. One need only go a little farther into the text of the presentation to understand quite clearly that if a careful reading of the encyclical does not suggest the note of infallibility and irreformability of the papal decision, it does not follow that it is quite simply a reformable pronouncement.

At this point Lambruschini adds a technical clarification explaining the various levels of authority that a teaching can have:

In theological language there are various grades and nuances in categorizing the documents of the magisterium of the Church. The content is said to be of divine faith when it is clearly implied in revelation. It is said to be of Catholic faith when the extraordinary magisterium of the Pope or of an ecumenical Council, or the ordinary magisterium of all the bishops, unanimously and constantly declare that it is found in revelation, at least implicitly. The content is proximate to the faith when theologians see a very strict connection between the formulation and the definition. None of these three theological qualifications apply to the decision of Paul VI. His decision however, although not of divine faith, nor of Catholic faith, nor even proximate to the faith, is an act of the authentic magisterium—all the more valid because it confirms and crowns a century-long tradition, and particularly the teachings of the last three popes as Paul VI himself mentioned in his address of Wednesday, August 1, 1968 at Castel Gandolfo. While not of Catholic faith, the Pope's teaching on birth regulation can and must be said to be Catholic doctrine, such as to bind the consciences of all Christians.

It may be noted that Lambruschini introduces a new concept in this his second statement on the encyclical—that of the *authenticity* of the pontifical document. As we shall see, this is an important concept, particularly in relation to the nature of the assent due to the encyclical.

The clarification regarding the noninfallibility of the encyclical was immediately taken up, rather than by the press, by the theologians, who are always intent on making such clarifications. In fact, many other serious questions depend on these clarifications, such as the type of assent, obedience, and acceptance to be given to the document, as well as the question of reflection on and criticism of this document.

We are dealing with what is technically called a *theological note;* that is, the intrinsic and normative value of the document. Once it is recognized and established by all that *Humanae Vitae* is a noninfallible document, the problem is to decide its real value and to define the authority it possesses. Here we set sail on the wide sea of theological reflection on which there may be found opinions varying from the most rigid to the most free. Naturally these opinions depend on the general positions adopted by the individual theologians—positions which were arrived at even before the publication of the encyclical, either in relation to this specific problem or in a wider theological and moral context. In his commentary on the encyclical (*L'enciclica "Humanae Vitae,"* Milan, 1968) G. B. Guzzetti, after recognizing the noninfallibility of the encyclical, attempts to anchor its exact authority. This he does in the following statements:

In the encyclical we have, not a prudential directive or a positive determination by the Church as to how a couple should behave in their sexual life, but a teaching and a doctrinal proposition both on the nature of the marriage act in relation to fertility and on the morality of onanism. . . . We do not have a statement by the Church on natural or revealed law as is the case with the obligation to hear Mass on feast days, for example, or to fast before receiving communion, or to go to confession if one is certain that he has committed a serious sin. . . .

In the encyclical we have a teaching and a doctrinal proposition on the marriage-fertility relationship. . . . It is not a case of *certitude* or *probability*, but of a *certain interpretation* of reality, or of the nature of the marriage-family relationship and of the morality of onanism. It is not a case of *certain* teaching, or of teaching which does not contradict revelation; as, for example, when a person is to be considered living until there is sufficient certitude that he is dead. And it is not a case of a freely acceptable, even if not definitive, teaching, as is, for example, the teaching on the immediate origin of the first man from organic matter rather than from inorganic matter. On this point note is to be taken that the Church has for some time allowed the theistic-evolutionary thesis, leaving room for the acceptance in the future of an ecclesiastical teaching different from that of the present.

Here we have a certain interpretation on the nature of marriage and on the morality of onanism. . . .

We do not have here a doctrine proposed as the personal teaching of Paul VI or of the preceding popes, but the constant doctrine of the Church. It is the doctrine of Christ himself.

To prove his statement, Guzzetti quotes various texts from

the encyclical itself and then makes two further statements which are likewise proved by texts from the encyclical. Guzzetti says:

The Pope is restating a doctrine after ample consultation, mature reflection, and assiduous prayer in his capacity as Vicar of Christ and assisted by the Holy Spirit, in order to give an adequate reply to the doubts and questions which have arisen in the Church in our time. . . . Since the publication of the encyclical the Pope has strenuously defended its teaching against all attempts to devalue it, as may be seen on reading the Pope's discourses and the position taken by *L'Osservatore Romano.*

After various affirmations regarding the encyclical's *truth* and *irreformability* Guzzetti concludes:

The doctrine proposed by *Humanae Vitae* is therefore true and irreformable. This was clear to many even before the encyclical was published, and had the Pope decided differently it would have created grave problems concerning the very mission of the Church which they —or at least the present author—would only have solved by recourse to faith in the Mystery of the Church. One thing, then, is clear regarding the new contribution made by the encyclical: in order now to change the position taken by the encyclical, it would be necessary to overcome the previous difficulties which Paul VI himself has not been able to overcome . . . not to mention the new difficulties that have arisen as a result of the Pope's pronouncement.

For Guzzetti, therefore, the encyclical is not infallible, but because of the motives which led to its publication it must be considered as practically *irreformable.* Moreover, it suggests an even greater degree of doctrinal affirmation. Hence, Guzzetti experiences a certain difficulty—this seems particularly true when he states that a different statement by the Pope would have created grave problems—in admitting noninfallibility. For this reason he asks a rather unusual question and proceeds to give his own reply to it:

Why did the Pope not make an infallible definition? It is difficult to give a precise answer merely from a reading of the encyclical or from a study of the subsequent statements of the Pope or of *L'Osservatore Romano.* It could be thought that—*salvo meliori judicio!*—for reasons that may be hinted at or according to the custom of the Church, the

Pope did not want to place too heavy a burden on those who would have denied his teaching or have hesitated obstinately, for they would then have had either to accept the encyclical or to be called heretics.

This is a rather curious reply, considering that the same reasoning could be used to show the unsuitability of even restating the teaching, especially when it was known—and the Pope himself said this—that many would not be willing to accept it. If it had appeared as a teaching "of faith" to the Pope, he would certainly not have hesitated to invoke infallibility.

The problem is to define the encyclical's theological "qualifications," considering that the Pope must certainly have had graver reasons than those suggested by Guzzetti for not invoking infallibility. It is the task of theologians to define the extent of the encyclical's qualifications, and this fact itself suggests that the encyclical has not shut the door to all investigation. This is recognized even by *L'Osservatore Romano* when it answers *some queries related to the encyclical "Humanae Vitae"* (November 24, 1968, signed P. Z.). It says among other things:

With regard to the doctrine of the present encyclical, true experts in theology are able to recognize the special theological note that belongs to it for the following reasons: the Pope made his declaration while a very special situation of incertitude and discussion was prevalent; it is a doctrine constantly transmitted by the Church, and repeatedly proposed by the predecessors of Paul VI; the encyclical has the consent of the bishops throughout the world, who not only maintain the bond of communion with the successor of Peter, but who also have expressed a unanimous opinion among themselves. These bishops, for at least a century and a half—that is, from the time when the abuse of marriage began to spread in the West—have propounded their authentic teaching on the matter in both national episcopal conferences and special pastoral letters.

The theologian in *L'Osservatore Romano* also insists on the unanimity of the doctrine and consequently on the "common doctrine." But he recognizes that it remains an open question for theologians to determine the exact theological note of the encyclical. Whatever this note is, it cannot be that of infallibility; and hence the question of reformability or irreformability remains an open one.

"Ordinary" Teaching and "Authentic" Teaching

Once infallibility has been excluded, the investigation narrows down to two points: the *ordinary* magisterium and the *authentic* magisterium. Here again, the interpretations range from the maximalist to the minimalist.

An editorial in *Renovatio* (the periodical of theology and of culture) of December 1968, while admitting that the document is noninfallible as regards "ex cathedra" teaching, makes an attempt at affirming that the ordinary magisterium can be infallible:

In discussing the value of *Humanae Vitae* we are obviously dealing with its theological value, since this is what is under discussion. In other words, the question we are asking is whether the affirmations of *Humanae Vitae,* especially those condemning all methods of contraception, are reformable or not—do these affirmations enjoy the guarantee of infallibility or not? It is important for the faithful to know if this is a matter of divinely guaranteed certitude. It is obvious that without absolute certitude the document would lose much of its force. One thing is certain: *Humanae Vitae* is not an ex cathedra definition. This means in principle that its reformability is not excluded. Hence the question may be restated in the following way: Given that the document is not an ex cathedra definition, does it possess infallibility and consequently irreformability from another source, and if so, what source?

First, whatever one's opinion, the teaching of Vatican II in paragraph 25 of *Lumen Gentium* must be kept in mind: "This religious submission of will and of mind must be shown in a special way to the authentic teaching authority of the Roman Pontiff, even when he is not speaking ex cathedra. That is, it must be shown in such a way that his supreme magisterium is acknowledged with reverence, the judgments made by him are sincerely adhered to, according to his manifest mind and will. His mind and will in the matter may be known chiefly either from the character of the documents, from his frequent repetition of the same doctrine, or from his manner of speaking." This text is a condemnation of those who have not shown sufficient consideration, respect, reverence, or sincere adhesion. It affirms that the document in question is at least an act of the authentic magisterium, but it does not solve the point in question, which is an entirely different one. In fact, "authenticity" does not imply infallibility or its consequence, irreformability. The faithful wish to be absolutely certain, and rightly so.

To present as the only possible alternatives, in the case in question, either an ex cathedra definition (which has been rejected), or a solemn or authentic magisterium (which of itself does not imply infallibility) is to fall into sophistry and grave error, because there is another alternative: that of the ordinary infallible magisterium. It is strange how some seem to have avoided speaking of this at all costs. The ordinary magisterium is the Church's sure, everyday food, while the solemn magisterium is rare and does not always succeed in arresting heresies in their first cautious and obscure manifestations. This is so mainly because it requires long and careful preparation, but also because it is exercised by the Roman Pontiff or by the episcopal college in union with the Roman Pontiff.

Objectively, the question can be stated thus: Granted that the document is not an act of the infallible magisterium, and that in itself it does not therefore possess the guarantee of irreformability and certitude, does it not perhaps have the guarantee of infallibility which belongs to the ordinary magisterium under the specific conditions already mentioned? In this case the substance of the document would not be irreformable by reason of the document itself, but the substance of the document would have the guarantee of infallibility of itself and from elsewhere.

Now it seems we must reply as follows: the substance of the document is already guaranteed by the ordinary magisterium, and for this reason it is irreformable. Even in the first century the *Didache* mentions "the killers of children." The same words reappear in the letter of Barnabas (20:2); Clement of Alexandria speaks particularly against contraceptives (*Pedagogus* 2:10; 41:2). We can also read Minucius Felix (*Octavius* 30:2), Lactantius (*Divinae institutiones* 6:20, 25), Justin (*Apologia* I, 29), Athenagoras (*Legatio pro Christianis* 33). This tradition is continued in the later Fathers, especially in the writings of St. Augustine, which were the basis of canonical legislation. The whole line of patristic and theological tradition is characterized by these same concepts. In this way we come to the encyclical *Casti Connubii* of Pius XI (December 30, 1930) which summed up the ancient and common teaching. All the conditions necessary for the ordinary irreformable magisterium would seem to be fulfilled here.

The present situation of widespread inquietude is a recent phenomenon, which is no reflection on the many centuries of serene acceptance. It is always necessary to remember that between the solemn

377

magisterium and the simply authentic magisterium lies the ordinary magisterium endowed with the charism of infallibility.

Renovatio then concludes by asking what authority the encyclical would have over Catholics' consciences if it were reformable.

By exploring the "note" of the *common magisterium,* it is possible to bring in the "qualification" of infallibility properly so-called. This is done in place of the solemn magisterium which does not apply in this case, but it is sufficiently strong to safeguard the encyclical's authority.

Without attempting to retain the idea of infallibility, but in an effort to establish the doctrinal certitude that the encyclical possesses despite this fact, the Dominican theologian M. R. Gagnebet speaks of the *Certitude of the encyclical's teaching* in *L'Osservatore Romano* of September 4, 1968 in a series of his articles entitled "The Authority of the Encyclical *Humanae Vitae.*" He speaks of the concept of certitude and of infallibility without using the latter to establish the former. Gagnebet says:

Some object that the encyclical *Humanae Vitae* is not a document of the infallible magisterium. Hence its teaching cannot lay claim to the guarantee of absolute certitude which alone could put an end to all discussion. It is possible, therefore, to recognize the authority of the Pope, without accepting this teaching.

Let us note, first, that according to the last Council, the doctrinal authority of the Pope and the bishops is not limited to definitions of faith.

After quoting the text from the Council already quoted by the writer in *Renovatio,* Gagnebet continues:

Let us apply these criteria to the recent encyclical. It is the obvious intention of the Pope to call a halt to a controversy which has called into question the teaching, traditional throughout the centuries, of theologians who have been approved by the magisterium. Pius XII did this in just such a case in his encyclical *Humani Generis*—"the question is no longer open to the free discussion of theologians"; moreover, Paul VI introduced nothing new into the question. Without wishing to go any farther back into the past, it may be noted that the teaching of the Holy See in this matter has not changed since the time of Pius VI. . . . The Council did not touch on this matter, which was reserved for the Supreme Pontiff, but it did affirm the principle: "With regard to the regulation of births, it is not permitted for the sons of the Church to use methods that the magisterium, in explaining the divine law, disapprove of." Finally, the document in which the Pope proposes his teaching is an encyclical addressed to the universal Church. . . .

In using the noninfallible nature of this document to deny the certitude of its teachings, some seem to forget the fact that there are teachings in Catholic doctrine which are certain without being the object of an infallible definition. At the last Council the doctrine of collegiality was proposed as a certain teaching contained in Holy Scripture, but was not proposed as a defined doctrine which had to be believed by divine faith. It is without doubt an infallible doctrine, but it was not defined because the Council did not want to promulgate any new dogmas of faith.

To restrict the divine assistance to a few extraordinary acts of the solemn magisterium drawn up through the centuries, would be to forget that Christ promised to be with his Church all days, even to the end of time. In any case, it is a certain theological doctrine that the Holy Spirit assists the Church in promulgating moral and disciplinary laws. This divine assistance guarantees that when there is a case of "laws imposed on the universal Church," these laws cannot be contrary to revelation or to the natural moral law. The constitution *Auctorem Fidei* condemned a proposition of the pseudo-Synod of Pistoia according to which "the Church governed by the Holy Spirit could impose a disciplinary law that would be not only useless and so burdensome as to restrict Christian freedom, but also dangerous and harmful." If this is true for disciplinary laws, it must be *a fortiori* true for the moral laws imposed by the Church on all the faithful. Such assistance is exercised in the encyclical *Humanae Vitae,* which is an authentic interpretation of natural law.

Even though it is not explicit, obviously Gagnebet would like to apply infallibility in some form to the encyclical. His last statement introduces another serious problem; namely, the competence of the ecclesiastical magisterium to interpret the natural law "authentically."

This longing for a precise definition of the doctrine of the encyclical is also apparent in the thought of Cardinal Charles Journet who wrote on the theme "The Light of the Encyclical" in *Nova et Vetera,* September 1968, in Lucerne. He proposed the hypothesis of a definability, or at least that there are sufficient elements on hand for such a definability. He also makes use of the idea of the *ordinary magisterium* of such a type that the Pope was able to say: "We have no doubt that it is our duty to make a statement in the express terms of the present encyclical." About this Journet states:

One thing is certain: the ordinary magisterium of the Supreme Pontiff is here being fully exercised. Any theologian who reflects on the seriousness of the issue, the light which has been thrown on the subject to clarify it, and the precision and certitude with which the reply was given, will probably realize that he is facing—such is our personal opinion—a point of moral doctrine which is further definable and which, in the future, will be verified by a consensus of divine faith.

The personal opinion of Cardinal Journet is of particular value and significance, all the more so because he is recognized as a theologian of importance, especially in ecclesiology.

Listening to these theologians one could get the strange impression that all the other theologians suffered an unforeseen mnemonic lapse or made an unexpected error which caused them to forget the basic principles of theological methodology with regard to the infallible, ordinary, and authentic magisterium. It seems that these theologians who go to great pains in clarifying and defining terms know that it is not so easy to apply them to the present question. There are many theologians, in fact, who, once they have admitted the encyclical's noninfallibility, immediately pass on to the concept of reformability. For example, on June 30, 1968, 87 theologians from various American faculties, published a declaration in which they said:

The encyclical is not an infallible teaching. History shows that a number of statements of similar or even greater authoritative weight have subsequently been proved inadequate or even erroneous. Past authoritative statements on religious liberty, interest-taking, the right to silence, and the ends of marriage have all been corrected at a later date.

This is a far cry from Gagnebet and Journet.

Having admitted that there is no case for infallibility, most theologians do not try to recover this by employing the concept of the "ordinary" magisterium. Beginning with the fact of noninfallibility, they try to establish on what grounds the doctrine of the encyclical, although demanding respectful assent, remains open to positive criticism and hence evolution.

The opinion of the North American Jesuit theologian R. McCormick, as reported in the *National Catholic Reporter,* is important on this point:

We can reject a pontifical document that is not infallible only if the arguments used for sustaining a doctrine are clearly inadequate, or at least if one has serious doubts about them. Now, many years of study and clarifying effort on this subject have led me to the conclusion that the traditional teaching is placed in strong doubt by virtue of both extrinsic and intrinsic reasons. This does not mean certainty on my part, except to the extent in which I remain open to further investigation . . . and to the authentic teaching of the magisterium. . . . Loyalty to the magisterium, however, cannot consist of blind submission—quite the contrary. Acceptance permits criticism and dissent, always provided that these are made with a sense of responsibility.

As can be seen, the brief statement of the American theologians is in a completely different vein from that of the "Roman" theologians, but it cannot be called any less Catholic because of this factor. We can see in it a greater sense of the dynamism and responsibility which is necessary for theological investigation, and also a greater taste for the problematic and dialectical approach, which are both outstanding characteristics of the theological work of our times.

Is Criticism a Right?

If the opinion of R. McCormick represents that of a great many North American theologians who willingly take up a dialectical position before a noninfallible document, even though an "authentic" one, there are still many who would maintain that one should behave "as if" the encyclical were infallible. It is enough to quote the intransigent stand of the North American magazine *Triumph,* which typically represents the so-called right-wing position. In an editorial it asks priests who do not agree entirely with the encyclical to be sincere and loyal to themselves and to the Church, and to leave the Church because they are automatically schismatics by not accepting the Pope's words. In the same September issue of the magazine we read:

A doctor made the following comment on the day after the publication of the encyclical: "Your Church has lost two members; my two Catholic colleagues have declared that they will abandon the Church because they say they find the mentality of the Pope incomprehensible and inacceptable." The same day a priest came to ask us whether in loyalty to his own conscience he ought not to abandon the priestly ministry, seeing that he could not possibly agree with the encyclical. This traumatic experience, together with the enormous danger of a mass desertion of the Church, has led many theologians to give great emphasis to the fallible character of the encyclical and to take up a strong position.

From this, it would appear that many theologians have adopted, in a very general way, this position regarding the "fallibility" of the encyclical—with the logical consequences deriving from it—merely because of the sudden shock it delivered to their still-developing investigations, or for fear of mass desertion from the Church.

The North American theologians are not the only ones to face both the possibilities and the inherent dangers in a criticism of a noninfallible encyclical precisely on account of and on the basis of their critical function within the Church. This is probably even more true of the European theologians. Theology has flourished in recent years, and this is mainly due to the rediscovery of its critical role. Hence the theologian Franz Böckle in *Neue Zürcher Zeitung* of August 4, 1968 could observe:

Now that Pope Paul VI has intervened in the question of birth regulation, the question being asked is what significance this pontifical declaration has for the freedom of discussion and for the personal obedience of theologians and the faithful in the Church. How valid is the old phrase *Roma locuta, causa finita?* Does a word from Rome put an end to the struggle or the discussion?

Böckle goes on to analyze the significance of the magisterium and obedience within the Church in order to show the constructive force of criticism within the Church and as the function of theology:

382

Ecclesial obedience properly understood and characteristic of adult persons, must not be a "corpse-like obedience." Because of love for true obedience we must be ready to take our criticism to the competent authorities. We must recognize, above all, that a noninfallible teaching can be false, or at least incomplete, and therefore urgently in need of correction. How can this be corrected, however, unless by means of a critical analysis, and eventually through opposition? This is the task proper to theology. It is the fundamental task of theology when faced with noninfallible declarations of the magisterium to show the reformability or relativity of such declarations by comparing them with scripture and tradition. Once again theology is called to pursue this task with relation to the encyclical.

The fundamental tasks of theology, therefore, are criticism, comparison, and eventually opposition. These tasks are extremely positive because they tend toward the same objective as the magisterium itself: direct comparison with scripture and tradition.

If this is true, then there is little sense in asking whether a right to criticize exists. In fact, criticism becomes a duty because it is a necessary service. The very fact that a document is not infallible is a sign that even the magisterium implicitly recognizes it has not yet arrived at a full understanding of the truth in question. Hence the faithful must help this magisterium to better understand the truth, especially those who are the specialists in this field; namely, the theologians.

While theoretically speaking, there is no problem in admitting all this, in practice things are not so simple, especially when the noninfallibility of a document or teaching calls other deeper issues into question. This is why *Humanae Vitae* recalled many old questions on which whole libraries had already been written, but which were suddenly seen in a completely new light. Theologians attribute this to the fact that, unlike a juridical question which can be definitively decided, a question of faith can never become a closed question.

While for many theologians it is pointless to ask whether they have the right to criticism, because for them this is the very function of theology, this same right is subject to rather violent attack from other quarters. Here again, naturally, it is based on a predetermined idea of the magisterium, of theology, and of obedience.

For example, Dietrich von Hildebrand in his book *Die Enzyklika "Humanae Vitae"—ein Zeichen des Widerspruchs*, Regensburg, 1968, replying to the question, "Does obedience require infallibility?" says that there is no longer room for other opinions:

One often hears it said that an encyclical is not infallible. In the first place it must be stated that infallibility is not restricted only to dogmas which are expressly declared "ex cathedra," but is extended to the official doctrine of the Church concerning important problems of faith and morals (cf. *Lumen Gentium* Nos. 3, 25). The ban on artificial birth regulation, solemnly proclaimed by recent popes and repeated in *Gaudium et Spes* (No. 51), is evidently an official doctrine of the Church and a tradition of the magisterium. Finally, *Lumen Gentium* (No. 25) states that every Catholic is bound to "internal and external obedience" with regard to the moral law contained in a teaching which is not ex cathedra, but at least *authentic*. In the case of the encyclical *Humanae Vitae*, this obedience is morally binding because, as is generally recognized, it is an expression of the "authentic magisterium" of the Church. The obligation is *independent* of the question of infallibility.

In view of this it would be senseless to consider the encyclical *Humanae Vitae* as the personal opinion of the Pope, and to oppose it with the opposite opinions of individual theologians and even laity as if being equally authoritative.

It would take no small effort to find anyone among the theologians who would "oppose" the personal opinion of the Pope with his own opinion, since they acknowledge that here we are dealing with an *authentic* magisterium which must be respected, but then the theologians note that the document *is not infallible* and consequently begin debating it. Hence the whole dialectic of the question does not seem "senseless" as von Hildebrand would make out. The position expressed by the theologian R. McCormick is a good illustration of this point.

When viewing the question in a more technically theological context, it is essential to keep in mind the position as delineated by the Vatican theologian Lambruschini at his press conference. His basic theme also is that the question as such is closed and with it all avenues of criticism. All that remains is the possibility of a deeper understanding of the motives for the doctrine together with the possibility of forming one's conscience on the basis of that doctrine. Lambruschini states:

By communicating his decision, the Pope has put an end to the question of the licitity or otherwise of contraception for the purpose of birth regulation, and it cannot be doubted that he has spoken after due consultation and mindful of the duties of his high office. The faithful are bound in conscience, and theologians may not continue discussing the question as if the Pontiff had not spoken.

A little earlier Lambruschini quoted a "noted author," J. M. Reuss, who in 1967 published *Verantwortete Elternschaft Gesammelte Ausatze zur Frage des Empfangnisregelung*, in which he asserts that

moralists agree that all methods of contraception which are used for egoistic or hedonistic motives or from mere caprice must be rejected. They would be more likely to allow methods, however, apart from periodic abstinence, in common enough, concrete cases—abortion being the only exception. He then declares that a decision of the pontifical infallible magisterium contrary to this tendency is not only undesirable but impossible, and that even a noninfallible decision in the present circumstances is full of difficulties. The pronouncement has come. It is not infallible, but it does not leave the question of birth regulation in a vague problematical condition. Assent of theological faith is due only to the definitions properly so-called, but there is owed also loyal and full assent, interior and not only exterior, to an authentic pronouncement of the magisterium, in proportion to the level of the authority from which it emanates.

Lambruschini's ideas on the possibility of discussion are even more decisively presented in his book which has been quoted already. On p. 60 he states: "Theologians and laity may not discuss contraception as though no new factor has entered into the discussion." He goes on to admit the possibility of further reflection but always for a "greater understanding" of the doctrine already established:

The authentic pronouncement of the Pope demands full submission of intelligence and will, because it was made to preserve the faith of the ecclesial community and of each individual member. This does not restrict theological reflection and a deepening of the understanding of the reasons which promoted it, both leading to greater understanding. I can understand, without necessarily justifying it, the open opinion of some theologians and laity; but I cannot understand how they could persist in holding this opinion after such a mediated, clear, and strong pronouncement. The encouragement given by the press to noted theologians to continue holding their opinions, almost as if these opinions, which are in open contrast with the teaching of the Sovereign Pontiff, were endowed with valid operative probability on the theoretical and practical moral level, constitutes a defiance of good Catholic sense, as well as of the supreme authority. . . . I ask myself under what pretexts these theologians claim to serve the Church, when they undermine her institutional bases which were willed and founded by Jesus Christ.

Are these theologians and faithful, therefore, who still lay claim to the possibility of criticism, guilty of "defiance"? This is not how it appears to the moral theologian Bernard Häring. In an article in *Commonweal*, September 6, 1968, describing the work of the commission of birth control, Häring said: "If my judgment of the situation is correct, the reason Pope John set up a small commission of theologians for a leisurely study of this issue was in order to open up discussion." Häring says this must continue because it throws light not only on the specific problem but also on a much larger one. This opinion is voiced by many theologians besides Häring. When theologians claim—for example, Böckle, as we have seen—that criticism is the task of theology, they are concerned not merely with the present problem of contraception but with a deeper problem. This particular doctrine, and the whole process of the Pope's decision, fit into a broader context. It is difficult to separate the two issues. In the same article Häring defines and delineates the sense of criticism in such a way that it is not restricted to the specific theme of the encyclical as would appear in the way Lambruschini and von Hildebrand presented the problem. In fact, Häring says:

In discussing *Humanae Vitae* and the developments of the last two years, the meaning when all is said and done, is really, "When you have come to yourself, you must lend strength to your brothers (Luke 22:32)." What is needed is an enlightened understanding of the spiritual office of the successor of St. Peter, as it appeared so remarkably in Pope John, against the most bitter opposition of that curial group which at the moment is triumphant, a group which, despite the era of internationalization in which we live, was powerfully strengthened at the last consistory by the appointment of 12 Italian cardinals. What is needed is the liberation for this ecumenical era of the Papacy in the direction in which Pope Paul VI himself has already made such giant strides. Call to mind the visit on two occasions of Paul to the patriarch Athenagoras, before Paul ventured to invite him to a visit in Rome. That was a sensitive and delicate touch, a special sign of humility of Paul with the patriarch.

What is needed now is for all men of the Church to speak out unequivocally and openly against these reactionary forces. This alone can prevent the reactionary forces from pushing the Pope in the opposite direction, back to that worldly narrowness exemplified in the *Syllabus* and the Church prohibition of Italians from voting in their own country, which lasted from 1870 to 1929. Despite this many will say: In this question it is not a matter of power; it is simply a matter of understanding Christian marriage. At first sight this may seem to be so; but if one looks more closely, it is clear that an outmoded understanding of curial power is the real issue, and in conjunction with it, the issue of noncollegial exercise of the teaching office, and the inadequately explored issues of how the Pope teaches.

An "inadequately explored" issue: here we have the point of view of those theologians and faithful who claim the right to criticize, not as something new, but as something inherent in their very function and vocation as Christians.

Häring develops his position along these same lines in a small book, *The Crisis Surrounding "Humanae Vitae,"* published at the end of 1968 in Germany. After tracing out the lines of the encyclical which followed those of *Casti Connubii,* he recognizes the fact that *Humanae Vitae* is attempting to follow the direction of Vatican II in what concerns the value and the meaning of conjugal love:

"The conjugal act preserves in its fullness the sense of true mutual love and its ordination toward man's most high calling to parenthood" (No. 12). Differing from preceding conceptions, here love is mentioned before the procreative objective of marriage. In concluding, however, once more the statement is made that married love cannot be authentic if it does not integrally preserve the biological structure of the marriage act. Now, this way of seeing things certainly cannot be the final word of the Catholic Church. The encyclical *Humanae Vitae* ought not, then, be reason for panic. It is wrong to think that one should leave the Church or refuse allegiance to the successor of Peter because one is unable to act in accordance with the Pope's way of thinking.

The reactions of many theologians and lay persons, as well as of non-Catholic Christians and others, have already shown that the Pope was extremely optimistic in thinking that modern man was particularly disposed to agreeing with his viewpoint. Everyone in the Church will give great weight to the Pope's words. It is not the first time, however, that an important section of Christianity has appealed to the Pope to revise a noninfallible teaching. In this case the appeal is none other than that the search after truth continue in the context of the widest possible collegiality.

The question can still be said to be open. It is here that the dynamic character and the "itinerant" situation of the ecclesiastical magisterium, as well as of theological science, can be seen. It was a providential fact that the Council did not descend to casuistry (solutions of particular cases), but only gave the nucleus of the fundamental directions along which married love finds its realization.

Openness to the teaching of the magisterium, even when an infallible pronouncement is not involved, is fundamental to the Christian life. This magisterium, however, cannot be isolated from Christians' understanding of their faith and understanding of life, and cannot be considered independently of the understanding of the faith within the universal Church. In times of dynamic development and evolution, not only courage but also the gift of discernment is required. Progress in discernment is at the service of these values which the Church has always been diligent in protecting.

"Progress in discernment" is a very clear formula and, at the same time, extremely balanced even if for this reason it may be contrary to the ideas of some theologians who do not admit of "opinion" and much less of criticism. If Häring's discourse may appear rather harsh, perhaps because it is ambiguous, the problems which it presupposes are extremely alive and realistic ones. In all probability, nothing would have been solved, nor would it even have been possible to assimilate the doctrine of the encyclical itself, unless there had been a period of calm review and discussion.

The Quest for a Style of Criticism

After the initial period of bitter criticism and reactions some definite form had to be given to all the constructive research and criticism claimed in the name of the very magisterium of the Church and as the duty of the faithful and the theologians.

The original clear, penetrating judgment by Häring was modified in a later declaration which he issued in Rome in December 1968, and in which he said:

Given the attitude of the Pope as expressed during his trip to Bogotá where he said that theologians have the right to continue freely their research on birth control and that the discussion provoked by the encyclical will allow for a more profound knowledge of the will of God, the time of polemics and declarations against the encyclical has by now come to a close. Theologians should now go on to a serious study of the positive aspects of the Pope's teaching: authentic married love, the dignity of the person, the dignity of the married act, and responsible parenthood.

This declaration may give the appearance of being a return to an earlier position. In reality, this is not so, since basically it takes cognizance of the possibilities opened to theologians on account of their recognized right to free research. Moreover, research, and this is a confirmation of its sincere goodwill, does not intend per se going *against* the encyclical, but simply taking up again the themes of the encyclical from its own point of view. Häring is not saying that a long and more profound examination need necessarily arrive at conclusions which coincide with those of the encyclical. In fact, even for Häring, while saying that the time is past for *opposing* the encyclical, these same difficulties of which he had previously made an honest exposition, still remain. Continuing his interview, Häring in fact states:

I cannot conceal the fact that my difficulties regarding the authentic interpretation of the natural law, the openness of every marriage act to procreation, and the responsibility of the man and the woman before their reproductive powers remain unchanged. Nevertheless, I think that the contributions made by several of the episcopates represent a valuable step forward. Without minimizing the Pope's fundamental concerns, they have given rise to important distinctions and developments.

Häring has in mind here the declarations made by various episcopal conferences. These have been interpreted in a rather scandalous manner as opposition to, or criticism of, the encyclical. In reality, while they may not be interpreted as opposition, they certainly may be viewed as criticism, but only in the positive sense already mentioned. It is in this sense that they may be said to be linked with the responsible criticism and "progress in discernment" about which Böckle and Häring have already spoken. They do, however, introduce one original fact. Never before has any encyclical been so much criticized by entire episcopal conferences. To say that the episcopal explanations give perfect approval *sic et simpliciter* would be to ignore the facts of the matter. They do give perfect approval in the sense that they embrace those same basic concerns expressed by the Pope, but they do otherwise insofar as they do not simply repeat what the encyclical states. Moreover, why are there so many declarations if they were written for that sole reason?

In reality, what this episcopal "criticism" put forward, as Häring himself recognizes, was a suggestion and a direction for a "style" of criticism. Considering that the themes, concerns, and aims are common to all, whereas the means and interpretations are not, then a style or criticism is undeniably beginning to appear also in the Church. A better-planned culture, a possibility for more comprehensive statements, a diminished fear of reprisals, a far different idea of the function of authority—all these lead to a criticism which is naturally becoming more open and loyal, but no less respectful and constructive on account of these factors.

The outlines of this style will gradually become clearer and will be seen in detail case by case. The "case" of *Humanae Vitae* is one of the more significant of them. If, in fact, all that was said on Vatican Radio after the Pope's "Credo" of June 30, 1968 is completely true ("The Holy Father has put an end to the confusion which has been reigning for 5 or 6 years by cutting short all useless theological discussion"), it would provide a reasonable foundation for the remark which circulated half the globe and which was then reiterated by Jacques Chatagner in *La Lettre* of November 1968: "Let us now close all theological schools and they can send us a disc from Rome!" Matters, however, are slightly more complex and the positive, valuable function of criticism must be reinstated.

On the Sunday following the promulgation of the encyclical, the theologian Hans Küng was invited to speak on the program "A Word for Sunday" over the Swiss Radio. Küng in a few minutes outlined a possible style of criticism:

The encyclical is an authentic—that is, an *official*—statement of the Pope after long reflection. It would be illusory to think it might be withdrawn or corrected in the foreseeable future. It is a *fallible* statement. This is admitted also in Rome. To the surprise of Rome, it has come up against the unanimous rejection of world publicity outside the Catholic Church and has simultaneously led the Catholic Church into the most serious internal *crisis* of recent decades. Many in our Church—bishops, theologians, priests, men and women—are shaking their heads, are in doubt, perplexed; some openly and publicly oppose it. The Pope found himself compelled to defend his encyclical as soon as it had appeared, and in some countries the bishops' conferences are meeting to find a solution.

"Here—at this difficult time for the Catholic Church, when we are dependent, too, on the understanding and aid of Protestant Christians—we shall attempt to give a word of *help*. What is to be done? How will it continue?

First of all: it *will* continue. The Catholic Church, her renewal, ecumenical understanding, will continue. Do not be misled here; do not give up hope. As we have already survived many crises, we shall survive the crisis, and in fact—if I understand the situation rightly— even profit by it: the decisive argument for the Pope was that he felt bound by the official teaching, given out as definitive, of his predecessors and of the episcopate of the first half of the century. This will lead our Church to a critical overhauling of her ideas of authority, magisterium, doctrinal formulations, dogma, and particularly of infallibility.

Will not the Church's infallibility in future have to be seen in the light of scripture, not so much in particular propositions or doctrines as in the assurance of faith that the Church will be preserved— indeed, will be constantly renewed—by the spirit of God *in spite* of all errors, throughout all errors of popes, bishops, theologians, priests, men and women? These and similar questions we shall now have to ask, together with Protestant Christians, for whom, with the doctrinal contradictions in their own camp, the same questions must likewise be raised in another perspective. And this will be very useful in bringing us together.

Things will go on then. And *what do we have to do?* Three things:

1. We shall take seriously and respect the conscientious decision of the Pope.

2. We shall consider and loyally discuss his arguments. We shall therefore not suppress but express our misgivings, in order to help ourselves and the Church to reach clarity: and at the same time we shall not indulge in mutual condemnation, but try to understand one another.

3. Those among us who after serious, mature reflection alone, with wife or husband, before God, come to the conclusion that for the sake of maintaining their love and for the sake of the continuance and happiness of their marriage, they must act in a way which is different from what the encyclical lays down: those are bound in accordance with traditional teaching, even of the popes, also to follow their conscience. They will therefore not accuse themselves of sin when they have acted in good faith. But, calmly and secure in their conviction, they will share in the life of the Church and of her sacraments. They may certainly rely on the understanding of their priests.

The emergence of our Church from the crisis in a new maturity and responsibility will therefore depend on each one of us. And this is just what will help, not only our own Church, but all Churches.

The direction outlined by Küng is one of extreme loyalty and clarity and, at the same time, a courageous one. It is with an outlook like this that a line of conduct or a "style" of positive and constructive criticism becomes possible. We ought to note as well how an ecumenical outlook is given a clearly visible place in Küng's treatment. On one side the internal "crisis" of the Catholic Church could be overcome through a criticism which Evangelical Christians could teach Catholics. On the other, Catholics, by their criticism, could help Evangelical Christians overcome a series of well-founded doubts about authority, the magisterium, infallibility, doctrinal formulations, and dogmas.

A development in this style of balanced criticism, which is at the same time clear and unambiguous, was put forward by the Argentine theologian Jorge Mejia in *Criterio* of August 22, 1968. After speaking of the encyclical's intrinsic value, he asks himself:

From what has been said, should we conclude that the Catholic is to believe and be silent? St. Paul, unexpectedly, says the opposite: "I believed, and therefore I spoke (2 Cor. 4:13)." Are we to exclude all possibility of the faithful, in a situation like the present one, manifesting an opinion which is contrary to the teaching of the encyclical? In principle, the answer cannot be negative. If it were so, I fear that we would have arrived at the point of stifling every possibility of dialogue in the Church. However, to paraphrase the text just quoted from St. Paul, I think that as regards criticism we should start from a fundamental attitude of faith. Criticism, in fact, is not to be identified with outbursts of anger or disillusionment. On the contrary, so that criticism be acceptable in the Catholic communion, it must start with the principle of this communion.

Now the principle of this communion is the Pope. We begin by accepting that the Pope has the right and, in the last analysis, also the duty of expressing a teaching contrary to that which may be personally considered as true. Starting from there it must then be admitted that the attitude in the Church on this teaching has completely changed. It is no longer possible to remain aloof from this transformation which is now taking on a definite outline, and a loyal movement in this direction must begin. While this movement is progressing, however, I do not see why it is not possible to express one's own point of view in the right manner. It is to be done at the very heart of the communion and not at its edges. It may also be that someone has reasons for holding that in his personal case it is only right for him to make his opinions known.

The procedure one adopts here is important. The normal channel of communication for a Christian with his brothers or superiors is not the daily paper, the news magazine, television, or radio. In the paragraph (*Lumen Gentium*, No. 37) which the Council devotes to this subject, it is stated that the laity are to make known their opinions on matters connected with the well-being of the Church "through the agencies set up for this purpose." The same applies to clerics. . . . To occupy cathedrals, publish statements, and call press conferences cannot solve anything.

Doctrines may and must develop even after the appearance of the encyclical. The price of this progress is free discussion. By this I do not mean to say that the subject matter of *Humanae Vitae* is still the object of discussion. Personally, I think it is not. However, I think it is possible to express opinions on the encyclical and its arguments, which, nevertheless, safeguard sincere acceptance of the teachings put forward. For centuries theologians have discussed the interpretation of the dogmas of faith without having denied them on account of this. . . . I am sorry to have to say this, but absolute silence cannot be imposed, today more than ever, without perpetrating an act of persecution. Such a persecution, however, would kill the spirit of Vatican Council II, and the Church has far more responsibility in safeguarding this good than the uniformity of an army or cemetery.

The position of Jorge Mejia is extremely balanced and at the same time, realistic and theologically grounded. In fact, he brings down to the level of practical attitudes of criticism and discussion all of what has been claimed by others on a theological level and for theological reasons. Of great importance, then, is the principle affirmed by Mejia of the possibility of criticism made from within the "communion" and not from its periphery. This principle is full of practical consequences regarding what is likely to happen in the criticism of the encyclical. Much of the criticism held to be offensive and radical is, after all, made from within the ecclesiastical communion. This is a datum of fact which is far more objective and positive than the facile accusations of schism and heresy hurled at those who voice these criticisms.

A concrete example to illustrate this comes from the country which for some time has alarmed many within the Catholic Church: Holland. The reactions and the criticisms have been extremely strong and clear without half measures. Yet the Primate of Holland, Cardinal Bernard Alfrink, responded in an interview full of common sense and theological maturity to the special correspondent of *Corriere della Sera* in Holland on August 10, 1968. The Italian correspondent immediately introduced the problem by mentioning the customary fear of schism and heresy, and referred to the letter of August 4 which the Dutch bishops had addressed to their priests and in which, among other things, it was stated that "in the formation of conscience an authoritative place is to be given to the teaching of the magisterium, even if in this case the infallible magisterium is not involved." The Italian correspondent then objected:

But by affirming that in the last analysis birth control is a matter for the husband and wife, doesn't it seem that the declaration implies a solution to the problem which differs from that given by the supreme magisterium? Could not someone accuse the Dutch bishops of ambiguity or straight-out divergence for the lines indicated by the Pope? In other words, having admitted that they insist on this as their position, would not the Dutch bishops seem to desire to head toward a schismatic situation or, at least, a de facto separation of the Dutch Church from that of Rome on one of the more important doctrinal questions?

Unfortunately the mentality presupposed by this line of questioning is sadly inadequate in its understanding of theological and ecclesial problems, not to mention the last phrase in which the problem of *Humanae Vitae* is "one of the more important doctrinal questions"! The cardinal immediately replied by raising the discussion to a level which devotes much more attention to problematical points of theology and the real issues affecting the ecclesial communion which cannot be reduced to a question of insignificant skirmishes or less:

The time of schisms has passed. The position that the Pope occupies in the Church is clear, especially after the Council. It is not possible to remain in communion with the Church without the Pope. Even the Pope, certainly, can be criticized, but whoever has received a solid theological formation can never be in favor of a schism. If someone here among us has at times spoken of a schism, it has happened because some essential elements have been left out of consideration: for instance, that a notable part of the Church accepts the encyclical.

An equally theologically grounded ecclesial sense, as well as corresponding common sense, was shown by the Dutch Jesuit Fr. Blets of Amsterdam:

The Dutch Catholics are seeking dialogue with Rome and lament not having found as yet a common language. However, they look on Vatican resistance as a passing historical phenomenon. They believe in the Holy Spirit and his action in the Church. The reason that they do not want a schism is because by breaking with Rome we could become a new Christian sect. It would be like going back a century in history.

What is necessary, therefore, is criticism beginning from within and remaining within the ecclesial communion. In his rather radical criticism of the encyclical, Gabriel Arnaud in *Terre Entière* of October 1968 also recognizes this:

395

A schism is very unlikely. On one hand the criticism comes above all from within the Church: priests, theologians, and laity do not wish to abandon the Church but desire to change it even if sometimes they arrive at the point of temporally refusing to participate in its present institutional life. On the other hand, in spite of the pressures brought to bear by the Curia, the authorities will not dare launch a frontal attack against all adversaries by confronting them with the choice of either "submitting or getting out," because such an attitude would not enjoy the consent of the entire episcopacy—and certainly not even of its majority. The hope remains that a new Council would possibly find a solution to the crisis. The new Council, convoked and inspired collegially—that is, with the participation of bishops, priests, and laity on all levels—would reexamine the question of birth control and "natural law" as well as (and especially) authority, responsibility, and freedom in the Church.

"Not a schism but a Council." Is this illusion or realism? It would seem more realistic to favor the second. In fact, a true criticism cannot lead to a schism but rather to a deepening of dialogue in the Church, insofar as the Church is above all the community of "the hearers of the Word." True criticism is a common coming to awareness of the true meaning which the Word of God has today. A Council is nothing other than the Church in its role of listening to the Word in the community. Thus a developed criticism in a real ecclesial sense cannot lead to a schism but to a Council; that is, to a "self-criticism" of the Church itself, its institutions, its exercise of authority, and its methods of teaching and learning.

This criticism has already begun. Never before has it happened like this; and *Humanae Vitae*, coming after the experience of a Council, has been the underlying motive for it. As yet we do not have available detailed and thoroughly examined criticisms, but some are beginning to appear on single issues under discussion. This already indicates the possibility of further discussion. The Jesuit theologian Giovanni Blandino, a specialist in the biological sciences, commented on two particularly interesting points: Under what circumstances is the use of progesterone lawful, and what are we to say of its implications when used for solving the problem regarding population? These are two issues clearly prompted by the encyclical. Blandino treats them with the extreme caution of the specialist, with respect for the doctrine proposed; but within these limits he attempts to discuss themes which the encyclical has not closed definitively. In this sense his research is a useful concrete example of calm and constructive criticism:

An Example of Interpretation: the Use of Progesterone and the Population Problem

The encyclical *Humanae Vitae* takes up the doctrine of Vatican II (*Gaudium et Spes,* No. 51) on the twofold objective of the marriage act, an objective which serves to unite the husband and wife and a procreative objective. It also affirms that these two are inseparably connected and that consequently it is not lawful to attain the former objective by excluding the latter. The central point and the essential aim of the encyclical lies in this affirmation: "The Church, calling men back to the observance of the norms of the natural law, as interpreted by her constant doctrine, teaches that *each and every* marriage act must remain open to the transmission of life" (No. 11). Thus the use of contraceptives—and, more so, sterilization and abortion—is illicit even when the couple have valid motives for not desiring more children.

The line of reasoning used by *Humanae Vitae* is based on the classical doctrine of acts against nature: the marriage act which is not open to the transmission of life is against life. Therefore, it is intrinsically evil and may not be licit for any possible reason.

However, the encyclical adds that "the Church, on the contrary, does not at all consider the use of those therapeutic means truly necessary to cure diseases of the organism, even if an impediment to procreation, which may be foreseen, should result therefrom, provided such impediment is not, for whatever motive, directly willed" (No. 15).

The encyclical, like Vatican Council II, upholds the obligation of responsible parenthood. It upholds, that is, the obligation and licity of a birth regulation which is, at the same time, generous and prudent. However, as means for such regulation, it allows only the use of the rhythm method. The encyclical exhorts scientists to study methods for making the rhythm method more reliable and easier to use.

The encyclical *Humanae Vitae* is not a document of the infallible and irreformable magisterium. However, it is a document of the authentic magisterium of the Church, and calls for "loyal internal and external obedience" (No. 28). The Holy Father explicitly notes that "obedience, as you know well, obliges not only because of the reasons adduced, but rather because of the light of the Holy Spirit, which is given in a particular way to the pastors of the Church in order that they may illustrate the truth" (No. 28).

Although not infallible, it would be a mistake to underestimate the value of *Humanae Vitae* on the doctrinal level. Certainly this document does not increase the probability of the opposite opinion, but clearly diminishes it. The encyclical, however, does not take away from scholars the right and the obligation to continue their studies. On the practical level, then, the norm given by *Humanae Vitae* obliges all Catholics in conscience. We do not see how it is possible to deny that in practice it obliges also those Catholics who from personal study, continue to be convinced that the opposite norm is probably the correct one. We say "probably" because we do not believe that a serious scholar feels he could arrive at complete certainty, given only human intelligence, on such a difficult question demanding the evaluation of an enormous number of biological, psychological, and social factors.

Indeed, in arriving at a knowledge of the morality of an act, a Catholic has at his disposal not only the method of direct, personal investigation with his own intelligence but also, and principally, the guidance of revelation and the magisterium of the Church. A number of works seem to show a misunderstanding of this point. It is absolutely true that every man must act according to his conscience; that is, according to the moral judgment which he forms. It is fundamental to the Church's doctrine that if a person thinks an action is good, he does well in doing it (even if that action in reality is bad) and that if a person thinks an action is bad he acts wrongly in doing it (even if that action in reality is good).

But the question which interests us here is another one and precedes the former: it is the question of the formation of one's conscience; that is, how one may arrive at forming a judgment concerning the morality of a certain kind of act: for a *Catholic* the forming of one's conscience must be effected not only by directly considering the kind of act, by the use of one's own intelligence, but above all through the teaching of revelation and the Church; the teaching of the Church must determine a person's actions when it is an infallible teaching or even when, while not being infallible, it is proposed by the Church as obliging on all with no evidence to the contrary. Clearly all this does not apply to the non-Catholic.

From the pastoral point of view the encyclical and all other episcopal documents which followed it recommend comprehension, patience, and kindness to confessors with an insistence that is striking. The teaching of *Humanae Vitae* has an influence in two areas: (1) on the married life of couples who wish to live in a Christian manner, and (2) on population control carried out by governments and other agencies. With regard to the influence of the encyclical in the former area it is fitting to indicate briefly here some theological opinions which, in some cases, moderate the austerity of the general norm. While opinions such as these are not contained in *Humanae Vitae*, they still fall within the limits of its teaching.

According to many theologians the use of progesterone (Pincus and Rock's "Pill") is lawful in order to regulate the female cycle where this cycle is irregular. In these cases the use of progesterone is held to be lawful because it is taken as a therapeutic means to rectify an abnormal situation. The importance of the regularity of the cycle for the use of the rhythm method is evident. Also Msgr. Ferdinando Lambruschini, professor of moral theology at the Lateran University, when officially presenting the encyclical to the press, spoke of this lawful use of progesterone.

Various theologians consider the use of progesterone also lawful in the following instances: (1) in case of depressive phobia during pregnancy—obviously this concerns only the typically pathological state; (2) in case of rape; (3) in the case where a woman because of a serious health condition, cannot support another pregnancy and where she has a heedless and incontinent husband (this case and the preceding one are justified as legitimate defense); (4) in case of duties which are limited to certain days (for example, examinations) and which require a delay in menstruation which would otherwise weaken the person; (5) during the period of lactation.

For a complete moral judgment in all these cases it is necessary also to evaluate whether and to what extent the medications used may damage the woman's physical health and if these, besides having an anovulatory action, also have an abortive action.

A theological opinion of a completely different kind but of more general interest for the serenity of the married life of Catholic couples states that if a couple who have valid motives for not having further children and who have a fundamental desire to respect the moral law, commit an occasional fault through human frailty against the natural use of the marriage act, this fault does not constitute a grave sin, but is only a slight imperfection, and therefore the couple do not lose the grace of God. Certainly this much is clear: of all the possible unlawful sexual acts, intercourse is the least unlawful. Nor may we conclude with certainty that this fault is serious for the simple reason that it is against nature. Even according to traditional reasoning there can exist acts against nature which are only slight faults—for example, lying. Nor must we think that the more the gravity of a fault is stressed, the rarer it will become. It may perhaps bring about exactly the opposite effect, such as the neglect of the sacraments, carelessness with regard to sins and increasing their number.

I would like to observe that such a situation is not only injurious for the husband and wife but also detrimental to the children's up-bringing. The couple feel far from God in the very period when they must carry out their whole educative role. Perhaps they encourage the children to receive the eucharist but they themselves do not receive it and the children are aware of this. Also, their interior state of spiritual malaise often makes the husband and wife express themselves with a certain amount of bitterness toward religion, and this has a penetrating, corrosive effect on the children's religious formation. It is ideas of the kind mentioned above which are responsible for certain "gems" of reasoning contained in the old manuals of moral theology. For example, Merkelback (in *Quaestiones de Castitate et Luxuria*, 3rd ed., Liège, 1929, p. 58) says that if masturbation were to be forbidden as only a slight sin, many would seek to avoid the obligations of marriage and would not marry.

The theological opinions here have greatly varying degrees of probability. The first is highly likely (while requiring some clarifications concerning the extent of its application). The least likely in the present circumstances is the last. In this regard there is in the document published by the Austrian bishops on September 22, 1968, a passage which, while leaving things unclear for more reasons than one, is a very interesting expression of the thought of a group of bishops. The passage is as follows: "Finally we wish to recall attention to the fact that the Holy Father does not mention mortal sin in his document. If anyone, therefore, falls short of the teaching of the encyclical, he should not feel in every single case separated from the love of God and may, as a result, go to communion without having been to confession."

However, in every case further study is necessary, and an eventual clarifying statement from the ecclesiastical authorities is to be hoped for. We shall now pass on to outline more fully the influence which *Humanae Vitae* has had on the second area; that is, on population control in countries with a high birth rate and with serious problems of food, health, etc.

It is well-known that there have been many reactions to the encyclical, both favorable and unfavorable. It is important to note that the unfavorable reactions on the part of representatives of the political world, non-Catholic religions, cultural interests, etc., were motivated clearly and preeminently not by the influence of the teaching of *Humanae Vitae* on the married life of Catholic couples, but by its influence on population control. In the often violent criticisms against the encyclical it was said that the doctrine which the encyclical put forward made effective population control virtually impossible, considering that the rhythm method is difficult to apply, especially among peoples of a low cultural standing. The Church was accused of proposing, in the face of the painful problems of so many underdeveloped, underfed peoples, only utopian solutions which could not be realized in practice.

On the other hand, it was to be expected that the vast majority of the criticism would take this direction. Moreover, we heard from reliable sources that Pope Paul VI himself during his long and painful personal travail before publishing *Humanae Vitae*, hesitated principally on account of the seriousness of the population problems of underdeveloped nations.

To us it seems that while firmly maintaining the central affirmation of the encyclical—that only those marriage acts open to a generation are lawful—and employing traditional moral principles, it is perhaps still possible to admit the lawfulness of propaganda on the part of governments and other agencies for the purpose of promoting birth regulation.

It is true that in various magazines and newspapers, statements can be found to the effect that *Humanae Vitae* does not intend to interfere with the population-control programs being conducted in various states. Generally, however, there is no proof given to support these statements, or they are motivated only by a general kind of reasoning which is not always acceptable. We, however, maintain that a precise line of reasoning is possible.

The exposition of our opinion is the principal aim of this work. At the conclusion of this article we shall try to compare our conclusions with what the encyclical itself expressly states on population control (No. 17). We must state from the beginning, however, that we shall arrive at no state of certitude and we shall not be in a position to resolve the question as to whether our opinion is valid or not.

Premise. In the encyclical *Populorum Progressio* (No. 37) it was explicitly admitted that public authorities are allowed to ensure population control "through the diffusion of appropriate information and the adoption of adequate measures, while in conformity with the demands of the moral law and respecting absolutely the legitimate freedom of couples." No similar statement is to be found in an explicit way in *Humanae Vitae*. However, there is no reason to think that the Holy Father has changed his mind. Therefore, it can be said by way of confirmation of the Holy Father's thought that a government may lawfully appeal for birth regulation and disseminate information about the rhythm method if, for example, the people are beset with serious problems of malnutrition and hunger. Let us now consider two points:

1. The encyclical does not discuss the question whether, for a couple who do not have the means of feeding their own children (supposing that we are dealing with a condition of very serious poverty), it would be a greater evil to use contraceptives or to give birth to another child.

Could it be that the use of contraceptives in cases of this kind would be a lesser evil? Here a clarification is called for. We are not asking whether in these circumstances the use of contraceptives is lawful. The encyclical is explicit in this regard: it is unlawful. We are asking, however, whether such a procedure would be *less* unlawful than giving birth to children in serious conditions of poverty, just as it is certainly *less* unlawful than resorting to abortion.

2. If the answer to the foregoing question is positive, would it be lawful for a government, after having attempted to inculcate what was the right and worthy way for man to regulate births, to teach also those people who because of their own fault (at least objectively), were not disposed to use that method and if, by using contraceptives rather than giving birth to children in conditions of extreme poverty, it would separate them less from the moral law?

In this case, the government is not to desire or to approve the use of contraceptives. It would be a genuine case in which a person, in choosing between two evils desired by others but disapproved of and advised against by him, counsels that at least the lesser be the one acted upon. The encyclical *Humanae Vitae* in No. 14 speaks of an invalid argumentation based on the criterion of the "lesser evil." What is involved, however, is a case completely different from what is proposed in our question. The encyclical, in fact, discusses the case of a person who commits evil to avoid another evil, or, more exactly, who performs a morally bad action to avoid a harmful event.

What answers can we give to the foregoing questions?

According to us, the affirmative answer to the first question is the probable one. That is, it seems to us that if the conditions of poverty are truly extreme, the less serious fault would be the use of contraceptives, a more serious fault would be having another child, while the use of abortion would still be more serious.

The reasons which lead up to this conclusion are the following:

1. Above all, we must consider the aim of human life on earth in the divine plan. God created man to make man happy in his love. Thus, he wished that this happiness be not only his gift but also a conscious and free conquest on the part of man. For this reason God placed man in a period of testing, which is exactly equivalent to the length of our earthly life.

Thus, according to the divine plan—that is, according to the natural order—the end of procreation, per se, is not that of commencing another life which then ought to come to an end quickly (we said "per se" because procreation "per accidens" sometimes cannot accomplish the realization of its perfect end), but is that of beginning a life which can attain physical and psychic maturity in a truly human condition. To understand the natural order it is not sufficient to consider only a small part of the divine plan, but it is necessary to consider it in its entirety—which often is extremely complex. By a truly human condition we mean a condition that is not psychologically depressed and almost degraded but a condition in which a person succeeds in knowing, evaluating, and selecting spiritual values to a degree which is not too far removed from that which his natural faculties permit. It is only in this condition that the natural faculties of that person are not wasted and that he can undergo the test and overcome it according to the divine plan.

On the other hand, experience teaches us, and it is commonly affirmed in the Church's teaching, that in situations of extreme poverty a man can develop his intellectual and moral capacities in a harmonious fashion only with difficulty. From this it follows, we feel, that the procreation of children in conditions of extreme poverty is less at variance with the divine plan—or the natural order—than the use of the marriage act which is not open to procreation. These conditions of extreme poverty are a harsh reality for many men. Paul VI in *Populorum Progressio* (No. 45) says: "Today no one can be ignorant any longer of the fact that in whole continents countless men and women are ravished by hunger, countless numbers of children are undernourished, so that many of them die in infancy, while the physical growth and mental development of many others are retarded, and as a result whole regions are condemned to the most depressing despondency."

2. In the procreation of children in conditions of extreme poverty there are, then, facets of responsibility and culpability which the use

of the Pill does not involve. In fact, in the first case, prolonged distress as well as physical and psychic suffering in a human being will occur in all probability. This does not apply in the second case. The difference between the two cases is not of secondary importance but is of *primary* and *enormous* importance. We will not delay on this aspect because it concerns matters which we consider self-evident.

3. Furthermore, the birth of more children in conditions which are already severely limited lends to the suffering of those already born who, if it were not for overpopulation, would have been able to attain a higher human level.

In short, the following are the reasons for which we think it possible to conclude that the fault of procreating children in situations of extreme poverty is more serious than that of using contraceptive means:

(a) The first fault is no less opposed to the natural order than the second.

(b) The first fault brings about, in all probability, the physical and moral distress of the human beings who are born.

(c) The first fault is responsible for a decline in the physical and moral situation of those already born.

It is clear that abortion is still more serious because abortion is a direct action against an already existing being. In the case of abortion there are, as well, other more complicated and general motives which would be out of place and too lengthy to discuss here.

Some theologians could object to the foregoing conclusion and hold that to procreate children even in conditions of extreme poverty is less serious because existence is always a gift: "It is better to be than not to be."

This principle was frequently used by moralists in the past. But in recent decades, in the broadest and most indiscriminate interpretation, it has been denied, directly or indirectly, even by the popes and by the Council. Pius XII himself said that in certain cases the procreation of a child could constitute a fault. Vatican Council II and Paul VI have also often spoken of the obligation of responsible parenthood. In *Humanae Vitae* the Pope clearly affirms the legality, when there are valid motives, of the use of the rhythm method. All this would be meaningless if it were true that in any situation "it was better to be than not to be." What is more, if this principle were always valid, the use of abortion would be less culpable than the use of contraceptives.

What is the intrinsic reason that this principle is not unreservedly true? It seems to be as follows: Simple existence alone has no importance for man, but what is of primary importance is the material and spiritual level of that existence. When the number of individuals becomes too great, the material and spiritual level is lowered. The excessive increase in the number of individuals brings about a decrease in the level of their standard of living—a decrease which probably affects not only the individual but also the group. This would mean a less perfect realization of the divine plan for the material and spiritual elevation of man.

We shall now try to answer the second question.

Because we think an affirmative answer to the first question is probable, it seems to us that an affirmative answer to the second question is likewise probable.

The possibility of public authorities or other agencies being guilty of abuses as regards propaganda for population control must, however, be kept in mind. Unfortunately, these abuses are not an unlikely possibility but a frequent reality.

This propaganda can be diffused licitly only when there is a real necessity and when at the same time proportionate efforts are made to increase production and to improve health and education facilities. This propaganda cannot be disseminated for capitalistic interests either by using force or by spreading the practice of sterilization or the use of abortion.

In various countries ecclesiastical and lay figures have denounced the fact that governments devote disproportionate amounts to the campaign for birth regulation with the tacit aim of protecting those in socially privileged positions and avoiding the pressures of the popular masses. It is to be noted that some propaganda relies above all on abortive means such as the IUD (intrauterine devices).

We have the impression that if the Church, for the reasons outlined above, admitted the lawfulness of governments spreading population propaganda of the kind indicated in our second question, it would perhaps be advantageous for the Church to exert more influence against the kinds of propaganda for sterilization or abortion.

Possibly another psychological advantage would be gained: that of helping Catholic couples in the personal observance of the moral norm. Indeed, the norm indicated by the encyclical is an austere norm and, therefore, it is understandable how there appears a tendency among Catholic couples who labor under the pressure of personal difficulties to criticize the validity of that norm. Moreover, even in their criticism Catholic couples often make little effort to examine critically the difficulties which the norm causes for population control in countries where hunger is rampant. It is completely natural that when wanting to attack the validity of a norm one tries to do so in that area which seems to be its weakest point—its Achilles' heel. This procedure implies that if the couple can prove that the rule does not apply in the population sphere, they can also conclude that it does not apply to them as married people within their own personal life.

If the norm indicated by the encyclical had not rejected the lawfulness of effective birth control propaganda, then Catholic couples would have found it easier to recognize the validity of the norm and put it into practice. It is necessary to recognize the difficulty of putting an austere rule into practice if it does not spring from personal conviction but is based solely on motives from authority. Before this material was written, various theologians were asked for their views on these two questions. In general they were all in favor of the answers we gave, with the exception of one. This theologian held that it was necessary to reply in the negative to the first question, giving as his reason that the use of contraceptives is against nature while the procreation of children in conditions of extreme poverty is not.

We have already outlined what we think of such a view. It seems to us that the second fault is no less opposed to the natural order than the first. In any case, there are other more important reasons for judging that the second is more serious than the first. It is simply not true that sins against nature are always more serious than all other sins. For example, it is commonly admitted in moral textbooks that masturbation is less serious than adultery. We now have to compare our conclusions with what *Humanae Vitae* explicitly said about propaganda for population control.

In speaking of the serious consequences which would result if the lawfulness of contraceptives were admitted, the encyclical (No. 17) states: "Let it be considered also that a dangerous weapon would thus be placed in the hands of those public authorities who take no heed of moral exigencies. Who could blame a government for applying to the solution of the problems of the community those means acknowledged to be licit for married couples in the solution of a family problem? Who will stop rulers from favoring, from even imposing upon their peoples, if they were to consider it necessary, the method of contraception which they judge to be most efficacious? In such a way men wishing to avoid individual, family, or social difficulties encountered in the observance of the divine law, would reach the point of placing at the mercy of the intervention of public authorities the most personal and most reserved sector of conjugal intimacy."

Are these words meant to censure both the argumentation and type of propaganda which we have outlined above?

Thus, we are asking ourselves whether the argumentation we gave above has possibly already been considered and rejected by the theologians who prepared *Humanae Vitae*. We have reason, however, for thinking otherwise. As was said before, our reasoning was shown to some theologians; of these, at least three were members of all the Papal Commissions for the preparation of the encyclical and one most probably was directly involved in the final draft. Moreover, one of these theologians said this explicitly of his own initiative. For these reasons we are still uncertain as to whether our conclusions are unacceptable or not.

Thus, there is nothing else to be done except to put forward our findings for the consideration of theologians while waiting for further examination and, possibly, more exact indications and clarifications on the part of ecclesiastical authority. In his discourse to the faithful on July 31, 1968 at Castel Gandolfo, the Pope himself said that the encyclical "is not a complete treatment of what concerns human beings in the sphere of marriage, the family, the integrity of customs—an immense field to which the magisterium of the Church could and perhaps should return with wider embracing, more organic and synthetic aims."

If ever the various theological opinions and the reasoning outlined in this book were to be judged valid, or at least extremely probable, the central aim of the encyclical *Humanae Vitae* would remain intact. This is, according to the mind of the Pope, to indicate the norm of behavior truly worthy of man. However, the teaching proposed would become much less severe than it could have appeared to be at first glance.

The Possibility and Significance of Further Development

The reflections of Blandino were not explicitly intended to criticize the encyclical, but they were used as a *critique of* the encyclical; that is, a reflection on points which *should* still be discussed and those which *must* be discussed. When reading some theologians who are preoccupied with establishing the truth of the encyclical, one almost has the impression that the problems have been solved and that the only problem remaining is that of finding ways and means of having the solution accepted. It will be realized very quickly that if the word of the magisterium is accepted in the manner in which it was put forward, facing up to new problems or new aspects of a problem will be imperative, and the encyclical will of necessity become the subject of discussion. To affirm without any shadow of doubt that the encyclical is not to be discussed or criticized is to render a disservice to the magisterium itself. It would be as if its development had ground to a halt in time, blocking any further evolution it could undergo. Thus, one of the first technical examinations like that of Giovanni Blandino, which is balanced and respectful but still reveals problems that do not seem to have been entirely cleared up by the encyclical, is a gesture already to be followed in itself.

But is it undeniable that to conduct discussions on the encyclical will raise the prospect of an "evolution"? When a theologian hears this word, the whole complex of problems connected with the question of the *evolution of dogma* comes to mind. However, *evolution* here means a continuously developing understanding of dogma; that is, of truth. All dogmas have undergone this phenomenon—including, for example, the dogma of the Trinity. If we were to compare the faith of the apostolic Fathers, of Tertullian, or of Origen with respect to the Trinity, with what we hold and believe today, we would term their belief heretical or at least imperfect. The truth is to be found in what theological science, influenced by ever new cultural forms and by the needs of the community, has continued to clarify and deepen in the meantime. How will all this, however, come about in the future with respect to *Humanae Vitae*? Something can be done if we admit that there is room for reform in the document; that is, that there exists the possibility of a greater development of the doctrine.

There are those who deny the possibility of such development being produced by changes in historical realities, and thus in human attitudes. They exclude from the outset the possibility of scope for reform in the document. In this line is G. B. Guzzetti (quoted previously) who is opposed to the idea of the possibility of the document's being changed and emphasizes the truth of the papal statement. He says:

I fail to see how it is possible to deny or cast doubt upon the truth or the immutability of teaching of such a nature without casting doubt on or denying the very mission of the Church as a teacher in matters of faith and morals, and faithful messenger of Christ's doctrine. I see how it is possible, without compromising the mission of the Church, to doubt or reject the advisability of certain pastoral directives which were not presented as seriously binding in conscience . . . in the same way as it is possible for certain directives of a political nature. I see how, with a change in circumstances, certain amplifications of the natural or revealed law even seriously binding in conscience can also be modified without compromising the mission of the Church. One thinks, for example, of highlighting the penitential character of Friday, the preparation by fasting for Mass and Holy Communion, and so on. Since such modifications are made in the light of a given historical reality it is obvious that, with a change in the situation, they can or simply must change.

I understand how, in the light of new knowledge, teaching given as temporary, probable, or "safer" can change without compromising the mission of the Church. I see how teaching given by the Pope as personal opinion can change. I understand how teaching given by this or that bishop, by the Pope himself in one case, or in an isolated document, or to a group of faithful, and so on, can change without making the mission of the Church the subject of discussion.

But I do not see how it is possible to change—without compromising the mission of the Church—teaching given as the constant doctrine of the Church with explicit reference to the Church's role as authentic bearer of Christ's doctrine, with the assistance of the Holy Spirit, demanding internal and external assent, put forward again after extensive deliberation, mature reflection, heartfelt prayer, and with the aim of clearing up doubts.

Following these abundantly clear statements, Guzzetti later speaks "with respect to an eventual possibility of change in the position of Paul VI." He observes:

A few have declared that the doctrine of *Humanae Vitae* is true but is not unchangeable. Wherefore, it can happen that in the future it will be abandoned. In this connection it seems necessary to make the following point: if a stand which is true for today can be reformed, it should be a cautionary directive, a clarification of a legislative nature made by the Church, or teaching put forward as probable. The statement that a position proposed as teaching of a nonprovisional kind, explaining the nature of marriage, can be true today and changeable in the future, is a contradiction. We are faced, therefore, with a choice: either we say that the position of the encyclical is not doctrinal in the sense explained above or we say that it is already false today or we say that it cannot be reformed.

By affirming its unchangeability in this way one thereby rejects all possibility of development. The distinction made by Lambruschini is more subtle. Having said in the presentation of the encyclical to the press that it is not infallible, he could have given the impression that it could be modified. Therefore, in the comment already quoted, he makes a distinction which is not a simple play on words: "To say that the papal decision is not irreformable does not mean that it can be modified on the level of theological reflection or of public opinion when it is more or less skillfully led. The irreformable nature of the condemnation of contraception is not weakened but strengthened by the encyclical."

On the level of theological reflection or of "public opinion" it is not possible, therefore, to think of further evolution in the doctrine, at least in the sense of a deeper understanding, which would thereby create a certain feeling of impermanence in the present doctrine—which does not mean that it does not have any importance or that it puts the mission of the Church in doubt, as Guzzetti maintains.

There are, in fact, other specialist theologians who clearly see the possibility of a development and thus of a modification of the document. We note in passing that "development" refers to the document as it is, while "possibility of modification" refers to the document in its formulation of the doctrine. Clearly the two are connected.

Apparently, however, not only theologians are involved. Figures of high standing and responsibility also share the opinion favoring a development. This was brought out by the Danish press in the first few days of September 1968, and specifically by *Katholiek Nederlands Persbureau* of September 4. Here is given a declaration of Cardinal Michele Pellegrino, the Archbishop of Turin, who was in Copenhagen at the time when he held a press conference. From the communiqué issued afterward by the Danish agencies it could be taken that Cardinal Pellegrino had said that "the Pope's encyclical on birth control is not an infallible statement. Furthermore, he underlines the fact that the principles contained in documents of this type can be changed and that a future pope can express them differently. When the Pope declares his opinion in an encyclical, Catholics ought to accept it with respect. Nevertheless, they are free to decide what position to adopt." Probably these final statements were much more precise in Cardinal Pellegrino's original speech. The incompetence of some journalists and the synthesis made by the press has rather distorted the thinking of the cardinal, which we can only guess at in its completed form. The first statement, however, on the possibility of evolution was certainly not entirely invented by a journalist.

"The principles contained in documents of this type can be changed and a future pope can express them differently." The reasoning is developed along the line of logic that if it is not infallible, a document can naturally be reformed. We have seen that Lambruschini makes a more subtle distinction on this point. But that line of logic was followed instead by other theologians, as for example, Bernard Häring, in his article in *Commonweal* of September 6, 1968. He seems to look ahead to that future time conjectured by Pellegrino, and gives a less optimistic opinion as we shall see immediately. Furthermore, by admitting that Lambruschini recognized its noninfallibility, he seems to go farther by saying that a revision of the text is not to be excluded. This was not said by Lambruschini, but is perhaps only Häring's personal conclusion. Häring says:

Msgr. Lambruschini, the curial official appointed by the Vatican to explain the encyclical to the press, emphasized that it was not an infallible statement, and that the possibility of a revised statement, if new data appeared, could not be excluded. However, the tone of the encyclical seems to leave little hope that this will happen in Pope Paul's lifetime—little hope, that is, unless the reaction of the whole Church immediately makes him realize that he has chosen wrong advisors and that the arguments which these men have recommended as highly suitable for modern thought are simply unacceptable.

At this point Häring tries to support this possibility of revision:

Noninfallible but very authoritative statements of popes were in the past officially corrected only after a relatively long delay. Even when they were strongly criticized within the Church, the criticism became known only slowly. But the radical change which rapid communication has brought about in the modern world has created a totally new

411

situation for authoritative Church statements, which are not infallible. The dialogue with the rest of the Church, which formerly took decades to unfold, takes place now in a matter of days or weeks. No significant theologian can write or express his opinion on an important issue without its being known almost the same day by anyone in the world with enough curiosity to learn about it.

In the past things were different. It took centuries before the extraordinarily dangerous "teaching" of the direct power of the Pope over all temporal matters was rejected. It demanded courage for Friedrich von Spee finally to speak out openly and forcefully against the persecution, torture, and burning of witches, a practice which had been recommended and doctrinally justified by a very authoritative encyclical of Innocent IV. For a long time the moralists did not dare to explain that the castration of the Vatican choir boys was immoral, since it had strong papal approval. The Council of Vienna explained in 1311 that theologians who tried in any way to justify usury were to be "imprisoned in iron chains" for the rest of their lives. And as late as the eighteenth century, moral theology textbooks published in Italy had to print the warning. Pius IX's *Syllabus* lay undigested in the Church's stomach and in her relationship to the world until the *Declaration on Religious Freedom* and *The Constitution on the Church in the Modern World* of Vatican Council II.

The immorality of torture, which was justified for so many centuries by the popes, and practiced in their name, was condemned by a papal statement only after a long period of time. Pius XII declared unequivocally that it was against the natural law. The "Holy Inquisition" and "holy wars" could have been wiped out from the picture of the Church if the prophetic spirit and the courage to speak out openly with Christian freedom had been more highly valued in the Church. When the popes and their curial theologians so frequently and so emphatically defended temporal power and the Vatican States as a divinely commissioned right and a spiritual necessity, this critical Christian frankness should have been more in evidence. Not only those who denied the implications of "Thou art Peter," but precisely those who believe in the spiritual mission of the office of Peter, must keep in mind the warning of the Lord against an earthly conception of the Messiah: "Away with you, Satan; you are a stumbling block to me. You think as men think, not as God thinks (Matt. 16:32)."

Häring, then, foresees no revision within a relatively short space of time, but observes that from history it appears that repeatedly emphasized concepts, and those defended with theological arguments, afterward in fact were revealed to be either partially true or completely false. Perhaps he did not intend applying the meaning of this evolution also to *Humanae Vitae*. In fact, he does not reject the encyclical as such but has strong doubts about its arguments and, therefore, thinks that a revision will come about when criticism reveals the unfounded nature of these arguments. It is clearly impossible to make any forecast as regards the time when this will happen, even if the observations made by Häring on the staggering speed with which criticism these days spreads and penetrates can already give some extremely significant indications. How can a doctrine, however, put forward time and again with so much emphasis and authority, be developed from within?

It is interesting to note in this regard the thesis held by Prof. John Noonan of the University of Notre Dame in the United States. He was one of the 6 American members of the Papal Commission and reacted strongly to the publication of the encyclical, as we have seen. His thesis is all the more interesting insofar as he maintains in his voluminous book *Contraception* that the condemnation of contraceptive practices by the Church is not a thing of recent times. In the 500 pages of his book he compiles a summary of the doctrinal development in the Church from the early centuries till today.

Noonan shows that the condemnation of contraceptive practices can be retraced without a break to the first centuries of Christianity. Doubts began to appear only during the nineteenth century and have found a real theological formulation only in the last 40 years. Therefore, Noonan only uses for his own purposes those who speak of the constant and continuous tradition on which the papal decision as faithful to tradition is based. This contribution of Noonan is of even greater importance insofar as this constant tradition is referred to only in a general fashion while the same encyclical quotes in a special way the immediate predecessors of the present Pope. The theological and practical doubts are minimized insofar as they only go back to a time relatively close to ours.

This, however, is precisely where Noonan places his theological interpretation. He observes that Chrysostom, Jerome,

Augustine and the other Fathers would have been shocked if they had heard what theologians, even the most conservative, teach today on marriage. These Fathers taught, for example, that the marriage act during menstruation was a grave sin, that the marriage act was to be used only for procreation, and that only one position was permissible during the marriage act. It is obvious today that no one accepts these theses. Therefore, Noonan, after an accurate study of the theme of contraceptive practices and the motives which led to their condemnation, asks whether this absolute condemnation could not also possibly go the way of the other condemnations. While in other cases factors which permitted doctrinal evolution and theological reflection intervened, in the case of contraception this has not happened with the same ease. Moreover, approximately 40 years ago when the doubts and the reflection first appeared, tradition was systematically opposed to them, and when reflection was revived in our day it found itself face-to-face with an encyclical. Noonan, therefore, concludes:

Could it be that we are really dealing with something quite different from a kind of sacralization of the absolute value of the conjugal act? That we are really dealing with values peculiar to marriage, such as children, their education, the sanctity of life, the personal dignity of the marriage partners, etc.? In order to safeguard these values the Church has constructed a wall around them—a wall whose significance and function is relative to the times. But is it really quite impossible to demolish this wall when it is ending up by becoming a prison?

Here is the reason that Prof. Noonan has gone to such lengths to show that there has always been an aversion in the Church to contraceptive practices. He holds that this datum of fact does not contribute toward proving that contraceptive acts are truly against nature or against the divine law. Therefore, he admits that an evolution is possible which will overcome this difficulty by appealing to all those fundamental values of marriage which the encyclical *Humanae Vitae* wishes to safeguard by condemning interference of a contraceptive nature. As a result, Noonan said in a press conference immediately after the publication of the encyclical that "in the end it will be considered as another error of the Papacy, just like the medieval condemnation of interest on loan capital and the declaration made by Pius IX that the existence of the Papal State was the will of God."

A truly interesting fact is that *L'Osservatore Romano* of August 5–6, in an article signed simply "C," which bears the title "How to Read the Encyclical," and which wishes to contribute toward a correct reading of the papal document by suggesting the main lines along which the encyclical was constructed, affirms that "above and beyond personal and casual interpretations, which more or less faithfully reflect certain situations, we believe we have been able to affirm that the encyclical of Paul VI merits more attentive reflection than can be afforded by a necessarily hurried and perhaps also biased reading." For this it suggests a "deeper reflection" which

leads to the consideration of the document not as a stone of a mosaic taken out of its surroundings but together with the deposit of Catholic doctrine which the Church has inherited from Christ and from the apostles. This is so because the encyclical is precisely this: an act of the supreme magisterium of the Church which is an integral part of the deposit of faith.

This last affirmation goes on to say that

in the context of this doctrine it will easily be seen how the Catholic Church of the twentieth century cannot profess a faith different from that of the primitive Church or that of the apostolic community. In like fashion, the Catholic Church of the twentieth century cannot teach a complex of moral laws different from that taught by the primitive Church or by the apostolic community.

It is to be noted that here we have a declaration concerning the *identity* of dogma and moral teaching; an identity admitted by all, even if an evolution of dogma and therefore of moral teaching, is to be admitted along the lines we have mentioned.

The interesting principle, however, precisely because it is derived from the reaffirmation of the value of the encyclical as "an act of the supreme magisterium of the Church" and as an act of fidelity to the teaching of the apostles, is, besides that of *identity*, that of *progress* in the possession of truth.

In fact, it is said:

This principle of identity does not exclude legitimate progress in the

415

possession of truth and an increase in faith. But progress and increase in faith as a moral evolution are not open to intrinsic modifications. They hark back to the subjective and extrinsic aspect in the sense that, on the part of man and the community of believers, a deeper penetration of the truth contained in the sacred deposit of faith and revealed once and for all by Christ is arrived at gradually under the influence of the Holy Spirit and the safe guidance of the magisterium.

Certainly, the writer outlines this possibility of a *progressive forward movement*, which is to say that in this sense the doctrine put forward by the encyclical is a greater penetration of the truth "contained in the sacred deposit." But at this point those who admit of a certain possibility of change in *Humanae Vitae*, seeing that it is not infallible, can ask whether such a process in the theme in question is now finished. But they can only say that it is finished if the encyclical is infallible. If it is not, this means that it leaves room for continuation of "legitimate progress in the possession of truth and increase of faith."

Is this possible? The question goes far beyond the particular concern of *Humanae Vitae* because if one insists on saying that this encyclical is not infallible and yet cannot be modified, he will be forced to apply the same criterion to other documents which, like *Humanae Vitae*, do not enjoy a qualified theological characteristic like infallibility, but on the other hand do not enjoy the honor reserved to *Humanae Vitae*. And this could be dangerous for the future of the Church and also of humanity.

If the decision given by *Humanae Vitae* is not the final one, then this encyclical has brought a very positive problem into the spotlight; namely, that of asking how and in what sense a faith can evolve and be rendered more sensitive and less bound by historical and cultural factors. A reply to this question is of vital importance for being able to say whether a faith has any possibility of survival for the man of the future.

Therefore, it seems that the old problem has taken on a new face. It is curious that an encyclical which was considered by many to be conservative and to represent a step backward, re-proposes the problems completely anew. Thus we could agree with Norris Clarke, professor of philosophy at Fordham University, who said in October 1968, that

416

such a clear and immediate disagreement with the encyclical of a pope is unique in the history of the Church. More than we know, perhaps, this is a historical moment in which a crucial change has taken place. More than ever before, this is a serious beginning of the evolution of the dogma.

While knowledge of the full truth comes by way of "legitimate progress," a "serious beginning" to evolution also has a place. Perhaps now as never before this paradox has become apparent: while a restricted question makes us think fearfully of the final definitive statement, all other more fundamental questions have experienced a "serious beginning." Roma locuta, causa finita? From what has followed after Rome has spoken it would seem not. It seems that the declaration of Rome has virtually provoked the expression of everyone's ideas, even those who were previously silent.

Chapter 8 The More Serious Problems Are Left for the Future

Biological contingency, natural law, and the moral order

"Natural law" and "Christian doctrine"— the alternatives for theology

"Eros," sex, and sin: legacies of the past and present realities

Are we still Catholics? Church of authority and Church of conscience

The issues which have once again been brought to the fore by the encyclical cover a far wider range than originally intended —or better, the kernel of all these issues is already contained in the encyclical. This is not surprising; for even though the Christian "fact" is not an ideological system, it has nevertheless an interior logic, whereby, if even the smallest aspect of it is touched or moved slightly, the rest must immediately be adjusted to fit into line with it. It is also true, however, that in certain instances of the encyclical, not to mention the basic issues, the "casuistry" which in the last few years has been so abhorred even by Catholic moralists, has been resurrected. The procedure which has been adopted is to begin with either the problem that the encyclical leaves unsolved or a particular expression in the text and then attack the encyclical from within by using this Trojan horse hidden between the lines. In *Il Regno* of September 1, 1968, Renzo Franchini, after giving two examples of this procedure, observes:

These two indications are sufficient to open up an interminable series of very human questions which casuistry, however, can obfuscate in perfect pharisaical fashion. This continuous, lamentable attempt to lead consciences astray is unquestionably a cure worse than the very evil which it attempts to avoid. This is not to deny the ethical validity of casuistry; it is simply to hope (today more than ever) that it will be supported by a strong moral force which allows it to develop into the art of choosing and not of merely dispensing. Prescinding from the theoretical discussions which are always possible but hardly of any concrete help when it comes to living and not just discussing—how should the Christian act who does not want to accept this self-righteousness of conscience couched in various legalistic loopholes?

In fact, a casuistry like the one disapproved of here would not only lead consciences astray by removing the possibility of their making a mature choice but would also entertain a far wider issue, which lies at the basis of the point made or reopened by the encyclical, hidden behind the legalistic issue. The only way in which consciences will not be distorted by the subtle game of legalistic casuistry is, as Dr. Scherer has already observed in his speech at the *Katholikentag*, by "discussion on the encyclical which will give us the opportunity to train ourselves in dialogue, on which so much is being said in the Church. Even in the future, so it seems, we shall have no more effective resource than this."

The best resource for the future is that offered by dialogue, but only if it centers on the fundamental theme of the encyclical and deepens those delicate points which the encyclical has challenged. Here we shall only dwell on some of those issues which appear to be more urgent and important. They arise precisely from within the very fabric and on the basis of the encyclical and then branch out to issues farther afield.

Biological Contingency, Natural Law, and the Moral Order

This is the first particularly serious element to emerge from the doctrinal fabric of the encyclical. This fabric is composed of two intersecting threads: the strictly theological contained in Nos. 7 and 8 of *Humanae Vitae*, and that based on the concept of "natural law."

On reading the encyclical it will be found that this theme emerges on several occasions, and as is generally admitted, it leaves no room for doubt as to the encyclical's precise intention of deducing from it the conclusion that all contraceptive methods are to be excluded. Whereas on the strictly theological theme the agreement has been unanimous, the second theme provoked a debate which shows no signs of abating even after the publication of the encyclical.

We may note the following texts of particular interest on this topic:

In the task of transmitting life, therefore, they (the couple) are not free to proceed completely at will, as if they could determine in a wholly autonomous way the honest path to follow; but they must conform their activity to the creative intention of God, expressed in the very nature of marriage and of its acts, and manifested by the constant teaching of the Church (No. 10).

God has wisely disposed natural laws and rhythms of fertility which, of themselves, cause a separation in the succession of births. Nonetheless, the Church, calling men back to the observance of the norms of the natural law, as interpreted by her constant doctrine, teaches that each and every marriage act must remain open to the transmission of life (No. 11).

That teaching, often set forth by the magisterium, is founded upon the inseparable connection, willed by God and unable to be broken by man on his own initiative, between the two meanings of the conjugal act: the unitive meaning and the procreative meaning. Indeed, by its intimate structure, the conjugal act, while most closely uniting husband and wife, capacitates them for the generation of new lives, according to laws inscribed in the very being of man and of woman. By safeguarding both these essential aspects, the unitive and the procreative, the conjugal act preserves in its fullness the sense of true mutual love and its ordination toward man's most high calling to parenthood (No. 12).

Hence, one who reflects well must also recognize that a reciprocal act of love which jeopardizes the disponibility to transmit life which God the Creator, according to particular laws, inserted therein, is in contradiction with the design constitutive of marriage, and with the will of the Author of life. To use this divine gift destroying, even if only partially, its meaning and its purpose is to contradict the nature both of man and of woman and of their most intimate relationship, and therefore it is to contradict also the plan of God and his will. On the other hand, to make use of the gift of conjugal love while respecting the laws of the generative process means to acknowledge oneself to be not the arbiter of the sources of human life, but rather the minister of the design established by the Creator. In fact, just as man does not have unlimited dominion over his body in general, so also, with particular reason, he has no such dominion over his generative faculties as such, because of their intrinsic ordination toward raising up life, of which God is the principle (No. 13).

As can be seen, the encyclical's manner of proceeding follows a strict, inner logic based on an understanding of the "divine plan inscribed" in the laws of life, seen as manifestations of the divine will that man may neither oppose nor interfere with for the sake of frustrating it.

The encyclical, however, foresees an immediate objection which can be raised and answers it in No. 16 where it affirms the licitity of employing the infertile periods:

To this teaching of the Church on marriage morals, the objection is made today, . . . that it is the prerogative of the human intellect to dominate the energies offered by irrational nature and to orient them toward an end conformable to the good of man. Now, some may ask: In the present case, is it not reasonable in many circumstances to have recourse to artificial birth control if, thereby, we secure the harmony and peace of the family, and better conditions for the education of the children already born? To this question it is necessary to reply with clarity: The Church is the first to praise and recommend the intervention of intelligence in a function which so closely associates the rational creature with his Creator; but she affirms that this must be done with respect for the order established by God.

The text is very interesting because it asserts that the Church does not hold the practice of birth regulation as an offense against the moral order, but states at the same time "this may not be done by either opposing or avoiding "the order established by God." This "order," then, is given by the "particular laws" which God has "introduced" in relation to the "design constitutive of marriage" (No. 13). More concretely:

In relation to the biological processes, responsible parenthood means the knowledge and respect of their functions; human intellect discovers in the power of giving life biological laws which are part of the human person (No. 10). While a rather general statement on the "law of nature" is more or less generally accepted, the real objections begin rearing their heads when reference is made to "biological laws which are part of the human person" and which then become "the creative intention of God, expressed in the very nature of marriage and of its acts" (No. 10).

It is for this reason that the encyclical is said to take the tone of "biologism" and the theological reasoning based on this biologism, which in turn gives rise to what may be called a "mythical" vision. Mention has also been made, on a harsher note, of "another Galileo case" on account of the encyclical's invasion of territory where the strictly religious magisterium, although possessing a certain competence, cannot pretend to possess it completely. Also bound up with this problem are the concepts of nature, evolution of nature, and intervention into nature. Mention has also been made of a confusion apparent in the encyclical between "revealed" elements and "anthropological" elements.

It is interesting to note at this stage, the criticism made by Marc Oraison, who is both a doctor and a priest, widely known for his studies and publications. In *Le Monde* of September 7, 1968 he made a clear, general summary of the present state of affairs. His article bears the heading "The Need to Look Clearly." He initially notes that after a few months the essential problems are now beginning to become clearer. He adds that now is also a good moment to lay them out clearly and simply, and to strip them as far as possible of anything resembling "pious" or metaphysical verbiage. He then goes on to observe that "a certain number of reactions seem to indicate that those who express them cannot bear the thought of imagining that there are disputable issues in the encyclical"; and he mentions the attempts which have been made (which we have also noted) to prove that "even if the encyclical is not infallible, one must act as if it were and reflect on it no farther." He also alludes to the accusations leveled against theologians, doctors, and psychologists for their criticisms, and the strong pressure brought to bear by bishops on dissenting priests. As a consequence Abbé Oraison has this to say:

Nobody any longer understands just what is happening. The authorities inform us that the encyclical is not infallible, but one should act as if it were. What pagan, magical idea of the Pope is this? What a sad reflection on their faith and of the idea they hold of the Church and its organization. Some react with a "holy terror" as if the Pope were a "half God, half man," along the lines of the oracles of Delphi or elsewhere.

Oraison also quotes the case of the first assembly of the apostles at Jerusalem reported in Acts (chapter 15), which gives an entirely different picture of the relation existing between the apostles, the community, and Peter.

We must discover, then, the central problem and forget about this holy terror of criticism. Oraison hence asks:

What, then, is the point under discussion? Are contraceptive methods, which mean more than just the Pill, against nature? Approximately 80 percent of theologians say No; the other 20 percent say Yes or are uncertain. Hence, the controversy is over the concept of "nature," and not over the general idea that human love must tend toward the good, which I think would be admitted by all. Now, by definition, nature is precisely that which is not "supernature." It is what we can know about the world and human reality without revelation. It is not *explicitly* revealed. It should not be a matter for surprise, then, that a document which makes many of its statements on this level, will find that these statements are liable to be disputed. I do not see why this should lead anybody astray or menace "faith in the Church." Exactly the opposite is true. By wishing to palm off what is not revealed as revealed, one puts the Church, the successor of Peter, and the successors of the apostles in a bad light, and this leads the men of our age to dissociate themselves from it.

The encyclical has been referred to as a "new Galileo case." This is not altogether false for, in many ways, the problem is the same: in the name of a "comprehensive view" in which theology properly speaking was confused with cosmology, it could not possibly have been admitted that the earth is in orbit. . . . Likewise, in the name of a comprehensive view of the notion of nature, which in fact takes us back many centuries, the achievements of modern anthropology could not possibly be admitted in the present document. This is where the confusion begins.

Marc Oraison repeats a question that the theologian Hayen had already asked in *Informations Catholiques Internationales* of September 1, 1968: "Is it so certain that every contraceptive practice dissociates love from life, and implicitly rejects creation?"

Oraison observes that the root of the question lies here, and states:

The competent reply to this question must not come from theology as such, but from anthropology. If anthropology in answer to this question were to reply, as in fact it does, "Not necessarily in itself, since it depends on the manner in which contraception is employed, and hence on the meaning given to it," then moral theology's task would simply be to determine the expression of this "manner" when placed alongside the demands of the gospel.

For Oraison (but let it be noted that it does not apply to him alone), the difficulty springs from a type of reasoning used by Gustave Martelet, one of the principal collaborators on the encyclical. This difficulty may be summed up as insufficiently distinguishing between what is "revealed" and what is "anthropological," which in turn leads to a confusion that forces one to reject the anthropological aspect. Oraison then observes that the direct result of this is that one slips into a subtle casuistry—"licit and illicit" does not mean "allowed or forbidden"; the Pill is condemned, but not those who use it. Oraison concludes in a rather brusque way: "But these subtleties are no longer acceptable to a man of today."

Martelet himself, however, faces these objections of the confusion between the revealed and the anthropological and between the encyclical's "absolutism" and the "biological contingency" on which it is based, and defends the encyclical against them. In his article in *Nouvelle Revue Théologique* of December 1968 he treats the theme "Biological Contingency and the Truth of Man," taking cognizance of the fact that

the strongest objection which can be leveled at the encyclical is that it *absolutizes* natural functions which, on at least two counts, are relative. Not only is the ovarian rhythm in many cases quite capricious, but moreover the very existence of such a cycle is purely contingent. How can the value of a *norm* be attributed to such a relative being which is in turn enclosed within a series of others which simply multiply the contingency of each of these beings? In our time there has sprung up a new "danse macabre," not of mortality on its imaginary fifteenth-century background tapestry, but of contingency on the background of the objective sciences of the twentieth century.

In fact, the very existence of the galaxies and the stars, the solar system and the moon's orbit around our planet, is a contingency. The cooling of the earth and the formation of its primeval waters is a contingency. The appearance on the earth of the first syntheses leading to the slow evolution of life from bacteria to the diplodocus is a contingency! To restrict ourselves to man in this rapid evolution of the world's universal contingency, we could even say that man's upright stature is also a contingency. The liberation of the forelimbs for the purpose of learning is a contingency. The decrease in size of the face and the cortical development which led to the covering of the anterior cerebral formations, be they vegetative or motor, is a contingency. Likewise, the powers of thinking and speaking are a contingency. The genetic code is all the more a contingency. "The instructions necessary for the synthesizing of the component cellular contents of DNA [deoxyribonucleic acid] in the form of linear sequences of four chemical roots" (quoting J. Monod, *Leçon inaugurale* of November 3, 1967 to the College of France) is a contingency.

The hormonal system and the cerebral hypophysis are no less a contingency. In a word, man himself is a contingency (the author of Ecclesiastes would have said "vanity"), especially in his strictly biological makeup! "It is not necessary that the whole universe rise up in order to crush him—a gas, a drop of water, are enough to kill him" (J. Monod, *ibid.*). On the other hand, this very "drop of water" or the salt or sugar levels which either support life or put it in mortal danger are a contingency. The duration of pregnancy and the woman's cycle are a contingency. Of the hundreds of ova, that proportion which can be fertilized and which, in fact, will be fertilized by the millions of spermatozoa which are emitted, is a contingency.

This merry-go-round of contingencies of which man is made can go on and on to the point of making us dizzy. Yet, from this formidable totality of relative events, as well as from the depths of this galaxy of improbabilities, which is what life in the cosmos amounts to, there has emerged a meaning or at least one questionable fact: man himself—this integral, living product of a series of chance events continually following one after the other; "the product of an incalculable sum of fortuitous events" (*ibid.*, p. 27). Is man to say "he should despair? Should he refuse a science which has burdened him with all these notions?" (*ibid.*, p. 28). We say that he certainly should not. This prodigious accumulation of chance cases has made possible not only "the odyssey, andromeda, or the passion according to Matthew" (*ibid.*, p. 27) but even Homer, Racine, and Bach themselves; in a word, every human being. For each one of these chance cases, myriads of cells, each possessing a number of elements which is great enough to fill the heavens, form morphological and functional complexes whose permanent integration guarantees man not only the biological power of living but also the quite human ones of thinking, speaking, willing, loving, acting, and hoping.

Yes, human *contingency* is truly infinite, but since it is also the terminus of an immense adventure of improbabilities, it is the contingency of *man*. If it is not necessary that "the whole universe rise up in order to crush him" with the weight of its conditioning factors and infinite probability, then "when the universe is crushing him, man will still be more noble than what is killing him because he knows that he is dying, but of its advantage over him, the universe knows nothing." Pascal then concludes in a perspective which is too exclusively intellectual in appearance but which in fact intimates the totality of human *originality*: "Hence our dignity consists in thought. It is this which we must take as our point of departure, and not space and duration which we may not succeed in surpassing. Let us work, then, to think well—this is the principle of morality" (*Pensées*, ed. Brunschvicg, No. 348).

Culture is coming to be more and more characterized by a growing respect for man's contingency. The more man discovers his fragility, the more he feels himself to be respectable. A sense of the human demands absolute respect for the fragility of its greatness. In this way man overcomes the temptation to contempt with which he risks enclosing himself, and enters into a "veneration of man" without which there will never be a planetary ethics of the human.

For this reason, the Council explains, "whatever is opposed to life itself, such as any type of murder, genocide, abortion, euthanasia, or willful self-destruction, whatever violates the integrity of the human person, such as mutilation, torments inflicted on body or mind, attempts to coerce the will itself, whatever insults human dignity, such as subhuman living conditions, arbitrary imprisonment, deportation, slavery, prostitution, the selling of women and children, as well as disgraceful working conditions, where men are treated as mere tools for profit rather than as free and responsible persons—all these things and others of their like are infamies indeed. They poison human society, but they do more harm to those who practice them than to those who suffer from the injury. Moreover, they are a supreme dishonor to the Creator" (*Gaudium et Spes*, Nos. 27, 3). Martelet also quotes here No. 26 of the same conciliar constitution and then concludes:

In short, the deeper the culture, the more it respects man's extreme fragility. In this way man's biological condition is integrated with this effective respect for man. When one thinks, speaks, and acts in this fashion, one is not espousing naturalism. One is recognizing the concrete conditions necessary if all that is human is to have a beginning. To omit this in theory and especially in practice, is to forget that man is not the highest or even the sole value in the universe unless he expresses himself in a manner which, at first sight, betrays him. I am obliged to respect the biologically destructible human being; but I am not obeying the biological, but the human. The two things are, however, so profoundly connected that not to respect man in his concrete conditionings is to injure him in his very person.

It would be difficult for anyone not to agree with Martelet's reasoning so far. In fact, it is precisely from reasoning such as this that many hold, as a consequence, that to exclude all contraceptive methods without exception is to injure man in his very person. Martelet is well aware of this since it is from these strictly theological reflections that *Humanae Vitae* initiates the reasoning process which leads to their exclusion. Martelet, therefore, continues his reflections by applying these considerations directly to the realm of sexuality. He says:

These considerations must now be continued in the realm of sexuality where there are found to be contingencies as basic and as structurally vital for the human person as sexual dimorphism, the hormonal system, the ovarian cycle, and all the genitality which married love incorporates in its language. The teaching of the Church, which here as elsewhere is an axiology and not a system, consists in bringing attention to the significance of contingencies such as these and thereby safeguarding men and women from possible self-contempt which they could be led into by knowledge, strength, and enjoyment, but also by suffering and a type of deviant humility. While Church teaching recognizes that the couple is responsible for its fertility and never questions the obvious right and duty they have of intervening in this sphere for their own good (Nos. 16, 2, 24, 37), it does lead them to a respect for themselves and for the true meaning of love.

This teaching states: The exercise of the powers which the couple possess in married union is to be measured in human terms by the respect that the couple should bear for the life contained in their love. It urges men to consider the disasters which can result from an inhuman type of intervention which breaks the *golden rule* which we spoke of. This golden rule, however, is not primarily the structure of the cycle; *it is the duty to itself which love recognizes of not undertaking anything which could lessen its life-giving powers.* The encyclical appeals along these lines to "insurmountable limits" (Nos. 17, 3) which are of an organic nature and therefore contingent. They are insurmountable, however, only if in them there is perceived the letter of a law of which love alone can discover the meaning in order to freely appropriate this law for its own ends. No longer, then, is the contingency of nature presented as a norm for love; rather, love itself discovers in this contingency which is man the respect due to human existence from its very origins. From this respect it then makes its law.

A message such as this clearly presupposes that the human conscience rediscover the meaning of man's structures at the very heart of his projects and that man integrate his biological contingency with the human qualities of his aims or, as the encyclical says, that "human intellect discover in the power of giving life, biological laws which are part of the human person" (Nos. 10, 2). Doubtless it is absolutely true that the integration of the biological with the human is human only to the extent that man discovers in it a good, worthy of himself. To do this rightly in the area now under discussion requires a still deeper understanding of the significance of anthroposophy which is at present undergoing growing pains. It will not come about, says the encyclical, by despising the significance of the structures which outline man's contingency. On the contrary, the humble conditions for true greatness are to be found there. An objective element of civilization cannot be seen in contraception as such. Rather there is an unconscious negation of it.

In its very structure, in fact, contraception is directed *against* a life-giving power. . . . As a means of opposing the duty of giving existence to a life—a duty which must simply be carried out—contraception is of itself a disorder in love's primordial relationship to life. This disorder does not always necessarily take extreme forms, but does not exclude them on account of it. In fact, this disorder potentially pre-contains them all. Therefore, the man who refuses to judge contraception from the very beginning as an anomaly, is exposing himself to the risk of not being able to dominate its harmful effects later.

The inordinate character of contraception is not in *the* intervention of man as such, but rather it is *this* particular intervention which destroys the relationship existing between the loving union and its life-giving powers. Nature and the laws which contraception transgresses, therefore, are nothing other than the *pure condition of love.* Respect for them is respect for love itself and the human principle in the world. To agree to assume this respect is hence to fulfill oneself, not to lessen oneself, so that the encyclical can say: "Man cannot find true happiness, toward which he aspires with his whole being, other than in respect of the laws written by God in his very nature—laws which he must observe with intelligence and love" (No. 31). When understood at this anthropological level on which it rightly belongs, the rejection of contraception is not a lack of appreciation for any of the human values found in knowledge and love.

Martelet then faces the problem that

the bond which unites the expression of love and the gift of life is not an absolute but a partially rhythmic one, and therefore is not *normally* present on every occasion. Since it varies from subject to subject, this rhythm, therefore, follows certain laws and it is hence possible to speak of a disrupted cycle. This is a vital point. It signifies that the unity of love and life which is by principle a partially rhythmic unity can become a real anomaly when it occurs outside of all rhythms. The rhythm is recognized as frequent, and possibly it will become gradually even more so. In any case, the burden of a disrupted cycle may not be left solely on the shoulders of a person's freedom. Therapy also has its role to play here. Its raison d'être is the fact that *normally* the encounter between love and life is not the constant law of married life. To attempt to reestablish a real balance so that the sole expression of a love's fruitfulness is derived from the normality of the cycle is not the same as practicing contraception.

Here Martelet has foreseen the difficulty voiced in several fields by those who consider the recognition of the therapeutic use of contraception and the use of infertile times as a subtle subterfuge.

Martelet therefore quotes No. 15 of the encyclical on this point. Martelet then goes on to affirm that

the idea of nature which to some appears inhuman at first sight, is really liberating. By introducing the notion of normality it limits the areas in which freedom and technology may be applied in such a way that freedom neither avoids its responsibilities before technology nor underestimates the legitimate help it can offer.

Martelet's article is an excellent commentary designed to justify the encyclical's reasoning. In the first text quoted it deals with the encyclical's theological reasoning as such, and in the second there can be seen an insistence on reasoning which is more strictly philosophical, dealing with the serious objection directed against the concept of "law of nature." Martelet's commentary is undeniably provocative, and only if it is read in its entirety can a wide-enough idea be obtained of the atmosphere of thought in which it was formed. It may be noted, however, that the entire reasoning is based in every case on *probabilities* and *suitabilities* even though these probabilities and suitabilities may at times acquire a very convincing force, the weight of which is at least equal to that of the opposing arguments. The whole issue, however, rests on the fact that no matter how suitable the motives and the reasons may be, when they are not really compelling they always leave a margin for interpretation and discussion. This could easily be demonstrated by individually examining Martelet's arguments, which, we repeat, are not to be despised.

Since they are based on theological reasons of convenience and on philosophical reasons taken from an anthropological perspective, it is easy to see why no one less than a well-known philosopher like Nicola Abbagnano, professor at the University of Turin, has taken up the same arguments from the philosophical point of view and contrasted them with the concrete situation of humanity and the various problems this involves. It must be admitted that conscious as Martelet is of the reality of man, he nevertheless gives the impression at times of having before his eyes a "universal humanity," so that humanity with all its concrete, present problems in all their extreme difficulty and harshness almost disappears.

In any case, Abbagnano faces the question from a purely philosophical point of view, and it is interesting to note that this contribution published in *La Stampa* of August 7, 1968 provoked a controversy with the Vatican newspaper which directly replied to the philosopher in one of those rare discussions held directly between the organ of the Holy See and an author. Abbagnano confronts the subject as follows:

The philosophical principles which inspired Paul VI's encyclical *Humanae Vitae* are easily recognizable because they are openly stated in the encyclical itself. They may be summarized as follows: (1) The natural law and the divine law coincide. (2) The natural law orients the sexual union to the procreation of offspring. (3) Hence every plan, project, or direct artifice to avoid the natural effect of sexual union —namely, the procreation of offspring—is against the divine will. The first thesis is an extremely ancient one of pre-Christian origins. It was expounded and defended in all its rigor in ancient Stoicism which presupposed as a principle of moral life the duty of conforming oneself to nature. By means of the Fathers of the Church and medieval Scholasticism, this principle entered into the Christian tradition and it was adopted as the basis of canon law.

It is sufficiently obvious that, if taken literally—that is, in its full rigor—every direct intervention by man for the sake of modifying or controlling the effects of the natural law would need to be considered as a rebellion against the divine will. In every case, not only birth limitation (whatever the means used, including the Ogino-Knaus method) but also the continuous struggle undertaken by man against sickness, death, famine, and evils of all kinds which assail him, there would be rebellion against the workings of the cosmic order willed by God.

As for man, he would have already disappeared from this earth many thousands of years ago (presuming he could have appeared) unless he had done in every sphere of activity exactly what Paul VI's encyclical condemns in the field of the marriage union: to foresee, plan, project, and prepare for himself in advance, ways of fighting the evils of nature—cold, bad weather, hunger, sickness, and the continual threats which nature hangs over his head at every moment. In no field can man afford to refuse to use the only effective weapon at his disposal, which consists in foreseeing the probable effects of the natural laws and regulating his behavior accordingly.

A refusal of this kind would be equivalent to committing suicide. There is no doubt, from the enormous amount of information available on the subject, that the indiscriminate multiplication of births which today is becoming a worldwide tendency, is one of the greatest dangers which the modern world faces. This proliferation is similar to what cancer is for the organism: a disordered and uncontrolled multiplication of cells which results in the death of the whole organism.

When we consider the moral side of the problem, further doubts and difficulties emerge. If the procreation of offspring is the essential aim of marriage, marriage itself (as Kant noted) is morally, hence also juridically, null when this procreation does not occur and is not envisaged as possible.

If the purpose of sexual union is procreation, two persons who come together are only *means* for the preservation of the species; that is, they do not have the value and dignity of *ends*. Correctly speaking, they are not persons but solely instruments which "the genius of the species" (which Schopenhauer spoke of) employs for his own purposes. For a human being to ask another to unite with him solely for this purpose would hence mean that he implicitly or explicitly considers the other as an instrument; that is, he reduces him to the level of a thing. That which grounds the dignity of the persons in the marriage union is their free choice and the project of a life in common in which both partners have a value not simply as means but also as ends.

If one outlaws family planning, matters become even worse from the children's point of view. A child which is born by chance, who is not desired or is unwanted, for whom there are no means available of saving him from deformity or a premature death, or of giving him an upbringing or a reasonable education, undergoes a condemnation which is unjust and outrageous for a human being. Nor can it be ignored that the number of induced abortions, illegitimate births, and abandoned children is growing at an increasing rate and that it is of little comfort to make an appeal for chastity, which "nature" itself more often than not, rejects.

Nor can the fact be ignored that sexual unions do not occur solely within the realm of valid and successful marriages and that it is morally unjust that a human being should be brought into the world and given a difficult existence just because two other human beings capriciously happened to meet each other. In theses cases the two do not perceive the dignity of the human being in the child but only the accidental, uncomfortable, and even threatening effect of an act which was only intended as an appeasement of a momentary need. On the other hand, the sexual union of two persons who love each other is the final and not instrumental expression of their love, and only for this reason does it enrich and integrate their moral personalities. Only deliberate, planned procreation safeguards the dignity of the person brought into the world as well as that of the couple.

It is clear that it is for science to pronounce on the effectiveness and safety of contraceptive methods. There are and there will be research, discoveries of new methods, verification, improvements, and discrediting. It is certain, however, that the use of such means must be left exclusively to the conscious choice of the individuals themselves—to the consciences, duly enlightened on the fundamental data of the problem, of the persons responsible. Neither the state nor the Church nor any other authority may today vaunt the right of impeding the exercise of this choice by means of bans or restrictions or forcibly produced ignorance.

It is easy to understand and respect the motives which led the Pontiff to confirm by means of his authority a thousand-year-old tradition of which he feels himself to be the guardian. The fact cannot be hidden, however, that an appeal to this tradition cannot offer any solution today to the social and moral problems which have arisen from the indiscriminate proliferation of the human species. It must also be remembered that the appeal to peace and the brotherhood of men becomes pure rhetoric unless it comes to grips which the basic situation which threatens this peace and brotherhood: the desperate, inhuman clashes between hungry and unlearned masses who have nothing to lose.

The themes raised in Abbagnano's criticism have already appeared in different places on different occasions. Now, and this is what interests us here, they are taken up again by a very serious and well-known philosopher. Nonetheless, it is obviously easy to bring the reasons put forward by Martelet to bear against them, and it is equally possible to remain hesitant for a long time before the two positions. The last few observations of Abbagnano should also be contrasted with what came to light in our reflection on the problems of the Third World.

Whereas Abbagnano respectfully limits himself to a mention of the difficulties involved, others take these reactions to greater extremes, as, for example, Dr. P. Prudon of Amsterdam in *De Tijd* of August 10, 1968 where he writes:

It is almost indecent to preach ascesis to people who barely, if at all, have a life worthy of man, by talking to them of harmonious development. Ascesis is possible for us well-fed men. . . . We are not justified in using arguments from moral theology to face a question in which the solution rejected by the encyclical is the sole basis for the hope of a better future for the majority of man. . . . The theological position, moreover, is not strong. We must not allow ourselves to be dominated by our instincts. Why, then, should we submit to a biological process like that of the fertility cycle?

It will be noticed here that the biological cycle is understood as the sole basis on which the concept of the law of "nature" is founded. This is the point which usually provokes the largest number of objections, in spite of Martelet's refined explanations.

Several others, however, think that there should not be such a rigid and fixist concept of the law of nature which they accept as the basis for the solution advanced by the encyclical. Thus, for example, Dr. A. L. Hupkens of Arnhem, in the same issue of *De Tijd*, observes that

the term "natural law" in the encyclical is to be interpreted in a wider sense. There is a law defined in the Bible: the ten commandments and the Sermon on the Mount. Then there is a law which "is impressed on the hearts of men." This is exactly what St. Thomas means by the natural law. That the Pope intends this latter law and not only the biological ordering is clear from the words themselves.

The distinction mentioned by Dr. Hupkens is, in any case, today quite well-known, and has been advanced notably by experts in the biblical sciences, especially of the Old Testament. Some hold that it is difficult to find a true concept of the law of nature in scripture since every concept of law is based solely on God's intervention in the covenant. Others hold that the Bible witnesses to the existence of a natural law which can be known and must be put into practice even without knowledge of revelation. The divergencies arise, then, over the extent to which these natural imperatives contained in the Bible are revealed. An even

434

greater number of exegetes are tending to think that the moral imperatives, taken both as a whole and individually, were assimilated and taken from the moral ideas of neighboring countries—even if the new divine revelation had purified them—as, for example, Egyptian and Babylonian notions, Hellenism, Stoicism, and possibly even other sources. They think, therefore, that the moral imperatives expressed in the Bible do not make up part of revelation but are to be included under natural law and hence must be interpreted according to the rules for the interpretation of natural law.

On the very same day that Nicola Abbagnano published his article, *L'Osservatore Romano* intervened, letting it be understood that the concept of the law of nature criticized by the philosopher goes to compose part of the "basic reasons" for the encyclical and that therefore these are in a far closer relationship to revelation than many exegetes and theologians would like to think. *L'Osservatore Romano* says:

Nicola Abbagnano adopts a position on the encyclical *Humanae Vitae*, declaring that he dissents completely from the basic reasons underlying the pontifical document. He challenges, in fact, the identification of the natural law with the divine law, an identification which belongs, as he puts it, to a primitive cosmology no longer tenable today even though limited to the biological world rather than the entire physical world. The fact that man has survived is due solely to the fact that during his extremely long sojourn on earth he did exactly the opposite of what the encyclical maintains: foreseeing, modifying, planning. Man cannot reject this, his true "liberty," without destroying himself, since the greatest danger looming over the society of man today is the proliferation of the human race in a way similar to that in the individual organism where a disordered multiplication of cells has fatal results. Up to here we are dealing with statements in which it is easy to discern a considerable confusion between the physical and biological orders in spite of the pains to which the author goes to keep them separate.

The Vatican newspaper after criticizing Abbagnano's understanding of the purpose of marriage, continues:

Prof. Nicola Abbagnano is a well-known philosopher. If, however, the present author, who does not pretend to be a philosopher, may be permitted his humble opinion, it seems that in his article, apart from the misunderstandings arising above all from a monistic, not to say animal, understanding of man and from a conviction that an earthly paradise is within reach, he in fact views union simply in terms of a coupling to which individuals are driven by an inevitable and hence uncontrollable instinct.

The Christian understanding of man, however, and also of marriage, is quite different. Man is the responsible master of himself, his own prerogatives and destiny, as a subject and not an object. Even though the outside world conditions him to a certain extent, he still has the power, and hence the possibility, of dominating it as long as he naturally knows how to dominate himself. The first few verses of Genesis narrate that at the dawn of creation Yahweh told the first human couple: "Subdue the earth." The condition for this conquest of the natural physical world, however, to which God placed no limits, is, in Christianity, the dominion and mastery of oneself and the rational use of the reasoning and spiritual faculties.

The Vatican newspaper then goes on to criticize the solution, apparently the only one advanced by Abbagnano, for safeguarding the dramatic tensions of our time—namely, the regulation of the development of humanity—with the observation that it lies, on the contrary, in the "promotion of man and the awareness that peacefulness in the realm of 'things' presupposes a daily struggle which is fought and won within each individual conscience."

If it must be admitted that Abbagnano's text is lacking in the nuances expected from such a philosopher (but keeping in mind that he is writing within a limited space), it must also be admitted that possibly *L'Osservatore Romano* attributes much more to him than he himself actually says, especially when it criticizes him for his view of man. When the text is read, it is not necessarily as "monistic" and "animal" as the Vatican newspaper supposes. It is certainly easy to then go on to contrast the Christian understanding with that of the philosopher if it is so rapidly reduced to a schematic form. There is also the verse of Genesis which is a little disquieting since it appears to be used to prove the criticisms raised against Abbagnano's statements, which, however, he could direct back at the accuser. Specifically, if the Creator says, "Subdue the earth," could not this command also be extended to a realm like that of natural laws, since they are based on biological cycles which are certainly equally part of the complex created by God?

While Abbagnano treats the theme from the philosophical point of view, theological thought is no less direct in its treatment. Its approach centers on the understanding of creaturehood revealed by God himself in the form of his Word contained in Genesis: "Subdue the earth."

"Natural Law" and "Christian Doctrine"— *the Alternatives for Theology*

While in philosophy the difficulty is one of accepting a teaching based on the concept of "nature," on which other philosophical categories sit in judgment, the discussion which has been initiated in theology is no less difficult. In fact, the whole debate over the relationship between "natural law" and "Christian teaching" has been reopened. To what extent is one connected with the other? To what extent, therefore, can one be based on the other? Consequently, how far may the authority of the magisterium intervene when the question under consideration is one of an ethico-religious teaching which has also a certain basis in the realities of nature or, more generally, in the natural law?

The question has not simply been reopened. It has become a crucial one ever since *Humanae Vitae,* with its teaching and its reasoning, suddenly appeared in the middle of a debate that had been very widespread in the theological field, which had just begun arriving at definite conclusions and which now is certainly handicapped, not so much by the encyclical's statements of principle but rather by its concrete decisions that presuppose a certain number of convictions concerning basic principles. The debate in progress did not have the question of birth regulation as its immediate object, but was certainly made all the more urgent on account of it. In fact, the only possible way to avoid the difficulty of an evolution of the traditional teaching was to discover what its basis was and to what extent this basis was both logical and legitimate.

Possibly the most important representatives of this debate, of the hundreds who dealt with and wrote on the subject, have been Prof. Franz Böckle (among whose various articles on the subject must be noted especially the volume *Das Naturrecht im Disput* written in collaboration with Arntz, Kaufmann, and van Melsen and published in Düsseldorf in 1966) and Prof. Jakob David who in 1967 wrote a book (*Das Naturrecht in Krise und Läuterung*, Cologne, 1967) where he puts the debate in its correct perspective and outlines also the conclusions to which his personal research has led him.

The discussion, even as it appears in David's book, is extremely interesting and has already reached such an advanced stage that not a few theologians were astounded by the encyclical and they reproached it for not having taken into account the breadth and the depth of the discussion which was in progress. Moreover, it is evident from the so-called Majority Document of the Papal Commission that the present issue had already emerged on several occasions in the commission's study.

It is impossible to synthesize more than briefly the question as studied by David. First he notes that the evolution of the discussion on natural law has taken a paradoxical turn. While on one side the natural law teaching, especially in the form given it by the Catholic Church, was receiving greater attention in non-Christian circles (favored in this by the threat to humanity which the totalitarian forces of bolshevism, national socialism, and fascism represented), on the other side among Catholics themselves, voices which were becoming more and more prudent, diversified, and even critical were being raised. It was more clearly recognized that a historical coloration surrounded a number of statements which up to that time had been accepted without question or criticism, and which had given rise to problems which were extremely difficult to resolve on the basis of those statements. David then goes on to examine the basic principles and presuppositions of natural law and the questions regarding the possibility of this right changing. Finally he deals with the question which interests us more directly here; namely, the statements on natural right made by the magisterium.

David comes to the conclusion that all the reasons which may justify the Church's intervention into natural law when it is connected with the sciences and philosophy "only prove that the

438

Church, on account of its *pastoral* task, has the right, competency, and even the duty insofar as it is a moral one, of proclaiming and teaching the natural law in times when all humanity finds itself in a state of confusion. This does not prove, however, that these teachings are of a theologically binding nature."

At this point David mentions that Prof. Joseph Fuchs had already observed in 1935 (in his work *Lex naturae. Zur Theologie des Naturrecht*) that in modern times far more than in the past, the doctrinal documents of the Church refer to natural law. The motives for this seem to be the following: (1) Contemporary Church documents deal more frequently with issues of moral theology. (2) In a secularized world, arguments based on natural law have more force than those based on Church teaching or divine revelation. (3) In the face of contemporary positivism, it is necessary to insist on natural rights.

David notes:

These motives are correct. They show at the same time, however, that the Church's teaching on natural law is connected more with her pastoral than with her doctrinal function. . . . After reading, for example, Pius XII's statement on natural law and the competence of the Church in this field, no one will be able to deny that the Church— the entire Church and not just the hierarchy—has the right and the duty to take an interest in the natural rights of man, draw concrete norms of behavior from them, and especially today, fight with all her strength and with full awareness of her responsibilities in order to discover the natural rights of man and to urge him to put them into practice. When on one hand, however, it is held that theology has its source in revelation, and on the other, that it is desirable to have natural law included within the doctrinal competency of the Church, no one will be able to deny that the conclusions, which attribute the Church with doctrinal competence in this sphere, surpass the premises.

In his conclusion David states:

It is quite obvious that the traditional teaching on natural law has gone considerably too far in its categorical affirmations, has too often applied to the whole of humanity very limited experiences and trends of thinking of Western Greco-Christian origins which can be pinned down to a given geographical region and to a clearly outlined historical period.

These are the reasons, observes David, for which

when one comes down to concrete facts, all human problems are found to be very complicated. One cannot hope to solve all the different elements one by one. One must bring together a whole series of elements so as to obtain a coherent synthesis and one which is amenable to application.

For this reason, David concludes:

It must be granted that when it goes beyond fundamental affirmations to formulate more concrete imperatives, natural law is no longer as simple, clear, and natural as was thought by some of the representatives of a rigid school of natural right whose scientific value did not always equal its fervor for the faith. If the historical character of man and humanity, which is rooted in the depths of the human person, is taken seriously, then the search for imperatives of natural law becomes all the more laborious and difficult and demands incessantly new efforts, but at the same time becomes more noble and flexible and contributes to man's greater honor and to his dignity.

It is true then that we are faced with a natural law, but it is also true that of all the things considered for so long to be natural law, very few are fundamental realities of universal and perennial value, inherent in the very essence of man and humanity. This is because man's condition is so strongly marked by his historical and environmental state. When this is transposed to the level of Christian doctrine, we can logically expect to see happening what David himself mentioned; namely, the Church taking a "pastoral" interest in these matters, without however, raising to the value of perennial doctrine anything which could be bound up with cultural and environmental conditions, no matter how ancient and venerable it may be. For this reason the problem of distinguishing between natural law and Christian doctrine has become an even more serious one for theology.

This, in fact, is the criticism which has been made of the encyclical, almost continuing, in a way, the criticism which the philosopher has begun in his own sphere. Thus Prof. C. P. Sporken in *De Tijd* of August 3, 1968, after listing some of the difficulties which arise from reading the encyclical, highlights one which is indicated in the encyclical itself when the Pope states that one of the principal reasons that he opposed the Majority Report of

440

the Papal Commission was because the criteria it employed differed from the doctrine on marriage proposed with constant firmness by the magisterium of the Church (No. 6). Dr. Sporken then goes on to indicate how this particular difficulty consists in the following fact:

The history of the elaboration of the encyclical and the reactions which arose after its publication have clearly shown that the teaching contained in it cannot be considered unquestionably as "the teaching of the Church"; that is, one representing the whole community of the faithful, priests, theologians, and bishops. We know that among these there are some who have different ideas than those of the encyclical on marriage morality, and that some follow a different line of pastoral care. At the basis of this question, however, there is a still more serious one: Is it possible to revise this ethic and this form of pastoral care which has now developed in the Church? Is it possible to halt the sun, hoping that it will quietly go back to circling our planet?

The problem, then, for Sporken, whom we have taken as representative of this line of criticism which has arisen over the problem of the relationship between Christian doctrine (or Church doctrine) and natural law, arises precisely from this inner contradiction in what the encyclical has proposed as the teaching always held in the Church, but which is based on a concept of natural law and which is therefore in itself subject to the gradual evolution of this concept, as Jakob David has indicated.

Sporken, therefore, goes on to say that

all these difficulties are, so to speak, concentrated and clearly revealed in the view on the natural law as it has been taught in the encyclical. The Pope states that the marriage teaching as he has proposed it is based on the natural law, illuminated and enriched by divine revelation (No. 4). It is here, in my opinion, that the most fundamental objection is to be found, that which affects the very foundation of the encyclical: the notion of natural law as the basis of moral norms. On reading the encyclical and attempting to understand exactly what the Pope means by the term "natural law," and consequently what he feels bound to teach as the basis of natural law on marriage, one makes an almost disconcerting discovery. In theory it is recognized that procreation must be considered "in the light of the integral vision of man" (No. 7), but in fact this integral vision is nullified by the interpretation of the notion of natural law.

The encyclical reduces the global vision of man exclusively and in a one-sided way to the physical aspects which then take on the role of a norm. The encyclical in fact defines natural law in exclusively physical terms: "the respect due to the functions of the biological process" (No. 10), "the biological laws of the physical (sexual) functions" (No. 3), and "the integrity of the human (sexual) organism and its functions" (No. 17). This biological legalism is simply put on the same level as the ethical norms.

In my view, few philosophers and moral sts subscribe to this opinion today. Theologians of world repute have shown that only an anthropological understanding of human and rational nature can serve as the basis of morality; for example, Rahner (in 1961), Schillebeeckx (in 1963), and Janssens (in 1966). The text of the encyclical is very much reminiscent of Cardinal Ottaviani's statement: "The basic norm of moral theology is to be found in the natural law, and both Pius XI and Pius XII have based their statements in matters of marriage morality principally on the natural law. Those who talk as if it is necessary to speak of rational and truly human nature are only searching for escape routes" (1966).

Would it not be more to our advantage, however, to look for the fundamental norms of our Christian morality in Christ and in his gospel? Personally, I prefer in every way the opinion of another cardinal who said also in 1966: "Maybe we are not always fully conscious that the Church must take the path which Christ took, listening to the inspiration of his Spirit who reveals himself to us in and through the world we live in, and who directs his call to us in this way. True fidelity hence consists in a continually growing adhesion to the initial gift and in continually advancing to ever newer stages. Immobility is opposed to the deep meaning of life and the gospel message. True fidelity consists in maturation and in a continuous rejuvenation, in continuity with what has gone before. Possibly we do not sufficiently understand that actions which are materially alike can in fact take on very different meanings in different periods. Changes are justified above all by the need for expressing permanent values in the forms proper to each age." Thus did Cardinal Suenens speak.

Human nature is always concretized and hence formulated in a culture and according to one particular culture. The history of moral theology and of moral decisions on the part of the Church hierarchy presents itself as undeniable evidence that a large number of "natural laws" came to be seen in the end as "cultural laws."

Luypen showed (in 1966) that the natural law in its origins really derives from the divine will. The way in which philosophers and

Thomistic theologians have spoken of the natural law as the expression of the will of God is simply disrespectful toward God. Knoll (in 1962) presented a comprehensive view of what "being in conformity with the natural law" was considered to be in the Church through the centuries. It is history which leaves us perplexed. Here is a single example: It is obvious how much slavery is opposed to the gospel demand of love, and yet St. Thomas himself taught that it is "in conformity with the natural law" for slaves to be slaves and not to make up part of the rest of the human community! It must be kept in mind, too, that according to Thomistic theology, natural law is the expression of the will of God! When slaves were being imported into America, Catholic theologians did not protest in the name of the gospel, but spent their time in debating the price to be paid, in justice, for the slaves!

What is sufficiently obvious is that the encyclical's real point of departure—namely, the assimilation of the biological law and the natural law on the moral level with the divine law—is very questionable both from the philosophical point of view and from the theological point of view.

Does not the Pope, however, explicitly recall the assistance of the Holy Spirit? I am convinced that the Spirit of God assists the ecclesial community and those who have the burden of authority in it. This does not imply, however, that by starting out from the message of salvation the Church can claim a monopoly of the divine rights when interpreting the "natural law" and "human dignity" in detail.

Cardinal Suenens' opinion, which we have just quoted, is fully subscribed to by many theologians: the inspiration of the Spirit of God cannot be revealed to the Church and its official magisterium unless in and through the world through the living faith of the whole Church. This in turn implies that the Holy Spirit's field of action includes not just the sentiment of Catholic believers but also the moral sense of Reformed Christians and all non-Christians. We get the impression however, that the encyclical has not kept this very much in mind. Even worse, since the encyclical posits in such a categorical way the biologial laws as the ethical norm of human dignity, it is in fact accusing many Catholics, the greater part of Reformed Christians, and all other men of goodwill of abiding by a marriage ethics unworthy of mankind. For this reason it seems to me that the encyclical could appear to them to be pretentious and disparaging, to say the least, and that it holds out little hope of contributing to the growth of ecumenism.

Sporken's reasoning is linear and follows a theological course which begins with the concept of "doctrine of the Church" and then outlines the difficulties of admitting a concept of "law of nature" as such—a concept which can, in reality, be subject to historical and cultural conditioning.

Following these lines of theological reflection, and at the same time deepening them with an observation of the theological value of the encyclical's reasoning, is the judgment that the moralist Bernard Häring gave in the September 1968 issue of *Commonweal*:

The encyclical is quite optimistic about the force of the arguments it proposes and the information provided by the Pope's advisors so that "the magisterium could give adequate reply to the expectation not only of the faithful but also of world opinion" (No. 5). Nevertheless, when the Pope speaks to "his own children" and to his "sons, the priests," optimism about the force of the arguments diminishes somewhat. He asks for "loyal internal and external obedience to the teaching authority of the Church" and then adds: "That obedience, as you well know, obliges not only because of the light of the reasons adduced, but rather because of the light of the Holy Spirit, which is given in a particular way to the pastors of the Church in order that they may illustrate the truth" (No. 28).

There can be no doubt that our obedience of faith to the Church rests on the confidence that the Church enjoys the special assistance of the Holy Spirit in the explanation of the gospel and the guidance of the Church. But it is not possible to make the Holy Spirit responsible for everything which in past centuries was loudly asserted in an authoritative tone by men of the Church. However, in *Humanae Vitae* the central argument is clearly and unambiguously a thesis of the natural moral law, and therefore a truth which is to be proved from human experiences and arguments of reason. If the Holy Spirit gives a very special grace in the composition and promulgation of this document, then one may legitimately expect that this grace will manifest itself in the way the question itself is handled—that means in the solid presentation of proofs from human experience and with good arguments. In my opinion, this is not true in the present instance. Therefore, it is no insult at all to the Holy Spirit if we continue to express our doubts.

After the appeal to the Holy Spirit there follows an exhortation that for the sake of peace in the Church "all should speak the same language" (No. 28). This admonition is followed by the words of

St. Paul (is this an accurate translation?) that there should be no difference of opinion among Christians. Paul opposed Peter to his face and expressed this difference of opinion openly (Galatians 2) when Peter had closed the doors to the spread of the gospel, yielding in a moment of weakness to the pressure of the Jerusalem Curia. The theologians and bishops who now raise their voices are not doing so out of "quarrelsomeness" but because if they do not, the credibility gap will be increased for the Catholic Church and many will find it impossible to belong to the Church because of the emphatic assertion of a constant human tradition in the Church. If, when all is said and done, the Pope abides unyieldingly to the conclusion of his encyclical, that in the Catholic Church only this one language of argumentation, mentality, and commands may be spoken, then the voices of many men and women who love the Church must fall silent, and this one language will reach the ears of only a few, and not the ears of men with whom the future lies.

The argumentation of *Humanae Vitae* rests mainly on two points: the first is the constant teaching of the Church; the second is the absolute sacredness and inviolability of the biological functions in every use of marriage, so that every act must remain open for procreation, whether or not procreation can at this moment be undertaken responsibly.

Humanae Vitae differs from *Casti Connubii* by no longer making the effort to base the teaching of the Church in this matter on Genesis 38. It no longer tries to base its proof on scripture. For every layman knows today that the intention of that text was to insist on the obligation to raise up children from the wife of one's dead brother—an obligation which is now forbidden by the Church. The text is not dealing with the absolute sacredness of the sperm. So the only argument which remains is the fact that the Church has always taught this doctrine ("constant firmness by the teaching authority of the Church" [No. 6]).

In a chapter on tradition in one of my books I have attempted to show that the tradition is not so unequivocal as many think. Attention must also be given to the historical context in which the teaching was presented. But if the argument from tradition is to play so important a role, we must call to mind Jesus' struggle against the important role assigned to human traditions. "He also said to them, 'How well you set aside the commandment of God in order to maintain your tradition (Mark 7:9).'" When the legalists asked the Lord, "Why do your disciples break the old-established tradition?" Jesus answered, "Why do you break God's commandment in the interest of your tradition? (Matt. 15:2–3)."

The encyclical must provide the opportunity for a better, more historically oriented understanding of tradition and also of language. Think again of the insistence in the Credo of Paul VI that "transubstantiation" is the most suitable word to express the real presence of Christ. This is to cling to words. Take as an illustration the word establishment. When I learned English, *establishment* was defined as "that which rests on a solid basis and therefore generates confidence." If someone in today's world wants to say that the Church rests on a solid basis and generates confidence by simply saying, "The Church and the papacy are an 'establishment,' " then he has chosen the wrong word. Words must be understood in their context. Answers to the vital questions of a period are not magic formulas which can simply be "applied" over and over again.

The second argument is the biological understanding of the inviolable laws of nature. In the "hierarchy of values" (No. 10), the biological seems to rate very high on the scale. The whole purpose of the act in its "metaphysical structure" is directed, so the argument goes, toward procreation, and therefore every act must remain open to procreation, even in cases in which it would be absolutely meaningless and irresponsible to bring new life into being. "In relation to the biological processes, responsible parenthood means the knowledge and respect of their funct on; human intellect discovers in the power of giving life, biological laws which are part of the human person" (No. 10). I believe that biological functions are one part of man; but these biological functions are often upset, and the art of healing is possible if only man is a responsible steward of these functions and can intervene.

It has not been proved that the biological functions connected with the power of procreation are absolutely untouchable and sacred, especially since they are often upset, and even according to the teaching of the Church, measures to restore health may be undertaken. The biological functions must be subordinated to the good of the whole person and marriage itself. This is, if I am not mistaken, by far the most common opinion in the Church.

Pope Paul's advisers hold to an absolutely biological understanding of the natural law. They have not even progressed from a very materialistic style of medicine to man-centered medicine, which views medicine not as the art of restoring biological functions, but of serving the whole person.

Pope Paul asserts that an intervention in the biological process necessarily destroys married love. This assertion has no more proof to back it up than the assertion of *Casti Connubii* that it is necessarily against the dignity of a woman for her to have some occupation outside the home.

Häring notes that the Council had confronted the problem from another point of view by positing the idea that

birth control is evaluated quite differently in different circumstances. It is one thing if it is practiced as the result of a conscientious decision that new life cannot responsibly be brought into being here and now; it is quite another if it is a simple rejection of the parental vocation. Since Pope Paul makes the analysis of the act his starting point, this fundamental distinction does not appear. The evil seems to consist exclusively, or at least principally, in the violation of sacred biological functions. The encyclical also fails to see that abortion is a much greater problem than the methods of birth control. In the encyclical, abortion is rejected only in passing; the Council put its principal emphasis on a condemnation of abortion. So the encyclical, from a pedagogical standpoint, is rather confusing.

Häring also underscores the fact that

the encyclical gives an extraordinarily great significance to the rhythm between fertile and infertile periods. "God has wisely disposed natural laws and rhythms of fecundity which, of themselves, cause a separation in the succession of births" (No. 11). Practically the only method permitted for responsible birth control is periodic continence. "It is then licit to take into account the natural rhythms immanent in the generative functions, for the use of marriage in the infecund periods only" (No. 16). Father Lestapis, S.J., and Father Martelet, S.J., who are clearly among the superconsultors, have called the rhythm between the fertile and infertile periods *le mystère sexual* ("the sexual secret of mystery"). When I asked, ironically, some years ago, "What happens when the sexual mystery is not functioning properly?" without noticing the irony, the scholar answered, "Then only asceticism can help."

Here is the problem of the present teaching: women whose periods are regular, who can use all the necessary means including the possibility of an undisturbed temperature reading, and if necessary, seven doctors at their disposal, can live in accordance with the teaching of the Church. What about the poor, the uneducated, when their periods are irregular, or when because of their level of culture, they are simply incapable of understanding these methods? What happens if these methods not only fail biologically, but lead to severe psychological disturbances?

Over the years I have received at least fifty letters that present cases in which unsuccessful use of rhythm led to psychoses for these women and required treatment for them in mental institutions. Just a week before the encyclical appeared, an English doctor wrote me that the confessor of a woman for whom he had prescribed the Pill had refused her absolution when she had been released from a half year of treatment in a mental institution after a pregnancy psychosis. And the superioress of an American hospital told me that the chaplain refused absolution to a severely ill woman who had taken the progesterone Pill for the most valid reasons. He refused because she was not prepared to promise that she would take no more after her convalescence. The encyclical *Humanae Vitae* is so apodictic and absolute that no exceptions of any kind may be permitted for objective reasons.

At this point Häring reintroduces the grave psychological difficulties involved in both the uncertainty of the permitted methods and in the long periods of abstinence between husband and wife, which have a negative repercussion on the essential values of married and family life. Bernard Häring's reaction may leave us surprised on account of its clarity and sharpness which excludes all possible subterfuge of ambiguity. It must also be kept in mind, however, that he is one of the best and most well-known, present-day moralists, and that he has as well a wide experience outside of pure theoretical research. His way of speaking is certainly an example of honesty which excludes all possibility of false or questionable prudence and ambiguous submission.

The theologians on this occasion have really shown themselves to be the "enfants terribles" which many today consider them to be. In fact, the strange situation has developed where on the one hand we have the "good Catholic people" who are scandalized and concerned over the attacks against their "simple and ancient faith" and on the other, the bad-child theologians who take great delight in chasing sacred cows, and who grieve the hearts of the sacred hierarchy and are responsible for the good faithful being scandalized.

For this reason it is interesting to note what the professors of theology and moral philosophy at the Catholic University of Louvain and in various schools and seminaries of theology in

Belgium have to say. At the beginning of the declaration on a common reflection on *Humanae Vitae* and on the Belgian bishops' statement of August 30, which they drew up on September 4, 1968, together with other specialists in theology and philosophy who were present, they stated:

As the teachers on this problem and as those who must critically reflect on it by nature of their scientific tasks, we consider it our duty to make public our conviction that we do not wish to give rise in any way to unhealthy agitation but rather to contribute to the formation of opinion and open dialogue within the Church.

After making this declaration which was certainly necessary even if not well understood (as we shall see later), the theologians at Louvain continue:

We note with astonishment that the encyclical considers married life in a perspective which a large number of persons feel to be both obsolete and mistaken. The constitution *Gaudium et Spes* had, in any case, consciously rejected this perspective and had therefore by its openness given rise to hopes of an entirely different nature. The difference in perspective is strongly determined by the point of departure chosen. If a personalist position is chosen as the point of departure, the conclusions arrived at will necessarily be different from those where biological integrity comes first.

We must declare in conscience that we do not see the validity of the outlook which considers the biological laws of the process of procreation as dominant laws valid in themselves, disconnected from the comprehensive aim of marriage and the family. As for the concrete question of methods, we realize that every statement in this regard is relative. Therefore, we respect the opinion of those who consider periodic abstinence as the sole method allowed. Beginning from a personalist vision, however, we cannot understand the specifically moral distinction made between the use of infertile periods on the one hand and the use of methods which temporarily impede fertility on the other. Both methods can be used for good and for evil. In fact, in the last analysis, the moral value of a method is determined by its relationship to the truly human project of love in responsible parenthood.

At this point the Belgian theologians examine the significance of the Belgian bishops' declaration, which was the first to be produced collegially and also one of the most important since it unambiguously recognized the value and the significance of the personal conscience before the dictates of *Humanae Vitae*.

The same theme, more directly connected, however, with the question of the significance of the collegial authority of the magisterium, is very much stressed in the declaration of 20 theologians from Germany, Austria, Belgium, France, Holland, Ireland, Switzerland, and Czechoslovakia who met in Amsterdam on September 18–19, 1968 to discuss the encyclical. In their "consensus paper" they first evaluate the encyclical's content:

For several years, a large number of theologians from various countries have devoted themselves to developing new perspectives in the doctrine of conjugal morality. In these studies it has been their desire to avoid every form of laxity, which would be nothing but a capitulation before egoism and hedonism. They have desired, on the contrary, to invite the faithful to live their marriage in a more conscious manner and with a heightened sense of their responsibility in the service of the essential values—both moral and religious—of man. They have been able to find these new perspectives stated in the chapter of the pastoral constitution *Gaudium et Spes*, which concerns marriage and the family, and they have dedicated themselves to pursuing their reflection in the light of the Council's teaching.

In this context, we note with surprise that the encyclical *Humanae Vitae* does not respond to the expectations which the pastoral constitution *Gaudium et Spes* has awakened. In effect, the encyclical represents the conjugal life in a perspective which, according to the judgment of a great number of competent persons, appears to be inadequate.

The theologians then continue their criticism from the personalist point of view as the Belgian theologians had already done. It must be kept in mind that among these 20 theologians at the meeting in Amsterdam there are some of the most outstanding names in contemporary theology in the field of morality: Aubert of Strasbourg, Auer of Tübingen, Beemer of Nijmegen, Böckle of Bonn, Janssens and Franssen of Louvain, Mádr of Prague, Schoonenberg of Nijmegen, Groot of Amsterdam, McDonagh of Maynooth (Ireland), etc.

In another declaration, 87 theologians of the Catholic University of Washington, after stating that "as Roman Catholic theologians we respectfully acknowledge a distinct role of hier-

archical magisterium (teaching authority) in the Church of
Christ," note that in any case, "Christian tradition assigns
theologians the special responsibility of evaluating and interpreting pronouncements of the magisterium in the light of the
total theological data operative in each question or statement."
Next they recognize the "many positive values concerning marriage expressed in Paul VI's encyclical." However, they state:
"We take exception to the ecclesiology implied and the methodology used by Paul VI in the writing and promulgation of the
document. They are incompatible with the Church's authentic
self-awareness as expressed in and suggested by the acts of
Vatican Council II itself. The encyclical consistently assumes
that the Church is identical with the hierarchical office. No real
importance is afforded the witness of the life of the Church in its
totality; the special witness of many Catholic couples is neg-
lected; the encyclical fails to acknowledge the witness of the
separated Christian Churches and ecclesial communities; it is
insensitive to the witness of many men of goodwill; it pays insufficient attention to the ethical import of modern science.

The theologians go on to observe that "the encyclical betrays
a narrow and positivistic notion of papal authority." They then
speak of the encyclical's doctrinal content and reasoning which
are the source of almost universal difficulties for theologians:

We take exception to some of the specific ethical conclusions contained in the encyclical. They are based on an inadequate concept of
natural law: the multiple forms of the natural law theory are ignored
and the fact that competent philosophers come to different conclusions
on this very question is disregarded. Even the Minority Report of the
Papal Commission noted grave difficulty in attempting to present con-
clusive proof of the immorality of artificial contraception based on
natural law.

Other defects include: overemphasis on the biological aspects
of conjugal relations as ethically normative; undue stress on sexual acts
and on the faculty of sex viewed in itself apart from the person and
the couple; a static world view which plays down the historical and
evolutionary character of humanity in its finite existence, as described
in Vatican II's pastoral constitution *Gaudium et Spes*; unfounded
control"; indifference to Vatican II's assertion that prolonged sexual
assumptions about "the evil consequences of methods of artificial birth

abstinence may cause "faithfulness to be imperiled and its quality of fruitfulness to be ruined"; an almost total disregard for the dignity of millions of human beings brought into the world without the slightest possibility of being fed and educated decently.

In actual fact, the encyclical demonstrates no development over the teaching of Pius XI's *Casti Connubii* whose conclusions have been called into question for grave and serious reasons. These reasons, given a muffled voice at Vatican II, have not been adequately handled by the mere repetition of past teaching.

As can be noticed, the declaration of the theologians at Washington, in spite of its conciseness and simplicity, keeps account of the strictly "theological" objections, and it will not be long before they are further developed in theological thinking.

There is an obvious question, however, in the face of all these criticisms by the theologians. It has been formulated by Prof. W. M. C. Klijn, associate professor of ethical theology at the Higher School of Amsterdam, in *De Volkskrant* of August 17, 1968. Prof. Klijn says:

The basic question, and its moral and theological repercussions cannot be avoided, is the following: Is the Pope's teaching objectively correct or not? And does this judgment of the Pope express the sole, authentic thought of the Church as such? Second, there are many who ask how this state of affairs could have come about in 1968. The text of the encyclical gives ample material for a reply. One of the reasons could be the fact that in the debates of the past few years too little consideration was taken of the type of ideas, thought, and reasoning used by the defenders of the traditional teaching. Hence the Pope found no reassuring answer for his profound concern over the finality of marriage.

The encyclical contains no unexpected element in its theological reasoning which could be the source of further reflection. Nor does it contain any reasoning which has not been deeply studied and even refuted by capable and competent men during these past few years. This papal document on birth control shows many similarities with that dealing with priestly celibacy, not only on account of the subject matter which in both cases refers to marriage and sexuality, but also on account of its literary composition. It begins by recalling the present evolution of the subject. It then notes the difficulties and objections of the persons who hold a different opinion, but it does not go on to offer any satisfying solution or exhaustive reply. The last part of the document then makes an appeal for the generous efforts of all, for fidelity to the magisterium and to divine grace, as well as mentioning the pardon obtainable in the reception of the sacraments. This is all the more tragic if it is placed against the background of the immense seriousness with which the Pope has fought during the last few years to clarify the problem.

The theological content of the encyclical remains below standard and is not on a par with the intense feeling of responsibility which is driving the Pope, at his age, to again take up the study of the matter in order to be able to put himself forward as the judge of a majority of competent men's thought.

One thing must be remembered in any case: the Pope expressly rejects, and this is in accord with the Council, all downgrading of marriage and woman's sexuality. He does not seem to be aware, however, that the use of artificial contraceptives does not necessarily harm these values but can, on the contrary, protect them. This becomes all the more evident when he reacts against certain arguments of the supporters of the new, deepened perspective on marriage morality.

His reasoning follows a vicious circle since the premises already fully contain the conclusions by holding as untouchable data what is yet to be proved. Thus the Pope recalls the following theses: (1) Fertility as the goal of marriage must be considered within the framework of married life seen as a whole. (2) The marriage act intentionally made infertile may be morally good by the fact of constituting a single whole with the fertile acts which precede and follow it. (3) The marriage act intentionally made infertile may be good on account of the intention behind it: to guarantee harmony and peace in the family, and the education of children already born. The Pope's answer to these theses states that an end which is good in itself does not justify illicit means and that one is not permitted to do evil so that good may come from it. These arguments have hence been understood by the Pope as so many attempts at legitimizing what, in his thinking, has already been condemned. One asks why, but to understand this we must go deeper into the Pope's way of thinking.

It may be useful first to indicate a traditional *non sequitur;* namely, that the use of the Pill for therapeutical reasons is judged to be licit. Why does the end—that is, healing—here justify the means and the function pertaining to the means, which is that of temporary sterilization? Why in this case is the end included in the intrinsic evaluation of the means? The question centers on a traditional principle in moral theology which has been introduced here—a principle

453

which practically speaking, gravitates between two ideas: the intention and the material act. This principle has been strongly and rightly criticized in the past few years.

There appears to be another contradiction in the fact that on one hand, encouragement is showered out to promote research, while on the other hand, the couple are urged not to escape their responsibilities by putting their trust in technical means. On one hand, the integration of human intelligence and will is explicitly judged as good, while on the other, this integration must be limited to the observance and regulat'on of the woman's periodic rhythms and to dominion over one's sexual desires.

All these considerations lead us to ask a very important question: What is it that induces the Pope to judge the method of periodic abstinence as licit? He recognizes a certain analogy between periodic continence and the other contraceptive methods. All these methods are based on the desire to limit the number of children by avoiding pregnancy. He sees a vital ethical difference, however, in the fact that the method of periodic abstinence consists essentially in *continence* during the fertile periods while the other methods, are an *interference* with the biological processes. He practically *identifies* the "natural law" as a "moral category" with the "biological laws" of procreation. But what is this identification based on? It is based on the nature of each particular marriage act which the encyclical considers in the light of the unbreakable unity of the *twofold* significance of the sexual act: mutual love and fertility.

I think that this is a fundamental and precious aspect but only if this twofold *significance* of the marriage act not be unquestionably identified with the *biological* act. It seems to me that the marriage act between husband and wife, in its physical aspect, can and must be the sign of the deepest meaning of sexuality—love and fertility. The human dimension, however, must not be entirely absorbed by the biological laws of the transmission of life.

This, however, is exactly what the encyclical does—and hence it hinders the couple from seeing what the real possibilities are; namely, that it is precisely the procreative aim of sexuality which can justify contraceptive methods and that to avoid interference in the biological process can be identical to opposing human procreation. To summarize, the twofold meaning of sexuality does not allow us to make any hard and fast conclusions on the moral worth of certain methods.

Prof. Klijn's reasoning enters most directly, therefore, into the crux of the considerations made possible by the encyclical.

His reasoning moves explicitly within the limits of the precise difficulties that present-day theology has raised in regard to the encyclical's reasoning. For this reason Prof. Klijn continues:

All this leads us to the heart of the encyclical's reasoning; namely, a given theological understanding of every human person in relation to God. I suspect that the determining factor here is a certain mythological representation which does not belong to the essence of faith but which simply const tutes a nonbiblical and historically conditioned veneer; namely, the direct *infusion* here and now of the individual soul. From the moment when the marriage act takes place man loses all right to interfere in the biological process since it is forbidden for him to interfere in the divine liberty carrying out its creative work "from within" this process itself.

Prof. Klijn observes that we must not play down any of the biblical data such as the mention made of John the Baptist in the womb of Elizabeth, and of the other men of God in the Old Testament, called by God "right from their mother's womb," as well as the reference, for example, to Psalm 139 where God is thanked for having clothed the psalmist right from his mother's womb, since this, as he says, is a great mystery, the marvel that he is and the marvel of God's works.

Prof. Klijn observes, however, in line with contemporary theological thinking:

These texts have no intention of teaching us a theological biology, although they do express admiration at the unfathomable mystery of creation. They tell us of the unique position of the human person on account of the fact that God establishes a direct relationship with him by a total calling which embraces his entire existence "from his kidneys and his mother's womb" to his death itself.

These texts, however, do not tell us that the creating "hands" of God operate solely in the necessary biological process and exclude the power granted to man by the Creator to make a conscious and responsible use of medical techniques. It is precisely in this way, in the name of the Creator, that human liberty and, together with it, the liberty of the Creator himself will be found to have been forced.

After these observations of a more strictly theological nature, Prof. Klijn expresses the problem involved in interpreting the psychological and sociological arguments introduced by the encyclical to justify "a posteriori" the exclusion of all "unnatural" contraceptive methods. He observes:

Moreover, the Pope supports his opinion with a certain number of psychological and sociological arguments: all forms of constraint would be eliminated and hence there could arise infidelity, promiscuity, and abuse by governments. This concern of the Pope is by no means an unrealistic one, but the dangers must be avoided by other means; namely, moral education. The fear of possible abuses must never be a reason for forbidding the good use of things. Infidelity cannot be caused merely by the Pill: periodic abstinence can also contribute to it and disguise it. The encyclical seems to believe that artificial contraceptives remove all barriers to egoistic abuse of the woman on the part of the man. This clearly contradicts the facts: the use of these techniques *can* be the expression of a real, human culture, a sense of responsibility, and a profound mutual respect.

Experience proves that in this case the couple must face just as many moral demands as if they were to resort to the use of periodic abstinence. Every form of birth control requires in one way or another that love "in reserve" which has been so perceptively described by Doctor Terruwe.

For many persons the full acceptance of this encylical's teaching will have weighty consequences—possibly too weighty consequences. Numerous are those who will find themselves put before a dilemma and unable to find a solution in either the grace of God or the sacraments. This certainly applies to those urgent cases where the choice must be made between the marriage union and the reception of the sacraments and where periodic continence is excluded on account of the extremely serious risks involved.

Prof. Klijn examines this difficulty farther, finally arriving at the problem of overpopulation which he mentions in a few words, but then proceeds with a very interesting observation or, better still, a question which he leaves unanswered but to which all contemporary theology has been attempting to find a solution: "The people in developing countries will have to make their choice between the alternatives of demographic explosion and sin, between extending the population or multiplying the sin. Could not precisely this insight represent the will of God for them? Is it really a lack of Christian spirit?"

A question is implied here which reechoes that of whether the vehicle of the will of God for man can be understood as principally or almost solely the natural law or also the historical conditions in which man comes to find himself—conditions which are much more variable than can be imagined.

This is the problem which lies at the base of the theme treated in *Frankfurter Allgemeine Zeitung* on August 13, 1968 by the Dominican Anselm Hertz, associate professor of philosophy at the University of Frankfurt. Prof. Hertz gives his article a title which is already significant in itself: "Metaphysics of Natural Law or Message of Salvation?" In other words, the difficulty of a theology which moves between "natural law" and "Christian doctrine" is formulated more precisely in the question of whether a metaphysics of natural law of itself can become the theme of the message of salvation (since the encyclical's reasoning is based on this natural law).

Prof. Hertz notes that

the formal aspect of the encyclical's reasoning already refers to its basis in natural law when it mentions "the principles of the moral teaching of marriage founded on the natural law, illuminated and enriched by divine revelation" (No. 4).

The institution of marriage is described in a material way in the encyclical within this formal outline. In accordance with tradition, this description encompasses the two elements of married love and responsible parenthood. . . . The problem is still open, however, as to whether the words "to collaborate with God in the generation and the education of new lives" (No. 8) lay stress on the preeminence of the mission of procreation. . . . As for the material aspect of the reasoning on natural law found in the encyclical it is surprising to see the concept of natural law limited to biological principles. Within the framework of these biological principles the encyclical has developed an elevated "ethos" of married love which, however, precisely because it is based on biological principles, finally becomes a metaphysics of natural law, and culminates in an outlook typical of this way of viewing the value of human effort: "for the attainment of a perfect dominion of self" (No. 21). . . .

How debatable this concept of nature is can already be seen from the problem of the infertile periods. . . . In reality, the fact is that by means of hormonal preparations it is possible to bring about the infertile periods even individually. This, however, is a question of milligrams: a couple more milligrams of hormones prevents ovulation and is therefore against nature, a couple of milligrams less and the period follows normally and is therefore in accord with nature. The distinction between natural and unnatural has become a question for the microscope.

Prof. Hertz discusses this point at length and then passes on to reflect on the reasoning of the encyclical which we called a posteriori and whose weaknesses were revealed by Prof. Klijn. Prof. Hertz evaluates these weaknesses in a different way. He notes:

It would be a false interpretation of the spirit of the encyclical to consider these references to the consequences which would flow from a liberalization of contraceptive methods as a reason for banning them. The moral principle *abusus non tollit usum* ("abuse of a thing does not take away its use") is always valid. Therefore one may not ban the use of contraceptive means for the simple fact that there is danger that they will be used for an evil purpose. . . . It is also the fear of free will in human actions which determines the encyclical's pastoral tone. . . . The much-acclaimed technical progress becomes an instrument which free will uses in cases where the human spirit must encroach on biological principles. This fear of human arbitrariness is certainly justified. There is always the danger of man being manipulated and this is equally true in the biological field. This danger cannot be avoided, however, through metaphysical reflection on natural law rooted in an image of the world which belongs to antiquity, but rather demands a concrete ethics of human brotherhood, which for the Christian flows from the message of Christ.

Prof. Hertz then observes that since the document is not "ex cathedra," these enunciations of the ecclesiastical magisterium are not infallible or free of error "a priori," and therefore the discussion on the reasons pro and contra can continue even in the future.

With regard to the situation now created by the possibility for further discussion, Prof. Hertz has some interesting and penetrating comments to make. He says:

The encyclical makes no reference to the situation which would arise if priests and lay people were to find that they have strong arguments against the doctrine presented in the document. This, however, is exactly the situation in which many Catholics find themselves. It is particularly well-known that the majority of the theologians in the Papal Commission declared themselves to be in favor of a revision of the attitude to contraceptive methods. In such a case, to demand only exterior obedience would be to create a very problematic situation. . . . The Pope foresaw the reaction and the rejection, as he himself says in the encyclical. He also adds that by remaining steadfast in its prohibition of contraceptive methods, the Church becomes a sign of contradiction.

This show of personal courage is worthy of admiration except that one asks the question whether these human and moral efforts should be exerted simply to defend, by appealing to the concept of a Christianized natural law, a natural law which has its roots in an ancient philosophy, or whether it would not have been better to have put in place of this metaphysics of natural law a "message of salvation" which has been spread spread by the spirit of the gospel of Christ in a far stronger way than a Christianized natural law could ever be spread.

This last observation of Prof. Hertz leads us directly to a theme which has appeared on a number of occasions in the other theological contributions: the theme of the perspective on sexuality, chastity, and sex as such, which appears to be at the basis of the encyclical's treatment, one which is intimately connected with the concept of natural law. This theme, although prompted by the encyclical, refers back to the far wider problem of the understanding of sex and sexuality in Christianity and, more specifically, in Catholicism. At the same time it is connected with the concept of sin or guilt in general. It is a subject which has already been widely examined in the various criticisms against Christianity, but is also present in theological thinking, and here also in a rather critical way.

"Eros," Sex, and Sin: Legacies of the Past and Present Realities

The magazine *Planète* of October 1968 speaks of a relationship between the attempt to arrest the growing phenomenon of sexual liberty which the encyclical represents and the moral order necessary for the preservation and exercise of power. It is along these lines that the opening theme of the encyclical is directly connected with the general phenomenon of the contestation of values, which up to now were held to be untouchable but which are not interpreted as part of a system which is attempting to survive. A discussion on this theme would be broad and interesting since it would directly include not only the questions of sex and human sexual behavior, but above all the not always clear motives for ecclesiastical pronouncements in the realm of sexuality when seen from the standpoint of faith. In any case, when introducing the topic of "Catholic morality, science, politics, and metaphysics of sex" in relation to the encyclical (note the interesting range of topics possible in a discussion on *Humanae Vitae*), *Planète* observes:

Patriarch Athenagoras was explicit in his declaration to the Agence France Presse: "Paul VI wants to save both the moral law and the interests and the existence of the family and of nations. The encyclical helps preserve the moral order necessary for power. Sex is the door by which the individual flees from collectivity, and to claim sexual liberty is to put all the cultural structures in question. Within the Church itself the encyclical refuses to trust the Catholic to make good use of his liberty."

This point warrants further examination. Chastity is a spiritual way of life. It is not a brake on the flesh; it is a struggle against the invasion of sexual images; its aim is to prevent sex from introducing its demands to the detriment of interior unity. It is possible to make love very chastely. Continence is a doing without sex. The encyclical imposes this temporary privation as a "lesser evil" for Catholics, who are considered incapable of real, interior, and individual behavior.

It introduces the notion of quantity, whereas it is quality which is the basis of the relationship. If the good thing to do is to *deprive* oneself several days a month, then the evil things consist precisely in *doing* it. We are back in a Manichaean idea of sexuality which considers it as a terrifying freedom. How is one to reacquire the values of *agape* before the growing domination of *eros* on the basis of these principles? It is a tragedy for those Catholics who tried to reinstate human life in its unity of flesh and spirit.

It seems that with this encyclical the Pope wanted primarily to erect a defensive barrier against the general risks which are incurred when sexual liberties are set free in Western civilization. This is an attitude which is typical of governments in general. A group of psychiatrists at the University of Wisconsin, after two years of study on American campuses, recently published some findings which are in striking agreement with the findings of "natural theology." In their view, "sexual liberty" is as much a cause as an effect of psychic disturbance in those who uphold it. This liberty provokes the disturbance when it is not already one of its symptoms. It is therefore "antinatural"; nature is what is "normal." What is normal is what is lived out by the great majority of people—it is the collective *consensus*. Consequently they hold that "parents, educators, doctors, journalists, have the task of more strictly abiding the truth of facts—not the exceptions, but the collective or representative facts.

What *Planète* says on the idea of continence is possibly disputable, since it is not exactly the Christian understanding; but it must be recognized that the encyclical does tend toward this view. And we shall see that Catholics themselves reproach the encyclical for this. Even more interesting is the relationship existing between sexual behavior, sexual education, and the social order of the established structures. In fact it is interesting because it is more correct today to reflect on the subject of sex in this concrete relationship than on a purely abstract level. The reference to the American psychologists' research is also very illuminating and cannot be left out of the reflections occasioned by the encyclical. Impressive on this issue is the report of Dr. Escoffier-Lambiotte in *Le Monde* of August 8, 1968 in which, referring to the research of the University of Wisconsin, the point is made that those persons who are in any way responsible for the education of the new generation or the masses must follow

the strictest adhesion to the truth of collective representative facts which entails: diffusion of this truth and this truth alone; systematic criticism of distortions, abusive generalizations, and the myths fed by mass media, that of sexual liberation as well as that now in the process of disappearing, of Victorian-type restrictions, both of which are a source of anguish and anxiety; the growth in reflection on and the continuous gathering of information about the simplest ethical norm (deep, lasting affectiveness) on which the youth of today may base themselves in this period of "sexual revolution" and which will also serve as a safeguard against the most serious disillusionments and excessive anxiety.

The commentator in *Planète* has these statements of Dr. Escoffier-Lambiotte before him when he observes that

when the wave reaches Soviet Russia one will be able to read a text like this in *Pravda*. It is to these incertitudes of the public powers

461

menaced by the "libertarian unleashing of eros" that the encyclical offers help. No doubt it is in this general perspective that its content must be considered. To have admitted the legitimacy of a carnal act which is voluntarily made infertile would have amounted, as some exegetes of the encyclical say, to unhinging the very foundations of dogma and the sacraments. It still remains to be discovered what these foundations are in relation to sexual morality.

Here, then, is a new judgment on the underlying motives or "whys" of the encyclical. Even though a questionable one, it would not in fact be entirely useless to debate this judgment in greater detail since it has also received attention from Catholics. The relationship between the foundations of dogma and religion and sexual morality is in fact one of the issues which most worries theologians after the encyclical, and we have already seen several aspects of the question.

It is not an entirely new problem, since there has already been considerable discussion on the Church's understanding of sexual morality. We have already observed that in the past few years theologians have spoken of it in a rather critical fashion, exposing either the Church's unwarranted preservation of past theories and ideas, or its equally unwarranted interference into fields which, in themselves, do not directly concern the "foundations" of dogma or of Christianity. Since the former criticism implies that there has been theological revision, and hence an evolution of the moral judgment, it is logical for those theologians who support this view to be particularly sensitive to the problem after the publication of *Humanae Vitae*.

Possibly the most radical, comprehensive expression of these criticisms resulting from previous research has been that of Julius Evola in his work *Metaphysique du sexe*, Paris, 1958. We indicate this type of research so as simply to reveal in its most open form the basic position which then became the starting point for various further revisions of the outlook on sexual morality, and also for reflection on the difficulties which still remain regarding the conception of sexual morality, or better, of sex in general, in *Humanae Vitae*. Julius Evola's understanding of sexuality with regard to Christianity, and hence his practical attitudes, are obviously quite different from ours, and therefore there will be no need to attempt to correct the "outrageous statements" which appear in his study.

In the chapter of his book dedicated to Christianity and sexuality, Evola states that the Church's sexual morality does not belong to its revealed base. It is to be seen rather as the result of a degeneration in the metaphysical content of the divine teaching, and as a decline and distortion of this teaching into a simple, repressive, sexual morality. The traditional religions have always recognized two laws: one concerns life in the world, which is not rejected but rather sacralized; the other concerns the small minority who have an ascetic vocation and to whom the way of detachment has been revealed. According to Evola:

In contrast to ancient Judaism, Mazdaism, Veda Hinduism, and Islam itself, Catholicism confused the two orders and introduced ascetic values into the sphere of ordinary-day life. One of the consequences of this has been the condemnation of sex, which has led to a real theological hate for sex.

Evola continues by saying that in the gospels the distinction was still evident. In Luke, for example, it is said: "The children of this world marry and are given in marriage. But those who shall be accounted worthy of that world and of the resurrection from the dead, neither shall they be able to die any more, for they are equal to the angels, and are sons of God, being sons of the resurrection (Luke 20:34–36)." This is not sexual Manichaeism but simply the recognition of a mystical life based on continence for those who "have been considered worthy" of this form of life.

Evola then observes that indications of this hate for sex are already evident in St. Paul. The sexual experience of primordial unity was designated to the level of "fornication" and "shamelessness," and marriage became a lesser evil: "It is good for man not to touch woman. Yet for fear of fornication, let each man have his own wife, and let each woman have her own husband. Let the husband . . . ; but if they do not have self-control, let them marry, for it is better to marry than to burn (1 Cor. 7:1–2, 9)." Sexuality, which has been sacralized in the pure, spiritual tradition as a symbol of unity, now becomes sin, and a confusion creeps in between the mystico-ascetic way and the "moral order" of society.

Evola can see no basis in the text for any relationship between sexual union and "original sin." In Genesis 2:24 mention is made of two, Adam and Eve, who became one flesh before sinning and when they were still unashamed of going naked. Post-evangelical Christianity equated all aspects of sexual life with sin. In fact, sex was allowed only within marriage and only for the sake of procreation. Marriage understood as a "sacrament" should have become a guarantee of this order, and the sacralization of sexuality should unify the recognition of the transforming value of sex. This value was rejected. Eros became a simple, impure, and natural function for continuing the species. Hence there remained only the social side of the Christian religious precept, and a simple, mediocre, and blunt check imposed from outside on the human animal who, from the standpoint of spiritual realities, was of no interest.

Evola's thesis is certainly open to criticism from various sides —and besides there are not a few historical inaccuracies in this chapter dedicated to the Christian understanding of sex. For example, Evola states that marriage as a sacrament goes back only to the twelfth century. Nevertheless, discounting the generalizations and the radical element in his judgment, it cannot be denied that, generally speaking, there has been a certain amount of distortion of the meaning of sexuality in the Christian tradition. Nowadays these distortions are felt all the more strongly, and the encyclical has simply been the catalyst which has again precipitated these issues.

Thus, for example, Patrick O'Donovan, writing in *Time* of August 19, 1968 on the subject "Sex, Sin and Catholics," observes that

in condemning artificial birth control, the Pope has done nothing other than give expression to an attitude as old as Christianity. However eloquently they may protest, Christians are ambivalent when it comes to sex. They tend to disapprove not only of every undue form of sexual relationship, but also of the matrimonial one. Naturally, this is not the official teaching; in fact, the Christians have placed marriage into the ambit of a great sacrament and they take it so seriously that they can annul it only in very exceptional circumstances. Furthermore, the conjugal act between man and woman is itself an essential part of the sacrament. The priest, moreover, does not have an essential part in the sacrament; the sacrament is a contract of love between two faithful, and it is so solemn that all the priest can do is to bless it. . . . But—and this is unique among the religions—in Christianity there is hostility and suspicion with regard to sex. It is strange that this should be so; the religion of the Christians had its origins among the Jews, who saw the blessing of God in the number of their children, and were capable of the most sincere acceptance of human sexuality. But right from the beginning there has been a peculiar puritanism among the Christians; perhaps this was a reaction against the legendary excesses of the Roman Empire. In any case, it was certainly a search for purity, and purity in its highest expression has nothing whatever to do with sex. St. Paul is generally considered responsible for this concept. . . .

Some of the Church Fathers wrote about the virtues of sex in their fanciful way which might well have been used by a fiery Hindu guru; but they did this with repugnance, while the guru would have seen it as one of the ways of encountering God. They also taught that the total refusal of the sexual act and pleasure was the only solution, up to the point that the great Origen emasculated himself and lived to regret it. One could continue with a long list of famous saints who saw the question of sex with intolerant repugnance and accepted it as an unpleasant necessity; for example, SS. Gregory, Augustine, and Ambrose. It would be wrong to feel shocked at the excesses of the past. There is not a single saint in the whole of the calendar who could today be admired without reservation—not even St. Francis would meet with full approval . . . ; and the great Francesco Saverio would be considered as a very rigid leader who tended toward religious imperialism.

I consider it to be very easy to justify the idea that self-control and even a certain measure of austerity are a prerequisite for every form of high spirituality. . . . Nevertheless, it would seem that in this matter there has been a tragic cleft in Christian practice. In medieval Europe one began to think that the only really good Christians were to be found in the monasteries; the monks of the golden period of Irish monasticism were obsessed by the dangers of the flesh. There are few saints—and this is surprising—who lived a normal married life; even St. Thomas More, who loved children, married twice, and had the great gift of a realistic sense of humor, still regretted that he had not been called to become a Carthusian monk. It may be that this is all due to the strength of the Manichaean heresy, which is the most fundamental and ancient error of our civilization; it holds that there are two great principles in life: evil, which is identified with the material creation, and good, which is represented by the spirit. This is an error of a delightful and seductive simplicity, and it is very far from being dead.

After having carried his considerations farther by giving illustrations of the forms which this Manichaeism can assume, O'Donovan states that

in a certain sense we can say that the Pope has strengthened the splendor and the sanctity of marriage. But he has also asserted that it is not for pleasure and not even essentially for the continuity of a happy relationship between the partners; the essential thing is procreation, and it therefore has a utilitarian purpose. The majority of Christians have been saddened by his decision, but this decision ought not to have surprised them. The appearance of the Church may have changed in a surprising manner, but the tradition that is at the basis of what this decision represents is still as solid as a rock.

This last observation of O'Donovan's could at the same time be either a simple contestation—and this is done even by Catholic theologians either in the hope that this rock remain firm or that it be dislodged—or an evaluation. We have already noticed that it is this evaluation which is, in practice, at the basis of the theological disagreements with the encyclical.

An interesting reaction has come from Charles Davis, the well-known English Catholic theologian who created a sensation several years ago when he announced he was leaving the Catholic Church. It is clearly obvious that at the bottom of his reaction lies the same fundamental judgment which led him to make his decision and which he described in his well-known book *A Question of Conscience*, London, 1967. Commenting on the letter of Cardinal Heenan on *Humanae Vitae*, Davis said:

It offers the hope that medical science will come to the rescue of the teaching of the Pope, and will perfect the Pill for completely regulating the menstrual cycle, thereby facilitating the use of the cyclic method. To rely on a hope of this kind only heightens the crude biological reference to natural law and matrimonial ethics contained in the encyclical. It leaves Catholic sexual morality in the bog from which the contemporary theologians have tried to rescue it. What is implied is not only the refusal of contraceptives, but rather the rejection of the considerable progress in Catholic moral thinking which had led to their being accepted. We might add that the appeal for science to find a heaven-sent solution to the dilemmas created by bad theology has not so far had any success in the history of Christian doctrine.

Davis' reaction and judgment are harsh, but no less harsh than those of lay people who write in a theological vein as, for example, Jean Marie Paupert, author of several theological essays. In *Le Monde* of August 11–12, he observes, after criticizing the treatment of natural law, that

in the second part of the encyclical, the only fine and positive section of it, every pastoral consideration is devoted to the defense and illustration of Christian chastity. The whole appearance, then, is as if the true motive behind the Pope's choice was his fear of an erotic explosion and a fear that man will not be able to make a moral use of the Pill—although it would certainly be wrong to minimize the danger. The theology of nature would, in this case, have solely the role of a supporting theological structure for want of a better one. No matter how magisterial this text is . . . it seems to me one of the most unfortunate possible for various reasons. Certainly it is not because it is at loggerheads with the world. Surely the gospel is a scandal and Christianity a cross!

This scandal and this cross, however, must be put in their right context. By leaving them on the uncertain ground of a static view of nature, which sees biological technique in a Manichaean light, the Pope has chosen the easy way out. The difficult and the *true* thing for Christians to do is to teach the world how to make a human and moral (and hence, difficult) use of contraceptive techniques, whichever they may be (as also to teach it a good use of atomic energy). I am thinking here, as are numerous others, of the urgent need for a Christian "crusade" of "agape" against the liberation of "eros." The pastoral text prepared by the majority of the Papal Commission was refreshingly beautiful and true because, based on a true moral theology, it put demands on Christians by placing before them, together with responsible parenthood, voluntary continence, and thereby giving them the possibility of being models to the world of moral dominion over biological techniques.

The Pope did not trust Christians or others to use these techniques in a Christian or human way. Objectively, and in spite of his declared good intentions, this leads one to think of a lack of esteem. Lack of esteem, however, evokes just as much lack of esteem on the other side, and it is not healthy for authority to lose its esteem for any length of time. Militant Christians, good Christians, masses of well-disposed nonbelievers, all expected from the mouth of Christ not a license but a message of salvation, a human way of living. This reply has been refused them; the door has been shut in their faces as if they were curious children. Much more could still be said of the Manichaean confusion between chastity and continence, which without appearing on the surface, can be seen lurking underneath.

Another lay writer, Carlo Augusto Cannata, in the magazine *Momento* of October 1968 takes up an aspect which he considers to be a fundamental one of the encyclical, and voices his doubts about it. He has no intention, in fact, of making a speech on "those themes which must be the subject of an ecclesial dialogue, as ecumenical as possible." He states that he is restricting himself to fulfilling a duty, that of

expressing a doubt on a fundamental point of the content of *Humanae Vitae,* and which I put forward as the personal meditation of a Christian consciously reflecting on the problems of sexuality, and which I intend to be a contribution to the liberation of the Christian interpretation of sex from the superstructures of Hellenistic dualism which, from Augustine onward, entered into and obscured a clear vision of scripture. The vision that lies at the base of the affirmations contained in the encyclical sees sexuality as an instrument for procreating or, more precisely, as a physical and psychic situation which determines the action from which conception arises. An expression like that in No. 11 ("As experience bears witness, not every conjugal act is followed by a new life. God has wisely disposed natural laws and rhythms of fecundity which, of themselves, cause a separation in the succession of births") can only mean that in an ideal case, which is that really corresponding to nature as created by God, births should follow on from births, except during the sterile periods which spontaneously follow after each birth.

True, the document later views the use of infertile periods as licit. No one will deny, however, that given the premises, this is an astonishing admission, nor will he recognize the justification which the encyclical gives for it as convincing. . . .

Let us return to the vision at the base of the encyclical, since it is this which gives the deepest reasons for the sadness contained in the Pope's words. A vision which sees in sexuality a mechanism designed for procreation, with an effective life-span corresponding to the material possibility of fulfilling fertile actions, is a description of animal, not human, sexuality. The distance between two successive pregnancies of the female of an animal species does not correspond, in fact, just to her powers of supporting two successive pregnancies without danger (neither is it so for the woman today), but also includes the interval in which those born from the first pregnancy acquire the ability of existing independently of their parents. An animal's learning capacity is of a short duration as also is the period during which the young require family assistance (I use the word family like the earlier expression "learning capacity" in an approximate sense in order to make the comparison more evident) for nutrition and defense. There is no need to note the radical differences which man's position reveals, at least in the historical situation in which we are immersed, where the parents' dedication to each of their children is of such a length as to permit 6 to 8 pregnancies.

However, if the biophysical state of human fertility contrasts in such an evident way with the requirements for life in which it is inserted, how can one possibly not recognize that the perspective taken from purely biological data is completely inadequate as a basis for the moral interpretation of human sexuality? How can one not see that the situation, which is supposed to be "ideal," is really seriously pathological?

A further aspect of the difficulties inherent in the encyclical's view of sexuality becomes apparent here; namely, on the one hand its rather biological viewpoint, and on the other, the problem which it raises when it is viewed on the level of family life and the role that sexuality plays in it. Cannata gives further consideration to this point:

Imagine, for example, that a couple makes the decision to employ an initial period, of months or even years, in which each partner will use the other's sexuality to help deepen the possibilities of dialogue between them, thereby preparing as perfectly as possible that environment of love and security which is necessary for the development of the children who are to come. Then another period of time will be devoted for birth or births which will be suitably close together for the advantages that the brothers will obtain from being of a similar age, yet far enough apart to guarantee the mother the necessary physical efficiency, and limited to a number which takes into account "both their own welfare and that of their children, those already born and those which may be foreseen. For this account they will reckon with both the material and the spiritual conditions of the times as well as of their state in life. They will then consult the interests of the family group, of temporal society, and of the Church herself" (*Gaudium et Spes*, No. 50). Finally, there will be a period of time necessary for undertaking the work of education (keeping in mind that the education of children implies a continual self-education process for the parents themselves) by employing their respective sexuality so that they maintain a basis for the integral, harmonious development of each person making up the family group.

In this way sexuality is applied to the far wider area from which it must be viewed. As can be seen, the issue is not one of moral libertinism but rather of an acute sense of responsibility.

For this reason Gabriel Arnaud, in *Terre Entière* of October 1968, observes:

Sexual morality is a morality of relationships, of the whole relationship with the children who are or will be born, and of their relationship with other persons. To find a basis for an objective, sexual morality, one must first make an inventory of this entire system of relationships. It is not by chance that the problem of relationships is at the center of the debate on sexuality. On all the levels where man today attempts to discover a meaning to his life—in philosophical research, in holding a widely accepted outlook, or in immediate experience—relationships with the other are always present as the "place" in which life's meaning is revealed. The relationship between man and woman must be interpreted in all its dimensions and not be judged exclusively by its concrete, biological fertility.

Able Jeannière wrote: "The man is only man before the woman; the woman is only woman before the man. In spite of role mobility, when it comes to variations in values it is no longer a social creation; the human reality is defined by this fundamental reciprocity" (*Anthropologie sexuelle*, Paris, 1965). And Teilhard de Chardin: "If man and woman are primarily for the child, then the role and strength of love should diminish the more that human individuality decreases and the density of the earth's population comes closer to the saturation point. But if man and woman are principally for each other, then they will become more human and they will feel the growing need to come together all the more."

What has just been said, in opposition to the idea of sexuality which seems to emerge from the encyclical, is even further supported by the conception which is now becoming increasingly widespread in spheres of cultural and scientific research and which consequently has fully entered into modern theological thought. Marc Guéret, in *Le Revue Nouvelle* of September 1968, has drawn a description of it, which is perhaps still the most comprehensive treatment to date of the whole discussion on sexuality that has emerged since the appearance of *Humanae Vitae*. Marc Guéret says:

Sexuality is connected with the depths of the mystery of man for the simple reason that if it is to continue in existence it must go beyond the limits of the couple itself. It is also united to the depth of the mystery of the universe and the cosmic forces.

In any case, it is also frequently placed in relation to the world of the sacred. . . . This fundamental ethnological insight is expressed in far more scientific language by depth psychology. Psychoanalysis shows that sexuality encompasses a much wider field than genitality, taken here in the sense of reproduction. It brings the importance of the sexual instinct to light. One of the great merits of psychoanalysis is that it has destroyed a whole host of taboos which surrounded the phenomenon of sexuality. It shows that sexuality and aggressiveness are two indispensable drives and without them man has no dynamism. The sexual instinct, then, is not viewed with mistrust. It is seen to contain a source of energy which men must capture and dominate. Even the encyclical speaks of domination of the sexual instinct by the use of reason and free will.

Unfortunately, the term domination is understood here in two different contexts. In traditional Church teaching, domination consists in not dissociating sexual union from procreation. Certainly the Church recognizes the value of sexual pleasure willed by God but it does not wish this pleasure to be obtained outside of openness to the transmission of life, except in cases where "natural" infertility is utilized.

Psychoanalysis understands sexual self-mastery in another sense. It often speaks of sublimation. Sublimation of sexual energy can be achieved by assigning it to nonsexual objects as, for example, aesthetic and cultural activity. Sublimation can also be achieved through the intentions which man brings to his sexual behavior. We notice, for example, how important pleasure is in eating. Its morality depends on the finality which man assigns to it. Pleasure is either oriented solely to itself, and this is egoism, or this pleasure retains a broad openness

471

to the other, in which case it is moral. The same applies for married sexual union. The Church does not want to dissociate it from the transmission of life, but this pleasure has a broader openness than to its purely biological side. Everything depends on the intention which the subject confers on it. It can be extremely egoistic just as it can reach out toward the other; that is, toward the partner, toward the children, and toward society. Sexual pleasure is more than a concession made to the work of procreation. Its finality is far wider than that of biological life—it reaches out to the entire sphere of the couple's activity.

Obviously, an objection will be raised here on a point of principle: evil may not be done for the sake of good. But who says that pleasure is an evil? Does not this negative judgment, particularly in regard to sexual pleasure, spring from a certain outlook on the "nature" of things? Contemporary sexology shows that sexuality begins from birth and that its role is far more extensive than that of genitality and reproduction. Th s accords with the insights gained from an ethnological study of sexual behavior. Unfortunately, the sexual instinct still remains suspect, partly because it is something which is shared with animals. In reply to this, it must be said that one need not necessarily be an animal to live one's own sexuality. The characteristic which is proper to man is exactly that of being able to assign numerous finalities to his sexual life.

While the view of sexuality which seems to have emerged from the encyclical has been criticized, it is precisely this capacity of man which has been very much emphasized: a capacity already intrinsic to him which is a fountain of energy, of relationships, and of creativity on the level of the different dimensions of his life. Sexuality should, therefore, be understood more in this perspective even when judging concrete behavior in the realm of married life. Hence, from the difficulties put forward by the encyclical, a positive, far broader outlook has arisen and it certainly will not be long before its influence is felt on the whole of moral theology.

It is along these lines that Gabriel Arnaud has presented in *Terre Entière* of October 1968 some valuable observations which widen the horizons of the debate in such a way as to not permit the criticisms of *Humanae Vitae* to descend to the pamphlet level. Arnaud says:

472

It is the relationship with others which prevents the modern industrial society—or should prevent it—from becoming a pure consumer society. Industrial society promotes this relationship with all kinds of communications media, comforts, and pastimes, in the great concentrations with their "lonely crowds" as described by the American sociologist Riesman. On the other hand, the need to flee from the crowd means that the family, the group, the small basic community, gain in importance together with all the groupings "on a human level" in which man has an awareness of existing, because in these he establishes a true relationship with his fellowman and is in turn recognized by him. I construct myself as a living being by "recognizing" the other and by being "recognized" by him in recognition which obliges me to transform myself. Thus a real fruitfulness is one of the effects of the relationship, including the married relationship. It is at least equally as important as simple biological fruitfulness, which apparently has greater reality because the "product" is more visible since it dissociates itself from the couple and s nce it has as its object the preservation and the propagation of the species.

The coming of modern industrial society has reevaluated the relationship, not just as a constitutive element of the individual's existence, but also as an element in international relationships. Today we are ready to urge that a solidarity is necessary between the rich industrialized countries and the traditionally poor countries, and with all the more effort when we see it slowly slipping out of reach every day. This solidarity is a prerequisite of a mutual relationship: not only will rich nations not be able to help poor nations develop themselves unless they start questioning their own attitudes but it is also in the relationship, by looking in common at their present and their future, that rich and poor nations will discover the answers to their basic problems.

The interpersonal and "intersocietal" relationship is so much at the heart of the problems which face the man of today and has acquired such a dignity for Christians (their encounter with *other* in faith necessarily passes through their encounter with *others*), that we remain astounded before the simplistic traditionalism of the encyclical's vision. How could Paul VI make himself the advocate of international solidarity in the new, industrial society by publishing his encyclical on the development of peoples and then come forth with such a traditionalist anthropology? His understanding of the man-woman relationship, of the role and position of the woman within the couple, and of society, all bear, to a great extent, the stamp of the ancient culture of the Mediterranean basin which drags in with it a thousand sexual taboos. There are other cultural traditions in the world which assign far less importance to sex.

Moreover, the old Mediterranean culture must itself integrate the experiences and the questions of modern society under pain of seeing itself included among the objects of a curiosity shop. The man of today who sees himself as the maker of history, is attemtping to leave behind the mythical universe in which he found himself in the past—and where often today he still finds himself. In a word which is destined to become the key word of industrial society, he wants to be *adult,* continually becoming freer and more responsible for his personal and collective destiny. Paul VI has turned his back on this man and speaks to him in a language which he no longer understands.

The question of knowing whether the encyclical will create an additional obstacle to man's journey toward adulthood is not, on the other hand, a simple one. At the same time as he is desperately searching to affirm, both individually and collectively, his vocation to responsibility, man is afraid of liberty. He wants to liberate himself of the old myths which guided his journey but at the same time cherishes them as if he were afraid of losing them. This is true for every man, whatever his cultural level, and especially for the vast masses of people.

We do not have to look far to see the truth of this. Of the men of our old continent immersed in a Christianity bound up with the old Mediterranean culture, how many still remain under the protection of their childhood taboos and unconsciously seek to foster guilt feelings which will free them from their responsibilities? The more they feel themselves to blame, the easier it is for them to live in their mediocrity if they can discharge their guilt on a law which is exterior to them.

There still remains to be answered the question of whether it is the Church's role to liberate man instead of holding him under its protective wing in a universe full of dangers.

Are We Still Catholics? Church of Authority and Church of Conscience

All these questions, which began from a precise doctrinal point, have slowly spread like an oil spot. In this way they have touched the Church itself, its meaning, and its mission. The problems which *Humanae Vitae* has brought to light are showing themselves to be far more important than the doctrinal detail which it intended dealing with. On the other hand, the sum total of the difficulties which the encyclical has provoked now seems so heavy that the question which spontaneously comes to our lips is: Are we still Catholics? We must, in fact, keep in mind that the strongest criticism has come precisely from Catholics, and touches upon delicate sectors of the Church's very existence. The criticisms which come from outside are not so strong even though they give the appearance of being more radical. When they do, in fact, come from a Catholic, and all the more when from a theologian, it is like an expert looking into a mechanism of which he knows the most delicate points very well—we have seen this borne out during the course of the long discussion.

If one holds a monolithic idea of the Church, monopolizing ideas and consciences, unwilling to accept dissent and discussion within itself, the question will immediately arise as to whether we have not come to the point of having to choose between the Church and conscience.

One of the most interesting aspects of this question and one which undoubtedly gives us some idea of the true future of the life of the Church, is precisely the fact that by criticism the Church is revealed for what it is. A criticism which has been aroused by one of the Church's actions appears as one of the most alive and responsible ways not only of "living" in the Church, but above all of "being" the Church. It is nothing other, in fact, than the circulation in the community of the research and experience of faith. All this necessarily leads to crises, but afterward come purification and greater understanding.

Moreover, the focal, and at times tragic, point where all this takes place is in the very delicate meeting place between authority and conscience—between the authority of discipline and teaching and the consciousness of belonging in a living and responsible way to the Church and of being responsible before God and before man in the way in which this is lived out in our age. Obviously this consciousness will be transformed into critical awareness. What possibilities, however, and what duties remain open to a Catholic who finds himself in the Church with this critical attitude?

It is only too clear that the answer is a rather negative one.

For example, the Swiss bishop Nestor Adam states: "Whoever does not loyally and totally adhere to the teaching of the encyclical can no longer call himself a Catholic." The phrase, accurately reported by *L'Osservatore Romano* (without any further comment on its part—a surprising fact when one recalls that the same paper has criticized phrases far less close to heresy than this!), is the best we can think of to give a completely mistaken idea of the Church. It represents the attitude, however, of those who have made *Humanae Vitae* the touchstone of fidelity or infidelity to the Christian faith. It must be observed, however, that the Church is above all, the community of those who search together for the Word of God and its meaning *for today*, under the guidance of the hierarchy. In this case, it differs radically from the view put forward by the bellicose Swiss bishop—an ironical fact, given the long, pacifist tradition of his country! What, then, at closer quarters, does the critical dimension, which Catholics have entered on the occasion of *Humanae Vitae*, and which by now encompasses all sectors of the Church and all its expressions, signify?

Prof. C. P. Sporken, in his article in *De Tijd* of August 2, 1968 asks himself the same question which we have asked here, keeping in mind the encyclical's insistence on both external and internal obedience to the teaching which it has put forward. Prof. Sporken hence asks:

What are we to think if, in spite of the appeal to internal and external obedience, a considerable number of bishops, theologians, doctors, priests, and married persons end up finding themselves in a "heterodox" position in regard to this encyclical? Can a person continue to consider himself a Catholic and really to make up part of the Church if he believes he is following in conscience different norms from those indicated by the encyclical?

We know that generally encyclicals do not bear the guarantee of infallibility unless it is expressly stated. In other words, they need not be considered as infallible judgments, but as teachings toward which Catholics owe a respectful obedience, unless they have sufficiently grave reasons for thinking otherwise.

I feel that this could very easily be the case for this encyclical. When we consider the way in which it was drawn up, we see that it reproduces the thought of a very small minority of theologians—especially the Roman theologians—who neither quantitatively nor qualitatively represent the body of theologians in the Church. Besides, it is a declaration which according to the Pope himself, is not directly based on the gospel message but on a given interpretation of the natural law, even if relying on the light of divine revelation (No. 4). This interpretation, however, is very disputable, and is therefore found to be rejected by a great number of Catholics, priests, theologians, and bishops, as well as by the majority of other Christians and non-Christians.

Considering all this, we can say the following: the fact that the Pope chooses a particular interpretation of marriage morality does not take away from the other fact; namely, that a great number of Catholics hold another opinion which they base on very valid arguments. The present situation in the Church, then, entails at least the following:

1. On matters of birth regulation, each couple can and must make the decision to which they feel obliged according to their situation in married life—a situation in which personal factors play a far more important role than do biological laws.

2. Everyone must respect the ethical views of his neighbor and the judgments of conscience which flow from them.

If, however, as Cardinal Alfrink has said, the couple's personal conscience remains the ultimate norm, does not then all the Church's morality become shaky and abandoned to the whims of the individual?

Nothing could be farther from the truth. The following of one's personal conscience represents precisely a link with our human condition and hence with the whole, human community. For the Christian this means that his undertaking in the human community is placed in the perspective of evangelical charity; that is, in a human charity where God's love for man and man's love for God find their daily fulfillment. The concrete content of this fundamental ethical mission can only be discovered in life itself. If it is to be discovered in marriage, however, the basis cannot be biological sexuality but must be the human significance of sexuality as an expression of love. In other words, the truly human elements, like the mutual love and the structure of the family, will have greater importance.

To take personal conscience as the ultimate norm does not mean, therefore to search for escape routes so as not to obey the Pope. It has the positive significance of making oneself feel bound to what one considers in all sincerity to be the moral truth. I think I should say that the encyclical cannot be considered as the total, clear expression of the moral truth in matters of marriage and marriage morality.

Whether we are Catholics or not certainly does not depend on the fact of whether we are obedient or not to this encyclical. To be a Catholic or not to be one depends primarily on our will to remain in communion with the human community which loyally wants to believe in Christ and his gospel. It depends on whether we want to search, in communion with all persons of goodwill, for the moral task which this entails. It is in the moral conscience of the ecclesial community that we find, in my opinion, the true norm which binds the Catholic's conscience.

This is a view of Catholicity which comes far closer to the "truly Catholic" one than that traditional view held with a superficial fidelity, or at least not after serious reflection or personal conquest. It is a more dynamic, historical, religious, and human view. It is good to emphasize this because many today like to use the term "Catholic" or "non-Catholic" on the basis of an inhuman and ahistorical view of Christianity. This is all too easy, but also dishonest. It amounts to wanting to have one particular idea of Catholicism so as to be able to make use of it for one's advantages—faith does not enter at all into this—or to make a puppet of it and then pull it down when it no longer does the motions one demands of it.

It is difficult to see how a serious Catholic who has understood the objective dilemma which the encyclical has put before him, will be unable to accept, at least as a hypothesis, the views suggested by Prof. Sporken.

The theological group which issues the Argentine periodical *Presencia,* in a long, unpublished editorial, has gone deeper into this question. After establishing that the magisterium expressed by the encyclical is "intermittent" and authoritative, it asks how a Catholic is to face a magisterium of this kind in conscience. It says:

A magisterium of this kind can have three aspects according to the matter it deals with: (1) divine revelation and anything strictly connected with it; (2) the natural values of human, personal, and social life; (3) theological and biblical investigation. Obviously the encyclical refers to the second point.

The Canadian theologian Gregory Baum puts it in the following way: "The positions of ecclesiastical authority in this matter have only the single, pastoral objective, and one cannot exclude the possibility that the progress of science will have a strong influence in bringing about a change in the official position. . . . In the sector dealing with natural knowledge we can also find an evolution in the doctrine. The idea that man has of himself depends on many factors, both personal and social and for this reason it evolves in history. It must not be forgotten, therefore, that the Church's position regarding personal and social ethics has undergone a series of changes. The classic example is that of religious liberty. While the ecclesiastical magisterium of the last century totally rejected the idea that religious liberty is a right of the human person (Pius IX in the encyclical *Quanta Cura*), Vatican II formally declared that religious liberty is an inalienable right of man and that it must be respected by all institutions and societies."

The Catholic cannot in conscience doubt the Church's competency to interpret the natural moral law. The Church, however, is not the sole body qualified to give this interpretation. It is the official teaching of Vatican II that salvation is possible outside the Church for anyone who correctly interprets and follows the natural law. The German theologian W. Kasper observes as well that "the Church must show the dogmas not just as formally binding but also as full of significance in themselves, enlightening for man and attainable in the world today through faith." If this applies to dogmas, it applies even more to moral teachings.

The traditional teaching to be found in the encyclical, was adequate for a rural-type civilization with rigid social structures. Today, however, science, faith, and morality are very closely interconnected. The solution to the problem of responsible parenthood can no longer be reduced to a purely biological issue. We must take into consideration the contributions of psychology, physiology, chemistry, and in general all the sciences, the changes operating in our highly industrialized and mass-level society with its relatively complex series of economic, social, and psychological factors. Man has advanced in his knowledge of himself and his causal relationship to the society in which he is evolving.

By this we mean that in the expression of our personality we are not obliged, as Catholics, to give total assent to the Pope's encyclical. We can welcome it by virtue of obedience. This type of attitude serves as a witness to unity. It signifies that we recognize the authority of the Roman Pontiff in matters which in themselves are not dogmas of faith . . . but the history of salvation and the "prophetic" mission pertains to the entire people of God and every member participates in it with his own personality. It is a duty to listen to and to follow the hierarchical magisterium even though, in the final analysis, it is ourselves who are responsible for our actions. At times, therefore, when faith is an adult faith, liberty can go against obedience and precisely for this reason will strengthen and enrich the life of the Church. It is only in this way that any permanent *aggiornamento* of the people of God is possible.

In any case, a less radical and possibly more ecclesial position is also tenable. It consists in presenting a wider perspective on the formal content of the encyclical from within a position of open obedience. The problem is that of putting it in a "personalist" light if this is possible.

These are two different perspectives, but both are equally valid and both hold greater possibilities for growth and maturation than any simple statement of total obedience with no questions asked. The last choice would be equivalent to returning to the famous *perhinde ac cadaver* which, even though it did produce real men and real saints in former times, would today risk giving an inexact picture of the Church. Man lives in history and cannot be aware of how much history means to him for his way of living and thinking, and of living and thinking the message of salvation.

What, then, is the future of this crisis which has been further clarified and deepened after the appearance of *Humanae Vitae*?

Yves Seinlet, in *Frères du Monde* of January 1969, observes that

history will tell us if the crisis which we are now going through was the decisive test which was food for a renewal of the faith, or if it was nothing other than a dramatic period which threatened to dash the bark of Peter to pieces. One thing which is certain is that if from the human viewpoint we can know nothing of the future, then the present situation puts demands on our responsibilities.

Some, for the sake of the Church's internal cohesion, would like us to confuse blind obedience to the Pope's decisions with faith in Jesus Christ. Before a solitary Pope like this, whose metaphysical place would be between heaven and earth, man would be doomed to silence. We confess, frankly and simply, that we cannot accept this way of viewing the Christian's place in the Church. And we affirm our rejection in all tranquillity and peace of conscience.

We shall be accused of thereby contributing to the confusion which is at present deeply disturbing the Church. We are not ignorant of the fact that she is living through a crucial period. Like everyone, we sadly feel the crisis in all its gravity and breadth, and the incertitudes to which it has given rise. However, we shall continue believing that it is more dangerous and harmful, in the long run, to overlook the truth, avoid the questions which it puts before us, and keep silent about the difficulties of doctrine which, in any case, are public and known by all. It is certainly a fine thing to sacrifice everything to avoid dissent among believers. But unity can only become a reality by overcoming the living tensions in an authentic way and by not succumbing to the insipidity of fine sentiments.

It is evident—and no one tries to disguise this fact any longer— that *Humanae Vitae* did not bring about unanimous response in conscience to the teaching pronounced by the Pope. Besides those who for discipline or on account of conviction adhere to the official teaching, there are as many who, not only in good faith but also for objective reasons, cannot accept it. Unity of opinion within the Church has fallen to pieces. The conscience of a great number of Christians has opposed the conscience of the Pope.

We are forced to ask what the basic reasons are for this opposition. It would be dishonest to try to minimize them by alluding to the spirit of contestation or the widespread spirit of pleasure in our society. While they were waiting for the Pope's decision, Christians gave in to "illusions of convenience" (Msgr. Marty of Paris). Such a partial, distorted judgment betrays an ignorance of the very truth in question. Since in the last analysis, the encyclical has offended such a great number of Catholics, and among them some of the best and most dynamic Christian married couples, we must in strictest honesty suppose that this has happened for reasons which are more valid than those which have been suggested up to now. Let us clearly admit it: they have been unable to recognize in this text, which has escaped from another age, either the face of the Church as it appeared in the Council or the consciousness that man has of himself today.

No one has ever pretended that he expected the Pope to bring about a compromise with the truth to the extent of "calling licit a thing which is not" (*Humanae Vitae*, No. 18). The minimum honor that any opinion is entitled to expect is that the rectitude of its intentions be respected, even though it may upset a mind formed in another school of thought. Outside of these boundaries all dialogue is impossible and it is no longer a search for truth.

On the Pope's side, what suffocates this trust is the atmosphere of suspicion, so manifest in his last discourses—the unhealthy fear lest his authority be sneered at and offended. Stiffened by his transcendence, Paul VI has made his attitude so hard that he has become the man of monologue. This distortion of faith is sadly felt by many Christians.

They do not challenge the Pope's magisterium, they do not want to promote loose habits, nor do they want the Pill to be legitimated because they know that in this sphere science has far more to teach them than sexual morality. What has offended them has been the exercise of authority and the moral reasoning which have been inspired by an ecclesiology and anthropology which in no way agree either with their feelings, or with their understanding of human problems, or with their way of perceiving the realities of faith. They are asking themselves today, and not without anxiety: "Shall we feel ourselves to be strangers in the pastor's flock?"

Should we be scandalized at this uneasiness as if it were already a confession of apostasy? If not, what is to be done to ensure that the responsibility of which Yves Seinlet speaks becomes operative, without it falling into either childish aggression or comfortable indolence, which are no less offensive than open criticism or loyal discussion? These are the practical problems which the immediate future brings with it.

Georges Montaron, director of various committed Christian movements, in *Tèmoignage Chrètien* of October 17, 1968 gives us a vivid summary, which could well be made ours at the end of this long journey through the certitudes and incertitudes of an encyclical which has simply awakened the dialectic present in every living faith. Mantaron says:

Never has an encyclical given rise to so much discussion, so many attacks and adopting of positions as *Humanae Vitae*. Some have been scandalized. Others are troubled. As for us, we are glad of it.

The Pope is not a general who shouts out in accordance with his strategy, demand ng instant, blind obedience. He is not the mysterious head of any kind of "cominform" of Catholics. We have too much respect for the Bishop of Rome to treat him in this way. He is the Vicar of him who wanted to serve men, and he puts himself forward as an "expert in humanity." This is what makes his task so heavy and so respectable.

As for the Church, she is not an army in which everyone, like a robot, marches at the same pace. Nor is she the visible expression of simple ideology. We are part of the Church and we know that she is, to use the formula of Vatican II, the flock in which the sheep grows, the ground on which everyone discovers a place suited to his needs. She is above all a mother and a servant.

We also know that all men, and particularly Christians, are morally obliged to search for the truth and to adhere to it "by a personal assent." Hence an encyclical letter is primarily an invitation to reflection.

It must be said: The Church is not in crisis when her children dialogue, criticize, argue. On the contrary it is here that she affirms that she is very much a living body and is giving the world an obvious sign of her good health. She must be looked at not with the eyes of the reporter looking for the sensational or with the eyes of the conservative deeply concerned for the masterpieces of ancient stones which are now in danger. She must be looked at with the eyes of youth in the world today.

What scandalizes us, then, is not the discussion which is taking place in Germany, Holland, England, Latin America, etc., but rather the silence of other parts of the Church. It is the silence of the majority mixed with triumphant cries at the defeat of others. . . .

What also scandalizes us are those all-too-easy cries and those which show no sign of dignity or modesty. They are the cries of the enthusiastic prelates who talk of Paul VI's virile courage and this admirable encyclical, and of the integralists who had not yet finished their work of undermining the Council texts of Vatican II but who are now back and ready to sing their *Te Deum* because, in their opinion, Rome has finally shown its true colors once again. There are also the cries of those who would like to have us believe that *Humanae Vitae* is the encyclical "par excellence," the pole-star for all Christians, and that the Church's teaching on love and birth control embodies all its previous teaching since it is only in this matter that authentic sin and true morality are to be found.

On the other hand . . . other Christians are tempted to ignore *Humanae Vitae*. This is a mistake and it must be stated.

By refusing to listen to the word coming from Rome and by stifling it they are in fact behaving as conservatives. These in fact never opposed the social encyclicals or those on peace. They never even discussed them. They were happy to ignore them. In their daily life they continued acting as if they had not heard anything. By doing this it is possible that they put themselves outside the Christian community, but they saved their face.

We belong to the people of God and we intend to remain that way. We have heard these words of Paul and we have received them.

Certainly they appear disappointing. It seems that the Pope has drawn up a document to suit the rich. The rigor of the text does not correspond to present-day realities. The reasoning put forward does not take into consideration the needs of man. We shall say all this because, in conscience, we cannot give our total approval to the document. However, we shall not treat it with contempt, but we shall strongly say what we think. It is not a question of contesting for contestation's sake but one of revealing, no doubt respectfully but also clearly, what we think. It is a question, even more, of using Paul VI's text as a basis for drawing up for the men of our time and together with them a reflection on the transmission of life, on service to humanity and to God in marriage, so that each of us can be faithful to his calling.

The paths of silence and contempt will never be ours, nor will those of resignation. We intend being free and responsible men and acting with full awareness in all things. The encyclical is an invitation to dialogue. We will speak.

484

Conclusion

Humanae Vitae, which to many seemed like a meteorite that had unexpectedly plummeted down from another world and another age into our own world and age, will probably eventually be seen from another point of view. Even though it is an act of the religious magisterium it is still irremediably caught up in an undeniable moment of crisis for this magisterium and a moment also of profound rethinking of the data of religious truth and of its criteria of conceptualization, language, and expression. Even if *Humanae Vitae* continues to reecho in the sociological and cultural reality of the time, it is still undoubtedly caught up in the growing pains of our present-day society, the contestation of which—now that both the left- and right-wing ideological fashions and conformisms have fallen—will bring about nothing short of a complete reconstruction. And though a sign of research and help offered to the man of today, it is still inextricably part of the transformation of the very image of present-day man, who is already living his future in the tension between the old cocoon of the past in which he is still enclosed and that condition of life to which he already unconsciously aspires.

Since a document like *Humanae Vitae* is a little of all this, it is by no means surprising that it does not appear to be the last word, but rather the first word of a story which has just begun. In this sense, even though it may represent, objectively speaking, the last phase of an out-of-date story, it has become the first phase of a story which has yet to begin.

On the strictly religious and Christian level, it may be said that because of the influence of the conditioning factors of scholastic theological mentality and language, *Humanae Vitae* now becomes the impulse for a more decisive and unretractable facing of the essential values of the gospel message. The question will be asked if and how the divine law exists in the reality of man transformed by the experience of technology and by the discovery of laws which were once held to be unsurpassable and to which man can now apply his hand in the laboratory. The question will be asked: What is the radical, indestructible meaning of the Word, which in order to remain alive, must be applicable in the appropriate translation to the man of every age, even to the man capable of reconstructing "in vitro" what "nature" took thousands of years to construct with its not always lovable and almost always violent and fearful "laws"?

The question will also be asked: Cannot and must not a teaching which comes down from above take into consideration what comes from below, for the simple fact that every man is of his very nature and by divine calling a "hearer" of and a witness to the Word of God? Even if in the past a particular type of society almost demanded as a service and as a help the exercise of a magisterium given entirely from above, will not the fact of a culture which is based more and more on planning together with a growing awareness of man, lead to a redimensioning of it? Maybe the upheavals that are occurring today in the Church are an indication of this transformation and not, as some superficially tend to judge, of impatience and caprice, for the very fact that these upheavals are taking place is an irrefutable sign of vitality. And *Humanae Vitae* is not the promised land of "professional" theologians who finally have something to dispute, but it is evidence that men have something to live for.

From the Pill the discussion passes on to nature, and from this to the significance of sex, marriage, love, and the family. From here it continues to the personal responsibility of the individual conscience and then to the place of each one in a Church which only now is slowly beginning to lose its unfortunate seventeenth-century shackles of the Roman court. It then goes to the magisterium authority, the structure of the Church, the meaning of religiosity or, better, faith—which is quite different! Next, it considers the meaning and the value of the gospel of salvation, and finally comes back to man, who is at the center, just as it had been one of the problems of man which had given rise to all this turmoil—something far nobler than a simple squabble.

Some will see in this turmoil the proof of the decadence which set in the moment the "reins were loosed." Others, perhaps the majority, see it as the natural appearance of what has been consciously or unconsciously expected for a long time.

Thus *Humanae Vitae*, this monument to the work of old, architectonic mentality, will, in the end, become the first stone of a new construction of which the architect will no longer be a court gentleman, but he who loved man so much as to make himself like unto him in all things. Does not looking at the size of St. Peter's on the Vatican Hill always arouse contrasting feelings which give rise to a stream of new thoughts? Paradoxically, the monument that consecrated the apogee of the Roman Church's power became the first stone and the most imposing monument to commemorate the birth of the Reformation in the very heart of old Christendom.

What is more, whereas then the dividing line passed through the different Christian confessions, today it passes through the reality of the world in which the new image of man is being created. In fact, the issue is no longer one of religious doctrines that are fought over by the different churches, but of huge, unavoidable problems before which all the Churches are called and forced to justify themselves. Are they still bearers of an original message of salvation willed *propter nos homines et propter nostram salutem,* or are they rather splendid mausoleums to their own, past glories? *Humanae Vitae* thus becomes an unintentional but objective contribution to a new age of ecumenism, the post-ecumenical period which is already no longer characterized by wise equidistant, spiritual politics, but by that mysterious "omega" point which, in the end, is the same for all.

At times it is even humorous to think what Luther would have done with some of today's Catholic theologians. He would have at least called in the Grand Elector to expel them from his states. Would not Calvin also have taken the Bible in his hand to sanctify with the Word of God an occasional burning in the marketplace? But in this case it would no longer be Giordano Bruno or Michael Servetus, but some of the famous Catholic theologians with whom we are well acquainted. What is even stranger, it would happen for the very same reasons for which the Holy and General Inquisition burnt Giordano Bruno in the *Campo de' Fiori.*

An assembly such as that at Uppsala, which united all the Protestant and Orthodox Churches with the participation of the Catholic Church in July 1968, revealed this general tension of all the Churches, stretching out toward the grave problems of humanity to the point where it could be said that the World Assembly at Uppsala sinned by *horizontalism.* Is not this horizontalism, however, possibly in the very logic of Christianity itself?

On the other hand, and almost at the same time, it was said that *Humanae Vitae* sinned by *verticalism,* because of a kind of unconscious lack of understanding when it was faced with the real problems of man. But let us rapidly synthesize the lines of discourse which the encyclical has given rise to and we shall see that it really does sin by "verticalism." The statements which it provoked have become an energetic and possibly necessary corrective.

Four general lines have in fact emerged from a process which is moving in a continuous dialectic of opposition and tension, and which is in search of syntheses not on the abstract level but immersed in living realities:

1. *The content of the encyclical:* It is an affirmation on one hand of the supernatural and on the other of a law of nature. Opposed to this is the conviction that the law of nature cannot canonize a biological law and interpret it as a divine law.

2. *The ecclesial problems:* The magisterium is reaffirmed in all its fullness and competence, and authority is imposed both with moderation and comprehension. On the other hand, there have been brought back the themes of liberty, conscience, and autonomy before one's own responsibility, even if under the guidance and with the help of the magisterium and authority. As well, there is a renewed, deeper thinking on the meaning of public opinion in the Church, of theological research, and of the relationship between freedom of research and the intervention

of the magisterium. Practically everything is once again being brought into question, and nobody for the moment wants to give an abstract solution from his desk to a question which appears all the more alive the more one attempts to solve it.

3. *The problems of present-day humanity:* Development and underdevelopment, the population situation, the condition of the married couple and the family, the difficulties of educating children in a new social context, the relationship to government programs, the social and political commitments of states, scientific research (especially of a biological and genetic nature), the manipulation of man—there are just as many other chapters in this vast, complex issue of which we are all so well aware. The encyclical has practically put all of them in question again. When they did begin rediscussing these problems, and not within the closed confines of laboratories and specialized research institutions, everybody unexpectedly realized that they had believed themselves to be very much advanced in the solution of their problems. They are now bitterly aware that almost everything consisted of good intentions and ambitious projects, with few resulting, practical achievements.

4. *The comprehensive view of the world and man: Humanae Vitae* has been accused of holding an antiquated, fixist, unrealistic, and utopian view of the world and man. It is precisely this, however, which causes us to return to a basic question; namely, whether by chance there is anyone in the world today who has a better, more plausible, more acceptable, and more dynamic view. We have noticed that to refuse to have a "project man" on the drawing board can be dangerous. There is always someone immediately ready to profit by it for his own projects which are far less clean and certainly suggestive of dollars or something similar. The whole question returns, then, of whether a project man is possible and suitable and, hence, where to search for an outline of a philosophy of man and of his history. Technology will strangle man if he abandons himself to it with no idea of what he is or wants to be.

Does a question such as "For or against *Humanae Vitae?*" have any meaning at this stage? It is, after all, a senseless question. *Pros* and *cons* can be very convenient alibis—paradoxical, but all too often true—for avoiding our personal and collective responsibilities. I find it easy to be *against* it if it does not coincide with my small, egoistic interests, with the present state of my research, with my economic programs. I find it easy to be enthusiastically *for* it if it helps me to justify the quiet corner of my convictions that have been put in crisis by everything which is now on the move and which is calling me to move if it helps me safeguard any of my positions which have been attacked by an evolution of thought, if indirectly it approves of one of my actions whose greatness has yet to be recognized, if it supports me in a political operation even if that operation is honest and of service to others, if it exempts me from the obligation to search personally and responsibly for a moral attitude for my conscience and my actions.

In one case or the other, the attitude is no longer that of either fidelity to the teaching of our faith, honesty before our convictions, or loyalty toward ourselves and others: it is simply that small, everyday egoism which can take us to the point of using big and noble words in order to cover over our smuggling of not-so-clean interests under the guise of big and noble commitments. The world is full of this.

All of what *Humanae Vitae* has achieved, however, as we have already noticed, possibly makes us a little less pessimistic. Beneath even the strong words of rejection and delusion we can catch a glimpse of the secret love and maybe even a trace of nostalgia for the serious things awaiting us after the fun fairs with which the type of society we live in has tried to put us to sleep.

How strange that we owe this to a papal document like *Humanae Vitae*—or at least, we owe it among other things also to *Humanae Vitae*! Is it perhaps because it is more a question than a definition?